Terrorism, National Security and Economic Development

Terrorism, National Security and Economic Development

Dr. G.S. Rajpurohit

RANDOM

RANDOM PUBLICATIONS
NEW DELHI (INDIA)

Terrorism, National Security and Economic Development

ISBN 978-93-5111-970-8

Published in 2016 in India by

RANDOM PUBLICATIONS

4376-A/4B, Gali Murari Lal, Ansari Road
New Delhi-110 002
Phone : +9111-43580356, 011-23289044, 011-43142548
e-mail: sales@randompublications.com,
info@randompublications.com, randomexports@gmail.com

Type Setting by : Friends Media, Delhi-110089
Printed at : Sanat Printers

Preface

A modern trend in terrorism is toward loosely organized, self-financed, international networks of terrorists. Another trend is toward terrorism that is religiously- or ideologically-motivated. Radical Islamic fundamentalist groups, or groups using religion as a pretext, pose terrorist threats of varying kinds to U.S. interests and to friendly regimes. A third trend is the apparent growth of cross-national links among different terrorist organizations, which may involve combinations of military training, funding, technology transfer, or political advice.

Terrorism is the systematic use of terror, often violent, especially as a means of coercion. In the international community, however, terrorism has no legally binding, criminal law definition. Common definitions of terrorism refer only to those violent acts which are intended to create fear (terror); are perpetrated for a religious, political, or ideological goal; and deliberately target or disregard the safety of non-combatants (civilians). Some definitions now include acts of unlawful violence and war.

The use of similar tactics by criminal organizations for protection rackets or to enforce a code of silence is usually not labeled terrorism, though these same actions may be labeled terrorism when done by a politically motivated group. The writer Heinrich Böll and scholars Raj Desai and Harry Eckstein have suggested that attempts to protect against terrorism may lead to a kind of social oppression.

As terrorism emerges as one of the greatest threats to India's internal security, the government, policy makers and strategic community continue their efforts to find an anti-dose to counter the menace of terrorism. Poignantly, the Mumbai terror strike in 2008 exposed the fissures in the India's internal defense apparatus as it was caught unaware and unprepared. However, the incident provided the Indian government an important lesson to prepare itself and deal with the new-age terrorism. A stringent series of measures have since been initiated to revamp its existing homeland security apparatus to shield and secure the country against future terror aggressions.

This book is deals with the various forms of terrorism, operating in different parts of the globe, irrespective of their socio-political affiliations and economic conditions.

– ***Author***

Contents

1

The many Faces of Terrorism

The year 1967 was an important one in the Middle East, with its striking demonstration of Israeli military superiority. The Western perception of the 1948–49 war had been that of a young nation heroically defending its right to exist and snatching victory from the combined forces of three Arab states. In 1956, the Israeli army had romped its way to the Suez Canal, but that had been as a member of the Anglo-French coalition. The victory of 1967 had been unqualified, the humiliation of the Arab states complete. But the Arab defeat opened the door to the rise of al-Fatah, the Palestinian National Liberation Movement, or the PLO, which had up to then only marginal.

The PLO, after all, had been founded in 1964 in Egypt under the auspices of President Nasser, who had chosen as its leader a man, Ahmed Shukairy, whose only claim to representativity was his status as a Palestinian figurehead. After the 1968 debacle and the skirmish that year with the Israeli army at Karameh in Jordan, in which the fedayeen distinguished themselves, the Palestinians themselves were promoted to center stage as the redeemers of Arab honour. These events highlighted the fact that, territorially speaking, the Israeli-Arab conflict was essentially an Israeli- Palestinian conflict.

They also drove home the fact that, despite the guerrilla war against the Jewish colonizers from 1936 to 1939, Palestinian nationalism had been too weak to resist Transjordan's absorption of the West Bank (which had been part of mandate Palestine) and Egypt's mandate over Gaza. In one of history's little ironies, the PLO was finally ready by the late 1980s to assume sovereignty over territories that had been under exclusive Arab control from 1949 to 1967. Likewise, in 2002—three decades late—Saudi Arabia offered recognition and peace to Israel in exchange for the territories occupied after the Six-Day War. The full and comprehensive acceptance by the elite Arab leadership of realities on the ground would seem to have been singularly slow in coming.

Its grasp of the military disparities involved was equally tenuous. Thus, in late 1968–early 1969, following the adoption of the Palestinian Charter, the various movements that made up the PLO and its fringes were nourished on delusions. One of these was the dream of defeating Israel in a guerrilla war modeled on those in Vietnam and Algeria; another was the establishment, via the rejection of alliances with any Israeli faction, of a democratic Palestinian state over all the territory of Palestine, in which the Jews would enjoy only the rights of a religious minority. This dream represented a regression to the sectarian minority millet system of the Ottoman empire, to the status of dhimmi for Jews, to which the creation of a national state had been the explicit response.

The Palestinian resistance was flawed in its underestimation of the depth of Israeli nationalism. A Palestinian state was at best conceivable on the West Bank, and perhaps in Transjordan with the overthrow of the Hashemite monarchy. The PLO rejected that strategy and sought instead, with pan-Arab assistance, to undermine Israeli society through guerrilla warfare. Could the Israelis, like the Europeans of Algeria, be forced out of the country? To believe they could was a pipe dream. Indeed, Israeli leaders felt at the time that if the Palestinians wanted their own state, they had only to establish it on the far side of the Jordan River. And among the political elite, there were many who had no intention of restoring the 1967 borders, let alone revisiting the question of East Jerusalem.

The impossibility of fostering conditions conducive to guerrilla warfare on the West Bank, coupled with the interception of virtually all commando units crossing the river from Jordan, led the Palestinian organizations to focus on terrorism—just as, in Latin America, the failure of the focos had led to urban guerrilla warfare. The impossibility of waging guerrilla warfare caused the Palestinian organizations to fall back on terrorist activities. In July 1968, by diverting an El Al flight between Athens and Cairo, the Popular Front for the Liberation of Palestine launched what was at the time called "publicity terrorism." The Palestinian cause, born of dispossession, had been emphatically brought to the West's attention.

WHAT IS TERRORISM

Terrorism is the systematic use of terror, often violent, especially as a means of coercion. In the international community, however, terrorism has no legally binding, criminal law definition. Common definitions of terrorism refer only to those violent acts which are intended to create fear (terror); are perpetrated for a religious, political, or ideological goal; and deliberately target or disregard the safety of non-combatants (civilians). Some definitions now include acts of unlawful violence and war.

The use of similar tactics by criminal organizations for protection rackets or to enforce a code of silence is usually not labeled terrorism, though these same actions may be labeled terrorism when done by a politically motivated group. The writer Heinrich Böll and scholars Raj Desai and Harry Eckstein have suggested that attempts to protect against terrorism may lead to a kind of social oppression.

The word "terrorism" is politically and emotionally charged, and this greatly compounds the difficulty of providing a precise definition. Studies have found over 100 definitions of "terrorism". The concept of terrorism may be controversial as it is often used by state authorities (and individuals with access to state support) to delegitimize political or other opponents, and potentially legitimize the state's own use of armed force against opponents (such use of force may be described as "terror" by opponents of the state).

Terrorism has been practiced by a broad array of political organizations to further their objectives. It has been practiced by both right-wing and left-wing political parties, nationalistic groups, religious groups, revolutionaries, and ruling governments. An abiding characteristic is the indiscriminate use of violence against non-combatants for the purpose of gaining publicity for a group, cause, or individual. The symbolism of terrorism can leverage human fear to help achieve these goals.

ORIGIN OF TERM

"Terrorism" comes from the French word *terrorisme*, and originally referred specifically to state terrorism as practiced by the French government during the Reign of terror. The French word *terrorisme* in turn derives from the Latin verb *terreô* meaning "I frighten". The *terror cimbricus* was a panic and state of emergency in Rome in response to the approach of warriors of the Cimbri tribe in 105 BC. The Jacobins cited this precedent when imposing a Reign of Terror during the French Revolution. After the Jacobins lost power, the word "terrorist" became a term of abuse. Although "terrorism" originally referred to acts committed by a government, currently it usually refers to the killing of innocent people by a non-government group in such a way as to create a media spectacle. This meaning can be traced back to Sergey Nechayev, who described himself as a "terrorist". Nechayev founded the Russian terrorist group "People's Retribution" in 1869. In November 2004, a United Nations Secretary General report described terrorism as any act "intended to cause death or serious bodily harm to civilians or non-combatants with the purpose of intimidating a population or compelling a government or an international organization to do or abstain from doing any act".

DEFINITION

The definition of terrorism has proved controversial. Various legal systems and government agencies use different definitions of terrorism in their national legislation. Moreover, the international community has been slow to formulate a universally agreed, legally binding definition of this crime. These difficulties arise from the fact that the term "terrorism" is politically and emotionally charged. In this regard, Angus Martyn, briefing the Australian Parliament, stated that

- "The international community has never succeeded in developing an accepted comprehensive definition of terrorism. During the 1970s and

1980s, the United Nations attempts to define the term floundered mainly due to differences of opinion between various members about the use of violence in the context of conflicts over national liberation and self-determination."

These divergences have made it impossible for the United Nations to conclude a Comprehensive Convention on International Terrorism that incorporates a single, all-encompassing, legally binding, criminal law definition terrorism. The international community has adopted a series of sectoral conventions that define and criminalize various types of terrorist activities.

Since 1994, the United Nations General Assembly has repeatedly condemned terrorist acts using the following political description of terrorism:

- "Criminal acts intended or calculated to provoke a state of terror in the general public, a group of persons or particular persons for political purposes are in any circumstance unjustifiable, whatever the considerations of a political, philosophical, ideological, racial, ethnic, religious or any other nature that may be invoked to justify them."

Bruce Hoffman, a scholar, has noted:

- It is not only individual agencies within the same governmental apparatus that cannot agree on a single definition of terrorism. Experts and other long-established scholars in the field are equally incapable of reaching a consensus. In the first edition of his magisterial survey, 'Political Terrorism: A Research Guide,' Alex Schmid devoted more than a hundred pages to examining more than a hundred different definitions of terrorism in an effort to discover a broadly acceptable, reasonably comprehensive explication of the word. Four years and a second edition later, Schimd was no closer to the goal of his quest, conceding in the first sentence of the revised volume that the "search for an adequate definition is still on" Walter Laqueur despaired of defining terrorism in both editions of his monumental work on the subject, maintaining that it is neither possible to do so nor worthwhile to make the attempt."

Hoffman believes it is possible to identify some key characteristics of terrorism.

He proposes that:By distinguishing terrorists from other types of criminals and terrorism from other forms of crime, we come to appreciate that terrorism is:

- Ineluctably political in aims and motives
- Violent – or, equally important, threatens violence
- Designed to have far-reaching psychological repercussions beyond the immediate victim or target
- Conducted by an organization with an identifiable chain of command or conspiratorial cell structure (whose members wear no uniform or identifying insignia) and

- Perpetrated by a subnational group or non-state entity.

A definition proposed by Carsten Bockstette at the George C. Marshall Center for European Security Studies, underlines the psychological and tactical aspects of terrorism:

- Terrorism is defined as political violence in an asymmetrical conflict that is designed to induce terror and psychic fear (sometimes indiscriminate) through the violent victimization and destruction of non-combatant targets (sometimes iconic symbols). Such acts are meant to send a message from an illicit clandestine organization. The purpose of terrorism is to exploit the media in order to achieve maximum attainable publicity as an amplifying force multiplier in order to influence the targeted audience(s) in order to reach short- and midterm political goals and/or desired long-term end states."

Walter Laqueur, of the Center for Strategic and International Studies, noted that "the only general characteristic of terrorism generally agreed upon is that terrorism involves violence and the threat of violence". This criterion alone does not produce, however, a useful definition, since it includes many violent acts not usually considered terrorism: war, riot, organized crime, or even a simple assault. Property destruction that does not endanger life is not usually considered a violent crime, but some have described property destruction by the Earth Liberation Front and Animal Liberation Front as violence and terrorism.

Terrorist attacks are usually carried out in such a way as to maximize the severity and length of the psychological impact. Each act of terrorism is a "performance" devised to have an impact on many large audiences. Terrorists also attack national symbols, to show power and to attempt to shake the foundation of the country or society they are opposed to. This may negatively affect a government, while increasing the prestige of the given terrorist organization and/or ideology behind a terrorist act.

Terrorist acts frequently have a political purpose. Terrorism is a political tactic, like letter-writing or protesting, which is used by activists when they believe that no other means will effect the kind of change they desire. The change is desired so badly that failure to achieve change is seen as a worse outcome than the deaths of civilians. This is often where the inter-relationship between terrorism and religion occurs. When a political struggle is integrated into the framework of a religious or "cosmic" struggle, such as over the control of an ancestral homeland or holy site such as Israel and Jerusalem, failing in the political goal (nationalism) becomes equated with spiritual failure, which, for the highly committed, is worse than their own death or the deaths of innocent civilians.

Very often, the victims of terrorism are targeted not because they are threats, but because they are specific "symbols, tools, animals or corrupt beings" that tie into a specific view of the world that the terrorists possess. Their suffering accomplishes the terrorists' goals of instilling fear, getting their message out to an audience or otherwise satisfying the demands of their often radical religious and political agendas.

Some official, governmental definitions of terrorism use the criterion of the illegitimacy or unlawfulness of the act. to distinguish between actions authorized by a government (and thus "lawful") and those of other actors, including individuals and small groups. Using this criterion, actions that would otherwise qualify as terrorism would not be considered terrorism if they were government sanctioned. For example, firebombing a city, which is designed to affect civilian support for a cause, would not be considered terrorism if it were authorized by a government. This criterion is inherently problematic and is not universally accepted, because: it denies the existence of state terrorism; the same act may or may not be classed as terrorism depending on whether its sponsorship is traced to a "legitimate" government; "legitimacy" and "lawfulness" are subjective, depending on the perspective of one government or another; and it diverges from the historically accepted meaning and origin of the term.

Among the various definitions there are several that do not recognize the possibility of legitimate use of violence by civilians against an invader in an occupied country. Other definitions would label as terrorist groups only the resistance movements that oppose an invader with violent acts that undiscriminately kill or harm civilians and non-combatants, thus making a distinction between lawful and unlawful use of violence. According to Ali Khan, the distinction lies ultimately in a political judgement.

An associated, and arguably more easily definable, but *not equivalent* term is violent non-state actor. The semantic scope of this term includes not only "terrorists", but while excluding some individuals or groups who have previously been described as "terrorists", and also explicitly excludes state terrorism. According to the FBI, terrorism is the unlawful use of force or violence against persons or property to intimidate or coerce a government, the civilian population, or any segment thereof, in furtherance of political or social objectives.

Barack Obama, commenting on the Boston Marathon bombings of April, 2013, declared "Anytime bombs are used to target innocent civilians, it is an act of terror." Various commentators have pointed out the distinction between "act of terror" and "terrorism", particularly when used by the White House.

PEJORATIVE USE

The terms "terrorism" and "terrorist" (someone who engages in terrorism) carry strong negative connotations. These terms are often used as political labels, to condemn violence or the threat of violence by certain actors as immoral, indiscriminate, unjustified or to condemn an entire segment of a population. Those labeled "terrorists" by their opponents rarely identify themselves as such, and typically use other terms or terms specific to their situation, such as separatist, freedom fighter, liberator, revolutionary, vigilante, militant, paramilitary, guerrilla, rebel, patriot, or any similar-meaning word in other languages and cultures. Jihadi, mujaheddin, and fedayeen are similar Arabic words which have entered the English lexicon. It is common for both parties in a conflict to describe each other as terrorists.

On the question of whether particular terrorist acts, such as killing civilians, can be justified as the lesser evil in a particular circumstance, philosophers have expressed different views: while, according to David Rodin, utilitarian philosophers can (in theory) conceive of cases in which the evil of terrorism is outweighed by the good which could not be achieved in a less morally costly way, in practice the "harmful effects of undermining the convention of non-combatant immunity is thought to outweigh the goods that may be achieved by particular acts of terrorism". Among the non-utilitarian philosophers, Michael Walzer argued that terrorism can be morally justified in only one specific case: when "a nation or community faces the extreme threat of complete destruction and the only way it can preserve itself is by intentionally targeting non-combatants, then it is morally entitled to do so".

In his book Inside Terrorism Bruce Hoffman offered an explanation of why the term terrorism becomes distorted:

- *On one point, at least, everyone agrees*: Terrorism is a pejorative term. It is a word with intrinsically negative connotations that is generally applied to one's enemies and opponents, or to those with whom one disagrees and would otherwise prefer to ignore. 'What is called terrorism,' Brian Jenkins has written, 'thus seems to depend on one's point of view. Use of the term implies a moral judgement; and if one party can successfully attach the label *terrorist* to its opponent, then it has indirectly persuaded others to adopt its moral viewpoint.' Hence the decision to call someone or label some organization *terrorist* becomes almost unavoidably subjective, depending largely on whether one sympathizes with or opposes the person/group/cause concerned. If one identifies with the victim of the violence, for example, then the act is terrorism. If, however, one identifies with the perpetrator, the violent act is regarded in a more sympathetic, if not positive (or, at the worst, an ambivalent) light; and it is not terrorism.

The pejorative connotations of the word can be summed up in the aphorism, "One man's terrorist is another man's freedom fighter". This is exemplified when a group using irregular military methods is an ally of a state against a mutual enemy, but later falls out with the state and starts to use those methods against its former ally. During World War II, the Malayan People's Anti-Japanese

Army was allied with the British, but during the Malayan Emergency, members of its successor (the Malayan Races Liberation Army), were branded "terrorists" by the British. More recently, Ronald Reagan and others in the American administration frequently called the Afghan Mujahideen "freedom fighters" during their war against the Soviet Union, yet twenty years later, when a new generation of Afghan men are fighting against what they perceive to be a regime installed by foreign powers, their attacks were labelled "terrorism" by George W. Bush. Groups accused of terrorism understandably prefer terms reflecting legitimate military or ideological action. Leading terrorism researcher Professor Martin Rudner, director of the Canadian Centre of Intelligence and Security Studies at Ottawa's Carleton University, defines "terrorist acts" as attacks against civilians for political or other ideological goals, and said:

- *There is the famous statement*: 'One man's terrorist is another man's freedom fighter.' But that is grossly misleading. It assesses the validity of the cause when terrorism is an act. One can have a perfectly beautiful cause and yet if one commits terrorist acts, it is terrorism regardless.

Some groups, when involved in a "liberation" struggle, have been called "terrorists" by the Western governments or media. Later, these same persons, as leaders of the liberated nations, are called "statesmen" by similar organizations. Two examples of this phenomenon are the Nobel Peace Prize laureates Menachem Begin and Nelson Mandela. WikiLeaks whistleblower Julian Assange has been called a "terrorist" by Sarah Palin and Joe Biden.

Sometimes, states which are close allies, for reasons of history, culture and politics, can disagree over whether or not members of a certain organization are terrorists. For instance, for many years, some branches of the United States government refused to label members of the Irish Republican Army (IRA) as terrorists while the IRA was using methods against one of the United States' closest allies (the United Kingdom) which the UK branded as terrorism. This was highlighted by the Quinn v. Robinson case. For these and other reasons, media outlets wishing to preserve a reputation for impartiality try to be careful in their use of the term.

A WORKING DEFINITION OF TERRORISM

'Terrorism' has different meanings for different people. Terminology is always a matter of agreement for the purpose of common understanding. There is no point in searching for logic-based definitions of terms which belong to the realm of political or social science, especially when the term in question carries a negative emotional connotation. There is no way on earth by which the United States can logically prove that the Libyan-sponsored attack on the Rome and Vienna airports in 1985 was an act of terrorism, if some of the basic assumptions and semantics necessary for the definition of terrorism are not universally accepted. The United States assertion is certainly consistent with its own definition of terrorism, but Colonel Muammar al-Gaddafi may still maintain that the term 'terrorism' should be reserved for acts such as the US punitive raid on Libya and that the Rome and Vienna attacks are more properly described as actions of revolutionary violence, armed struggle, or fighting for freedom. Still, for students of political violence, classification of the phenomena that fall under this general category is an essential first step of research. Achieving a consensus on the meaning of the term 'terrorism' is not an important end in itself, except, perhaps, for linguists. It is necessary, on the other hand, to differentiate between various conditions of violence and to distinguish between diverse modes of conflict, whatever we name them, if we want to gain a better understanding of their origins, the factors which affect them, and how to cope with them. The purposes, circumstances and methods involved in state violence against its own citizens are entirely different from those that characterize violence exercised by states against other states or by insurgent groups against governments. The application of the term 'terrorism' to all three situations is obfuscating and disrupts academic research as well as addressing these problems in political action. As long as the term 'terrorism' simply denotes a violent behavior which is deplorable in the eyes of the user of the term, its utility is in propaganda rather than in research.

An interesting approach to the problem of defining terrorism was taken by two Dutch researchers from the University of Leiden, Alex Schmid and Albert Jongman. They collected 109 academic and official definitions of terrorism and analyzed them in search for their main components. They found that the element of violence was included in 83.5 per cent of the definitions, political goals in 65 per cent, and 51 per cent emphasized the element of inflicting fear and terror. Only 21 per cent of the definitions mentioned arbitrariness and indiscrimination in targeting and only 17.5 per cent included the victimization of civilians, noncombatants, neutrals or outsiders. A closer look at the assortment of definitions quoted by Schmid and Jongman shows that official definitions of terrorism are fairly similar. Thus, the US Vice-President's Task Force defined terrorism as '... the unlawful use or threat of violence against persons or property to further political or social objectives.

It is generally intended to intimidate or coerce a government, individuals or groups to modify their behavior or policies. The Office for the Protection of the Constitution of the Federal Republic of Germany definition is: 'Terrorism is the enduringly conducted struggle for political goals, which... [is] intended to be achieved by means of assaults on the life and property of other persons, especially by means of severe crimes as detailed in art. 129a, sec. 1 of the penal law book (above all: murder, homicide, extortionist kidnapping, arson, setting off a blast by explosives) or by means of other acts of violence, which serve as preparation of such criminal acts. A British legal definition contains the same ingredients in a more succinct form: 'For the purposes of the legislation, terrorism is "the use of violence for political ends, and includes any use of violence for the purpose of putting the public or any section of the public in fear."

There are three common elements in the definitions quoted above:

- The use of violence;
- Political objectives and,
- The intention of sowing fear in a target population.

Compared to official definitions of terrorism, those offered by academics are, unsurprisingly, more diverse, although most of them contain the three cornerstones of government definitions. Before we become overly euphoric about the evolving consensus about terrorism, let us remember that the sample of definitions brought by Schmid and Jongman reflects, by and large, the perceptions and attitude of Western academics and officials. Not only Syrian, Libyan and Iranian opinions of what constitutes terrorism are quite different, but, most likely, those of the many other Third World countries. The evolving Western consensus about the essence of terrorism is probably not shared by the majority of people on earth. Moreover, the three basic commonly-agreed characteristics of terrorism delineated above do not suffice to make a useful definition. As working definitions, the official ones quoted above are too broad to be useful. The main problem is that they do not provide the ground to distinguish between terrorism and other forms of violent conflict, such as guerrilla or even conventional war. Clearly, both conventional war and guerrilla warfare constitute the use of violence for political ends. Systematic large-scale bombing of civilian populations in modern wars were explicitly intended to spread fear among the targeted populations.

For example, a leaflet which was dropped over Japanese cities by American bombers in August 1945 stated:

- These leaflets are being dropped to notify you that your city has been listed for destruction by our powerful air force. The bombing will begin in 72 hours.
- We give the military clique this notification because we know there is nothing they can do to stop our overwhelming power and our iron *determination. We want you to see how powerless the military is to protect you.*
- Systematic destruction of city after city will continue as long as you blindly follow your military leaders...

The dropping of atomic bombs on Hiroshima and Nagasaki which ended World War II can also be viewed as a case which fits the definitions of terrorism, albeit on a huge scale. Clearly, these were acts of violence, committed in the service of political ends, with the intent of spreading fear among the entire Japanese population. The history of guerrilla warfare also offers ample evidence of systematic victimization of civilians in an attempt to control the population. During its struggle for the independence of Algeria, the Front Liberation Nationale (FLN) murdered about 16,000 Muslim citizens and kidnapped 50,000 others, who have never been seen again, an estimated number of 12,000 FLN members were killed in internal 'purges'. A Vietcong directive of 1965 was quite explicit about the types of people who must be 'repressed', namely, punished or killed: 'The targets for repression are counterrevolutionary elements who seek to impede the revolution and work actively for the enemy and for the destruction of the revolution.' These included, among others, 'Elements who actively fight against the revolution in reactionary parties such as the Vietnamese Nationalist Party (Quoc Dan Dang), Party for a Greater Viet Narn (Dai- Viet), and Personality and Labour Party (Can-Lao Nhan-Vi), and key reactionaries in organizations and associations founded by the reactionary parties and the US imperialists and the puppet government.' To be 'repressed' were also 'Reactionary and recalcitrant elements who take advantage of various religions, such as Catholicism, Buddhism, Caodaism and Protestantism, actively to oppose and destroy the revolution, and key elements in organizations and associations founded by these persons.

A more recent example is the Peruvian Sendero Luminoso practice of killing and maiming villagers for such offenses as voting in national elections. If the definition of terrorism is equally applicable to nuclear war, conventional war and guerrilla, the term loses any useful meaning. It simply becomes a synonym for violent intimidation in a political context and is thus reduced to an unflattering term, describing an ugly aspect of violent conflicts of all sizes and shapes, conducted throughout human history by all kinds of regimes.

If both the bombing in mid-air of a commercial airliner by a small insurgent group in peacetime and strategic bombing of enemy population by a superpower in a world war are 'terrorism', social scientists, policymakers and legislators can do nothing but sigh. If we wish to use the term 'terrorism,' in a political science analysis, we ought to limit it to a more specific type of phenomena, distinguishable from other forms of political violence. Despite the ambiguities and disagreements, the concept of terrorism in modern usage is most commonly associated with a certain kind of violent actions carried out by individuals and groups rather than by states, and with events which take place in peacetime rather than as part of a conventional war. Although the original usage of the term in a political context referred to state violence and repression (the 'Reign of Terror' period in the French Revolution), from a practical point of view the recent definition of the term by the United States Department of State is a better anchor. According to this definition "'terrorism" is premeditated, politically motivated violence perpetrated against noncombatant targets by subnational groups or clandestine state agents, usually intended to influence an audience. Practicality is the only reason why, in the remainder of this article, 'terrorism' will be used to connote insurgent rather than state violence. In the following sections I shall identify terrorism more precisely among the other forms of insurgent violence.

THE UNIVERSE OF POLITICAL VIOLENCE

Theoretically, there is an infinite number of ways to classify politically motivated violence. Nevertheless, with the criteria of utility and parsimony in mind, a basic classification that relates to the initiator of the violence and to its target, distinguishing between states and citizens. It encompasses, in a gross manner, all forms of political violence carried out by humans against other humans, while differentiating between their main types. Each one of the four cells includes a distinct category of truculent behavior. These will be described briefly in the following paragraphs.

STATES AGAINST STATES

Violence initiated by states can be conceptually divided into two main types:

- State violence directed against other states, and
- Violence that states inflict on their own citizens.

Aggressive actions of states against other states have often taken the form of conventional war: a clash of sizable regular armies; this has, undoubtedly, been the most consequential form of violence in history. Various aspects of conventional wars, such as military strategy and the laws of war have been studied extensively and have become recognized academic disciplines or sub-disciplines. Obviously, states have also used a plethora of lower levels of violence in their contests with other states, such as limited air force strikes, commando raids or the assassination of enemy agents. Yet, in all cases these acts can be characterized as organized and planned, and they reflect the capability of a large bureaucracy.

STATES AGAINST CITIZENS

The use of force by states against their own citizens includes two main subcategories. One is the ordinary, overt legal process by which states enforce their laws. The other is the clandestine use of illegal violence by a government, designed to intimidate and terrorize their citizens with the intention of preventing them from opposing the regime. Sometimes illegal state violence is exercised, in the context of an internal strife, in the name of efficiency: cutting corners of due legal processes which constrain the struggle against the insurgents. Examples are abundant: The most extreme instances have involved the enormous totalitarian regimes of Nazi Germany and Stalinist Soviet Union. 'Death squads', usually manned by members of the security forces in several Latin American countries provide a less efficient, albeit quite repugnant example of a different brand.

CITIZENS AGAINST CITIZENS

The most mundane form of citizens' violence against other citizens is, of course, common crime. Common crime is usually motivated by reasons that have nothing to do with political objectives. Much of it is committed for personal economic gain and another significant part is stimulated by personal animosities. Thus, the great mass of citizens' violence against other citizens is unrelated to the subject of this article, namely, political violence. There are, however, also phenomena of citizens' violence committed for political or social motivations.

Some of these are related to racial or ethnic rivalries or strives; others are associated with rightwing or left-wing social ideologies, and still others have to do with a variety of idiosyncratic issues, such as abortion, environment conservation or animal rights. A special case of citizens' violence, vigilantism, merits special mention. Vigilante violence has, sometimes, been associated with an unauthorized attempt to control crime, but sometimes - as the origin of the term meant - with violent activity against ethnic or political minorities.

CITIZENS AGAINST THE STATE

Citizens' violence against states may be organized or spontaneous. Sometimes it is an impulsive expression of discontent, having neither clear political goals nor organized leadership or plan. In its organized form citizens' violence falls under the category of insurgency, aimed at overthrowing the government. The main forms of insurgency are distinct strategies of uprising that differ from each other in several important characteristics. Before turning to examine them in greater detail, however, it is necessary to cope with the definition of terrorism and to distinguish between this mode of violence and other forms of conflict.

FORMS OF INSURGENT VIOLENCE

Insurgent violence may take various forms. These include revolution, coup d'etat, guerrilla, terrorism and riots. In recent years the term intifada gained publicity, referring to the Palestinian uprising in the Israeli-administered territories. With the exception of riots, these forms of political violence can be also viewed as strategies of insurgency. Before I turn to focus on the characteristics of terrorism as an insurgent strategy, let us describe briefly the other forms of insurgency, emphasizing their unique attributes.

Coup d'Etat

Coup d'etat is 'a sudden, forceful stroke in politics; especially, the sudden, forcible overthrow of a government'. It is the seizure of power by an individual or a small group of persons who control important positions in the state's machinery. Edward Luttwak, who wrote a highly informative and amusing book on coup d'etat, characterized this strategy as 'the infiltration of a small but critical segment of the state apparatus, which is then used to displace the government from its control of the remainder.' Usually but not always, a coup grows from the ranks of the military. In any event, for a successful completion of a coup, the rebels must insure the cooperation of at least part of the armed forces. The success of a coup depends upon surprise, in order to catch the government off guard.

It is, therefore, imperative that preparations for the coup are done in utmost secrecy. Compared to other strategies of insurgency, a coup usually involves little violence and, sometimes, it is achieved without bloodshed. A coup is always planned to be a swift event and is ordinarily a brief episode, regardless of its success, although failed coups have, occasionally, developed into prolonged civil wars. In sum, coup d'etat can be characterized as a planned insurgency at a high level of the state's ranks, by a few people, involving relatively little violence during a very brief period of time.

Leninist Revolution

Revolution is usually meant in the sense of a radical social, political or economic change. Unlike coup d'etat, revolution is a change of the system rather than a strategy. In some cases the revolutionary change of the system has been achieved with little or no violence (*e.g.*, the recent transformation of the form of government in Czechoslovakia, East Germany and Poland or, using a very different example, the industrial revolution of the eighteenth century in England). In other instances revolutions involved enormous bloodshed, as in the Chinese Communist Revolution. Some revolutionary changes have involved protracted convulsions and others were relatively quick. In short, as Brinton started his classic treatise, 'Revolution is one of the looser words.' In the context of this article, however, the term revolution is used in a much more limited sense, connoting a strategy rather than a social or political outcome.

Although revolutions in history have sometimes been spontaneous, unplanned events and have utilized a variety of forms of struggle, since this article's interest is primarily in the nature and implications of the strategy of insurgency, I shall focus on the Leninist concept of bringing about a revolution. The way by which the Social Democratic Party under Lenin's leadership, and especially its Bolshevik branch, sought to realize the Marxist revolution was through a thorough process of clandestine preparations. According to this strategy the period of violence was meant to be brief. The actual seizure of power was conceived as a cataclysmic episode which might involve immense violence. Before this final decisive confrontation, however, there ought to be a long, arduous period of groundwork designed to prepare the revolutionary organization.

The three most important elements in this preparatory period were recruiting, educating and organizing the revolutionary cadres. Upon the opportune moment, the prepared mechanism would be put to action. This moment, according to the Marxist theory, would come when the inherent economic characteristics of the capitalistic regime would bring its collapse. Of course, not all of the activity of the revolutionary party was clandestine. There were front organizations and other tools of propaganda which carried out the important task of preparing the hearts and minds of the people. But the Most important part for making a revolution was the tightly-knit clandestine party apparatus. The Leninist model of revolutionary strategy can, therefore, be characterized as an insurgency from below, involving numerous people. The period of preparation is very long, but the direct violent confrontation is expected to be brief.

Guerrilla

Guerrilla means 'small war'. This form of warfare is, perhaps, as old as mankind, certainly older than conventional war. Guerrilla is a diffuse type of war, fought in relatively small formations, against a stronger enemy. In numerous instances guerrilla warfare has merely served as an auxiliary form of fighting, especially behind enemy lines, whereas the main military effort took the form of conventional war. In many insurrections, however, guerrilla warfare was, at least for a while, the main form of struggle. As a strategy guerrilla avoids direct, decisive battles, opting for a protracted struggle, which consists of many small clashes instead. In some guerrilla doctrines, final victory is expected to result from wearing out the enemy.

Other doctrines, however, insist that guerrilla is only an interim phase of the struggle, intended to enable the insurgents to build a regular army which will, eventually, win through conventional warfare. Guerrillas try to compensate for their inferiority in manpower, arms and equipment by a very flexible style of warfare, based on hit-andrun operations. For this, the guerrillas utilize the terrain to their advantage, immerse in the population or, sometimes, launch their attacks from neighboring countries. The principle is always to prevent the government forces from employing its full might in the contest. Tactically, however, guerrillas conduct warfare in a manner similar to conventional armies. When guerrillas stage an ambush or attack a village, they do it in the same way that a regular infantry unit would.

Riot

Riot is mob violence. Riots are usually unorganized, in the sense that the rioters are not totally controlled by a leader nor are they organized in units or other hierarchical structure. However, riots have, sometimes, been intentionally incited by organized political activists, and at least partly directed. Unlike the other forms of violence discussed in this paper, riots cannot be characterized as a strategy of insurgency or a form of warfare. Although a major insurrection has, sometimes started by riots, such as in the cases of the French Revolution of 1789 and the Russian Revolution of February 1917, the spontaneous street violence was not part of a carefully planned scheme to topple the regime. In difference from guerrilla and terrorist struggles, riots are brief, unplanned episodes. They may recur over weeks or months, but they still constitute a spasmatic eruption rather than a planned, organized, protracted campaign.

Nonviolent Resistance

By definition, nonviolent resistance is beyond the scope of an article on political violence. It encompasses methods such as demonstrations, labour strikes, hunger strikes, merchandise boycott, refusal to pay taxes, and other variations of challenging the authorities without spilling blood. This form of uprising was the purpose of comparison with violent strategies. Because of the moral and practical importance attached to nonviolent resistance as an alternative to violent modes of uprising, however, a comment on this form of struggle seems in place. Famous examples of nonviolent struggles which succeeded in inducing a major political change include Gandhi's movement in India, Martin Luther King's civil rights campaign and, of course, the 1989 protest movements in Eastern Europe.

In view of these stunning successes, one should wonder why have they been so rare in history. A possible explanation may suggest that nonviolent resistance was only discovered after World War II. This is certainly not true. Gene Sharp mentions several cases in history which prove the contrary. A more plausible explanation is that nonviolent resistance is of practical value only when the challenged government refrains from using its power to break the resistance by force. In this sense, the change of political standards after World War II which has been expressed in a global recognition of the right of self-determination and in a general trend towards further liberalization in democracies, gave nonviolent resistance a better chance than ever before. Nevertheless, even in the second half of the twentieth century, there has not been a single case of a successful nonviolent challenge to a totalitarian regime or external power which was determined to face it by force. This lesson was learned, at a dear cost, by the Hungarians in 1956, the Czechs in 1968, and the Chinese students in 1989.

At a first glance, the success of the nonviolent movements in East Germany, Poland, Czechoslovakia and Bulgaria to change the regimes in these countries in 1989 seems to contradict this generalization. It should be remembered, however, that these movements were prompted by the liberalization in the Soviet Union, and they succeeded only because the USSR changed its previous policy of intervention and even refused to render the communist regimes of its former satellites minimal Political backing in their effort to retain power.

The difference between the successful Czech uprising in 1989 and the failure of 1968, or between the success in East Germany and the failure in China, cannot be attributed to the greater determination or capability of the insurgents in the successful cases, but to a lesser determination of the governments. The Iranian Islamic Revolution of 1979 and the failure of the August 1991 coup in Moscow are other seeming demonstrations of the effectiveness of nonviolent resistance. Yet in these examples too, the success of the unarmed civilians was a result of the rulers' indecisiveness and ineptitude. In all likelihood, greater determination from the Shah in Iran or the coup junta in the USSR, would have resulted in a bloody crushing of the resistance. In short, nonviolent resistance is a practical mode of strife only when the government allows it to take place. It is absolutely useless in repressive regimes determined to remain in power. In addition, only rarely has nonviolent resistance existed as the only mode of struggle. Alongside Gandhi's nonviolent struggle against British rule, there were numerous terrorism and rioting incidents. Black dissatisfaction in the United States in the 1960s was not only expressed in peaceful marches and sit-ins but in violent riots as well. A broad uprising is usually expressed in several concurrent forms, and it is hard to evaluate the effects of the various aspects of the comprehensive struggle singly.

TYPES OF TERRORISM

In early 1975, the Law Enforcement Assistant Administration in the United States formed the National Advisory Committee on Criminal Justice Standards and Goals. One of the five volumes that the committee wrote was entitled *Disorders and Terrorism*, produced by the Task Force on Disorders and Terrorism under the direction of H.H.A. Cooper, Director of the Task Force staff.

The Task Force classified terrorism into six categories:

- *Civil disorder*: A form of collective violence interfering with the peace, security, and normal functioning of the community.
- *Political terrorism*: Violent criminal behaviour designed primarily to generate fear in the community, or substantial segment of it, for political purposes.
- *Non-Political terrorism*: Terrorism that is not aimed at political purposes but which exhibits "conscious design to create and maintain a high degree of fear for coercive purposes, but the end is individual or collective gain rather than the achievement of a political objective."
- *Quasi-terrorism*: The activities incidental to the commission of crimes of violence that are similar in form and method to genuine terrorism but which nevertheless lack its essential ingredient. It is not the main purpose of the quasi-terrorists to induce terror in the immediate victim as in the case of genuine terrorism, but the quasi-terrorist

uses the modalities and techniques of the genuine terrorist and produces similar consequences and reaction. For example, the fleeing felon who takes hostages is a quasi-terrorist, whose methods are similar to those of the genuine terrorist but whose purposes are quite different.

- *Limited political terrorism*: Genuine political terrorism is characterized by a revolutionary approach; limited political terrorism refers to "acts of terrorism which are committed for ideological or political motives but which are not part of a concerted campaign to capture control of the state.
- *Official or state terrorism*: "Referring to nations whose rule is based upon fear and oppression that reach similar to terrorism or such proportions." It may also be referred to as Structural Terrorism defined broadly as terrorist acts carried out by governments in pursuit of political objectives, often as part of their foreign policy.

Number of failed, foiled or successful terrorist attacks by year and type within the European Union. Source: Europol. 1 person died in terrorist attacks from separatist groups in 2010.

Several sources have further defined the typology of terrorism:

- Political terrorism
  - Sub-state terrorism
    - i. Social revolutionary terrorism
    - ii. Nationalist-separatist terrorism
    - iii. Religious extremist terrorism
      - a. Religious fundamentalist Terrorism
      - b. New religions terrorism
    - i. Right-wing terrorism
    - ii. Left-wing terrorism
    - iii. Single-issue terrorism
  - State-sponsored terrorism
  - Regime or state terrorism
- Criminal terrorism
- Pathological terrorism

MOTIVATION OF TERRORISTS

Attacks on 'collaborators' are used to intimidate people from cooperating with the state in order to undermine state control. This strategy was used in the USA in its War of Independence and in Ireland, in Kenya, in Algeria and in Cyprus during their independence struggles.

Attacks on high profile symbolic targets are used to incite counter-terrorism by the state to polarise the population. This strategy was used by Al Qaeda in its attacks on the USA in September 2001. These attacks are also used to draw international attention to struggles which are otherwise unreported such as the Palestinian airplane hijackings in 1970 and the South Moluccan hostage crises in the Netherlands in 1975.

Abrahm suggests that terrorist organizations do not select terrorism for its political effectiveness. Individual terrorists tend to be motivated more by a desire for social solidarity with other members of their organization than by political platforms or strategic objectives, which are often murky and undefined.

DEMOCRACY AND DOMESTIC TERRORISM

The relationship between domestic terrorism and democracy is very complex. Terrorism is most common in nations with intermediate political freedom, and is least common in the most democratic nations. However, one study suggests that suicide terrorism may be an exception to this general rule. Evidence regarding this particular method of terrorism reveals that every modern suicide campaign has targeted a democracy–a state with a considerable degree of political freedom. The study suggests that concessions awarded to terrorists during the 1980s and 1990s for suicide attacks increased their frequency.

Some examples of "terrorism" in non-democracies include ETA in Spain under Francisco Franco (although the group's terrorist activities increased sharply after Franco's death), the Shining Path in Peru under Alberto Fujimori, the Kurdistan Workers Party when Turkey was ruled by military leaders and the ANC in South Africa. Democracies, such as the United Kingdom, United States, Israel, Indonesia, India, Spain and the Philippines, have also experienced domestic terrorism.

While a democratic nation espousing civil liberties may claim a sense of higher moral ground than other regimes, an act of terrorism within such a state may cause a dilemma: whether to maintain its civil liberties and thus risk being perceived as ineffective in dealing with the problem; or alternatively to restrict its civil liberties and thus risk delegitimizing its claim of supporting civil liberties.

For this reason, homegrown terrorism has started to be seen as a greater threat, as stated by former CIA Director Michael Hayden. This dilemma, some social theorists would conclude, may very well play into the initial plans of the acting terrorist(s); namely, to delegitimize the state.

RELIGIOUS TERRORISM

Religious terrorism is terrorism performed by groups or individuals, the motivation of which is typically rooted in faith-based tenets. Terrorist acts throughout the centuries have been performed on religious grounds with the hope to either spread or enforce a system of belief, viewpoint or opinion. Religious terrorism does not in itself necessarily define a specific religious standpoint or view, but instead usually defines an individual or a group view or interpretation of that belief system's teachings.

PERPETRATORS

The perpetrators of acts of terrorism can be individuals, groups, or states. According to some definitions, clandestine or semi-clandestine state actors may also carry out terrorist acts outside the framework of a state of war. However, the most common image of terrorism is that it is carried out by small and secretive cells, highly motivated to serve a particular cause and many of the most deadly operations in recent times, such as the September 11 attacks, the London underground bombing, and the 2002 Bali bombing were planned and carried out by a close clique, composed of close friends, family members and other strong social networks. These groups benefited from the free flow of information and efficient telecommunications to succeed where others had failed. Over the years, many people have attempted to come up with a terrorist profile to attempt to explain these individuals' actions through their psychology and social circumstances. Others, like Roderick Hindery, have sought to discern profiles in the propaganda tactics used by terrorists.

Some security organizations designate these groups as *violent non-state actors*. A 2007 study by economist Alan B. Krueger found that terrorists were less likely to come from an impoverished background (28 per cent vs. 33 per cent) and more likely to have at least a high-school education (47 per cent vs. 38 per cent). Another analysis found only 16 per cent of terrorists came from impoverished families, vs. 30 per cent of male Palestinians, and over 60 per cent had gone beyond high school, vs. 15 per cent of the populace. To avoid detection, a terrorist will look, dress, and behave normally until executing the assigned mission. Some claim that attempts to profile terrorists based on personality, physical, or sociological traits are not useful. The physical and behavioral description of the terrorist could describe almost any normal person. However, the majority of terrorist attacks are carried out by military age men, aged 16–40.

STATE SPONSORS

A state can sponsor terrorism by funding or harbouring a terrorist organization. Opinions as to which acts of violence by states consist of state-sponsored terrorism vary widely. When states provide funding for groups considered by some to be terrorist, they rarely acknowledge them as such.

STATE TERRORISM

As with "terrorism" the concept of "state terrorism" is controversial. The Chairman of the United Nations Counter-Terrorism Committee has stated that the Committee was conscious of 12 international Conventions on the subject, and none of them referred to State terrorism, which was not an international legal concept. If States abused their power, they should be judged against international conventions dealing with war crimes, international human rights and international humanitarian law. Former United Nations Secretary-General Kofi Annan has said that it is "time to set aside debates on so-called 'state terrorism'. The use of force by states is already thoroughly regulated under international law" However, he also made clear that, "regardless of the differences between governments on the question of definition of terrorism, what is clear and what we can all agree on is any deliberate attack on innocent civilians, regardless of one's cause, is unacceptable and fits into the definition of terrorism." State terrorism has been used to refer to terrorist acts by governmental agents or forces. This involves the use of state resources employed by a state's foreign policies, such as using its military to directly perform acts of terrorism. Professor of Political Science Michael Stohl cites the examples that include Germany's bombing of London and the U.S. atomic destruction of Hiroshima during World War II.

He argues that "the use of terror tactics is common in international relations and the state has been and remains a more likely employer of terrorism within the international system than insurgents." They also cite the First strike option as an example of the "terror of coercive diplomacy" as a form of this, which holds the world hostage with the implied threat of using nuclear weapons in "crisis management." They argue that the institutionalized form of terrorism has occurred as a result of changes that took place following World War II. In this analysis, state terrorism exhibited as a form of foreign policy was shaped by the presence and use of weapons of mass destruction, and that the legitimizing of such violent behaviour led to an increasingly accepted form of this state behaviour. State terrorism has also been used to describe peacetime actions by governmental agents such as the bombing of Pan Am Flight 103.

Charles Stewart Parnell described William Ewart Gladstone's Irish Coercion Act as terrorism in his "no-Rent manifesto" in 1881, during the Irish Land War. The concept is also used to describe political repressions by governments against their own civilian population with the purpose to incite fear. For example, taking and executing civilian hostages or extrajudicial elimination campaigns are commonly considered "terror" or terrorism, for example during the Red Terror or Great Terror. Such actions are often also described as democide or genocide which has been argued to be equivalent to state terrorism. Empirical studies on this have found that democracies have little democide.

FUNDING

State sponsors have constituted a major form of funding; for example, Palestine Liberation Organization, Democratic Front for the Liberation of

Palestine and some other terrorist groups were funded by the Soviet Union. The Stern Gang received funding from Italian Fascist officers in Beirut to undermine the British Mandate for Palestine. Pakistan has created and nurtured terrorist groups as policy for achieving tactical objectives against its neighbours, especially India.

"Revolutionary tax" is another major form of funding, and essentially a euphemism for "protection money". Revolutionary taxes are typically extorted from businesses, and they also "play a secondary role as one other means of intimidating the target population". Other major sources of funding include kidnapping for ransoms, smuggling, fraud and robbery. The Financial Action Task Force is an inter-governmental body whose mandate, since October 2001, has included combatting terrorist financing.

TACTICS

Terrorism is a form of asymmetric warfare, and is more common when direct conventional warfare will not be effective because forces vary greatly in power. The context in which terrorist tactics are used is often a large-scale, unresolved political conflict.

The type of conflict varies widely; historical examples include:

- Secession of a territory to form a new sovereign state or become part of a different state
- Dominance of territory or resources by various ethnic groups
- Imposition of a particular form of government
- Economic deprivation of a population
- Opposition to a domestic government or occupying army
- Religious fanaticism

Terrorist attacks are often targeted to maximize fear and publicity, usually using explosives or poison. There is concern about terrorist attacks employing weapons of mass destruction. Terrorist organizations usually methodically plan attacks in advance, and may train participants, plant undercover agents, and raise money from supporters or through organized crime. Communications occur through modern telecommunications, or through old-fashioned methods such as couriers.

RESPONSES

Responses to terrorism are broad in scope. They can include re-alignments of the political spectrum and reassessments of fundamental values.

Specific types of responses include:

- Targeted laws, criminal procedures, deportations, and enhanced police powers
- Target hardening, such as locking doors or adding traffic barriers
- Preemptive or reactive military action

- Increased intelligence and surveillance activities
- Preemptive humanitarian activities
- More permissive interrogation and detention policies

The term counter-terrorism has a narrower connotation, implying that it is directed at terrorist actors. According to a report by Dana Priest and William M. Arkin in the Washington Post, "Some 1,271 government organizations and 1,931 private companies work on programmes related to counterterrorism, homeland security and intelligence in about 10,000 locations across the United States."

MASS MEDIA

Media exposure may be a primary goal of those carrying out terrorism, to expose issues that would otherwise be ignored by the media. Some consider this to be manipulation and exploitation of the media. The internet has created a new channel for groups to spread their messages. This has created a cycle of measures and counter measures by groups in support of and in opposition to terrorist movements. The United Nations has created its own online counter-terrorism resource.

The mass media will, on occasion, censor organizations involved in terrorism (through self-restraint or regulation) to discourage further terrorism. However, this may encourage organizations to perform more extreme acts of terrorism to be shown in the mass media. Conversely James F. Pastor explains the significant relationship between terrorism and the media, and the underlying benefit each receives from the other.

- There is always a point at which the terrorist ceases to manipulate the media gestalt. A point at which the violence may well escalate, but beyond which the terrorist has become symptomatic of the media gestalt itself. Terrorism as we ordinarily understand it is innately media-related.—Novelist William Gibson

HISTORY

The history of terrorism goes back to Sicarii Zealots — Jewish extremist group active in Judaea Province at the beginning of the 1st century AD. After Zealotry rebellion in the 1st century AD, when some prominent collaborators with Roman rule were killed, according to contemporary historian Josephus, in 6 AD Judas of Galilee formed a small and more extreme offshoot of the Zealots, the Sicarii. Their terror also was directed against Jewish "collaborators", including temple priests, Sadducees, Herodians, and other wealthy elites.

The term "terrorism" itself was originally used to describe the actions of the Jacobin Club during the "Reign of Terror" in the French Revolution. "Terror is nothing other than justice, prompt, severe, inflexible," said Jacobin leader Maximilien Robespierre. In 1795, Edmund Burke denounced the Jacobins for letting "thousands of those hell-hounds called Terrorists...loose on the people" of France. In January 1858, Italian patriot Felice Orsini threw three bombs in an attempt to assassinate French Emperor Napoleon III. Eight bystanders were killed and 142 injured. The incident played a crucial role as an inspiration for the development of the early Russian terrorist groups. Russian Sergey Nechayev, who founded People's Retribution in 1869, described himself as a "terrorist", an early example of the term being employed in its modern meaning. Nechayev's story is told in fictionalized form by Fyodor Dostoevsky in the novel *The Possessed*. German anarchist writer Johann Most dispensed "advice for terrorists" in the 1880s.

A TYPOLOGY OF TERRORISM

If we are to have a full understanding of the term "terrorism," which encompasses a significant number of highly varied movements and groups, we need to establish a summary typology. Excluding state terrorism, we need to draw a distinction among terrorist groups based on left- or rightwing political ideology (in that regard, it is useful to recall that terrorism is a tactic and has no inherent political colouration); nationalist movements, either separatist or autonomist; and political-religious sects. In most cases, terrorism represents a political strategy. While warfare is based on physical coercion, terrorism seeks to have a psychological impact. In contrast to guerrilla warfare, terrorism is the negation of combat. It is about attacking an unarmed adversary, not about surprise attacks on elements of a regular army.

Among revolutionary terrorist groups, mainly on the left but also on the right, we find the following organizations or groupings:

- In the United States, the Weathermen and the Symbionese Liberation Army
- In the Federal Republic of Germany, the Rote Armee Fraktion, better known as the Baader-Meinhof Gang, led by Gudrun Ensslin and Horst Mahler in addition to the two principals for whom it was named; along with the tiny, more obscure anarchist group "Movement 2 June", whose name commemorates the date of the police killing of a student at a demonstration against the shah of Iran's presence in Germany
- In Italy, the Brigate rosse or Red Brigades, and, on the far right, various fascistic organizations
- In Japan, the Japanese Red Army

Among the separatist or autonomist ethnic movements in the West, we may cite:

- In Canada, the Front de liberation du Quebec (FLQ), short-lived but noted for its kidnapping and murder of a government minister
- In Ireland, the IRA, the most broadly-based of the movements on this list

- In Spain, the military wing of Euskadi ta Askatasuna (Basque Homeland and Freedom), or ETA
- In France, almost preposterous groups that assert that Corsica is a colony and playact the role of a liberation movement, exploiting the laxity of the French state

Autonomist or separatist movements that resort to terrorism are classified as terrorist movements by the U.S. government, although many are first and foremost guerrilla movements. That is the case in Latin America with two Colombian organizations, the Revolutionary Armed Forces of Colombia and the smaller National Liberation Army, as well as the Shining Path in Peru, or what is left of it since the arrest of its leader Abimael Guzman, known as President Gonzalo. In the Middle East, such movements include the Democratic Party of Iranian Kurdistan (PDKI), led, until his assassination by the Iranians, by Abdul-Rahman Gassemlou. From 1979 to 1984, when it was compelled to withdraw to Iraq, this group never went in for terrorist-type activity.

That is also true, to the best of our knowledge, of the Kurdistan Democratic Party and the Patriotic Union of Kurdistan, the Kurdish movements active in Iraq between 1968 and 1991. The Kurdistan Workers' Party (PKK), active in Turkey from 1984 to the arrest of its leader Abdullah Ocalan, known as Apo, was above all a guerrilla movement. Over its fifteen years of existence, the movement, operating across a large swath of south-eastern Turkey, compelled Ankara to mobilize up to 150,000 troops to stamp it out. The PKK also put terrorism to effective use in its struggle. The Turkish army, for its part, deployed death squads to eradicate all Kurdish opposition, including non-violent opposition. The Palestinians, whatever their political persuasion, have had little alternative to terrorism, being unable to launch a guerrilla war.

The Chechen insurgents are less easy to characterize than others. On the one hand, the movement indisputably harbours nationalists devoted to the idea of independence and fighting in a guerrilla context. On the other hand, Chechnya is a jihad attracting Islamist fighters from a number of countries, the best-known being the Jordanian Shamil Basayev, who tried unsuccessfully to drag Dagestan into the struggle. Moreover, Chechen nationalists or radical Islamists have resorted to terrorism, as illustrated by the 2002 hostage-taking in a Moscow theater. Beyond a shadow of a doubt, the world's most effective organization when it comes to terror is the Liberation Tigers of Tamil Eelam—the Tamil Tigers. But it is primarily a guerrilla movement and has even been able to mount conventional military operations against the Sri Lankan army. In Nepal, the Maoist movement is a guerrilla operation, as are the faction fighting for the independence of Aceh in Sumatra, Indonesia, and the weaker movements waging armed struggles on the ground in the Molucca Islands and Papua New Guinea. In the Philippines, the Moro National Liberation Front, or MLNF, on Mindanao, claiming to represent the Muslim minority of 4 percent within a vast Catholic majority, has been calling for autonomy, or even independence, for decades. Over the years, the movement has received assistance from Libya and other Arab countries. The even more extreme Abu Sayyaf Group split off from the MLNF in 1991. Since no typology can reflect the full complexity of reality, we must include here the sui generis struggle led, with no hope of success, by the Armenians between 1975 and 1983. Foremost among the political-religious sects resorting to terrorism are the militant radical Islamists who coalesced in Afghanistan and have participated in various armed struggles, some by no means limited to terrorist activities, in Bosnia, Algeria, Chechnya, Kashmir, and so on.

The long list of Islamist organizations includes some with memberships of just a few dozen and others that count thousands of adherents. Such movements have arisen in virtually every Muslim country, with the general exception of sub-Saharan Africa. The Hezbollah movement of Lebanon, deemed a terrorist organization by the United States, is above all a militant political movement. It is not chiefly characterized by acts of terrorism. Aum Shinrikyo, which gained renown with its 1995 sarin gas attack on the Tokyo subway, killing twelve and injuring thousands to varying degrees, is notable among millenarian sects (but hardly the only one).

Instances of state terrorism that took place during the same period include, in Latin America:

- The death squads in Brazil
- The systematic suppression of Indians in Guatemala
- The depredations of the Argentine military throughout its hold on power
- The early years, in particular, of the Pinochet regime in Chile
- The especially brutal counterterrorism and counterinsurgency operations in Peru under President Fujimori

In Africa:

- The Algerian army and its methods
- the use of terror during the fourteen-year dictatorship of Charles Taylor in Liberia
- The dictatorships of Francisco Macias Nguema in Equatorial Guinea and Idi Amin Dada in Uganda
- The civil war in Sierra Leone
- The terror in Burundi under Tutsi rule
- The genocide in Rwanda and its impact on neighbouring Congo

In the Middle East:

- State terror implemented by Turkey in the context of the counterinsurgency, including death squads and the policy of systematic deterritorialization in the Kurdish region
- The massacre of 10,000 Sunnis in Hama by the regime of Hafez al-Assad of Syria in 1982

- The systematic deployment of terror at every level by Saddam Hussein, especially with respect to the Kurds, including Operation Anfal,2 the use of poison gas against the Kurds in Halabja in 1988, and the 1991 suppressions of the Kurds and Shiites

In Southeast and East Asia:

- Genocidal massacres in Cambodia
- Terror in China's Cultural Revolution• and,
- Although occurring before 1968, the 1965 massacre of between 300,000 and 500,000 communists or suspected communists by the Suharto regime in Indonesia

This list is not, of course, exhaustive. Let us keep in mind that, as the political scientist Paul Wilkinson puts it, torture is the "extreme form of individualized terror."

THE JIHADIST MOVEMENT IN THE CONTEXT OF CONTEMPORARY TERRORISM

From 1970 to 1990, it was customary to divide terrorist organizations into three categories: revolutionary, identity-based, and manipulative. During that period, revolutionary terrorism was mainly the province of far-left European groups such as the Red Brigades or the Red Army Fraction. Cause-based terrorism was particularly influenced, at the international level, by Palestinian organizations, with their secular ideology and Marxist-Leninist leanings.

They had succeeded in forging active ties—in the areas of training, logistics, and mission subcontracting— with European revolutionary groups or other cause-based groups such as the Provisional Irish Republican Army (PIRA) and ETA. Finally, manipulative terrorism, or state terrorism—which uses undercover agents, mercenary groups, or other entities under its control—was considered characteristic mainly of the countries of the Middle East or of the Levant such as Iran, Syria, Iraq, and Libya. All of them, in the framework of their regional power strategies, had availed themselves of the services of PLO dissident groups.

Two trends emerged following the collapse of the Soviet bloc: the near-cessation of state terrorism and the end of Palestinian secular terrorism and of European far-left revolutionary terrorism. Islamic terrorism, however, began to pick up steam. Its many new manifestations either filled the vacuums that had been created—for instance, the Palestinian group Hamas took over from the Palestine Liberation Organization, now a state entity—or set out to fight new battles. Some believe that today's Islamic terrorism is simply a new form of anti imperialism and that it can be classified as revolutionary terrorism.

Others are of the view that it falls into a fourth category—religious terrorism. It should be emphasized that this essay does not aim to denounce Islam or its religious schools, nor does it claim to be a scholarly treatise on the struggles waged within Muslim or Muslim-influenced societies. Its more modest goal is to serve as a tool—a kind of filter, perhaps—to better understand the contemporary phenomenon of Islam-inspired political violence. To state that the phenomenon should be viewed as a holy undertaking smacks of propaganda. To insist that it can be explained solely on the basis of specific religious interpretations or selective analyses is to oversimplify the subject; specialists who make such claims can be very far removed from realities on the ground.

In the summer of 2002, an in-depth treatise was published by recognized authors which explained that there was no threat of jihadist terrorism in Southeast Asia. Yet on October 12 next, Bali was struck by the Jammah Islamiya in the deadliest attacks since those of September 11. The book—otherwise very good—has since been reissued with a different conclusion. It is thus important to move beyond a discussion of actual threats and to situate the mujahideen movement in its proper context in the history of political terrorism, so that its true nature can be fully understood and the full extent of the danger it poses accurately assessed.

This text therefore takes a different tack than do those that have been published since the end of 2001, which appear to favour sensationalism over facts. To view the events of September 11 as representing the emergence of a kind of super-terrorism, lumping together a shoddy analysis of events with a discussion of threats verging on apocalyptic fantasy, smacks more of a sales pitch than of a level-headed process of reflection. Gerard Chaliand, in denouncing the "anxiety sellers," points out that, while terrorism certainly kills large numbers of people, it does provide a livelihood for many others—consider the numerous experts offering erudite explanations who have come out of the woodwork in recent times.

But the subject of terrorism merits a more restrained approach, if only because of the respect due its victims. One thing is certain: jihadist terrorism cannot prevail, because, unlike Islamism, it has no genuine political vision and, as a result, does not engage in negotiations. It has a different goal: to push for mass radicalization in the context of a near-Messianic undertaking. In that sense, the jihadists' message is much more revolutionary than religious, and its approach more long-term than is generally recognized. The extent to which some authors overestimate the importance of the phenomenon is commensurate only with the depth of their silence in the face of its growing strength during the previous decade. The first attack against the World Trade Center was not the one of September 11, 2001, in which hijacked airliners slammed into it; the first attack took place on February 26, 1993, when a car bomb exploded in an underground parking lot beneath the Center.

Those topics have, however, been dealt with very insightfully by a number of serious-minded authors from various fields, all of whom have approached the topic of jihadist terrorism from a comprehensive perspective. They are listed in the bibliography, and the multidisciplinary approach taken here is greatly in their debt.

GUIDE TO TERMINOLOGY

It must be recalled that the term "Islamism" refers not to a theological doctrine but to the political use of Islam. In that sense, Islamism must be distinguished from fundamentalism, which advocates a return to the founding texts of Islam. Islamic fundamentalism becomes Islamism only when its ideology is used to impose a strictly interpreted model of original Islam based on sharia, or Islamic law, on society and on the state. I therefore use the term "political Islamism" to describe the beliefs of those movements that endeavor—by legal means—to use Islam to reform the institutional structure and sociocultural environment of a particular geopolitical grouping. I use the term "radical Islamism" when attempts are made to completely transform such a geopolitical grouping.

The term "activist Islamism" (or "militant Islamism") is used when movements resort to violence to achieve their goals. Finally, the phrase "Islamist terrorism" (or "jihadist terrorism") is used to describe a new stage of that third phase, in which Islamist activists use terrorism—indiscriminate or targeted—to impose their views, or in the context of identity politics. Thus the term "jihadist movement" encompasses previously fragmented Islamist activist groups that had, at an earlier stage, opted for jihad as a means to an end, but that later embraced it as their sole objective. The term "mujahideen movement," which is close enough to it in meaning that it is often used in its stead, places greater emphasis on individual action on the part of its followers, however, in the context of what is to them a holy undertaking. Finally, I shall avoid engaging in any kind of scholarly dispute; that I leave to the specialists. Inasmuch as I am addressing a readership that is curious about the realities of contemporary terrorism, and that, in general, lacks in-depth knowledge of Islam, I have chosen to limit references to texts to brief but informative quotations, placing them in the appropriate historical context. While it may seem to some that Arabic terms have been translated too simplistically, the goal here is for such terms to be as widely understandable as possible.

EGYPTIAN GROUPS MOVE FROM VIOLENT PROTESTS TO TERRORISM

In the 1970s, a number of small groups took shape, coalescing around charismatic leaders. Their acts of violence garnered widespread media coverage and piqued the interest of many young Egyptians from the religious middle classes, as well as from socially disadvantaged segments of society. Underemployed students determined to fight corruption among the elites, as well as impoverished farmers forced into rural exodus, joined different groups, depending on their social and geographical origins. This period saw the emergence of Saleh Sirriya's Organization for Islamic Liberation (al-Harakat al-islamiya lil tahrir), Sheikh Omar Abdel Rahman's Islamic Group (Gama›at al-Islamiya), and Mustafa Shukri's Muslim Society (Jamaat al-Muslimin), which the press soon dubbed "Takfir wal Hijra" (Anathema and Exile), or TWH, the name by which it is generally known—its use being either pejorative or positive, depending on the speaker. Shukri, an agricultural engineer from a modest background in the plains of southern Egypt, took his cue from the attitude of the Prophet at the time of his return to Medina. He believed that people who claimed to be Muslims but failed to devote themselves to waging holy war against apostate rulers were themselves heathens.

True believers—still a minority—had no choice but to "anathematize" (takfir) those Egyptians who accepted such a jahiliya type of existence, and to retreat (hijra) in order better to fight them. The first stages of the war ordered by Shukri were more along the lines of petty crime. Funds were needed to finance the organization, which was composed largely of illiterate Muslims from rural backgrounds.

The group therefore engaged in extortion, targeting wealthy farmers and businessmen, and robbed members of the Coptic community—incidents that usually involved some form of violence. All of this, of course, attracted the attention of the Egyptian security services (mukhabarat), which arrested several members of the group. In an attempt to win their freedom, Shukri ordered the kidnapping of key local personalities, including political figures and judges. During the resulting clashes with the police, a hostage was executed, and Shukri was soon identified and arrested.

He was condemned to death in 1974. After Shukri's execution, some of his followers emigrated to Algeria, where the authorities had recently begun an Arabization campaign and were looking for teachers. Influenced by their views, an Algerian movement led by Dr. Ahmed Bouamra adopted the underground name of TWH. A second wave of Shukri followers also went into exile in Pakistan in 1980; they were among the first to join up with those jihadist groups that were fighting the Soviet army in Afghanistan. They originated a form of TWH that, because it was internationalist in character, hewed more closely to the jihadist model; it met with violent opposition from the Salafist movement. Several dozen Algerians, veterans of the jihad against the Soviet army, returned to Algeria in late 1989, bringing with them their new ideology and giving fresh impetus to the jihadist spirit of Bouamra's Algerian TWH.

They were among the first to advocate the use of violence. Following the imposition of a state of emergency, many of those takfiris fled to Europe. There they established a number of networks—part criminal, part jihadist—which were subsequently dismantled by local police forces during the period 1993–2002. Most of their members subscribed to the group's school of thought in order to reap the benefits of ghanima—tolerated behaviour. Indeed, that obscure dispensation permits the commission, in the name of jihad, of illegal acts—such as theft, trafficking, even murder—against infidels as long as a portion of the spoils is handed over to the cause.

To add to the particularities of the international form of TWH—also known within the Salafist movement as the Muslim Society (Gamaat al- Muslimin)—its last leader, the emir Al Barkaoui, lost no time in proclaiming himself caliph in 1994, before being forced by other, hostile jihadist emirs to flee Pakistan for Europe. He was eventually edged out by Abu Kutada, the ideological leader of the local European jihadist movement, which the last of the TWH's militants drifted into joining. The Organization for Islamic Liberation involved mainly low-ranking officers whose nationalist ideals had been shattered following the Arab defeat by Israel in 1967.

It was decimated in 1974 in the wake of the Heliopolis garrison's aborted mutiny, but its work was carried on, in a sense, by al-Jihad, which had moved quickly to recruit members within specialized military units. The most famous of those recruits is, of course, Lieutenant-Colonel Khaled al-Istambuli, mastermind of Anwar Sadat's assassination during a military parade on October 6, 1981. His brother, Tawfik, later headed out to the Afghano-Pakistani zone, becoming a follower of Ayman al-Zawahiri and then of Osama bin Laden. The Gama›at al-Islamiya (GI) undoubtedly represents the most fully developed form of Egyptian jihadism and the one that underwent the most extensive transformation. It started out as a student organization, playing a pivotal social role in universities, while proselytizing heavily. Young students, made vulnerable by the isolation that can come with attending university and lured by cheap rent and free transport, soon came to embrace militant Islamism—a symbol of social solidarity.

The authorities quietly encouraged their activities so as to counterbalance the influence of the Marxist unions. In the late 1970s, the movement, led by Omar Abdel Rahman—a graduate of al-Azhar University known as the "blind sheikh"—had evolved into a highly structured organization comprising dozens of autonomous groups. They had considerable material and financial resources at their disposal, including buses, offices, a print shop, and health centers. Sadat was not viewed with hostility at the time, because he had made sure to enlist the support of religious circles, in particular at al- Azhar, so as to foil any attempted plots by Nasser's old guard. During the first part of his term, religion began to intrude into public life: the family code and the status of women were changed to reflect the rules of sharia.

The situation changed drastically when Sadat joined in the peace process with Israel, launched under pressure from the United States. His rule came to mean a corrupt regime; a rapprochement with the West, Israel's great champion; and the excesses of a leadership that left the Muslim people mired in poverty.

Thus Sadat became known as "The Pharaoh." The protests organized by the GI were brutally suppressed. Its property was seized and its offices shut down, depriving students of a number of social benefits and greatly angering them. Many of them, as a result, joined underground offshoots of Gama'at al-Islamiya and went on to wage urban guerrilla warfare against any and all symbols of power. Attacks and assassinations were rife. In the end, the sole result of such a harsh repression was the creation of a fresh crop of martyrs.

Sadat, who had understood the new dimensions of the threat, was more than willing to accept the American suggestion that he support the Afghan jihad, seeing that he might be able to get rid of the most radical of the militants by sending them off to Pakistan. But he was unable to reverse the revolutionary process that had begun in his country, which culminated in his assassination, before the eyes of the international press, during the military commemoration of the first victories of October 1973. His death sentence, which was carried out by al-Jihad members, had been authorized earlier by a GI-issued fatwa, probably written by Omar Abdel Rahman himself.

INDISCRIMINATE TERRORISM AND THE DEFEAT OF EGYPTIAN JIHADISM

The death of the Pharaoh was the first great victory achieved by the jihadist movement, whose strategy was now sketched out in blood. For the first time, an apostate leadership had been shaken to its very foundation. Egyptian paratroopers had to intervene, wresting control of the city of Assiout from the jihadists, who had proclaimed it an Islamist city.

By the end of 1981, all of the Middle East regimes were under threat, paralyzed by the failure of pan-Arabism and by their inability to create any kind of economic momentum despite the bonanza of their oil wealth. Syria's Hafez al-Assad had forgotten none of this when, a year later, he ordered his troops to retake, at any cost, the town of Hama, which had fallen to the local Muslim Brotherhood movement. An estimated 8,000 to 20,000 people were killed in the process—a new crop of jihadist martyrs.

The new Egyptian head of state, Hosni Mubarak, saw clearly that suppression—even when carried out with an iron rod—would not suffice. Nonetheless, in 1982, he sent 14,000 soldiers to the shantytown of Imbaba, in Upper Egypt, which had just proclaimed itself an Islamic republic; it took six weeks to retake it. Mubarak followed in his predecessor's footsteps in diverting Islamist demands by directly supporting the Afghan mujahideen. Most of al-Jihad's leaders were executed and their followers imprisoned. Most of the latter, once freed, chose to return to Pakistan.

That was the case of Ayman al-Zawahiri, a surgeon, and Muhammad Atef, a police officer, who went on to become the leaders in exile of a militant organization whose jihadist activities were focused more on other countries than on their own. Many of the militants who remained in—or returned to—Egypt were arrested in August 1993, just before a planned bomb attack against the minister of defence. However, it was probably al-Jihad members—veterans of the war in Afghanistan—who carried out the first major suicide bombing, using two vehicles, against the Egyptian Embassy in Islamabad on February 3, 1995. Al-Jihad was also responsible for the attempt on Mubarak's life during an official visit to Addis Ababa on February 19, 1995. Strangely enough, the GI was not as affected, probably because of the organization's size.

Omar Abdel Rahman himself, following a lengthy trial, was found not guilty of issuing the fatwa calling for Sadat's assassination. He went into exile in Saudi Arabia and later in Pakistan, and finally, in 1990, requested political asylum in the United States. Until his arrest three years later, he continued from there to guide the decisions of Egyptian leaders in the context of the armed struggle. Despite the purges carried out within the ranks of the army, soldiers remained who were open to jihadist ideas. Egyptian military officers forged ties in Pakistan not only with the Afghan mujahideen but also with the Arab volunteers who were being trained to fight the Soviet army. It was a long time before the regime could regain trust in its security apparatus, and it thought twice about positioning it in areas where there was support for the GI.

The Islamists took advantage of that state of affairs to strengthen their bases and move ahead with the recruiting process, while at the same time forming profitable relationships with their counterparts in neighbouring countries such as Libya, Somalia, Yemen, and Saudi Arabia. The first GI targets were local ones.

The groups attacked and robbed infidels—that is to say, Copts—and struck at symbols of power, in particular local authorities, so as to ensure security in Islamist-held areas. In the early 1990s, the Cairo cemetery, in which hundreds of thousands of marginalized Egyptians were living, served also as a GI rear base, which the police dared not enter. In the early part of the decade, however, the Egyptian security services gradually retook the ground they had lost.

The ulama, aware of the danger posed by the radicals, lent their support to the ruling authorities, taking a stance against the insidious but very real call that was being made to submit to the rules of Islam. Now the roles were reversed. Successive neutralization campaigns, coupled with the absence of any real external support, drastically undermined the strength of GI militant cells.

By 1996, the movement no longer had a strategy, and its seven jailed leaders finally agreed to negotiate a truce. Sheikh Abdel Rahman himself, from his American prison cell, called for an end to the fighting. For that reason, the last remaining active GI cells, in a senseless, lastditch effort to bring the government to its knees, began to target tourist areas, so vital to the Egyptian economy. In September 1997, a group of mujahideen carried out a grenade attack against a busload of tourists, killing nine German citizens. That November, a hail of bullets felled fiftyeight Western nationals, the majority of them Swiss tourists, at Luxor; survivors were stabbed to death.

The operation was masterminded by an Afghan veteran, Mehat Abdel Rahman, and probably directed, from Afghanistan, by Rifai Taha, head of the group's external branch. But the Egyptian jihadists, whose actions had doomed hundreds of thousands of Egyptians to many long months of unemployment, had played their last cards. Since then, the Islamist movement has not claimed responsibility for a single local attack. However, in the 1980s the fight being waged by Egyptian militants— precursors of the mujahideen movement—had acquired a new dimension through its support for external jihads. Forced to take refuge in Afghanistan in the mid 1990s, its militants openly joined forces with al Qaeda, for which it had always been a mainstay.

2

The Ideological Nature of Terrorism

The most important feature of terrorism, distinguishing it from other criminal acts or conduct during armed conflict, is the motivation of terrorists and the codex against which terrorists measure their conduct. Generally speaking, those perpetrating 'normal' criminal offences do so out of some personal, hedonistic motivation – whether that be the material rewards of a burglary, the thrill and high of challenging 'the system' or using drugs, or the desperation of stealing necessities where no alternatives appear to be available. Personal gain is the common feature of criminal conduct, setting aside crimes of passion and those of the mentally insane. In contrast, the primary motivation of terrorists is altruistic, motivated by a higher cause or ideology that is greater than his or her personal impulses or gains.

It should be recognised that the individual terrorist may not be motivated in this way, instead acting out of a sense of revenge borne out of the individual's personal or familial experience or perceptions of ill-treatment or humiliation, a matter recognised, for example, by the Israeli Security Agency and the Israeli Counter-Terrorism Bureau, and also implied in the United Nations Global Counter-Terrorism Strategy.

It can be generally said, however, that a terrorist (or at least the entity that recruited the individual) will act for the furtherance of an external cause (whether it be a localised secessionist movement or global jihad) and for the benefit this has to both the cause and the people of it. Combined with the honour derived from such conduct in this life, and the rewards in the next, the motivations of a terrorist are far beyond those of an 'ordinary' criminal offender. Consider, for example, the following description of rewards attainable by the

- *Shahid (suicide bomber) in the afterlife*: When the Shahid meets Allah, he will be forgiven from the first drop of blood. He is saved from the grave. He sees his place in heaven. He is saved from the great horror. He is given 72 dark-eyed women. And he is champion of the right for 70 members of his family. A crown is placed on his head, with a precious gem. That is better than anything that exists in this world.

Added to these distinct motivations are the standards against which terrorists measure their conduct. The fact that a terrorist act might be unlawful according to the law of the State in which the act is perpetrated, or under international law, is argued to be irrelevant to a terrorist. Terrorists measure their conduct against the codex of the ideology they are pursuing.

If the ideology mandates the killing of Jews or Christians, then that killing is not murder but, instead, a legitimate and appropriate act. The consequence of these features is significant. Standard criminology does not apply. The notion of personal deterrence is largely irrelevant, with the language of terrorists often entirely divorced from that of the 'normal' criminal offender. Moving from these more abstract ideologies, one can also categorise the impetus for particular terrorist acts as falling within one or more of the following four motivations: secession; insurgency; regional retribution; and the phenomenon of what has come to be known as 'the global jihad'.

Secession

It is an all-too-common assertion that one person's terrorist is another's freedom fighter. For instance, would a bombing carried out by a rebel group, which is directed towards the destabilisation of dictatorial authorities perpetrating horrific crimes against the local population (the Pol Pot Regime, for example), amount to a terrorist act or an act of a legitimate liberation movement? Such propositions have been the subject of much debate. Early resolutions of the General Assembly addressing the issue of terrorism contained express affirmations of the principle of self-determination. In the very first resolution of the United Nations on the subject of terrorism, the General Assembly expressed deep concern over terrorism, urged States to solve the problem by addressing the underlying issues leading to terrorist conduct, and then stated that

- *The General Assembly*: Reaffirms the inalienable right to self-determination and independence of all peoples under colonial and racist regimes and other forms of alien domination and upholds the legitimacy of their struggle, in particular the struggle of national liberation movements, in accordance with the purposes and principles of the Charter and the relevant resolutions of the organs of the United Nations;

A number of subsequent General Assembly resolutions echoed this affirmation, adding that such liberation movements should also be conducted in accordance with the Declaration on Principles of International Law Concerning Friendly Relations and Co-operation among States. One of the most problematic issues in this area is distinguishing terrorists from lawful combatants in legitimate struggles for selfdetermination. Here, States that do not recognise a claim to self-determination will commonly claim that those using force against the State's military forces are terrorists. The right to self-determination is the right of a people (sharing a common historical tradition, racial or ethnic identity, cultural homogeneity, linguistic unity, religious or ideological affinity, territorial connection, and or a common economic life) to determine their political status and freely pursue their own economic, social and cultural development. It holds a prominent position within various international documents.

However, the precise scope of this right, and in particular whether it includes a right to use armed force and engage in wars of national liberation, has always been a point of contention. This controversy, as recognised by the Special Rapporteur to the former Sub-Commission on the Promotion of Human Rights, has been the major obstacle to the development of a comprehensive definition of the term 'terrorism', and of the completion of work towards the Comprehensive Convention on International Terrorism. The Comprehensive Convention is to be considered, while the interface between terrorism.

What can be said at this point is that, since its adoption of the 1994 Declaration on Measures to Eliminate International Terrorism, the General Assembly has made it clear that self-determination does not legitimate the use of terrorism by those seeking to achieve self-determination. This is a point reiterated by the Special Rapporteur on the promotion and protection of human rights and fundamental freedoms while countering terrorism, in the context of the terrorist organisation ETA (Euskadi Ta Askatasuna) in Spain, whose proclaimed political goal is self-determination for the Basque Country.

Insurgency and Regional Retribution

The second and third motivations for terrorist acts are those arising out of the occupation of a territory by foreign military forces, either in the form of insurgency occurring within the occupied territory or acts directed towards occupying forces but occurring outside the territory. Insurgency and regional retribution have been portrayed by many as the prime motivations for terrorist events linked to the occupations in Afghanistan and Iraq during these early years of the twenty-first century. Examples include the attack on United Nations headquarters in Baghdad on 19 August 2003, which claimed the lives of the Special Representative of the Secretary-General, Sergio Vieira de Mello, and 21 other men and women. Following the commencement of the multi-national Operation Enduring Freedom in Afghanistan, a manifesto issued by Salem Almakhi and first aired on Aljazeera in October 2002, announced a warning to Christians and members of the alliance waging war against Afghanistan and Al-Qa'ida. A further example can be seen in a video statement of Noordin Mohamad Top directed to various nations, including Australia and the United Kingdom, and identifying senior members of the

- *Australian Government*: As long as you keep your troops in Iraq and

> Afghanistan and intimidate Muslim people, you will feel our intimidation... You will be the target of our next attack... Our enemy is America, Australia, England and Italy... We especially remind Australia that you, Downer and Howard, are killing Australia, leading it into darkness and misfortune and mujahedeen terror...

Islam and 'The Global Jihad'

Finally, closely linked to the ideological nature of terrorism, is the question of Islam and terrorism. An all-too-common and unfortunate expression is that not all Muslims are terrorists, but all international terrorists are Muslim. While that is not entirely correct, and certainly not advocated by the author, it is true that the modern phenomenon of international terrorism (in the form of what has come to be known as 'The Global Jihad') is perpetrated by radical Muslims. The adoption of terrorism by radical Islamic movements as their modus operandi stems, in part, from the historical development and subsequent manipulation of the Islamic faith. Islam began as a faith of a small community of believers during the seventh century in what is now Saudi Arabia.

It is based upon the belief that Muhammad, a respected businessman in Mecca in around 600 AD, received revelations from Allah (God) that were later written down in the Qur'an. A period of divisions followed the death of the prophet Muhammad, leading to the characterisation of two Muslim loyalties today: the Sunni (representing the vast majority of Muslims today under the Sunnah Islamic faith); and the Shi'ite (who treat Muhammad's sonin- law Ali as their caliph and subsequently elevated him to the status of prophet). Within what is now the main-stream Sunnah faith, four 'schools' of interpretation of the complex text of the Qur'an came to be accepted as legitimate (from liberal to radical): the Hanafi, Maliki, Shafi'i, and Hanbali. The greater majority of Muslims advocate and practice the more moderate interpretations of the Sunnah revelations of the Qur'an. For such Muslims, their faith advocates tolerance of others and their religious choices and customs. On the subject of those that are not Muslim, for,

- Example, the Qur'an instructs: And I shall not worship that which you are worshipping.
- Nor will you worship that which I worship.
- To you be your religion, and to me my religion.

The core of Islamic life for all Sunnah is said to be the 'five pillars of Islam': publicly bearing witness to the basic affirmation of faith; saying prescribed prayers five times a day; fasting during the month of Ramadan; giving a tithe or alms for support of the poor; and making a pilgrimage to Mecca at least once during the believer's lifetime, if this is possible. Calls for the killing of Jews and Christians by the likes of Usama bin Laden and Al-Qa'ida is based upon a radical reading of the already conservative school of Sunnah interpretation (Hanbali).

The motivation of Al-Qa'ida, for example, is the spreading of the Muslim faith and the elimination of what such groups see as the evil of modernity. The advancement of religious beliefs is not, in and of itself, problematic and is in fact a common tenet of almost all religions. Viewing modernity (democracy, capitalism, Statehood) as an evil that must be eliminated at all cost is, however, an extreme view and one that poses a threat to all western nations.

The World Islamic Front Statement of 1998, entitled "Jihad Against Jews and Crusaders", purports to be a fatwa (religious ruling) requiring the killing of Americans, and claims to base itself upon a call by Allah to "slay the pagans wherever ye find them, seize them, beleaguer them, and lie in wait for them in every stratagem (of war)".

- *The 1998 Statement concludes with the following direction*: We – with Allah's help – call on every Muslim who believes in Allah and wishes to be rewarded to comply with Allah's order to kill the Americans and plunder their money wherever and whenever they find it. We also call on Muslim ulema, leaders, youths, and soldiers to launch the raid on Satan's US troops and the devil's supporters allying with them, and to displace those who are behind them so that they may learn a lesson.

While this fatwa is particularly directed towards Americans, due to the purported occupation and plundering of the Arabian Peninsula by the United States during the 1991 and 1998 Gulf wars, the sentiment of the jihad is one that is opposed to modernity in general. Its desire is to eliminate modernity and return to the era when Islam formed a prosperous ummah (community of Islamic believers) in the Middle East and beyond, without restriction by State borders: an era in which modernity was absent in the region.

Following the commencement of the multi-national Operation Enduring Freedom in Afghanistan a further manifesto, issued by Salem Almakhi, announced a warning to Christians and members of the alliance waging war against Afghanistan and Al-Qa'ida. This most palpably applies to States participating in Operation Enduring Freedom, but is also of much broader application. It conceivably attaches to all members of the United Nations taking action against Usama bin Laden, the Taliban and Al-Qa'ida pursuant to various Security Council resolutions and the directions of the Council's 1267 Sanctions Committee.

The manifesto finally:

- *Instructs*: Anyone who possesses an arrow in his quiver, make haste and [shoot] it for the sake of Allah, and aim it at the enemies of religion – the Jews and the Christians [...].

Along the same lines, an audio tape aired by Aljazeera in 2003, a senior aide to Usama bin Laden, Ayman Zawahri, exhorted his audience with the following words:

- Oh Muslims! Carry out attacks against the embassies, companies, interests and officials of the US, Britain, Australia and Norway. Burn the ground under their feet.

- Opposed to this, writers such as Al-Muhajabah condemn the use of terrorism and point to the following Qur'anic versus as restricting the circumstances in which recourse to acts of aggression may be had: Permission to fight (against disbelievers) is given to those (believers) who are fought against, because they have been wronged. And what is wrong with you that you fight not in the Cause of Allah, and for those weak, ill-treated and oppressed among men, women and children. Allah does not forbid that you to deal justly and kindly with those who fought not against you on account of religion nor drove you out from your homes. Verily, Allah loves those who deal with equity... It is only as regards those who fought against you on account of your religion, and have driven you out of your homes, and helped to drive you out, that Allah forbids you to befriend them.

So it is that the one text of a relatively young religion has given rise to two Muslim loyalties, with four schools of thought arising from the more widely-practised Sunnah devotion of Islam. Of those four schools, the minority conservative school of Hanbali has been adopted and distorted by some to advocate jihad, through terrorist means, against modernity.

TERRORISM

How does terrorism fit into the spectrum of political violence? The customary modern usage of the term refers, at least in the West, to actions such as the bombing in mid-air of Pan Am Flight 103 in December 1988, the attacks on passengers in the Rome and Vienna airports in December 1985, and the seizure of the Saudi Embassy at Khartoum in March 1973. These actions represent a form of political violence which is different from guerrilla, conventional war and riots. Actions of this kind, when they are carried out systematically, constitute a distinct strategy of insurgency. This strategy should have a name, be it 'terrorism' or another, and retaining 'terrorism' has the advantage of familiarity. In fact, practitioners and advocates of this form of struggle have themselves often used the term to describe their method. Yet, the definitions of the term leave several questions to be answered. I shall now turn to examine some of the areas of confusion.

TERRORISM AND GUERRILLA

The terms 'terrorism' and 'guerrilla' are often used interchangeably. Apart from some carelessness in the use of technical terminology by the media, politicians and even academics, this faulty synonymity reflects confusion concerning the definition of terrorism and, often, a wish to avoid the negative connotation that this term has acquired. 'Guerrilla' does not carry a defamatory overtone and its usage, therefore, seems to many writers to carry an air of objectivity. As Walter Laqueur pointed out, the widespread use of the misnomer 'urban guerrilla' had probably contributed to the confusion. This term has been used by revolutionaries to describe a strategy of terrorism, as an extension of, or substitute for guerrilla warfare.

As strategies of insurgency, however, terrorism and guerrilla are quite distinct. The most important difference is that unlike terrorism, guerrilla tries to establish physical control of a territory. This control is often partial. In some cases the guerrillas ruled the area during the night and government forces had control in daytime. In other examples government forces were able to secure the main routes of transportation but guerrilla territory started as little as a few hundred yards to the right and left. In many instances guerrillas managed to maintain complete control of a sizable portion of land for long periods of time. The need to dominate a territory is a key element in insurgent guerrilla strategy. The territory under the guerrillas control provides the human reservoir for recruitment, a logistical base and - most important -the ground and infrastructure for establishing a regular army. Terrorist strategy does not vie for a tangible control of territory. Notwithstanding the fact that terrorists try to impose their will on the general population and channel its behavior by sowing fear, this influence has no geographical demarcation lines. Terrorism as a strategy does not rely on 'liberated zones' as staging areas for consolidating the struggle and carrying it further. As a strategy, terrorism remains in the domain of psychological influence and lacks the material elements of guerrilla. Other practical differences between the two forms of warfare further accentuate the basic distinction of the two strategies.

These differences belong to the tactical domain, but they are actually an extension of the essentially divergent strategic concepts. They relate to unit size, arms, and types of operations of guerrilla and terrorism. Guerrillas usually wage war in platoon or company size units and, sometimes even in battalions and brigades. There are well-known historical examples in which guerrillas even used division-size formations in battle. Terrorists operate in very small units, usually ranging from the lone assassin or a single person who makes and plants an improvised explosive device, to a five members' hostagetaking team. The largest teams in terrorist operations numbered 40- 50 persons. These, however, have been very rare.

Thus, in terms of operational units' size, the upper limits of terrorists are the lower limits of guerrillas. Differences in weapons used in these two types of warfare are also easily noticeable. Whereas guerrillas mostly use ordinary military-type arms, such as rifles, machine-guns, mortars and even artillery, typical terrorist weapons include home-made bombs, car bombs and sophisticated barometric pressure-operated devices, designed to explode on board airliners in mid-air. These differences in unit size and arms are merely corollaries of the fact, that tactically, guerrilla actions are similar to regular army's mode of operation. Because terrorists, unlike guerrillas, have no territorial base, they must immerse among the general civilian population if they do not wish to become sitting ducks for their hunters. This is why ordinarily terrorists cannot allow themselves to wear uniforms, while guerrillas ordinarily do. In a somewhat simplified comparison, therefore, one may say that whereas guerrilla and conventional war are two modes of warfare which are different in strategy but similar in tactics, terrorism is a unique form of struggle in both strategy and tactics.

METHOD AND CAUSE: TERRORISTS AND FREEDOM FIGHTERS

Terrorist groups normally describe themselves as national liberation movements, fighters against social, economic, religious, or imperialist oppression, or any combination of these. On the other side of the barricade, in an understandable attempt to degrade terrorism, politicians have presented the terms 'terrorists' and 'freedom fighters' as contradictory. Thus, Vice-President George Bush wrote: 'The difference between terrorists and freedom fighters is sometimes clouded. Some would say one man's freedom fighter is another man's terrorist. I reject this notion. The philosophical differences are stark and fundamental. Without passing judgement on the self-description of any particular group, trying to present the terms 'terrorists' and 'freedom fighters' as mutually exclusive in general is a logical fallacy.

'Terrorism' and 'freedom fighting' are terms which describe two different aspects of human behavior. The first characterizes a method of struggle and the second - a cause. The causes of groups which adopted terrorism as a mode of struggle are as diverse as the interests and aspirations of mankind. Among the professed causes of terrorist groups are social changes in the spirit of right wing and left wing ideologies, aspirations associated with religious beliefs, ethnic grievances, environmental issues, animal rights and specific issues such as abortion. Some terrorist groups undoubtedly fight for self-determination or national liberation. On the other hand, not all national liberation movements resort to terrorism to advance their cause. In other words, some insurgent groups are both terrorist and freedom fighters, some are either and some are neither. Terrorism and Morality The hero of the moralistic approach to terrorism is a Russian named Ivan Kaliayev. Kaliayev was a member of the 'combat organization' of the underground Social-Revolutionary Party which adopted assassinations of government officials as its main strategy in the struggle against the Tsarist regime. Kaliayev was chosen by the organization to assassinate the Grand Prince Sergei. On 2 February 1905 Kaliayev waited, a bomb under his coat, for the arrival of the Grand Prince. When the Prince's carriage approached, however, Kaliayev noticed that the intended victim was accompanied by his two young children. In a spur-of-the-moment decision Kaliayev refrained from throwing the bomb, so as not to hurt the Prince's innocent brood.

Two days later Kaliayev completed the mission, was caught, tried and executed. Kaliayev's insistence on a very strict definition of permitted targets of revolutionary violence gained him the status of a saint in the gospel of moralistic analysts of terrorism and something like a litmus paper for a quick identification of right and wrong in revolutionary violence. The most concentrated treatment of the question of the morality of terrorism has probably been offered by Walzer. His basic position can be summarized by the following quotation: In its modern manifestations, terror is the totalitarian form of war and politics. It shatters the war convention and the political code. It breaks across moral limits beyond which no further limitation seems possible, for within the categories of civilian and citizen, there isn't any smaller group for which immunity might be claimed...

Terrorists anyway make no such claim; they kill anybody. Walzer's morality litmus is the responsibility of the victims for acts that are the subject of the assailants' grievances. In line with this criterion he offers what one might call a crude scale of assassinability: government officials who are part of the presumed oppressive apparatus are assassinable. A case in point is Kaliayev's victim. Other persons in government service, who are not related to the oppressive aspects of the regime (*e.g.*, teachers, medical service personnel, etc.), make a questionable category. Walzer's somewhat ambiguous verdict is that because 'the variety of activities sponsored and paid for by the modern state is extraordinary... it seems intemperate and extravagant to make all such activities into occasions for assassination. The third category, that of private persons, is definitely not assassinable according to Walzer. These cannot spare their lives by changing their behavior. killing them is, therefore, unequivocally immoral. Walzer's analysis leaves several principal problems with no satisfactory answer. The most important one has to do with the essence of moral judgement. The fundamental question is whether moral norms in general and war norms in particular are absolute, unchanging over time and identical in all societies, or are they a changing reflection of the human condition and, therefore, varying across societies and perennially modified to fit new situations.

An absolute nature of moral norms may presumably stem from two sources: a godly edict or a universal psychological trait, common to men and women in all societies in history. In the first case, there is no point in arguing: Divine rules are not negotiable, they are a matter of belief. For those who believe in their divine source, they are fixed regulations of human conduct which do not change over time. Walzer admits that his treatise rests on the Western religious tradition, but it is not clear whether this attribution is a statement of cultural identification or an announcement of personal religious conviction. Cultural norms are certainly a powerful source of influence on attitudes, opinions and behavior, and can be portrayed as the cast in which personal values are molded.

But for claiming the status of an absolute value of the human race, it is necessary to show that the value under consideration is shared by all cultures. Given the tremendous diversity of cultures, the assertion that a certain value is universal must rest on the assumption that this value stems from a set of attitudes and emotions which prevail in all societies. With regard to the specific issue under consideration, namely, moral values related to political violence, the universality assumption is untenable. This is proven by the very fact that divergence from the moral code of war presented by Walzer as the absolute dictum, is so common. Flagrant breaches of Walzer's rules in modern history cannot be explained merely by the personal craziness or iffirnorality of some individuals, who happened to head totalitarian regimes which enabled them to act in contradiction to the will of most of their inhabitants. In many cases, the violations of morality have been supported by the majority of the population in the nation which committed them. Large scale departures from the laws of war have been practiced even by democracies, a form of regime where government action is limited by public will. Thus, the massive bombing of Japanese civilian population, with the intent of damaging the population's morale, and the total destruction of Hiroshima and Nagasaki by atomic bombs in World War II were, undoubtedly, supported by most of the American people.

It is obvious that in actual application, the moral code in general, including the rules of war, is a product of people's needs, perceptions and convenience, and is subject to cultural and circumstantial influences. Cultural differences concerning the status of noncombatants have been expressed, for instance, in the utilization of hostages. Whereas most Westerners regarded the usage by Iraq in 1990 of civilian hostages - men, women and children - as a human shield against the Possible bombing of strategic targets as a repugnant, immoral act, for many in the Arab world this was a legitimate, morally justified feat. It seems, however, that situational factors have a much greater role than cultural diversity in determining conduct in war.

The form of government is, perhaps, the single most important factor. The most severe violations of human rights in modern history have been committed by totalitarian Western regimes. Perceived necessity plays a major role as well. In fact, all states have repeatedly broken the rules of war. In almost all modern wars civilian populations have been victimized intentionally, and the magnitude of the transgression has been determined by capability and need as much as by moral principles. Terrorism is not different from other forms of warfare in the targeting of noncombatants. Yet terrorism, more than any other form of warfare, systematically breaches the internationally accepted rules of war. In guerrilla warfare and conventional war, the laws of engagement are often ignored, but terrorism discards these laws altogether in refusing to distinguish between combatants and noncombatants and, with regard to international terrorism, in rejecting the limitations of war zones as well. Unlike conventional and guerrilla wars, terrorism has no legal standing in international law (from the viewpoint of domestic law all insurrections are treated as crimes). For this reason, terrorism as a strategy and terrorists as a warring party have no hope of gaining a legal status.

Hence, terrorism may be correctly described as an illegal form of warfare, but characterizing it as an immoral one is meaningless. Terrorists wage war by their own standards, not by the standards of their enemies. Both sides' rules of conduct stem from capabilities and necessities and undergo changes for reasons that are basically pragmatic. Of course, people and states pass moral judgement on the justification of wars and on particular acts in war. Their judgement, however, reflects nothing but their own existing cultural norms at best and - too often - a partisan view, influenced by direct interests. Yet morality, although it cannot be coherently treated as an absolute value is, at a given time, society and context, a psychological and, therefore, a political fact.

Publics do pass moral judgements on persons, organizations and actions. They react by moral standards, no matter how emotional and irrational these may be. In fact, it is the emotional rather than the logical component that makes morally-based attitudes so powerful. Morality is a code of behavior which prevails in a certain society at a certain time. As such, morality closely corresponds to the existing law, but the latter has the advantages of clarity, precision and formality. As a reflection of current norms, terrorism is an immoral form of warfare in twentieth century Western societies. The power of this characterization, however, is weakened by the fact that in virtually all modern wars the moral code of behavior (and, indeed, the laws of war) has been breached by all parties on a massive scale, at least with regard to the targeting of civilians. In this respect, the difference between terrorism and other forms of warfare is a matter of comprehensiveness. Whereas terrorists usually dismiss the law altogether, without even pretending to abide by it, states pay tribute to law and norms and breach them only under extreme circumstances it should be noted that the relativity of morality has been also expressed in the changing rules of combating terrorism. If laws reflect the prevailing moral standards in a given society, one may find interest in the fact that all states, when faced with the threat of insurgency, have enacted special laws or emergency regulations permitting the security forces to act in manners that would normally be considered immoral. Indeed, under such circumstances states have even tended to sanction security forces' breaching of these laws or, at best, to punish such 'excesses' rather leniently.

ATTEMPTS TO DEFINE TERRORISM

Attempts to define terrorism have been made since before the establishment of the United Nations.

The Draft League of Nations Convention for the Prevention:

- *Punishment of Terrorism was to provide that terrorism comprised*: All criminal acts directed against a State and intended or calculated to create a state of terror in the minds of particular persons or a group of persons or the general public.

This Draft Convention never came into force as not enough States ratified it, due mainly to dissent over definition of the term. There have been suggestions that terrorism be defined as the peacetime equivalent of war crimes. In a report to the United NationsOffice on Drugs and Crime (UNODC), Alex Schmidt proposed taking the already agreed upon definition of war crimes (comprising deliberate attacks on civilians, hostage-taking and the killing of prisoners) and extending it to peacetime. Terrorism would then be defined as the "peacetime equivalents of war crimes". It does not appear, however, that this has gained any popular acceptance. Schmidt's earlier and more complex definition of terrorism is, on

- The other hand, cited by UNODC as representing "academic consensus": An anxiety-inspiring method of repeated violent action, employed by a (semi-) clandestine individual, group or state actors, for idiosyncratic, criminal or political reasons, whereby – in contrast to assassination – the direct targets of violence are not the main targets. The immediate human victims of violence are generally chosen randomly (targets of opportunity) or selectively (representative or symbolic targets) from a target population, and serve as message generators. Threat and violence-based communication processes between terrorist (organisation), (imperilled) victims, and main targets are used to manipulate the main target (audience(s)), turning it into a target of terror, a target of demands, or a target of attention, depending on what the intimidation, coercion, or propaganda is primarily sought.
- At the European Union level, the crime of terrorism has been defined by the Parliamentary Assembly of the Union as: Any offence committed by individuals or groups resorting to violence or threatening to use violence against a country, its institutions, its population in general or specific individuals which, being motivated by separatist aspirations, extremist ideological conceptions, fanaticism or irrational and subjective factors, is intended to create a climate of terrors among official authorities, certain individuals or groups in society, or the general public.

Three practical distinctions between terrorist and criminal conduct have been made earlier in this chapter, concerning the focus, participants in, and victims of terrorism. The two definitions of terrorism just cited contain three further common threads: firstly, that the victims or 'physical' target(s) of a terrorist act (a building, or people) are not the 'primary' target of the act (the target against whom a message is being sent, usually a government or international organisation); next, the purpose of the threat or violence is to intimidate and create a situation of fear or terror (hence the term terrorism) or to persuade or dissuade the primary target to do or abstain from doing something; and, finally, that this is done to advance an ideological, political, or religious cause.

OBJECTIVE VERSUS SUBJECTIVE DEFINITIONS OF THE TERM

The sticking point in achieving international consensus on a definition of the term is not so much with the technical wording of what physical conduct amounts to a terrorist act. The problem lies more with what the purpose of the conduct is. This, as discussed earlier, is particularly controversial in the context of secession and the boundaries of permissible conduct by a peoples in pursuit of their self-determination. A number of States argue that a subjective analysis and definition of such conduct (by considering its purpose) should therefore be made. The UN Office on Drugs and Crime reports that Arab States such as Libya, Syria and Iran have all campaigned for a definition that excludes acts of 'freedom fighters' from the international definition of terrorism by employing the argument that a justified goal may be pursued by any available means.

While these positions are firmly held by a small number of States, the majority of States adhere to an objective definition of terrorism (one which does not take into account the motives of the conduct). In 1994, the UN General Assembly adopted the Declaration on Measures to Eliminate International Terrorism. The Declaration was based on the notion of peace and security and the principle of refraining from the threat or use of force in international relations.

It pronounced that terrorism constitutes a grave violation of the purpose and principles of the United Nations. While it did not purport to define terrorism, it did say that criminal acts intended or calculated to provoke a state of terror in the general public for political,

- *Purposes are in any circumstances unjustifiable*: The States Members of the United Nations solemnly reaffirm their unequivocal condemnation of all acts, methods and practices of terrorism, as criminal and unjustifiable, wherever and by whomever committed, including those which jeopardise the friendly relations among States and peoples and threaten the territorial integrity and security of States.

In reaffirming the Declaration in 1995, *the General Assembly was even more precise on this point*:

- Reiterates that criminal acts intended or calculated to provoke a state of terror in the general public, a group of persons or particular persons are in any circumstances unjustifiable, whatever the considerations of a political, philosophical, ideological, racial, ethnic, religious or any other nature that may be invoked to justify them;

Of even greater value in this respect, according to the Executive Director of the International Policy Institute for Counter-Terrorism, is the Security Council's resolution 1269. While the resolution also fails to define terrorism, it clearly takes an objective approach to the question of terrorist conduct, stating,

- *That the Security Council*: Unequivocally condemns all acts, methods and practices of terrorism as criminal and unjustifiable, regardless of their motivation, in all their forms and manifestations, wherever and by whomever committed, in particular those which would threaten international peace and security;

Resolution 1373 also points to an objective approach, paragraph 3(g) of the resolution calling upon States to ensure that "claims of political motivation are not recognized as grounds for refusing requests for the extradition of alleged terrorists".

- *Security Council resolution 1566 further provides as follows*: Recalls that criminal acts, including against civilians, committed with the intent to cause death or serious bodily injury, or taking of hostages, with the purpose to provoke a state of terror in the general public or in a group of persons or particular persons, intimidate a population or compel a government or an international organization to do or to abstain from doing any act, which constitute offences within the scope of and as defined in the international conventions and protocols relating to terrorism, are under no circumstances justifiable by considerations of a political, philosophical, ideological, racial, ethnic, religious or other similar nature, and calls upon all States to prevent such acts and, if not prevented, to ensure that such acts are punished by penalties consistent with their grave nature;.

INTERNATIONAL CONVENTIONS RELATING TO TERRORISM

The number and scope of these conventions might, at first instance, seem impressive and comprehensive. They have, however, various limitations. To begin with, they only apply to States parties to the conventions. Beyond this, the conventions are of limited application because of the very precise subject matter of each treaty. The conventions are not of general application but, rather, relate to specific situations in which terrorist acts might have effect, whether on board aircraft, in airports or on maritime platforms. The only treaty with the potential to impact a wider audience and scope of activity is the International Convention for the Suppression of the Financing of Terrorism (the Suppression of Financing Convention). This is said for two reasons. Firstly, the Convention mirrors much of the suppression of financing obligations contained in Security Council resolution 1373. As a resolution binding upon all members of the United Nations, this has had a significant impact upon the status of the Convention. Prior to 11 September 2001, there were just four States parties to the Convention and, accordingly, the Convention was not in force. Due at least in part to resolution 1373 and the work of the Counter-Terrorism Committee, there are now 160 States parties to the Convention. The Suppression of Financing Convention is also of greater relevance because of the wording of article 2(1)(b) of the Convention. Although this provision does not purport to define the term 'terrorism', it explains (for the purpose of prohibiting the financing of terrorist entities or operations) what type of acts may not be financed:

- Any other act intended to cause death or serious bodily injury to a civilian, or to any other person not taking an active part in the hostilities in a situation of armed conflict, when the purpose of such act, by its nature or context, is to intimidate a population, or to compel a government or an international organization to do or to abstain from doing any act.

The Convention does therefore have some potentially wider application and is useful for States in determining the type of conduct they are to prohibit.

THE DRAFT COMPREHENSIVE CONVENTION ON INTERNATIONAL TERRORISM

Also considered in Chap. 3 is the work undertaken since 2000 towards establishing a comprehensive convention against terrorism. One of the expected sticking points in the progress of this work has been that of definitions, not just in terms of defining what amounts to a terrorist act (draft article 2), but also with regard to the wording of draft article 18, which concerns exemptions. In particular, the definition and/or inclusion of acts of "armed forces" or "parties" to a conflict (this being relevant to the proposed limited exemptions from jurisdiction and/or liability under the Convention); whether "foreign occupation" should be included within that category of exemptions; and whether the activities of military forces should be "governed" or "in conformity" with international law.

Draft article 18 has been described by the Chairman of the Committee as the crux of the Convention. Hinging upon these matters has been a lack of consensus on a preamble.

UNITED NATIONS HIGH-LEVEL PANEL DEFINITION OF TERRORISM

Albeit non-binding, mention should be made of the 2004 report of the

Secretary- General's High-level Panel on Threats, Challenges and Change in which terrorism

- Was described as:...any action, in addition to actions already specified by the existing conventions on aspects of terrorism, the Geneva Conventions and Security Council resolution 1566 (2004), that is intended to cause death or serious bodily harm to civilians or non-combatants, when the purpose of such an act, by its nature and context, is to intimidate a population, or to compel a Government or an international organization to do or to abstain from doing any act.

There are two problems with this definition, corresponding to each of the emphasised sections of text in the quotation. Firstly, the definition does not confine itself to the extant terrorism-related conventions. That is, it goes further than the description within Security Council resolution 1566, of acts to be suppressed in the fight against terrorism by expressing itself to be "in addition to" actions already specified within that resolution.

The UN Special Rapporteur on counter-terrorism has expressed dissatisfaction with this approach, instead advocating for precision by restricting 'terrorism' to the cumulative characteristics set out within resolution 1566. Furthermore, the definition within the High-Level Panel's report is potentially confusing because of its imprecise reference to "civilians or non-combatants". By doing so, the definition immediately invokes war-time terminology which has significant implications and consequences under international humanitarian law, whereas it has already been observed in this chapter that acts of terrorism predominantly occur during peacetime.

UNITED NATIONS RESOLUTIONS ON TERRORISM

The development of General Assembly and Security Council resolutions on the subject of terrorism and counter-terrorism. What is relevant, for the purposes of this chapter, is to recognise the absence of an express definition of the term 'terrorism' within any of those resolutions. This includes resolutions 1269 and 1373 of the Security Council, resolutions through which important obligations upon member States of the United Nations were established.

There is one resolution of the Security Council, however, which is of considerable value. Although it does not express itself as establishing a universally accepted definition of the term terrorism, Security Council resolution 1566 called on all States to cooperate fully in the fight against terrorism and, in doing so, to prevent and punish acts that have three cumulative characteristics.

The United Nations Special Rapporteur on the promotion and protection of human rights and counter-terrorism has expressed support for this approach. This is the subject of consideration next.

RATIONALISING A DISTINCT APPROACH TO TERRORISM

The need for a distinct approach to the criminalisation and suppression of terrorism should be apparent from the discussion of the nature of terrorism to this point. Approaching terrorism as a phenomenon justifying a distinct regime of counterterrorism law is not just supported by those features of terrorist conduct discussed. Such an approach is also driven by most States. The desire of States to take a special approach to the suppression of terrorism appears to be rooted in a combination of factors, not all of which are unique to terrorism, but which may cumulatively have been treated by States as calling for a different approach. The common thread in each factor, or at least in the way each factor can be perceived, is not unique: the political interests of States. The most apparent reason for States taking distinct action against terrorism is the fear-inducing nature of terrorist conduct and the attention this brings to terrorist events through the media and public alike. This in turn adversely affects the credibility of national executive administrations in the eyes of the national public, and also the credibility of the United Nations as an institution established to maintain international peace and security in the eyes of the international community. The more severe the terrorist act, the greater the terror induced, to the extent that the public may in fact be paralysed in a real sense, affecting their freedom of movement and association, and enjoyment of life. That again serves to adversely impact upon national and international 'executive' credibility.

As will be seen through the discussion of international documents on terrorism that follows, terrorism is therefore viewed as being a crime of 'international concern' (using the wording of the Rome Statute on the International Criminal Court) and contrary to the principles of the Charter of the United Nations. Terrorism was, in that regard, proposed to be included within the jurisdiction of the International Criminal Court, to stand beside genocide, war crimes and crimes against humanity. A further issue of concern to States is the transnational nature of terrorist offending. Whether through Embassy bombings on foreign soil or direct attacks within the territory of a State (such as the 2001 attacks in the United States and those in 2005 in London), national interest and national security are often affected.

Through an international framework on counter-terrorism, those interests can be arguably better protected through the ability to secure mutual legal assistance and the extradition of perpetrators of such attacks, and cut off the means by which terrorist organisations operate. A final and individual self-interest of States is that of combating revolutionary and secessionist terrorism, that is, terrorism occurring solely within a State and aimed at destabilising or overthrowing the established government of the State, or conduct aimed at 'breaking away' from the State. The established government has, in those circumstances, a very real and pressing desire to eradicate terrorism. The international community, in seeking to maintain the integrity of statehood and the stability of regions, also has a vested interest. Examples include the Basque Fatherland and Liberty movement in Spain, the Kurdistan Workers' Party in Turkey and the Liberation Tigers of Tamil Eelam in Sri Lanka.

DISSIDENT RELIGIOUS TERRORISM IN THE MODERN ERA

Dissident religious terrorism is political violence conducted by groups of fervent religious true believers with faith in the sacred righteousness of their cause. Any behavior in the defence of this cause is considered not only justifiable but also blessed. As discussed, most major religions—in particular, Christianity, Islam, Judaism, and Hinduism—have extremist adherents, some of whom have engaged in terrorist violence. Smaller religions and cults have similar adherents.

Among the ubiquitous principles are the convictions that they are defending their faith from attack by nonbelievers or that their faith as indisputable and a universal guiding principle must be advanced for the salvation of the faithful. These principles are manifested in various ways and to varying degrees by religious extremists but are usually at the core of the belief system. From the perspective of religious radicals in the Middle East, violence done in the name of God is perfectly rational behavior because God is on their side.

Many of the holy sites in the region are sacred to more than one faith, such as Jerusalem, where a convergence of claims exists among Muslims, Jews, and Christians. When these convergences occur, some extremists believe that the claims of other faiths are inherently blasphemous. Because of this sort of indisputable truth, some extremists believe that God wishes for nonbelievers to be driven from sacred sites or otherwise barred from legitimizing their claims.

Case: The Grand Mosque Incident

The framework for Muslim life is based on the Five Pillars of Islam. The Five Pillars are faith, prayer, charity (*zakat*), fasting during the month of Ramadan, and the hajj (pilgrimage) to the holy city of Mecca, Saudi Arabia. In November 1979, during their hajj, 300 radicals occupied the Grand Mosque in Mecca. Their objective was to foment a popular Islamic uprising against the ruling Saud royal family. After nearly 2 weeks of fighting, the Grand Mosque was reoccupied by the Saudi army, but not before the Saudis called in French counterterrorist commandos to complete the operation. More than 100 radicals were killed, and scores were later executed by the Saudi government. During the fighting, Iranian radio accused the United States and Israel of plotting the takeover, and a Pakistani mob attacked the U.S. embassy, killing two Americans.

Case: The Hebron Mosque Massacre

On February 25, 1994, a New York–born physician, Baruch Goldstein, fired on worshippers inside the Ibrahim Mosque at the Cave of the Patriarchs holy site in the city of Hebron, Israel. As worshippers performed their morning prayer ritual, Goldstein methodically shot them with an Israel Defence Forces Galil assault rifle. He fired approximately 108 rounds in about 10 minutes before a crowd of worshippers rushed him and killed him. According to official government estimates, he killed 29 people and wounded another 125; according to unofficial estimates, approximately 50 people died. In reprisal for the Hebron massacre, the Palestinian Islamic fundamentalist movement Hamas launched a bombing campaign that included the first wave of human suicide bombers.

Case: The Rabin Assassination

On November 4, 1995, Israeli Prime Minister Yitzhak Rabin was assassinated by Yigal Amir, who had stalked Rabin for about a year and shot him in the back with hollow-point bullets in full view of Israeli security officers. Amir was a Jewish extremist who said that he acted fully within the requirements of Halacha, the Jewish code.

Case: Sectarian Violence in Iraq

Iraq is a multicultural nation with significant but varying strong ethno-national, tribal, and religious identities.

The demography consists of the following are:

- Subpopulations: Arab: 75 per cent to 80 per cent
- Kurdish: 15 per cent to 20 per cent
- Turkoman, Assyrian, or other: 5 per cent
- Shi'a Muslim: 60 per cent to 65 per cent
- Sunni Muslim: 32 per cent to 37 per cent
- Christian or other: 3 per cent

Tensions that had simmered during the Hussein years led to difficulty in fully integrating all groups into accepting a single national identity. For example, many Arabs who had moved into northern Kurdish regions after native Kurds were forced out became pariahs when Kurds returned to reclaim their homes and land. Some violence was directed against the Arab migrants. More ominously, the Sunni minority—which had dominated the country under Hussein—found itself recast as a political minority when the country began to move towards democracy when an interim government was established in June 2004. Sunnis expressed their dissatisfaction when large numbers refused to participate in elections to form a Transitional National Assembly in January 2005.

Also in Iraq, religious extremists—it is unclear whether they are Sunnis or Shi'a—conducted a series of attacks on non-Muslim cultural institutions. These included liquor stores (often owned by Christians) and barber shops (that offered Western-style haircuts). Readers should be familiar with the essential distinctions between the Sunni and Shi'a Islamic traditions. These examples confirm that religious terrorism in the Middle East occurs between, and within, local religious groups. Radical true believers of many faiths attack not only those of other religions but also "fallen" members of their own. Attacks against proclaimed apostates can be quite violent.

Movement Case: The International Mujahideen (Holy Warriors for the Faith)

The mujahideen are Islamic fighters who have sworn a vow to take up arms to defend the faith. They tend to be believers in fundamentalist interpretations of Islam that have defined their jihad, or personal struggle, to be one of fighting and dying on behalf of the faith. The modern conceptualization of the mujahideen began during the Soviet war in Afghanistan, which dated from the Soviet invasion of the country in December 1979 to its withdrawal in February 1989. Although several Afghan rebel groups (mostly ethnically based) fought the Soviets, they collectively referred to themselves as mujahideen. To them, their war of resistance was a holy jihad.

Significantly, Muslim volunteers from around the world served alongside them. These Afghan Arabs played an important role in spreading the modern jihadi ideology throughout the Muslim world. Reasons for taking up arms as a jihadi vary. Some recruits answer calls for holy war from religious scholars who might declare, for example, that Islam is being repressed by the West. Others respond to clear and identifiable threats to their people or country, such as the Soviet invasion of Afghanistan, the U.S.-led occupation of Iraq, or the Israeli occupation of Gaza and the West Bank. Others may join on behalf of the cause of other Muslims, such as the wars fought by Bosnian Muslims or Algerian rebels. Regardless of the precipitating event, mujahideen are characterized by their faith in several basic values. The ideology of the modern mujahideen requires selfless sacrifice in defence of the faith. Accepting the title of mujahideen means that one must live, fight, and die in accordance with religious teachings. Mujahideen believe in the inevitability of victory; because the cause is being waged on behalf of the faith and in the name of God, both the faith and God will prevail. In this defence of the faith, trials and ordeals should be endured without complaint because the pain suffered in this world will be rewarded after death in paradise.

If one lives a righteous and holy life, for example, by obeying the moral proscriptions of the Quran, one can enjoy these proscribed pleasures in the afterlife. As applied by the mujahideen, the defensive ideology of jihad holds that when one defends the faith against the unfaithful, death is martyrdom, and through death paradise is ensured.

Organization Case: Al Qaeda's Religious Foundation

The most prominent pan-Islamic revolutionary organization of this era is Saudi national Osama bin Laden's cell-based Al Qaeda (the Base), which seeks to unite Muslims throughout the world in a holy war. Al Qaeda is not a traditional hierarchical revolutionary organization, nor does it call for its followers to do much more than engage in terrorist violence in the name of the faith. It is best described as a loose network of like-minded Islamic revolutionaries.

Al Qaeda is different because it:

- Holds no territory
- Has virtually no state sponsorship
- Does not champion the aspirations of an ethno-national group
- Promulgates vague political demands
- Has no top-down organizational structure
- Has a completely religious worldview

Al Qaeda's religious orientation is a reflection of Osama bin Laden's sectarian ideological point of view. Bin Laden's worldview was created by his exposure to Islam-motivated armed resistance. As a boy, he inherited between $20 million and $80 million, with estimates ranging as high as $300 million, from his father. When the Soviets invaded Afghanistan in 1979, bin Laden eventually joined with thousands of other non-Afghan Muslims who traveled to Peshawar, Pakistan, to prepare to wage jihad. However, his main contribution to the holy war was to solicit financial and matériel (military hardware) contributions from wealthy Arab sources. He apparently excelled at this.

The final leg on his journey towards international Islamic terrorism occurred when he and thousands of other Afghan veterans— the Afghan Arabs— returned to their countries to carry on their struggle in the name of Islam. Beginning in 1986, bin Laden organized a training camp that grew in 1988 into the Al Qaeda group. While in his home country of Saudi Arabia, bin Laden "became enraged when King Fahd let American forces, with their rock music and Christian and Jewish troops, wage the Persian Gulf war from Saudi soil in 1991." After the Gulf War, bin Laden and a reinvigorated Al Qaeda moved to its new home in Sudan for 5 years. It was there that the Al Qaeda network began to grow into a self-sustaining financial and training base for promulgating jihad. Bin Laden and his followers configured the Al Qaeda network with one underlying purpose: "launching and leading a holy war against the Western infidels he could now see camped out in his homeland, near the holiest shrines in the Muslim world."

Al Qaeda has inspired Islamic fundamentalist revolution-aries and terrorists in a number of countries. It became a significant source of financing and training for thousands of jihadis. The network is essentially a nonstate catalyst for transnational religious radicalism and violence. When Al Qaeda moved to Afghanistan, its reputation as a financial and training center attracted many new recruits and led to the creation of a loose network of cells and sleepers in dozens of countries. Significantly, above ground radical Islamic groups with links to Al Qaeda—such as Abu Sayyaf in the Philippines and Laskar Jihad

(Militia of the Holy War) in Indonesia—took root in some nations and overtly challenged authority through acts of terrorism.

Cult Case: Aum Shinrikyo- (Supreme Truth)

Aum Shinrikyo - is a Japan-based cult founded by Shoko Asahara in 1987. Its goal under Asahara's leadership was to seize control of Japan and then the world. The core belief is that Armageddon is imminent. One component is that the United States will wage World War III against Japan. As one top member of the cult explained, "This evil [of the modern age] will be shed in a 'catastrophic discharge'... [and only those who] repent their evil deeds... [will survive]." At its peak membership, Aum Shinrikyo had perhaps 9,000 members in Japan and 40,000 members around the world, thousands of them in Russia. Asahara claimed to be the reincarnation of Jesus Christ and Buddha and urged his followers to arm themselves if they were to survive Armageddon.

This apocalyptic creed led to the stockpiling of chemical and biological weapons, including nerve gas, anthrax, and Q-fever. One report indicated that Aum Shinrikyo - members had traveled to Africa to acquire the deadly Ebola virus. Several mysterious biochemical incidents occurred in Japan, including one in June 1994 in the city of Matsumoto, where 7 people died and 264 were injured from a release of gas into an apartment building.

The Tokyo Subway Nerve Gas Attack

On March 20, 1995, members of Aum Shinrikyo positioned several packages containing sarin nerve gas on five trains in the Tokyo subway system scheduled to travel through Tokyo's Kasumigaseki train station. The containers were simultaneously punctured with umbrellas, thus releasing the gas into the subway system. Twelve people were killed and an estimated 5,000 to 6,000 were injured. Tokyo's emergency medical system was unable to adequately respond to the attack, so that only about 500 victims were evacuated and the remaining victims had to make their own way to local hospitals. The police seized tons of chemicals the cult had stockpiled. Asahara was arrested and charged with 17 counts of murder and attempted murder, kidnapping, and drug trafficking.

A new leader, Fumihiro Joyu, assumed control of Aum Shinrikyo - in 2000 and renamed the group Aleph (the first letter in the Hebrew and Arabic alphabets). He has publicly renounced violence, and the cult has enjoyed new growth in membership. A Japanese court sentenced Shoko Asahara to death by hanging on February 27, 2004. Aum Shinrikyo - is an example of the potential terrorist threat from apocalyptic cults and sects that are completely insular, segregated from mainstream society. Some cults are content to simply prepare for the End of Days, but others—like Aum Shinrikyo—are not averse to giving the apocalypse a violent push.

3

Pakistan Taliban and Al Qaeda

Al Qaeda appears to have adopted a strategy of working behind the scenes to bring together different militant groups in three ways: (1) providing 'religious justification' for actions against Pakistani security forces; (2) providing militant expertise to given projects; and (3) serving as an interlocutor between disparate militant groups.Al Qaeda ratcheted up its media campaign against the Pakistani state following the military raid in Lal Masjid in Islamabad in July 2007.

Previously too, the group had made several personal attacks on Pervez Musharraf, which culminated in two assassination attempts on the former President. It had also called upon the soldiers of the Pakistani security forces to disobey orders and mutiny. Since the assault on the radical mosque, however, Al Qaeda has deliberately sought to blur the theological distinction between "near" and "far" enemy.

In its mass messages, senior Al Qaeda figure Abu Yahya al- Libi termed the United States, Afghanistan and Pakistan as "a single entity, a single enemy, and a single army."Al Qaeda's number two, Dr. Ayman al-Zawahiri, too urged ordinary Pakistani's to rebel against their government. Calling the Pakistan Army a "security service agency...which kills Muslims to please those who pay it, the neo-Crusaders in Washington," al-Zawahiri said that "beneath the ruins of the Red Mosque [Lal Masjid] the 'Theory of Pakistan' was buried and the goal of its creation was lost and over the dead bodies of those martyrs the American, Zionist and Indian flags were raised."

His calibrated speech was clearly intended to appeal to the distinct militant groups present in Pakistan.Immediately following the Taliban's defeat in 2001, thousands of Talibs and their international compatriots known locally as "Arab Afghans" escaped to safe shelters in the tribal areas straddling the Pak- Afghan border demarcated by the Durand Line. Between then and the commencement of military operations by Pakistani forces, the Taliban and Al Qaeda set up their centre in the border village of Angoor Adda, the site of a cross-border US commando raid later in September 2008.They closely interacted with their fellow Pashtun brethren and leveraged widespread discontent against the US invasion.

Financial incentives, along with the camaraderie that followed episodic raids by Pakistani forces further brought the Afghan rebels closer to their local hosts. The Pakistan Taliban's rise to power betrays its strong affiliations with Al Qaeda. Its growth trajectory coincides with Al Qaeda's expulsion from Iraq. Following the defeat of Al Qaeda in Iraq in 2007, the group shifted its focus to Afghanistan and Pakistan, the tell-tale signs being the eruption of suicide bombings in both the countries. Suicide bombing is alien to the fighting traditions of both the Pashtun and the Punjabi groups. In their ten-year fight to oust the Soviets, the Afghan militants never once took recourse to suicide bombings.

Al Qaeda has also been directly and indirectly involved in many militant attacks inside Pakistan. At least one of the two assassination attempts on Pervez Musharraf was ordered by Al Qaeda and carried out by Jaish-e- Mohammad. Local journalists insist that Al Qaeda played a key role in sabotaging many of the peace deals that Pakistan unsuccessfully tried to forge with local militants with the aim of isolating the foreign elements. In fact, following the death of Pakistan Taliban leader Baitullah Mehsud in a US drone strike in 2008, Zawahiri again urged Pakistanis to support militants in the tribal areas and in Swat. Not doing so, he said, "is in fact standing with, backing and supporting the Crusaders against Islam and Muslims."

PAKISTAN'S BID AT RECONCILIATION UNDERMINES US INTERESTS IN AFGHANISTAN

Recent media reports indicate that the Pakistan military is negotiating with Afghan President Hamid Karzai for a peace settlement in Afghanistan. While a genuine thaw in relations between the two countries would be welcome, the US needs to be directly involved in any effort to negotiate an end to the war in Afghanistan. President Karzai is negotiating from a position of political weakness and many Afghans believe he will not protect the position of Afghanistan's ethnic minorities in the negotiations.

According to media reports, the Pakistani military is offering to mediate a solution by bringing the deadly Jalaluddin Haqqani network into the negotiations. Meanwhile, the US continues to press Pakistan to take on Haqqani's forces in North Waziristan through military operations. General Petraeus, in a Congressional testimony in late June, told US law-makers that US officials had briefed Pakistan's military Chief General Ashfaq Kayani on information suggesting Haqqani fighters were involved in a raid on the US Bagram air base in mid-May.

The Obama Administration's lack of a clear policy on reconciliation is contributing to Karzai's unhelpful approach to reconciliation and the Pakistani confidence that it will play the final arbiter in an Afghan peace settlement. Karzai recently fired respected Afghan intelligence chief Amrullah Saleh over differences on the Taliban reconciliation issue. Saleh had said negotiations with the Taliban would "disgrace" Afghanistan. As Carl Forsberg of the Institute for the Study of War points out in his recent monograph, Politics and Power in Kandahar,"Serious questions surround the realism of the Karzai administration's vision for reconciliation in southern Afghanistan."

Forsberg notes that for both Hamid Karzai and his half-brother, Ahmed Wali Karzai, reconciliation has the "element of an exercise in escapism" from the fact that Ahmed Wali Karzai, in particular, lacks support from a large portion of the population in Kandahar.Senior US Administration officials have repeatedly said that any reconciliation with the Taliban must be Afghan-led, and they have failed to assert a clear US role and vision for this process.

The Administration must be more forthright about what a political settlement in Afghanistan should involve and take a leadership role in the process.

PAKISTAN ARMY AND TERRORISM

One of the most powerful institutions in the region, the Pakistan Army also happens to be perhaps the most radicalised of them all. In fact, it would not be wrong to believe that the birth and rise of jihadi ideology and groups would have been stillborn but for the Pakistan Army, which found in Islam a strategic instrument to unite disparate elements of the state during the early years of Pakistan's history.

It was Colonel Akbar Khan, Military Secretary to Prime Minister Liaqat Ali Khan, who first invoked the spirit of jihad and gathered tribesmen from the Mehsud and Waziri tribal strongholds in the Federally Administered Tribal Areas (FATA) (the same set of tribesmen now fighting the Pakistan Army) to launch an 'irregular war' to free Kashmir from India within months of independence.Those Mehsuds and Waziris, who were stopped short of Srinagar by the Indian armed forces, could be, perhaps, called the first set of non-state actors created by the Pakistan Army.

The 1953 anti-Ahmeddiya riots benefited the Army more than JI as it culminated in the first coup and takeover of the government by General Ayub Khan.Though Ayub kept groups like JI at arm's length, he was not shy of using religious symbols and clarion calls to encourage his officers and troops in the battlefield. During the 1965 War, (Field Marshal) Ayub Khan, in a broadcast to the nation, invoked the Kalimae- Tayyeba "to project the war as a virtual jihad: a conflict between Islam and Kufr".This was the first time that the jihadi theme found a place in a soldier's vocabulary. As Ayub struggled with a litany of failures, first the war and then the economy, JI took to the streets against his "modernist religious policies", adding to his woes and finally forcing him to hand over the reins to another Pathan officer, Yahya Khan.

Like his predessor, Yahya was also not enamoured of JI and its ideological persuasions either. One of his senior officers, Major General Sher Ali Khan, was of a different mould though; he was a strong JI supporter.So when Sher Ali Khan, after his retirement, was appointed by Yahya Khan as the Minister of Information and National Affairs, he took it upon himself to work for the glory of Islam. He persuaded the Army to recruit 'volunteers' from JI and its student wing, IJT to fight the Bengali insurgency in East Pakistan.A large number of these 'volunteers' were drawn from IJT cadres from Punjab University and were well-educated; these men were trained by the Army to crush secessionists — political leaders, journalists, artists, writers, activists and judicial officers — in East Pakistan. JI also formed peace committees in East Pakistan to facilitate intelligence gathering for the Army. In return, the Army rewarded JI with seats in the East Pakistan Assembly.

The Army had also begun using Islamic slogans during the East Pakistan crisis. For instance, during the fight for East Pakistan, the local commander, Lt. General Tikka Khan,quoted freely from Islamic texts in his talks to the beleaguered West Pakistani garrison, reminding his forces of "the great battles against infidels [are] a proof of what Muslims could do." Nicknamed maulvi (preacher) among his peers, it was Zia-ul Haq, son of an overtly religious Army clerk, who systematically and radically changed what was, till then, essentially a professional Army in the tradition of the British days.

He invoked the triple motto of Taqva (piety), Iman (Islamic faith) and Jihad-fi-Sabil-Allah (Fight in the name of Allah). To encourage a faster Islamic transformation of the Army, Zia saw to it that new mosques were built within cantonments and training areas; Islamic texts were introduced into training courses; staff college libraries stocked with books on Islam, Islamic military ideology and practices; and middle-level officers were made to study and give examinations on Islam and Islamic military doctrine. Islamic teachings were introduced in the Pakistan Military Academy, Kakul.

Changes were made in the curriculum at Staff Colleges where new officers began studying and researching Islamic military practices, doctrine and strategy. A lecture series run by officer-scholar Colonel Abdul Qayyum, at the Command and Staff College formed the intellectual basis for the Islamic drive. Qayyum lectured on Islamic theology and doctrine but adopted a more open and rationalist approach that made him a much sought after ideologue.

The post of Army 'mullah' was created to act as a bridge between the profession and faith. The mullahs accompanied units into combat zones. A Directorate of Religious Instruction was established at the General Headquarters (GHQ) and religious handouts were published occasionally for the troops. Zia was the first Army Chief and head of state to attend the annual meeting of the Tablighi Jamaat at Raiwind in Punjab. Zia believed that "nobody but Allah made him the Chief of Army Staff and that he was on a divine mission to impose Islam in Pakistan."He encouraged officers and troops to frequent Tablighi meetings more openly.

Zia encouraged his men and officers to pray, fast and distribute Islamic literature within the force.Those who prayed five times a day, though it was not mandatory, found themselves in the shortlist for promotions more easily than others. Religious fervour became a passport to higher ranks and membership of JI and IJT proved to be useful. In selection boards for officers, religious knowledge and habits received positive marks. Recruits during this phase were made to take an oath on the Quran and were taught Islamic subjects.

They were also tested regularly for their grasp of religious knowledge to raise the level of religious awareness among Pakistani troops and ensure indoctrination. Many officers in the Army became attracted to JI's ideology and Maududi's teachings. Zia, in fact, used to reward men and officers with a copy of Maududi's books. Zia even wanted to redesign the national flag by inserting Arabic inscriptions and shift the Independence Day from August 14 to its equivalent in the Islamic calendar. Zia also incorporated religious groups like JI as part of the Pakistan Army's broader strategic objectives, both at home and abroad — at home to control ethnic and sectarian separatists who challenged the Army's writ and outside (specifically India) to initiate a proxy war to annex Kashmir as part of an "unfinished agenda".

In 1977, Zia met with the JI leaders and discussed the party's possible role in Pakistan's Afghan policy. JI utilised its links with Afghan warlords like Gulbuddin Hekmatyar and helped Zia in crafting a policy that benefited the party's Islamic cause and fulfilled part of its objective of influencing, if not entirely controlling, the policies of the state.

'PUNJABI TALIBAN'

Since the Iranian Revolution, and the commencement of the Afghan jihad in 1979, the Islamic world has witnessed the spawning of innumerable radical militant groups. This is particularly true for Pakistan. These groups seek to make the country into an Islamist state by enforcing their interpretation of Shariah and, hopefully, create a transnational super-state, or a Caliphate.

Noted scholar Oliver Roy explains:

- The Soviet invasion of Afghanistan imparted a new dimension to the idea of Jihad in Pakistan, which till then had only been employed by the Pakistani state in the context of mobilizing the population against India. However, from the beginning of the 1980s, the concept of Jihad was to become 'privatised'. Radical groups emerged out of the large traditional movements and embarked on armed operations..... For the Jihadists, Jihad is the way by which Muslims can be united and recalled to the true practice of Islam. The view is that Jihad, even if it should fail, is instrumental and sets an example: this is because it allows the Muslim masses to be aroused to consciousness, and [to draw] a distinction between true Muslims and the rest.

Traditionally, militant groups based in Punjab, Pakistan's most important province, belong to two distinct orientations – sectarian, (anti-Shiite), and anti-India (pro-Kashmir). The first major sectarian group, Sipah-e Sahaba Pakistan (SSP) was created in 1985 with covert state support, as a bulwark against perceived Iranian interference. The group, affiliated to the political party Jamiat-e- Ulema-e-Islam, drew popular support from Punjab, especially its south.

It launched a systematic ethnic cleansing campaign by targeting Shia businessmen and professionals in Sindh and Punjab. Hundreds of Shias were killed in target killings carried out by SSP and its more violent progeny, Lashkar-e-Jhangvi (LeJ).. It was the first Punjab-based group to have moved base to Afghanistan immediately after the Taliban seized power in the mid-1990s. The two groups fought for the Taliban against the Northern Alliance and were jointly responsible for the massacre of the Hazara community as well as the killing of Iranian diplomats in the town of Mazar-e-Sharif in northern Afghanistan in 1998. Post 9/11 when the US began bombing the Taliban-Al Qaeda hideouts in Afghanistan, LeJ actively helped the fleeing Al Qaeda and Taliban cadres in finding shelter in Pakistan. LeJ, with its wide network of safe houses and associates, managed to camouflage the presence of Al Qaeda and Taliban leaders in Pakistan for several months. This alliance came out into the open for the first time during the investigation of American journalist Daniel Pearl's murder in early 2002. LeJ was finally banned in August 2002.

The India-centric groups have also nurtured relations with Al Qaeda that predate 9/11. In 1998, Osama bin Laden announced the creation of the international Islamic Front for jihad against the "crusaders" (Christians) and the Jews. Among the signatories of the fatwa were Lashkar-e-Tayyeba as well as Harkat ul-Mujahideen. Laden is believed to have personally provided seed money to raise LeT and spoke to the annual convention of the group between 1995-97 by phone. Immediately after 9/11, many prominent Al Qaeda leaders like Abu Zubayda, Ramzi Binalshibh and Khalid Sheikh Mohammad were arrested from LeT safe houses.

Over the past few years, several militant groups from Punjab, who had earlier refrained from carrying out acts of terrorism inside Pakistan, have grown increasingly impatient with Pakistan's decision to freeze cross-border militancy directed at Kashmir.

In 2004, Pakistan pledged to take greater counter-terrorism measures so as to facilitate better bilateral relations with India. As a show of good faith, many training camps, and infrastructure and recruitment programmes were shut down. But there was no sincere attempt to dismantle the terrorist infrastructure created largely by the Pakistan Army.

Thousands of militants were rehabilitated and training camps were relocated to lesser known places and given new identities and cover. Many of these camps worked as charities and schools. While the present whereabouts and the doings of the thousands of youth trained for the Kashmir conflict remain murky at best, what is sufficiently clear is that many of the Pakistan Army's former proxies have gradually turned against their former benefactor.

This turnaround was demonstrated first in December 2003 when the Punjabi group, namely Jaish-e-Mohammad, carried out an assassination attempt on Musharraf. This tacit and triangular collaboration of the Pakistan Taliban, Punjabi groups and Al Qaeda has witnessed rapid momentum since 2007. More than 200 suicide attacks shattered the incestuous relationship that traditionally existed between the state and its armed proxies. The local expertise was provided by the 'Punjabi Taliban'. According to former Director of the Federal Investigative (FIA) Agency Tariq Pervez, "Ideas, logistics, cash [come] from the Gulf. Arab guys, mainly Egyptians and Saudis, are on hand to provide the chemistry. Veteran Punjabi extremists plot the attacks, while the Pakistan Taliban provides the martyrs. And it all came together in the Marriott case."

TALIBAN-CRIME NEXUS

Insurgents generate funds through a variety of means–donations from local and foreign sources, confiscation and taxation, legitimate businesses and criminal activity. In theory, insurgent movements and organised criminal groups have contradictory objectives. Insurgents aim to replace the state with a parallel counter-state, and, hence, seek instability and chaos. For an insurgent, the best way to attract passive sections of the population is to discredit the government, create security deficits and ultimately offer a better option.Criminal groups, on the other hand, are driven by a profit motive and prefer to maintain the status quo.

After spending considerable time and energy to coopt corrupt officials and find loopholes within the existing framework, it would indeed make bad business sense for the criminal syndicates to forgo these assets and start all over again with an insurgent parallel state that is eager to build social capital among its new constituents. Other mutual disincentives also limit insurgent-criminal alliances. The criminal groups, that enjoy a degree of de-facto immunity from corrupt officials, risk inviting government prosecution once they ally with anti-state insurgent groups.

For insurgents, profit motives might corrode their political goals and 'seduce the faithful'. In fact, groups like Al Qaeda and Hezbollah have ideologically resisted direct involvement in criminal activity.Insurgent groups end up supporting crime because it generates far greater wealth than taxation. It also makes logistical sense to outsource collection of funds to auxiliary groups in exchange for protection and an expanded area of operation. A hefty treasury enables insurgents to project power and influence over the local population, attract more recruits,and undermine the writ of the state. Kidnapping, extortion, bank robbery and drug trafficking, hence, have become the favoured means of generating funds.Other criminal activities include money laundering, human trafficking, arms trade, contraband, smuggling and petty crimes. Crime and narcotics makes up for almost 90 percent of the Pakistan Taliban's revenue, officially put at ₹ 4 billion.

The group benefits hugely from poppy cultivation and the heroin industry in Afghanistan. Protection money from smugglers constitutes a major chunk of the group's funding. Besides narcotics, contraband trade in goods such as cigarettes has also added to the Taliban's coffers. It is also believed to have built capabilities to carry out high paying robberies. It has reportedly formed 'commando squads' for the purpose of committing robberies, vehicle snatching, and kidnappings.As a result, the frequency of bank robberies has increased dramatically in Pakistan. Forty-two bank heists occurred in 2007, as compared to six in the previous year, most of them in Karachi, Pakistan's financial capital. However, the exact nature of the Pakistan Taliban's alliance with criminal groups is difficult to ascertain. Emulating the strategy of the Afghan Taliban in the 1990s, the group has been harsh on criminals.

But, the same time, it has itself committed robberies and bank heists. Based on limited information, it appears that the Pakistan Taliban has adopted a strategy of allying with criminal syndicates in areas outside of its direct control while strictly opposing crime in areas under its writ. As an exception, it has unambiguously supported high paying criminal activities like drugs trade, illegal trade in timber, etc, irrespective of the area of operation. Several factors further corroborate this argument. First, Pakistan Taliban's rhetorical cause – enforcing Shariah rule – is Islamist in nature.

Many of its leaders belong to the conservative clergy and have generously used Islamic idioms in their public statements. Hence, in order to prove their credentials as 'better Muslims', they have made it incumbent to carry out vigilante acts against criminals. In doing so, they also present politically neutral sections of the population with a crime-free society. Second, by supporting petty criminals who operate in government controlled areas, the Pakistan Taliban creates further instability and serves to discredit the government.

Third, the Pakistan Taliban is a highly decentralised organisation, loosely framed along tribal allegiances. The result is that many criminal elements find easy entry into its rank and file. Fourth, the Pakistan Taliban, unlike the Afghan Taliban in the 1990s, is not known to enjoy state supportand, hence, is forced to explore all possible means to generate funds. Fifth, as a result, they have supported resourceful criminal groups like the timber mafia in order to generate revenue. Lastly, Lashkar-e-Jhangvi (LeJ), a crucial ally of the Pakistan Taliban, has historically been criminal in its composition.

Alliance with LeJ, has created a further influx of criminal elements into the Pakistan Taliban. The group's strategy of simultaneously opposing crime in 'home territory' and carrying out sophisticated crimes in 'away territory' also explains increased crime in Karachi even as it remains relatively immune from insurgency and suicide bombing. Police officials in the port city believe that 80 percent of bank heists are related to the Pakistan Taliban.

The squads' tactic of choice is to infiltrate the firms that provide security to the banks, gain access to the necessary contacts and on its strength carry out the robbery. Another remarkable feature of crime in Karachi is the fact that the 10 percent of kidnappings in the city that involve the group generate more ransom than the other 90 percent put together.In the recent years, the Pakistan Taliban has also exploited natural resources to generate funds. Swat, one of the 24 districts of the Khyber Pakhtunkhwa became affected by the insurgency in 2007. The region not only produces half of Pakistan's high end timber, but also possesses vast deposits of precious stones.

The Pakistan Taliban and its predecessor, the Tehreek-e-Nafaz-e-Shariat-e-Mohammadi (TNSM) long benefited from illegal trade in these resources. In 1994, TNSM launched an insurrection in Malakand, demanding Shariah rule. For five days, it blocked the only road leading to the valley. In less than a week, more than 80,000 logs of high quality timber were smuggled out of the region. In 2007, the Swat Taliban started to give protection to the timber mafia. Local sources say 70 percent of Swat's forest cover was deforested during the two years in which the insurgents were in control.

In March 2009, militants took control of the emerald mines in Swat and began to hire locals for mining, assuming the role of employers. A month later, they occupied the mines of the adjoining Shangla district, and employed 1,000 locals as against the 100 employed by the American firm which was operating the mines earlier. Besides earning Rs 4 million in a week, they made a huge gain in social capital amongst the locals.

THE AFGHAN NETWORK: ARAB MUJAHIDEEN JOIN THE ANTI-SOVIET JIHAD

On December 24, 1979, Russian special forces seized Kabul airport, clearing the way for the Red Army to conquer Afghanistan. Setting aside tribal rivalries, the Afghan resistance organized itself, and the international Muslim community mobilized in support of the mujahideen, who soon were receiving assistance from the United States, logistical support from Pakistan, and financial contributions from Saudi Arabia. Divergent interests were at stake in the context of that indirect strategy.

The United States, taking a containment approach, wanted to halt any progress by the two leaders of the anti-imperialist front, the Communist Soviet Union and Shiite Iran—a brand-new enemy since the fall of the shah and the hostage crisis at the American embassy in Tehran. Saudi Arabia—traumatized by a 1979 incident that took place at Mecca during Ramadan, in which young Sunni protesters took a number of hostages and 1,500 people died—decided to take charge of the Sunni radical movement in order to control its young fundamentalist members and prevent them from being manipulated by pro-Iranian Hezbollah.

It was supported in this by the wealthy Gulf petromonarchies, intent on increasing their prestige among the Muslim community.

Finally, Pakistan— whose traditional adversary to the east, India, was a Soviet ally—wished to maintain a buffer zone in Afghanistan, on its western border. Arab volunteers arrived in Pakistan, some by very circuitous routes, to join up with the Afghan mujahideen. Often they were receiving assistance from their own governments, which were more than pleased to see the last of potentially dangerous active political opponents. It is likely that, during the 1980s, more than 20,000 Muslims from the Middle East and the Maghreb were involved in jihad. Most of them were recruited by transnational Islamic networks, headed up by radical ulama with ties to the World Islamic League and to Wahabi foundations, who secured the necessary fatwas to ensure support for the anti-Soviet jihad from recognized theologians.

The largest battalions came from the Middle East. Their numbers likely included approximately 6,000 Saudis, 4,000 Egyptians, and 1,000 Yemenis, as well as several hundred Syrians and the same number of Jordanians of Palestinian origin. A smaller number came from the Maghreb— maybe 2,000 Algerians and a few hundred Tunisians, Moroccans and Libyans. Some hailed from farther afield, including a few Westerners and a handful of Indonesians, Malaysians, Filipinos, and Sudanese.

THE FOUNDING OF MAKTAB AL-KHIDMAT

Considerable and predictable funding was required to accommodate and organize all of the volunteers and provide them with combat training. The necessary resources were provided by the Saudi authorities or by wealthy private donors. A number of Wahabi nongovernmental organizations—restructured or created for that very purpose—were used to collect such funds anonymously. Furthermore, the hundreds of millions of dollars that were circulating discreetly in circles populated by arms dealers and traffickers—an ideal situation for embezzlement to take place—had to be managed by men who could be trusted.

The task was entrusted to a Jordanian of Palestinian origin, \Abdallah \Azzam (1941–1979). \Azzam, who had fought in the 1967 war, had broken with the PLO on the grounds that it had sacrificed the struggle against Israel in giving priority to acts of subversion against the Hashemite royal family, aimed at gaining gain control over Jordan. Following 1970's Black September, he obtained his doctorate from al-Azhar and taught the Qur›an at Jeddah's Islamic University. He thus became the educational authority within the World Islamic League, maintaining close ties with the leaders of the Red Crescent. \Azzam, a pivotal figure in the context of militant and religious Islam, in 1984 created a new organization in Peshawar to which, given the clandestine nature of its activities, he gave a fairly neutral name, Maktab al-Khidmat ul- Mujahideen ul-Arab (MUKUB), or "Bureau of Services for Arab Mujahideen." Most of its leaders were from the Middle East, aside from a small number of Algerians.

Two of \Azzam's appointees were Abu Tamin and Abu Sayyaf. To officially assist \Azzam—and, in all likelihood, to monitor his activities— Prince Turki al-Faisal, head of the Saudi intelligence services, chose the son of a wealthy entrepreneur with close ties to the royal family, Osama bin Laden. Bin Laden, who had been active in the family business, was a deeply religious man who had recently finished his training as an engineer. He had also studied not only under \Azzam but also under Muhammad Qutb, the Egyptian ideologue's younger brother. Soon MUKUB had at its disposal a veritable propaganda machine whose most visible activity was the regular publication of the Arablanguage magazine Al-Jihad, which served as a platform for \Azzam. In a document entitled "Join the Caravan," he stated that mujahideen combat in Afghanistan was an individual obligation for all Muslims, who were duty-bound, if they could not actually participate, to provide financial support for it.

He stated that when "the enemy has penetrated into Islamic territory, jihad becomes an individual requirement.... No parental permission is necessary.... Giving money does not exempt anyone from physical jihad, no matter how great the sum.... Jihad is a lifelong obligation." He obtained religious backing from eight high-ranking ulama, including Sheikh Bin Baz, who would become Grand Mufti of Saudi Arabia, and Dr. Saleh Abu Ismail, a member of Egypt's Majlis al-Shura.

He regularly welcomed to Peshawar charismatic leaders of the jihadist movement, such as Egypt's Omar Abdel Rahman. This period marked the emergence in \Azzam's writings of the concept of a standing international jihad army: "That obligation will not end with victory in Afghanistan, and jihad will remain an individual obligation until we have reconquered all Muslim lands and reinstalled Islam: we still have ahead of us Palestine, Bukhara, Lebanon, Chad, Eritrea, Somalia, the Philippines, Burma, Yemen, Tashkent, and Andalusia." It is noteworthy that, in speaking of future jihads, \Azzam gave priority to the Palestinian struggle. Indeed, the first intifada of 1987 marked the resurgence of Islamic fervour in the context of the anti-Zionist effort.

AN ARMY OF ARAB VOLUNTEERS

At the same time, a comprehensive training programme for militants was being set up. Requirements were minimal: some physical and weapons training, and the occasional shooting off of the odd round. Weapons and materiel were mainly reserved for the numerous Afghan militants, who knew the terrain well. To occupy the volunteers' time, religious education classes were held in hastily assembled structures, most of which were set up within the refugee camps in the area around Peshawar, which housed 2 million Afghans. The students were pleased to acquire some basic knowledge of the Qur›an, and it was an easy task for instructors to move on to more radical dogma, teaching them, in a rudimentary but inspiring manner, the views of the theologians of jihad.

However, a few volunteers actually participated in operations on Afghan soil. Early on, they served as reinforcements for specific units, because the Afghan mujahideen—few of whom were open to Wahabism— distrusted these impassioned, jihad-invoking foreigners. The Afghan resistance movement, based in Peshawar, encompassed seven main parties, of which four were openly Islamist. But the volunteers were for the most part accepted by the Pashtun groups Hizb-i-Islami-i-Afghani (HIA), meaning Afghan Islamic Party, headed by Gulbuddin Hekmatyar, and al-Ittihad (Islamic Unity), founded by Dr. Rasul Sayyaf.

A small number of them were integrated into the Jammaat-i-Islami-i-Afghani (JIA)—the Afghan Islamic Society—headed up by Professor Muhammad Rabbani, whose military adjunct was a Tajik, Commander Massoud. Those men, who were viewed either as specially qualified or simply as the most highly motivated—would see action. They included Arab fighters who successfully halted a Soviet offensive in the Paktar region in February 1987. Although the following month, they failed in their attempt to seize Jellalabad, their pugnacity earned them the respect and longstanding loyalty of the Afghan mujahideen.

Their names soon became famous in radical Muslim circles throughout the world. Among them were Osama bin Laden; Egypt's Muhammad Atef and Ayman al-Zawahiri; Saudi Arabia's Ibn Khattab; Jordan's Muhammad al-Maqdisi; and the Philippines' Abu Sayyaf. Ten years later, all of them would receive extensive international press coverage. The rest were assigned to tasks that were not so directly war-related but equally necessary, such as handing out food supplies to refugees, caring for the wounded, and transporting weapons and materiel to the Afghan border. Far from home and living in difficult material conditions, in an atmosphere of semi-secrecy, they were all participating in a thrilling adventure. They were building up faith in a crude, radical form of Islam, establishing a network of relationships, and acquiring the aura of combatants. Isolation and shared solidarity with other believers from different cultures and with different experiences accomplished the rest.

They felt that they were sloughing off their nationalities and forming a new community of holy warriors, like the Prophet's companions. No longer were they Saudis, Egyptians, or Algerians; they were Salafist mujahideen, in the vanguard of the warriors of Islam. At the same time, they came into contact with a shady underworld, populated by dealers of all sorts, passionate theologians, and secret service agents, notably those of Pakistan's Inter-Services Intelligence, which had close ties to the Deobandi madrassas.

Founding myths also emerged that blended fact and fiction. Some famous ones tell of the invincibility of certain mujahideen, who, although riddled with bullets, continued to advance against the enemy, or who could disappear at will. Others speak of the power of God, through which fighters were able to stop tanks by throwing sand at them—sand that instantly changed into fireballs. All these stories met with great success when, years later, the Arab mujahideen, having returned to their communities, recounted them to naive and fascinated audiences. The storytellers, however, intoxicated by their experiences, truly believed that they had brought the Russians to their knees—forgetting the important material assistance provided by the West.

THE END OF THE AFGHAN JIHAD

Following Soviet withdrawal, and under pressure from the American intelligence services, who knew that their efforts in Afghanistan had forged a double-edged sword, the Pakistanis made an attempt to exert greater control over the Arab mujahideen, who had, at war's end, been abandoned by their former friends. American and Saudi support had melted away. Their fate was of little interest to their Afghan brothers, who were busy looting their country, reaping the benefits of the opium trade, and engaging in inter-clan clashes with an eye to conquering Kabul.

The Arab volunteers had no choice but to consider three alternatives. The first group decided to return to their respective homelands, where they mostly served as radical spearheads for local Islamist movements, creating underground cells with the goal of preparing for jihad against their governments, which they deemed infidel and corrupt. The second preferred to leave for those lands that people of their ethnic origin had traditionally favoured—Europe in particular. Some of them found the prestige accorded them by dint of their reputation as mujahideen instrumental in converting to Salafism a second generation of marginalized youths in search of an identity.

The third category opted to continue on with international jihad by lending fresh logistical or operational support to mujahideen fighters at the camps located near the Afghan-Pakistan border. The list grew rapidly: Algeria, Bosnia, Kashmir, Chechnya... However, during that period the Arab volunteers' leaders were secretly making plans for the future of their international jihad army. Certain writers claim that jihadist leaders stood united under \Azzam until the end, agreeing to the long-term pursuit of his plan to support oppressed Muslims in order to recreate the ancestral umma, from Andalusia to the Philippines.

They say that al Qaeda was formed to replace MUKUB, which had become obsolete in the context of the fresh struggles that lay ahead. Others, such as Rohan Gunaratna, believe that it was the debate over the new jihadist plan that led to a parting of the ways between \Azzam— who was fully aware of the strategic danger involved in terrorist activities— and Osama bin Laden, who had been convinced by the Egyptian al-Jihad, with whom he had forged very close ties, of the need to start out by fighting apostate regimes.

There really is no definitive answer to that question. On November 24, 1989, \Abdallah \Azzam died, along with his two sons, in a car bombing in Peshawar. Some saw it as the work of bin Laden, who was known for being duplicitous and who might have wished to rid himself of a troublesome leader overwhelmed by the magnitude of the stakes now involved in jihad. Others believed that the responsibility lay with the Arab intelligence services, which were determined to eliminate the leader of an army of international terrorists before he could bring his fight to their doorstep. In any case, \Abdallah \Azzam became the symbol of the mujahideen movement—an exemplary Muslim killed while carrying out the jihad that he had helped to make a reality. He certainly took many secrets with him to the "Paradise in the shadow of swords." But beyond the creation of this mythology, the future was looking grim for the mujahideen movement.

Its members had dispersed, and the former combatants, although relieved that combat had ended, had, however, to face the harsh reality of returning to civilian life and receding into anonymity. Osama bin Laden, \Azzam's official heir, returned to Saudi Arabia with a plan that could not yet be carried out, given the realities of the time. Even the most highly motivated Salafist mujahideen had no choice but to go back to their old national projects.

It took bin Laden only seven years to rebuild the Afghan network, this time with new opponents in mind. In the meantime, it was Algerian Islamists, despite the fact that they had represented a minority in the Afghan conflict, who, beginning in 1989, gave additional impetus to the dynamic of jihad. That new struggle led to all-out civil war and to unspeakable horrors.

ANALYSIS – MAKING SENSE OF THE SWARM

In the past, the different militant groups were based in separate regions. Their membership was drawn along ethno-linguistic cleavages. Most importantly, their construction of the immediate enemy was almost entirely mutually exclusive. The likes of LeJ, belonging to southern Punjab, engaged in sectarian violence. JeM, from western Punjab, focussed more on the insurgency in Kashmir.

The militant 'Talibs', who emerged from the chain of madrassas in the Pashtun belt, almost entirely channelled their resources to aid the Taliban. Even though certain intermingling occurred – JeM participated in sectarian violence in Pakistan and LeJ found safe haven among the Taliban – these were exceptions rather than trends. In post 9/11 Pakistan, the militant groups in Pakistan have ceased to restrict themselves to their previous exclusive silos, and have found strategic unison in targeting Pakistan. Four major factors have contributed to this phenomenon. First, unlike in the past, most militant groups today view the United States as their principal enemy. Successive opinion pollshave made it clear that the invasions of Iraq and Afghanistan antagonised the diverse militant cadre into proclaiming America as their biggest enemy.

The presence of US troops in the region further encouraged these different groups to pool their resources to fight this new found common enemy. Concurrently, Pakistan's alliance with the US in Afghanistan since 2001, and its withdrawal of active support to the Kashmiri insurgency since 2004, further convinced the militants that the government and security forces of Pakistan were surrogate to the United States, and hence, as apostate entities, legitimate targets. Second, Pakistan's counter-terrorism strategy has a serious systemic constraint that is unlikely to change in the near future — inadequate resourcing.Rather than eliminating militancy, under-resourced military offensives have only expanded the militants' reach and encouraged them to network.

More than 80 percent of the Pakistan Army is placed along the border with India, which, given the current state of affairs, is unlikely to change. As such, much of the counter-insurgency has been carried out by the relatively poorly trained Frontier Corps. Till recent years, consistent victories of the insurgents over the paramilitary forces led to the former gaining control over the local population and carrying out greater recruitment. Tactical battlefield victories have also attracted the attention of militant cadre across Pakistan, thus, facilitating the different groups to network. The relative success of military operations in Swat and Waziristan, during 2009 had a positive impact on the public perception in these areas, particularly about the Pakistan Army's willingness and capability to protect the local population. But it must be kept in mind that many insurgents managed to shift bases to safer places and are playing a waitand- watch game with the security forces.

Third, the resource crunch is not the only factor that inhibits Pakistan's fight against the militancy. Pakistan, over the past eight years, has targeted only those groups that have become a security threat to Pakistan, while ignoring groups like LeT that have refrained from mounting attacks inside Pakistan. Rather, they have used Pakistan's territory, and perhaps, the active support of state elements to target India and Afghanistan. The extent of state support to these groups is a matter of debate among experts and cannot be authoritatively explained by using open source data. However, such a strategy, apart from debilitating regional security, has also become the Achilles' Heel of Pakistan's strategy. Pakistan's selective approach has two implications on its own drive against 'anti-Pakistan' militants.

The 'pro-Pakistan' and 'anti-Pakistan' militants certainly have different near-term agendas, vis-à-vis their selection of targets. They are most often ethnically homogenous and are drawn together through kinship and personal networks. Therefore, at any given time, militants pursued by the security forces have found shelter among the 'pro-Pakistan groups'. The Mehsud militiamen, after being attacked from three sides in October 2009, were able to avoid annihilation as they found shelter with militias lead by Hafiz Gul Bahadur and Mullah Nazeer in Waziristan, which enjoy immunity from military strikes under peace deals.

Pakistan's inability to persecute anti-state groups in Punjab, despite their involvement in many suicide bombings, can also be ascribed to the fact that the province is also home to several groups that Pakistan has used as state tools to coerce India, and arguably, continues to view favourably. An inevitable byproduct of expanded military operations will be an even greater collaboration between active and dormant militants. Besides, the history of the past eight years strongly suggests that contact between active 'anti-Pakistan' militants and dormant 'pro- Pakistan' militants has consistently led to the former influencing the latter. Progressively, many groups and individuals who were earlier allied with Pakistan have switched sides and participated in violence against the state.

The most notable examples are the cases of Omar Sheikh and Ilyas Kashmiri. Interior Minister Rehman Malik's recent indictment of JeM as an anti-state group is further evidence of this trend. Moreover, as frustration mounts over the fact that the security forces were targeting their fellow Muslim brethren, the rank and file of these dormant militant groups could sever their ties with their patrons, and become 'rogue'. Four, Pakistan's ability to enforce its writ over the people of Pakistan, channel dissent and prevent armed non-state actors from forging a parallel contract with the population has depleted over the years. Groups like the Jamaat-ud-Dawa have for long run a sophisticated system of schools, ambulances and other social services that has won them considerable goodwill. Continuous under-funding of these critical sectors means that these non-state actors have a significant head-start in the race for 'hearts and minds'.

Any attempts to nationalise the schools, madrassas and hospitals, therefore, will cause large sections of the population, that are currently politically latent, to mobilise in favour of these non-state groups. Such a scenario, if not handled carefully, can easily turn disastrous. As discussed earlier, a confluence of Punjabi extremists, Pashtun rebels, and foreign Al Qaeda militants has created a unique data bank of skills and seemingly endless resource pipelines that run deep into West Asia. Therefore, availability of skills, weaponry and finances has made militant groups in Pakistan relatively more difficult opponents.

AL QAEDA'S STRATEGY OF UNIFICATION (1989–2001)

Any number of theories have been advanced as to the origins of the name "al Qaeda" (the base), from a reference to a computer file revealing the identities of Arab veterans of the Afghanistan conflict (the database), to Osama bin Laden's alleged high-tech headquarters, deep in the mountains of Afghanistan (the secret base), drawings of which—impressive though entirely fictitious—were produced by the American media when U.S. operations began in October 2001.

The name al Qaeda, which instantly became the focus of media attention following the August 1998 U.S. embassy bombings, had long had mythical status. Osama bin Laden himself had contributed to the mystery surrounding the name by never uttering it prior to the events of September 11. The group's leaders, in their internal communications, usually referred to it as "the society," an intentionally neutral appellation. In fact, it was \Abdallah \Azzam who had named the organization. In 1988, at the first signs of a Soviet withdrawal from Afghanistan, \Azzam decided that he would not disband the army of Arab volunteers he had created four years earlier but would use it to undertake a much vaster mission—the reconquest of the Muslim world.

To that end, he needed a standing vanguard of fighters to serve as leaders of the umma. He coined the term al-qaeda al-sulbah (the solid base) for this, which was also the headline of an editorial he wrote in issue number 41 of al-Jihad, published in April 1988. The article stated: "Every principle needs a vanguard to carry it forward that is willing, while integrating into society, to undertake difficult tasks and make tremendous sacrifices. No ideology, celestial or earthly, can do without such a vanguard, which gives its all to ensure victory.

It is the standardbearer on an endless and difficult path until it reaches its destination, as it is the will of God that it do so. It is al-qaeda al-sulbah that constitutes this vanguard for the hoped-for society." A few lines down, \Azzam set out eight moral guidelines governing the behaviour of the devout, iron-willed members of such a "solid base":

- One must unhesitatingly face the hardest challenges and the worst difficulties.
- Leaders must endure, along with their men, the blood and sweat of grueling marches.
- The vanguard must abstain from base, worldly pleasures, and its distinguishing characteristic must be abstinence and frugality.
- The vanguard must translate into reality the great dream of victory.
- Will and determination are necessary for the march ahead, however long it may be.
- Three things are essential to this march: meditation, patience, and prayer.
- Two rules must be followed: loyalty and devotion.
- All anti-Islamic plots that are being hatched throughout the world must be foiled.

Azzam's violent death in Peshawar in 1989 deprived the mujahideen movement of a recognized, victorious leader who had conceptualized his ideology and formed a militant group. His murderers were never identified.

Many theories have been floated in that respect—from his killing being the work of Arab intelligence services, for reasons of state, to an internal settling of scores within the mujahideen movement. But the salient point here is that, by killing \Azzam, his murderers brought Osama bin Laden into the picture.

Bin Laden would give an impetus of a different sort to al Qaeda and a new direction to the jihadist strategy. Rohan Gunaratna believes that the car bomb that killed \Azzam—a highly professional job using a remote-controlled explosive device—was the work of Egypt's al-Jihad group, under the guidance of its new mentor, bin Laden. Indeed, in the wake of the Afghan jihad, bin Laden, eclipsed by \Azzam, had been unable to impose his views. Al-Jihad apparently managed to persuade him to concentrate on the struggle against corrupt Muslim rulers instead of on the reconquest of former Islamic territory.

That was a key shift, because al Qaeda, in the context of its new strategy of taking the fight onto national territory, adopted the terrorist techniques used by the Egyptians. \Azzam, who had been deeply involved with the Palestinian resistance and who had in 1970 strongly criticized the PLO for having abandoned the struggle against the Zionist occupier in favour of efforts to subvert Jordan's Hashemite government, could not allow his organization to experience another Black September.

AL QAEDA'S STRATEGY AT THE DAWN OF THE THIRD MILLENNIUM

The Failure to Follow Up

The mujahideen movement's strategy of using jihad networks resulted in a fourfold failure. After twenty years of struggle, no Salafist state had yet been created. The jihad movement had not taken root, either in Algeria or in Bosnia, Chechnya, Kosovo or Uzbekistan. Islamist states, which had been early sympathizers with the cause—in particular Sudan, Pakistan, and Saudi Arabia—had eventually caved in under pressure from America and set limits on the support they provided the movement.

The Taliban regime, which was becoming increasingly isolated within the international community, was unable to extend its authority to the whole of the territory of Afghanistan. Thus the assassination of Commander Massoud represented a kind of rent paid to the Afghan regime by the mujahideen. The vast majority of armed undertakings failed because mujahideen groups, still split by rivalries, used different strategies: attacks in Algeria, guerrilla warfare amounting to little more than banditry in the Philippines, urban combat by Chechen Islamists in Grozny, suicide attacks in the Horn of Africa, logistical assistance to sleeper cells in Western countries—all based on different philosophies and agendas. The links among al Qaeda's numerous mujahideen satellite groups were based on individual ties and not determined by any kind of pyramid structure. Operational groups were aware of increasing surveillance by international security services, while financial networks had been under scrutiny since the 1998 attacks against American embassies in Africa. In that connection, it is noteworthy that almost all local groups were financially self-sufficient, more as a result of criminal activity than of funds raised by sympathizers. Operations were financed, and a portion of the funds were sent directly to the mujahideen movement. Indeed, bin Laden, who had invested considerable sums in his Sudan and Afghanistan projects, was no longer the "terrorist billionaire" who had held such fascination for the Western media.

Jihad Takes on a New Dimension

Despite his previous efforts to safeguard al Qaeda, bin Laden, by striking at the American superpower and claiming responsibility, had put the group's very survival on the line. His plan was reminiscent of the terrorist doctrines of nineteenthcentury Russian revolutionary socialists: an armed group carries out attacks in a stable country; the resulting suppression affects the population; and the people, led by the armed group, revolt. Action, suppression, revolution; the pattern is identical. The armed group is al Qaeda; the authorities—corrupt though they may be—are those of the Muslim countries; and the people are the Muslim community. But did the plan to globalize the jihad movement by involving Muslim peoples have any chance of succeeding? Previous versions of it had failed. Western response continued to be measured, and Muslim states saw that they could potentially become the principal victims of Sunni Islamist radicalism. Al Qaeda sustained heavy losses, but Muslims did not rise up, despite the fact that some saw the war in Iraq and support for Israel in the Palestinian conflict as parallel forms of state terrorism and that bin Laden remained a source of fascination for them.

The Transition to Global Warfare

Many authors believe that the Bali attacks marked the beginning of a global terrorist war triggered by al Qaeda's strike against Western economic interests. But al-Jihad and the GI had since the 1980s been targeting tourist sites in a bid to weaken the Egyptian government.

Furthermore, the first jihadist attack against the United States involved a World Trade Center tower—not just the embodiment of U.S. power but also an economic symbol. In the wake of September 11, Ayman al-Zawahiri set three goals for future operations: to inflict maximum casualties, that being the only language understood by the enemy; to concentrate on martyrdom operations as the most successful way of causing damage to the opponent and the least costly to the mujahideen in terms of casualties; and to choose targets, as well as the type of weapons used, with a view to wreaking maximum destruction on enemy structures and thus making clear the true dimensions of the struggle.

Aside from the World Trade Center and Bali attacks, jihadist operations have always aimed more at terrorizing the masses than at massacring them.

This is no doubt due more to an insufficiency of funds than to any lack of will to engage in combat. Indeed, bin Laden stated in several interviews that the jihadist movement should have at its disposal the very same weapons of mass destruction as its American opponent. The vast majority of the attacks that have taken place since September 11 have been of a more conventional nature, due to the need for operational secrecy and the unsophisticated tools available to jihadists. However, upon closer examination, it becomes clear that they have taken place in a strategically consistent manner. Al Qaeda's goal is to spread terror using limited means. Its targets are chosen to give it the advantage of surprise over its opponent. Indeed, the West, whose wealth has grown excessive, has many weak points.

The mujahideen, who cannot possibly succeed in a direct attack against enemy interests, must aim for the spectacular in order to lower their opponents' morale and galvanize their own followers. Al Qaeda and its accomplices are engaging in psychological warfare. In that context, while it is true that the mujahideen movement has not fulfilled the predictions made by doomsayers over the past two years, it is inarguable that it has shown a formidable power of imagination. It appears to have a better grasp of the infidel world than the latter could possibly suspect. In the future, its capacity to surprise will serve as a better indicator of its state of health than will the extent of the destruction it inflicts.

This new form of warfare required, first of all, the adoption of a new communications policy, probably elaborated under the guidance of Suleiman Abu Gayth, a Kuwaiti national and a Bosnia and Chechnya combat veteran who had been appointed al Qaeda spokesman in August 2001. Given the West's interception capacities, al Qaeda was forced to revert to more basic means of communication.

The use of satellite phones and e-mail—even in coded form—was curtailed as much as possible, and other slower but safer methods were used, such as human couriers. Likewise, the mujahideen, in order to keep their positions secret, had to stop using a very effective tool: their many and ever-changing web sites. They took on the Western media machine by co-opting its methods and using the Arabic media, starting with the Al-Jazeera television channel.

The Western media monitored the channel, watching for news flashes and retransmitting, in real time, every minor Islamist threat. As a result, such threats took on disproportionate importance in the eyes of the public.

That strategy was not a new one: for years Egyptian—and later Algerian—militant groups had transmitted their communiques to London-based Arabic-language newspapers such as Al-Watan al-Arabi. Video and audiotapes, transmitted clandestinely, thus spread al Qaeda's message throughout the world.

Such messages supposedly always originated from the group's leaders but could not always be accurately dated.

Threats against countries such as Great Britain, France, Italy, Canada, Germany, and Australia, and periodic claims of responsibility, were all the more forceful in their impact given that al Qaeda took care never to boast.

Its goal in terrifying the infidel world with threats made in the name of Islam was to force the Muslim world into a clash of civilizations.

THE MUJAHIDEEN MOVEMENT REPOSITIONS ITSELF (SEPTEMBER 2001–OCTOBER 2002)

Al Qaeda's forces in Afghanistan appeared to crumble rapidly during military operations. Underequipped, poorly trained, grouped mainly by ethnicity, mujahideen units did not have at their disposal the modern infrastructure described by the Western media. Most of them did not keep their promise to die as martyrs.

Many died during the bombings or were killed in Afghan score-settling, and several hundred ended up in the American camp at Guantanamo Bay in Cuba, but most of them managed to disappear. It was believed at the time that the movement's traditional fallback structures had been neutralized. Most of the countries that had welcomed it had, like Pakistan, done a sudden political about-face and either joined the international alliance or agreed to "clean up" their territory. Yemeni special forces launched major military operations to defeat the Aden-Abyan Islamic Army.

The GNT and Somali clan leaders, under the watchful eye of neighbouring Ethiopia and of the United States, announced that they had control over Al-Ittihad al-Islamiya. The Bosnian authorities arrested dozens of mujahideen and stripped hundreds of others of their Bosnian citizenship. The seizure of bank accounts and the reaction of the financial world had thrown into disarray the movement's usual system of transferring funds, and, furthermore, the international community, under the auspices of the United Nations, was in the process of elaborating new international legislation to combat terrorism.

The only thing we can be sure of is that the movement, having lost its Afghan network, has been dispersed and no longer has a coherent geopolitical structure capable of providing training and safe haven. For the time being, anyway, no state appears to have the capacity to provide to the mujahideen movement with the kinds of facilities that had been available to it in Afghanistan. Furthermore, the effective action of the anti-terrorist coalition led by the United States, whose president was overly quick to use the expression "crusade of good against evil"—a disastrous choice—has been strengthened by regional agreements. Unfortunately, it has become clear that the mujahideen movement is still alive and well. Most of its leaders survived the aerial and ground campaigns on Afghan soil, and ways of smuggling them out to other, more secure areas had long been planned. Indeed, al Qaeda had very close ties with Pakistan's seven tribal zones, which, lacking confidence in their own security forces, were all the more resistant to control by the Pakistani authorities. In the space of a year, the movement quietly repositioned itself geographically. Its key leaders fled to Pakistan and Iran, where longstanding and influential networks existed. Its operational chiefs and their lieutenants regrouped along a second axis, formed by the geographical crescent spanning Georgia, Turkey, Syria, the Gulf states, Malaysia, and Indonesia. Mujahideen sleeper cells took a third tack, remaining in Europe and Asia as well as in the United States.

During that time, the movement continued its fight in traditional jihad regions—in Algeria, Chechnya, and Kashmir and in the context of Asian guerrilla warfare—but al Qaeda carried out relatively few attacks. As usual, none really succeeded, killing fewer than 200 people in total. But most of the attacks perpetrated by the movement had links to Pakistan: either they were committed there or preparations had been made in that country.

All of those undertakings had similar characteristics: determined individuals employed the usual methods against media-ready targets, through the now-standard suicide attack. In Pakistan, several particularly violent attacks—using automatic weapons and grenades—struck Christian communities. But the ones of greatest magnitude occurred in Karachi, a city of 16 million people, where al Qaeda networks had been in operation for twenty years. In January 2002, the American journalist Daniel Pearl was kidnapped and beheaded. On May 11, the bombing of the Sheraton Hotel killed fourteen passers-by, including eleven French naval experts.

On June 14, a car bomb was set off in front of the U.S. consulate, killing thirty or so Pakistani, civilians. In all of those cases, investigated inconclusively by Pakistani authorities, involvement by al Qaeda operatives was suspected. Other operations were planned in Pakistan, probably by Khaled Sheikh Muhammad himself, believed to have masterminded the September 11 attacks. He was arrested in 2002, shortly after the capture of other key figures, including Zein al-Abideen Abu Zubeida, of Jordan, and Ramzi bin Al Shib of Yemen.

On December 22, 2001, Richard Calvin Reid of Great Britain, the "shoe bomber"—pentrite was found in his footwear—failed in his attempt to blow up a Miami-bound American Airlines plane out of Paris. Reid had received assistance from Pakistani networks that until that point had devoted their efforts to supporting jihad in Kashmir. On April 11, 2002, on the island of Jerba, Nizar Nouar of Tunisia carried out a suicide mission against the oldest synagogue in Africa, killing nineteen people. The Islamic Army for the Liberation of the Holy Places (AILLS) claimed responsibility, as it had when the U.S. embassies in Nairobi and Dar es Salaam were bombed in August 1988. On June 23, 2002, Moroccan authorities arrested three Saudi nationals who were planning suicide attacks by boat against American and British warships off of Gibraltar.

AL QAEDA FRANCHISES ITS ACTIVITIES AFTER 2002

The Maghreb

It should simply be added that, while the security situation did subsequently improve— although the country remained deeply traumatized—the Casablanca bombings of June 9, 2003, took Morocco completely by surprise, making it all too clear that the threat was capable of taking new forms. A phenomenon had emerged whose danger had not yet been understood: the radicalization of isolated Islamists, lured, at the local level, by jihadist speeches relayed by representatives of the mujahideen movement, and reeled in by sleeper cells composed of Afghanistan veterans.

The Middle East

Following the events of September 11, the peoples of the Middle East did not give in to the temptation to radicalize, and, in late 2002, the situation seemed to be under control, despite continuing evidence of the existence of underground groups. In 2003, as hopes for a settlement of the Palestinian question faded once again, two pivotal events occurred that led to further destabilization.

The first, of course, was the war in Iraq, strongly condemned by the Islamic world. Poor handling of the situation in the postwar period, marked by Shiite radicalization and a surge in the number of attacks— some of which looked to have been committed by mujahideen who had infiltrated the area—created a new regional hotbed of tension. The second was the serious crisis affecting the Saudi regime, increasingly challenged by its constituents and viewed with suspicion by its Western allies.

The authorities, after denying for years that local groups with ties to al Qaeda were present on its territory—several attacks against British nationals having been classified by police as "score-settling between alcohol smugglers"—and after having been implicated directly in the U.S. Congress's report on the events of September 11, finally responded by arresting radical ulama and Islamist militants.

But they did not move fast enough: on June 4 and November 9, 2003, major suicide attacks were carried out in Riyadh, killing forty-two and thirty-eight people, respectively, including Western civilians. Also important is the still-latent threat posed by local Islamist movements to stable regimes. That is the case of Jordan and Syria, two countries weakened by a recent power succession.

The West

In Europe, the participation on a massive scale of British troops in Afghanistan made Great Britain al Qaeda's European enemy No. 1, ahead of France, which, for historical reasons, remained the primary target of North African mujahideen. Al Qaeda's leadership, aware of the fact that the British authorities were taking a sterner stance towards the activities of small Islamist groups in England, had actually considered a strike against the British Parliament. The plan had been to hijack a plane from a British airport and crash it into the building.

That operation, which was to have been carried out by Pakistani Islamists simultaneously with the World Trade Center attacks, was eventually cancelled. In any case, the decision to act against England, guilty of having opposed the mujahideen presence in "Londonistan," was announced on November 12, 2001, in a message said to be from bin Laden. The movement's hostility increased further in the face of British involvement in the second Gulf War.

However, in early 2003, the threat to England had become more concrete, as evidenced by a series of failed armed operations ranging from small-scale biological attacks using ricin to a plan to launch a homemade missile at a plane at Heathrow Airport. Thus al Qaeda, unable to strike at Great Britain on its own territory, chose to attack that country's interests in Turkey. On November 19, two car bombs destroyed the British consulate and a British bank in Istanbul, killing nineteen people. It was the second real show of force by the mujahideen movement in Turkey and testimony to al Qaeda's resolve.

It also made clear the movement's inability to carry out direct attacks in Europe. Its decision to shift the struggle to a neighbouring country that had served as one of its rear bases meant the sacrifice of logistical networks that had been operating for years with relative impunity.

The move also confirmed the fact that the jihadist threat against Europe was aimed primarily at its external interests, specifically at expatriates and tourists. That was the case of France, which, although it had been able, following December 3, 1996, to thwart all jihadist plots on its soil, was struck on several occasions beyond its borders.

The death toll included two residents and a tourist at Jerba on April 11, 2001; a sailor off Yemen on October 6, 2002; four tourists in Bali on October 12 next; eleven technical experts in Karachi on May 5, 2002; and three expatriates in Casablanca on June 9, 2003. Aside from the Karachi attack, in which French naval-engineering personnel appeared to have been chosen because their level of security was inadequate, the other French victims had not been selected specifically because of their nationality but were simply random targets.

Another new development was jihadist groups' choice of Western targets on the basis of regional criteria. Jamaa Islamiya preferred to strike at Australians, killing 132 in the Bali attacks. The group even recruited Australian converts in al Qaeda camps so as to set up local operational networks. That plan had been in place in Europe since the 1990s, with the ongoing recruitment of young, second-generation North Africans in Afghan camps. The trend became evident in December 2001 in the United States, with the capture, in the mountains of Afghanistan, of John Walker Lindh, a convert to Islam.

Lindh has since been sentenced to twenty years in prison for treason. On the American continent, an investigation revealed that the nineteen pilots had acted virtually alone. Since then, other mujahideen cells in the United States have been dismantled—groups in Detroit and Chicago, not to mention the case of Jose Padilla—but they were rather small and did not appear to have made the transition to an operational phase. Lacking the advantage of surprise, al Qaeda once again proved unable to strike. In fact, the only attack against the United States was committed by a troubled American adolescent a few days after September 11. During a flying lesson, he crashed his plane into a building in Atlanta, following an incoherent radio transmission proclaiming his support for Osama bin Laden.

Central Asia

In the early 1990s, the Muslim republics of the Caucasus that came into existence following the Soviet Union's breakup witnessed the emergence of radical Islamist groups. Paradoxically, some of their commanders had fought against the mujahideen while serving in the Soviet army in Afghanistan. In 1994, al Qaeda set up a support structure in Baku, Georgia, for Azerbaijani Muslims fighting Armenian troops for control of Nagorno-Karabakh. Several hundred Arab veterans of the anti-Soviet jihad had fought there as a unit until the 1994 peace accords.

In 1991, a former Soviet air force general, Dzhokhar Dudayev, who had been elected president of the Republic of Chechnya on October 29, issued a decree of Chechen independence. Dudayev, backed by the Islamic Liberation Party (Hizb ut-Tahrir)—a Chechen faction of the Muslim Brotherhood—had chosen as military commander Shamil Basayev, an Afghanistan veteran who had been close to bin Laden. The first Chechen war began in 1994. In early 1995, several hundred mujahideen, including veterans of the Azerbaijani and Bosnian conflicts, were fighting alongside Chechen irregulars against the Russians.

Their commander, Ibn Khattab, a Saudi national, and bin Laden had fought side by side during a 1987 battle known as the Lion's Den. Khattab soon became Basayev's operations chief. In June 1995, Basayev, at the head of a Chechen commando unit, carried out a spectacular raid in Russia that led to the Budyonnovsk hostage incident.

On August 31, 1996, the Khasaviurt Agreement put an end to the hostilities. Ibn Khattab, who wanted to continue the jihad in the Caucasus, supported Islamist guerrilla warfare in Inguchia and north of Ossetia.

Many local volunteers set off to be trained in Afghanistan's new camps. Basayev and Ibn Khattab, unable to score any decisive victories in neighbouring countries, attempted an incursion into Dagestan on August 7, 1999. During the period from 4 to 16 September, 300 Russian civilians were killed in five apartment building bombings, committed, successively, in Boinarsk, Moscow, and Volgodansk. No one claimed responsibility for the attacks, which Moscow authorities said were committed by "Chechen bandits." A month later, direct intervention by the Russian army marked the start of the second Chechen war.

The civilian population, a large percentage of which had fled to Georgia, was particularly affected by the brutality of the conflict; indeed, atrocities were committed by both sides. As had been the case in Afghanistan, the Muslim world backed the Chechens, specifically through Islamic non-governmental organizations. Some of them—such as the International Islamic Relief Organization (IIRO)—were used by al Qaeda to channel assistance to Ibn Khattab's troops. Thus the Chechen jihad followed on from the Afghan jihad.

That is why Ibn Khattab, in a September 1999 statement titled "Europe:

- We Are Still at the Beginning of Jihad in This Region," said, The West, and the rest of the world, are accusing Osama bin Laden of being the primary sponsor and organizer of what they call "international terrorism." But as far as we are concerned, he is our brother in Islam. He is someone with knowledge and a mujahid fighting with his wealth and his self for the sake of Allah.... What the Americans are saying is not true. However, it is an obligation for all Muslims to help each other in order to promote the religion of Islam... He fought for many years against the Communists and is now engaged in a war against American imperialism.

During this period, several dozen Arab mujahideen arrived in Georgia under the pretext of providing humanitarian assistance to Chechen refugees, settling in the midst of the Pankisi Valley camps. The valley had been chosen by the Georgian authorities as a holding center for Chechen refugees, because the local people—the Kists—were themselves descendants of Chechen migrants who had arrived there in the nineteenth century. While the presence of mujahideen groups facilitated jihad in Chechnya by providing external logistic support, direct assistance by Arab volunteers to Chechen guerrillas remained limited.

The local climate was not to their liking. They did not look Chechen or speak the language, so, unlike local mujahideen, it was hard for them to blend in with the locals. On the other hand, they played a pivotal role in carrying out criminal activities, in particular kidnappings of foreigners, a number of whom were supposedly held in the Pankisi Valley. In Chechnya itself, the Islamists' religious leader, Sheikh Amar, worked to organize external assistance. As the local head of a Wahabi NGO that had been very active in Bosnia—the al-Haramein Foundation— he had the support of Middle Eastern theologians.

The funds received were used to develop propaganda tools that included publications and a web site—"The Voice of the Caucasus"—which advocated the creation of an Islamic emirate in the northern part of the region. But despite financial assistance from the Gulf, in the end suppression got the best of the Chechen Islamists. Their communications systems were scrambled by the Russian forces, which also relied heavily on bombings and searches, with the help of Chechen loyalists. Basayev had to have a foot amputated in January 2000, and Ibn Khattab died a few months later, probably poisoned. On October 23, 2002, Chechen Islamists led by Musar Barayev with explosives strapped to their bodies—including widows and sisters of "martyrs"—took 800 people hostage in a Moscow theater, demanding the withdrawal of Russian troops.

The Russian special forces intervened, using a sedative gas. Forty-one guerrillas were killed along with more than a hundred hostages. Georgia, under pressure from the United States, cordoned off the Pankisi Valley—the Chechen mujahideen's last supply base. It is believed that the area also served as a safe haven for the 700 boiviki (fighters) led by Commander Ruslan Gelayev, who had in late 2001 failed in his attempt to trigger Islamist warfare in Abkhazia.

The network led by Abu Musab al-Zarqawi—a Jordanian of Palestinian origin—also had a presence there. Al-Zarqawi had set up a number of structures to train combat volunteers to fight against the Russian forces. Several members of his group who specialized in explosives and chemicals, unable to get into Chechnya, decided to return to France and to Great Britain to wage jihad there. The failures of those two European groups sounded the death knell for the Chechen network. Some of the other organizations in al- Zarqawi's network—which was located in Iranian Kurdistan, along with the Ansar al-Islam (Followers of Islam) mujahideen group—had been dismantled when the American bombings started, in February 2003. It is likely, however, that some of the survivors are actively participating in suicide missions against American troops in Iraq—missions that are operationally very similar to those carried out by the mujahideen movement.

Tensions remained high, however, in the Muslim republics of the Caucasus, where many Afghanistan veterans were believed to have found refuge, despite the preventive operations carried out by security forces against local jihadist groups. The security situation in Central Asia remained, in the medium term, closely linked to the development of jihadism in South Asia.

South Asia

Insecurity continued to prevail in the Afghan-Pakistani zone. Indeed, the considerable dollar sums provided following the lightning-quick American victory did not make the Taliban any more open to democratic values. While military operations in Afghanistan were carried out effectively, reconstruction was done on the cheap. Aghanistan's President Hamid Karzai, who narrowly escaped death in assassination attempts in 2002 and 2004, is arguably in control only of Kabul, and that only because of the presence of the International Security Assistance Force (ISAF) and of NGO activities. Almost everything needs to be rebuilt—the administration, the tax system, the educational system, public services, and transportation.

The Taliban's weakness was overestimated because of their sudden disappearance. But they had simply hidden their weapons and become Pashtuns once again. Have they lost sight of the ideology that kept them in power before the Americans' arrival? It is more likely that they are just waiting for them to leave. In the meantime, they are keeping busy, for instance by participating in the various kinds of trafficking that are once again endemic throughout the country—especially opium trafficking. The 2002 opium harvest was estimated at 4,100 tons—a record for Afghanistan, only ten months after poppy cultivation had restarted. Kabul is not yet safe from attacks. Isolated yet significant acts of violence have made it clear that the Taliban and the "Arab Afghans" have not vanished entirely and still want to participate in jihad.

The impenetrability of the tribal zone—where traditional Pashtun ties of solidarity have held fast against all foreigners—and the question of Kashmir remain unresolved issues in the crisis affecting the Indian subcontinent, where Afghanistan remains the weakest and most unstable link. That regional crisis, which had prevailed since the violent partition of British India in 1947, fueled the process of radical Islamization—with a primarily Deobandi influence—in Pakistan. The tensions that exist today in that country are but a new form of the "Great Game" that has long been played in the region by local factions and foreign forces. Before September 11, Pakistani militant groups had been engaged in two types of jihad, in the conflict in Kashmir and in sectarian fighting against the Shiites. Ties were forged with al Qaeda so as to facilitate the training of their followers. But Pervez Musharraf's outlawing of those organizations in August 2001—a courageous act—led to the formation of underground groups devoted primarily to a third type of jihad—one dedicated to providing support for the mujahideen movement. It is no accident that, as we saw earlier, all of the attacks committed between September 11, 2001, and October 6, 2002, either occurred or were planned in Pakistan, nor that key arrests among al Qaeda's operational chiefs were subsequently made there.

Musharraf, weakened by the conflict with India—which was quick to denounce the Pakistani origin of the attacks committed in New Delhi and in Mumbai—then witnessed the emergence of a legal Islamist opposition movement. Nor could he be certain that his security forces would be loyal, and, in fact, he narrowly escaped several attempts on his life. This was a considerable burden to bear for the ruler of a country in a deep economic crisis, forced by international realities to drastically switch alliances.

Sub-Saharan Africa

Often overlooked is the fact that a third of sub- Saharan Africa's 700 million inhabitants are Muslims. The jihadist influence became evident most rapidly in the Horn of Africa due to the assistance provided in the early 1990s by Hassan al Turabi to ten or so radical groups in Eritrea, Uganda, and Somalia.

In February 1988, Abul Bara Salman, deputy commander of the Eritrean Islamic Jihad Movement (Jamaat al-Jihad Eritrea) stated that "the Islamist strategy in the Horn of Africa is based on several factors: jihad and preaching; educating Muslims about Christian plots... the resolve of Arab countries in the face of the Jewish threat; the efforts made in the context of jihad in Palestine."

The most powerful militant group in the region was probably still Al- Ittihad al-Islamiya, which had provided considerable support in connection with the August 7, 1998, U.S. embassy bombings. It is likely that the group is the author of a communique issued on August 19, 1988— supposedly on behalf of the apocryphal Islamic Army for the Liberation of the People of Kenya—claiming responsibility for the Dar es Salaam bombing, specifying that "the fight against the United States and its allies, the Jewish people of Israel, is a fight to the death. Before the Nairobi attack, we warned Muslims to avoid any location where there were Americans.... We are waging jihad everywhere and at all times."

The Somali group was also involved in the two-pronged Mombasa attack of November 28, 2002. In the late 1990s, threats had emerged in South Africa in connection with the radicalization of an Islamist group known as People Against Gangsterism and Drugs (PAGAD). However, PAGAD is believed to have been neutralized following the bombing of the Planet Hollywood restaurant in Cape Town in 1998. The situation had become more worrisome in Nigeria since the twelve northern provinces, with a mostly Muslim population, voted for the application of sharia despite opposition from the federal government. Several thousand Christians were killed during the rioting as the international community looked on with indifference.

Two Salafist centers—in Kano and Katsina—were located in that area. They both played an active part in arms trafficking in the sub-Saharan region, in support of Algerian militant groups. Nigerian Islamists had close ties—based on the call to jihad as well as on smuggling activities—with a number of groups that were flourishing in the Chad-to-Mauritania geographic crescent. It is worth noting that the Algerian GSPC carried out two operations in that region and that the aborted January 2001 attack against the Paris- Dakar-Cairo rally, as well as the March 2003 hostage incident involving thirty or so European tourists, also took place there.

Southeast Asia

The first signs of al Qaeda's presence in Southeast Asia appeared in 1995, following the arrest of Ramzi Yussef in Manila. At that time, Muhammad Jamal Khalifa, a Saudi national, had set up a financial holding company for al Qaeda in the Philippines, so as to finance the activities of local Islamist groups and forge ties with the mujahideen movement. But Khalifa was not just an average Saudi businessman; he was a veteran of the anti-Soviet jihad and Osama bin Laden's brotherin- law. In the 1990s, Southeast Asia was a convenient rear base for al Qaeda, which operated from its Afghan fortress. It was a safe area where new volunteers could be recruited, funds raised, fatwas obtained, and forged documents as well as technology procured.

The presence in the area of many tourists—particularly Middle Easterners—as well as ineffective security systems, undermined by corruption and excessive bureaucracy, made it an ideal place for a brief, or longer, stay, because they could go about their business unnoticed. For al Qaeda, Southeast Asia was also a fallback zone. As early as 1997, the organization knew that its strategy of secretiveness—to threaten, strike, and praise but claim no responsibility—was not viable in the long term, and it planned to withdraw to Southeast Asia when the Taliban regime fell.

In order to do so, alliances were required, and Asian mujahideen trained in Afghan camps heading back to their respective homelands were given messages for the leaders of their local groups, some of whom were veterans of the anti-Soviet jihad. Camps specializing in explosives training were needed, so al Qaeda sent instructors with particular skills in the area of the building and use of homemade bombs. As routes to Afghanistan, Pakistan, and Iran were under close surveillance, some of the new recruits were sent for training to Moro Islamic Liberation Front (MILF) camps in the Philippines. One of those recruits, a Frenchman by the name of Claude Sheikh Boulanouar, was arrested in December 1999 at Manila airport as he tried to board a plane with a detonator fuse hidden in his backpack.

The first attack in the Philippines by mujahideen was committed in 1997 on the island of Mindanao by two Arab mujahideen sent by al Qaeda to serve as MILF instructors. Militant Islamism in Southeast Asia has its roots in a clandestine Muslim organization—the Darul Islam (Islamic Unity)—that emerged in Indonesia following World War II. Its primary goal was to secure independence from its colonizers, but it also aimed to create a republic founded on Islam—present in the region since the fourteenth century— that would encompass the Muslim peoples of the region: Indonesia, Malaysia, southern Thailand (the Pattani region), and the southern Philippines (the Mindanao archipelago). Such a state was to be ruled by sharia law and would unite the local umma (community of believers), but Darul Islam did not at the time aim to conquer non-Muslims. Two of its leaders, Indonesians by the name of Abdallah Sungkar and Abu Bakar Bashir—both wanted in their homeland for subversive activities— took refuge in Malaysia in 1985. There they founded an Islamist movement similar to Wahabism, which advocated jihad and evolved into Darul Islam.

Their goal to was to agglomerate the various local conflicts pitting Muslims against Christians or the central authorities In the mid 1990s, several dozen of their followers—mostly Indonesians and Malaysians—headed to the Afghan-Pakistani zone to train in militant Islamism. They managed, if not to actually surpass their instructors, to persuade them to give their stamp of approval to a new dynamic similar to that of the Afghanistan-based mujahideen network, whose ideological bases were located, once again, in Pakistan and in Saudi Arabia. When he returned to Indonesia in 1999, Abu Bakar Bashir became the undisputed leader of the new Jamaa Islamiya (JI) (Islamic Group), a clandestine transregional organization whose goal was to impose Darul Islam through jihad.

At the same time, he founded, quite openly, the Indonesian Mujahideen Movement (MMI), an organization of fundamentalist activists that served as an inspiration for the activities of religious militias and as a JI recruiting ground. Bashir, though a declared Salafist and despite his incendiary sermons preaching jihad and his sympathy for bin Laden, was more of an ideologue than a fighter. For that reason, he charged his follower of fifteen years, Riduan Isamuddin, aka Hambali—a member of the JI's Majlis al- Shura—with the task of building up the military branch of the organization. The branch quickly zeroed in on three mantiqis (zones of action). The first included Singapore, Malaysia, and southern Thailand—an area of wealth sure to benefit a future Islamic state.

The JI had been founded there, and the armed branch's secret headquarters were there as well. The second zone, given the long-standing presence of MILF structures, was used for training. The third, Indonesia, was to be the battleground. Indonesia, however, was not prepared to act alone. Muslim guerrillas were focusing primarily on local conflicts—in Aceh, Molucca, and Celebes. Hambali, during several clandestine meetings held in Indonesia and Thailand, endeavored to standardize combat practices at the transregional level.

Filipino militants affiliated with the MILF or with Abu Sayyaf; Malaysians belonging to the Kampulan Mujahidin Malaysia (KMM) (Malaysian Mujahideen Movement); Indonesian guerrillas from Celebes, Molucca, and Java; Burmese members of the Rohingya Front; and ethnic Pattani Thai nationals participated in the creation of a coordinating body, the Rabitatul Mujahidin (Mujahideen League), along with, in all likelihood, representatives of the Afghan-Pakistani movement. The first attacks planned in Indonesia (against priests and presidentto- be Suhartoputri) came to naught. Amrozi, an Indonesian national who would later be involved in planning the three-pronged attack in Bali, was one of the protagonists. Malaysian mujahideen members of the KMM then launched a series of holdups and attacks against military posts to procure the necessary funds and explosives for future attacks.

They also assassinated a state assemblyman, Joe Fernandez, deemed too close to Christian circles. The jihad waged by the JI thus began in Indonesia. On December 24, 2000, approximately sixty bombs exploded in Christian churches throughout Java, killing forty civilians, including priests. On August 16, 2001, a car bomb went off in Jakarta, wounding the Philippine ambassador and killing four of his aides. No one claimed responsibility for either attack, in a strategic move reminiscent of al Qaeda's modus operandi. However, the Asian mujahideen movement was not as experienced as al Qaeda. In late 2000, the capture in Malaysia of Abu Jibril, an Indonesian who was one of JI's leaders, led to the identification of Hambali, who was running mantiqi 1 directly from Kuala Lumpur.

He fled to Pakistan in January 2001, where he was given new instructions, presumably by Khalid Sheikh Muhammad. Hambali had been the mastermind of the Bali attacks. Indeed, Bali was a perfect "soft target," because the island, with its mainly Hindu population, was a popular tourist destination for Westerners and for many nationals of Australia—Indonesian fundamentalists' bete noire since Timor-Leste's independence. The three-pronged attack was a complete operational success. Although only a third of the 1,100 kilograms of homemade explosives contained in the car bomb detonated in front of the Sari Club, everything within a 100-meter radius was destroyed. The first bomb had gone off a few minutes earlier in Paddy's Bar, 300 meters away, and people had gathered in the area where the second explosion was to take place.

The final death toll was 202, including 88 Australians. The third attack, which caused only material damage near the U.S. consulate, presumably was the operation's anti-American facet. Evidence soon surfaced of a double suicide bombing and of cell-phone detonation—a technique taught in the camps of Afghanistan—that pointed to a local group with ties to al Qaeda. It took a few weeks to break up the network, and in the process the JI's regional dimensions became apparent. There could be no doubt that for al Qaeda Southeast Asia had become a key strategic zone.

The possibility of getting some of Asia's 300 million Muslims to engage in armed protests was especially appealing to the organization since throughout the areas where jihad had traditionally been waged operational cells were being dismantled and high-level chiefs arrested. In hindsight, the Jakarta attack of August 5, 2003, was a failure. The suicide bomber was unable to get past security checkpoints and blew himself up too far away from the Marriott Hotel to do any damage. Of the twelve people killed, ten were Indonesian Muslims, which deprived the bomber of the status of shahid (martyr).

However, the regional organization for the first time claimed responsibility— a striking similarity with al Qaeda's strategy in the wake of September 11. The goal was probably to ensure a harsh sentence for Abu Bakar Bashir, set to go on trial August 10 for his role in the Indonesian bombings of 2000, which would anger Asian fundamentalists. But the Indonesian justice system responded in a measured and pragmatic way. The aging ideologue was sentenced only to four years in prison for his intellectual responsibility for JI's strategy of violence. For followers of the mujahideen movement, the warning was clear; the Indonesian people as a whole rejected the violence advocated by the organization and its official entities.

On August 11, President Bush's announcement that Hambali had been arrested in Thailand was a major setback for the jihadist strategy in Southeast Asia. His capture was the result of a series of operations that took down a logistical group in Cambodia, al-Qur›an (the Holy Book), and an operational group in Thailand, the Jamaa Salafiya (Salafist Group), which had been planning local attacks against five embassies and three tourist sites. In early September 2003, the organization's treasurer, Tawfik Rafke, was arrested. As a result, authorities were able to foil another plot and to identify a number of the group's members on the run from Indonesia.

However, in Southeast Asia the threat remains very real, with Indonesia and the Philippines as the weak link security-wise. Thailand, formerly a safe haven for clandestine groups, has taken decisive steps in the anti-terrorist struggle, given that its drawing power as a tourist attraction makes it a potential future target. Malaysia and Singapore, well protected within their borders, are concerned about threats to their external interests. Ultimately, Cambodia and Burma, and even Vietnam and Laos, all of which feature important sites which Westerners visit—look to be the new safe havens for jihadists on the run.

AL QAEDA'S STRATEGY TO ATTACK THE UNITED STATES

In late 2000, a series of meetings were held among al Qaeda's leaders and a number of highly placed mujahideen at which they decided to take action against their common adversaries. Each would be free to set goals and choose the means to achieve them, and each could count on support from the others. The mujahideen movement was thus joining forces with bin Laden. But that did not result in the creation of an organization with a pyramid hierarchy. Bin Laden made no attempt to openly impose his authority but established himself as a presence to be reckoned with in Afghanistan.

His experience and personal charisma, his ties with radical Saudi ulama, his wealth—all earned him respect. A prudent strategist, he refused to support massacres, and he never claimed responsibility for any attacks. He seemed more of a messenger than a guide. Indeed, bin Laden showed no evidence of personal ambition. Backed by al Qaeda's Majlis al-Shura and its experienced mujahideen, he called for jihad, which they viewed as the only means of restoring the caliphate and reuniting the Muslim community so as to make it a single political and religious entity.

The communications strategy he developed would make him worldfamous, enabling him to disseminate information through the American media and securing the loyalty of a number of Muslim journalists. While his strategy focused mainly on the Arabian peninsula, through threats against Americans, his message was a purely Salafist one calling for support for all oppressed Muslims, including Asian and Chechen Islamists and the Palestinian people. Bin Laden's closest aides were in charge of training camps. Recruitment was more effective that way, and volunteers were placed individually— usually in groups of thirty or so—in progressive stages, starting with basic military training and moving on to more specialized lessons about various poisons, electronic devices for use in bombs, and other techniques. In between training stages, mujahideen were either placed in accommodations known as "reception houses" (beit), usually with individuals of the same ethnicity, or they would go for religious instruction. Volunteers for suicide attacks were generally recruited in the early stages of military training, during rousing propaganda meetings run by the movement's leaders. Others were chosen for specific projects because of their particular operational profile—nationality, technical skills, or local connections. The final stages of training lasted for nearly a year. Those who went through it became very effective fighters, and a new caste of sorts was formed, most of whose members had seen combat alongside Taliban fighters against the Northern Alliance. Training structures were reorganized and further compartmentalized, becoming increasingly professional with the arrival of a new generation of war-savvy instructors, most of them Yemenis under the age of thirty. All participants were given new, several-thousand-page instruction manuals— available at the outset on diskette and later on CD-ROM—titled Encyclopaedia of Jihad, in which translated passages from Western military instruction guides alternated with detailed chapters penned by experienced mujahideen.

By early 2000, the Encyclopaedia of Jihad was available on various Internet sites set up worldwide through a complex relay system by mujahideen computer experts. Once trained, some of the volunteers settled in the area, either sending for their families or marrying Afghan women, and helped to train new arrivals. Others went back to countries where jihad was under way, or they participated in operational missions. Most of them, however, returned to their respective homelands, forming sleeper cells and providing logistical support while awaiting orders to make preparations for, or to participate in, attacks.

That was the scenario in Europe, where restructured mujahideen networks concentrated on four principal missions. First, recruiting efforts—which had resumed in 1997—were intensified, aimed at signing up volunteers for military training camps, located mainly in Afghanistan but also in the Philippines and in Yemen. Their second goal was to purchase specific items—including computers, communication materials, medicines, and certain kinds of clothing—for militant groups in jihad countries, particularly in Chechnya. Thirdly, they had to somehow secure the considerable financial resources required. That was accomplished through resort to organized crime—trafficking in forged documents, counterfeiting, credit-card fraud, and the drug trade—as well as burglary and armed robbery. Their fourth mission was to provide logistical support to mujahideen operatives in transit through Europe. Starting in 2000, Europe, too, became the target of operations. In earlier years, marginalized militants who in the past had been close to the mujahideen movement had independently planned and carried out attacks against France. They believed that, as they were working for the cause of jihad, they were free to act in the absence of specific instructions. New fatwas were therefore no longer necessary.

It is likely that their previous involvement in GIA-linked groups led them to target France, given its long-standing status as the principal external enemy of true Muslims. On December 3, 1996, a bomb exploded at the Paris RER train station Port-Royal. Given its timing—the Marrakesh network trial was due to begin on December 12—and its operational similarities with the July 25, 1995, attack, it was concluded that the perpetrators were lone individuals based in Europe with close ties to the mujahideen movement. The situation became clearer when, on March 5, the Brussels authorities broke up the group led by Farid Melouk—a French veteran of the war in Afghanistan—and Muhammad Chaouki Badache, an Algerian also known as Abu Qassim, who had been an MUKUB leader in Peshawar from 1992 to 1995. The group, which had been planning an attack in France during the soccer World Cup, was also involved in the trafficking of forged documents, which it needed in order to send its volunteers— who were mostly Moroccans—to the Afghan camps.

The mujahideen movement's involvement in attacks against Europe became evident on December 24, 2000, when German police arrested four Algerians, Afghanistan veterans all, in Frankfurt. They had in their possession weapons and an explosive device of the kind Afghan camps trained volunteers to build. A videocassette was also found showing locations around and in the city of Strasbourg—clear evidence that the group was planning an attack, probably on French soil, before January 1, 2001. The subsequent investigation, during which the contacts made by the Frankfurt group during the preceding three months were tracked down, made it possible to identify a significant percentage of European mujahideen networks. European police proceeded to dismantle them—little knowing that al Qaeda was gearing up for the most ambitious terrorist operation ever committed on American territory.

In Great Britain, on February 28, Abu Doha, an Algerian, was arrested for having provided logistical assistance in the Ressam case. The Italian subgroup of the Tunisian Fighting Group (Jamaa al-Muqatila al- Tunsia) (GCT), led by Afghanistan and Bosnia veteran Sami Ben Khemais Essid, was dismantled on April 4 in Milan. Evidence was unearthed of the pivotal role played within the GCT in Belgium by the group led by Taarek Maaroufi of Algeria, two of whose close associates were responsible for the assassination of Commander Massoud on September 9, 2001. The two had been recommended as journalists, slated to cover the Northern Alliance, by the Islamic Observation Center, a London Islamist propaganda group headed by Yussef al Fikri, an Egyptian, who had been sentenced in absentia in his homeland ten years earlier for his participation in GI activities. In Germany, where Islamist militants had been keeping a low profile, major judicial operations were launched, followed a few months later by investigations into the assistance provided by the Hamburg group to Muhammad Atta's group of pilots. In July, the arrest in Dubai of a French-Algerian, Jamel Beghal, tipped off the authorities to a suicide bombing being planned in Afghanistan by Zein al Abideen Abu Zubeida, whose target was probably the American embassy in Paris. All of those undertakings were part and parcel of the broad-based plan devised by the mujahideen emirs during meetings with bin Laden and his associates. But the emirs were in the dark as to al Qaeda's overarching goal: to attack America on its own territory and to humiliate it in a twofold, symbolic manner, striking at targets representative of its power and using its own equipment against it. The plan, which was elaborated under conditions of absolute secrecy over a period of more than a year, had been fine-tuned by bin Laden himself. He had entrusted the various stages of the operation's implementation to specific cells in Asia, Europe, and North America, chosen for their effectiveness and discretion.

CONCLUSION: THE AL QAEDISATION OF THE MILITANT TERRAIN

In spite of its brutality in carrying out fratricidal violence, the strategic brilliance of Al Qaeda's plan becomes evident in the changing nature of militant networking in Pakistan, along with the near unison in the militants' understanding of the enemy. To borrow counter-insurgency guru David Galula's terminology, Al Qaeda has been successful at converting the accidental mosaic of the disparate militant terrain in Pakistan into an intentional mosaic; has identified the US as its enemy, and views the government and military of Pakistan as an equal enemy. Through conviction that the government and the military of Pakistan is a mere 'puppet of the crusader enemy', traditionalist, nativist local groups have, for all practical purposes, become pseudo agents of Al Qaeda without even explicitly making that realisation. If the bitter experiences of the past eight years can in any way foreshadow future pattern of terrorism and counter-terrorism, it becomes clear that a greater counter-terrorism mandate in Pakistan will arguably lead to widening of the militant human terrain. Dynamic networking among the militant groups will act as a force multiplier, thus, requiring Pakistan to further broaden its counter-terrorist mandate. Paradoxically, more expanded counter-terrorist actions are likely to generate greater militancy, thus, developing into a negative feedback cycle. Clearly, this does not augur well for Pakistan, its neighbours and the United States.

4

The Evolution of Counter-terrorism Legislation

THE OPERATIONAL IMPACT OF COUNTER-TERRORISM LEGISLATION

Certain counter-terrorism laws have had an immediate impact on Islamic charities, particularly after 9/11, affecting their levels of funding and burdening them with administrative delays, such as the freezing of bank transactions. Since 2007 the impact has become more general across the humanitarian sector. This is due to multiple factors, including the judgement in the Holy Land Foundation case, the fact that donors, in response to pressure from domestic constituencies, have focused more closely on the issue, and allegations of high levels of aid diversion to designated terrorist groups, particularly in Somalia and the occupied Palestinian territories (oPt). The research carried out for this study suggests that counter-terrorism laws and measures have had an impact in five key areas.

FUNDING LEVELS

First, counter-terrorism legislation has directly affected levels of humanitarian funding. This has been particularly acute for Islamic organisations, as they have come under greater scrutiny than others, with many of their private donors becoming afraid of the possible consequences of indirectly funding designated groups or individuals. The impact on local NGOs, such as in oPt and Pakistan, has been especially severe. For example, several small organisations which ran sponsorship schemes for orphans in the Gaza Strip using private donations from Gulf donors have had to stop their operations. This has been partly as a result of specific restrictions introduced by governments such as Saudi Arabia, which has sought to counteract accusations by Western governments that it has allowed its citizens to support international terrorism through Saudi charities.

The impact has not been restricted to Islamic organisations. Donors that in the past had quietly accepted the risk of some aid diversion as 'the cost of doing business' in volatile environments have profoundly lowered their levels of tolerance when it comes to designated groups, often without taking into consideration the level of need. They now require firm assurances that the risk of aid being misappropriated is minimised and that no benefits are going to designated groups. When donors have considered these assurances inadequate funding has been stopped. Examples provided in interviews for this Policy Brief include OFAC licences not being renewed for specific projects in Gaza, despite the organisation in question receiving licences for other projects and having individually screened all project beneficiaries and undergone rigorous external auditing for the project.

The inability of aid agencies to provide firm assurances against the risk of misappropriation of aid has been particularly problematic in south-central Somalia, an area largely controlled by Al-Shabaab, an Islamist group that was designated as a terrorist organisation by the US government in 2008 and subject to UN sanctions from April 2010. Fears that Al-Shabaab was benefiting from the influx of humanitarian assistance, particularly food aid, led OFAC to suspend over $50 million in humanitarian aid for Somalia in 2009.28 These concerns were compounded by a report by the UN Monitoring Group on Somalia in March 2010 that alleged that three contractors were diverting over half of all food in Somalia — allegations that were contested by the World Food Programme (WFP).

ADMINISTRATION

Second, the administrative burden introduced by counter-terrorism legislation has affected the timeliness and efficiency of humanitarian aid, and can even deter aid actors from operating in high-risk areas. Delays in the transfer of funds and other administrative complications have become the norm for most Islamic humanitarian organisations, including those that are in full compliance with counter-terrorism laws. Islamic NGOs encounter tremendous difficulties in transferring monies received from donors, including Western bilateral and multilateral donors, to their country offices in places such as Pakistan. Bank transactions are frequently stopped without explanation and organisations have to wait for up to three months while an investigation is carried out. They are often asked to bear the costs of these investigations, even if they are cleared of any wrongdoing. Non-Islamic humanitarian organisations interviewed did not report similar problems with bank transfers, but they too have faced a significant increase in administrative procedures.

While many organisations already implement measures to minimise the diversion of aid, substantial staff time and financial resources are being devoted to applying for exemptions, checking lists (both of donors and partners) and otherwise ensuring compliance. Large amounts of information need to be collected and monitored as some donor regulations require organisations to vet, not just their staff or the staff of partner organisations, but of their partners' partners too. In interviews for this Policy Brief organisations detailed the number of extra staff hired at headquarters or in specific contexts such as Gaza to collect this information and ensure legal compliance. The same point came out of a consultation process between donors and humanitarian organisations in Somalia organised by WFP and supported by HPG in June 2011. Staff from Islamic organisations also reported screening all donations above $8,000, both from individuals and organisations, despite the very significant administrative burden this imposes.

Whilst humanitarian organisations clearly consider risk mitigation measures important,29 many also feel that they have become too cumbersome and are preventing them from taking the necessary risks to assist communities in need. Interviewees felt that funding shortfalls and the difficulty of complying with counter-terrorism laws in countries like Somalia have led some organisations to scale down their presence in areas controlled by designated terrorist groups.

RELATIONS WITH LOCAL COMMUNITIES

Third, the vetting of partners and beneficiaries is undermining relations between humanitarian organisations and local communities. USAID partner vetting requirements envisage collecting and reporting personal information about partner and contractor staff to the US government – a requirement that is invariably seen as invasive and accusatory by locals.30 Organisations are also concerned that the policy lacks clarity and transparency.

Other donors have tried to insert clauses in funding contracts requiring recipients to disclose personal information on partner organisations and beneficiaries. These measures undermine the neutrality of humanitarian organisations and make local acceptance harder to achieve, thereby potentially compromising access to people in need.

As noted by one commentator, 'through complying [with] national legislation, US [funded] organisations are seen by partners on the ground as endorsing the political view of the government ... particularly in its conception of terrorism and who deserves assistance'. In Somalia, two US organisations, International Medical Corps (IMC) and CARE, were expelled from areas under Al-Shabaab control in 2008 for allegedly spying and gathering intelligence that led to the assassination of Al-Shabaab leader Sheikh Maalim Adam Ayro in a US air strike.

NGOs with large non-state funding, such as MSF, have refused to accept these clauses and have replaced them with more generic clauses or inserted additional text stressing that nothing in their donor agreements 'shall be interpreted in a way that prevents MSF from fulfilling its mission as an impartial humanitarian actor bound by medical ethics'.

TRANSPARENCY

Fourth, the lack of clarity on the implications of the legislation and donor policy has led to decreased transparency and accountability in the way humanitarians operate in contexts where they have to interact with designated groups and individuals. In Gaza, for example, minutes are often not recorded at cluster meetings to avoid officially acknowledging any engagement with proscribed organisations.

Donors have given policy advice on non-headed paper. Charitable giving too has become less transparent as individuals turn to less regulated routes to avoid falling foul of counter-terrorism legislation, *e.g.* cash donations, which are more difficult to track. Several interviewees for this Policy Brief felt that, in the wake of the Pakistan floods, concerns about banking restrictions affecting transfers to and from Islamic organisations may have led the UK diaspora to give large amounts of money in cash to individuals or 'briefcase NGOs', which were not registered with the UK Charity Commission and did little if anything to comply with counter-terrorism legislation.

COORDINATION

Fifth, the threat of criminal sanctions has impeded transparent discussions between humanitarian actors and the development of a coordinated response to the issue of counter-terrorism. Due to the risk of criminalisation and potential prosecution of staff, many individuals and organisations are reluctant even to discuss this issue, let alone to discuss particular concerns or develop associated responses with other humanitarian organisations. Agencies have been reluctant to share information at cluster meetings and other coordination fora. This reluctance is also evident among donors, with many also preferring not to discuss this issue openly, or, as already noted, providing policy advice on non-headed paper.

Various initiatives have been undertaken by the IASC and individual organisations to document the impact of counter-terrorism legislation, but with little uptake. According to several interviewees, some organisations may be reluctant to admit that they have agreed to certain conditions or restrictions – or have operated in violation thereof. Counter-terrorism laws have affected humanitarian operations globally, but it is in Somalia and Gaza where the impacts have been most felt by the humanitarian community.

INTERNATIONAL LAW

Although the threat of terrorism has been on the international agenda since the League of Nations, agreements on countering terrorism at a global level date from the 1960s. A total of 14 international conventions exist, including the 1979 International Convention Against the Taking of Hostages, adopted in response to the US–Iran hostage crisis, and the 1980 Convention on the Physical

Protection of Nuclear Material. It has proved easier to reach agreement on these specific acts of terrorism than on a general definition of terrorism, and hence on a global anti-terrorist convention. As terrorist activities are mostly defined in opposition to the state, there has been a fear that such a convention would be used to suppress the right to self-determination. The events of 11 September 2001 gave some new impetus in this area. The 2005 World Summit Outcome Document included a commitment to conclude a comprehensive convention on international terrorism, and the UN General Assembly adopted a global counter-terrorism strategy in September 2006. Despite this, no progress has been made in the finalisation of the Comprehensive Convention.

Within the UN Security Council (UNSC), the events of 9/11 also led to new levels of consensus on dealing with terrorism. On 28 September 2001 the Council passed Resolution 1373 under Chapter VII of the Charter. Whilst terrorism is not defined in the Resolution, UN member states are ordered to refrain from providing any form of support to terrorist groups and individuals, and to implement measures to suppress terrorist acts within their jurisdiction. These include enhanced financial and border controls, international judicial cooperation, bans on the granting of asylum to terrorists (specifically, people who have 'planned, facilitated or participated in the commission of terrorist acts') and ensuring that 'any person who participates in the financing, planning, preparation or perpetration of terrorist acts or in supporting terrorist acts is brought to justice'. Member states are obliged to give effect to the Resolution at the national level through national law and other measures. Resolution 1373 also established the Counter-Terrorism Committee, comprising all the members of the Security Council, to monitor and report on the implementation of the Resolution.

Supplementing this overarching Resolution are specific sanctions regimes imposed by the Security Council in response to specific threats to international peace and security. These target particular actors, such as non-state armed groups in Somalia (under UN Security Council Resolution 733 of 1992) and groups in Afghanistan (based on UN Security Council Resolution 1267 of 1999). The Somalia sanctions regime targets Al-Shabaab and associates, and the Afghanistan regime, established in the wake of the August 1998 bombings of US embassies in East Africa, targets Al-Qaeda and the Taliban. Although these sanctions regimes are not necessarily characterised as counter-terrorism measures, the individuals subject to UN sanctions are often brought within the ambit of national counter-terrorist laws.

The open-ended nature of Resolutions 1373 and 1267 in particular has been criticised as being potentially ultra vires, or beyond the authority of the Security Council, including by the former UN Special Rapporteur on the Promotion and Protection of Human Rights and Fundamental Freedoms while Countering Terrorism. It has been claimed that the measures imposed by these Resolutions are disproportionate in countering any specific threats to peace and security, which is the mandate of the Council, in particular by imposing permanent sanctions over unlimited geographical areas on specific individuals.

REGIONAL AND NATIONAL LAW

Counter-terrorism laws have developed at different paces in different jurisdictions, reflecting the political environment in each case. In the UK, for example, counter-terrorism laws developed in response to the situation in Northern Ireland. A 12-month Prevention of Terrorism Act introduced in 1974 was renewed every year until 2000, when it was replaced with a permanent version in response to the more varied and open-ended terrorist threat deemed evident in attacks in Luxor, Dar es Salaam, Nairobi and Omagh. In Australia, the offence of terrorism was introduced in 2002, in response to both 9/11 and the Bali bombings of that year, in which 88 Australians were killed. Counter-terrorism legislation existed in the US prior to 9/11, with events such as the 1995 Oklahoma City bombing prompting a tightening of the law.

However, 9/11 can be said to mark a turning-point in national legislation in general, with counter-terrorism measures being stepped up across the board (partly in implementation of Resolution 1373). Additional controls have been introduced on the use of state funds, and a range of activities connected with terrorism have been criminalised where these were not specifically addressed before, including not only carrying out terrorist acts themselves but also providing resources or support to terrorist groups or individuals.

A number of groups and entities have been designated as terrorists by the Security Council, as with the 1267 regime, and these and others have also been designated as such by individual states. The designation of Hamas as a terrorist organisation by the US and the European Union (EU), for example, is not based on a Security Council Resolution but on national and regional policy decisions. The EU also maintains a list of 'persons, groups and entities involved in terrorist acts', established as an immediate response to Resolution 1373,5 as well as a list that reproduces the Security Council list under the 1267 regime. Individuals and organisations are included in some lists and excluded from others.

There have been numerous complaints and challenges – including successful legal challenges – to the accuracy of the various lists, and the lack of transparency and due process around listing and de-listing procedures.6The precise scope of the notion of 'support' to terrorist groups varies across jurisdictions. The EU Council Framework Decision on combating terrorism, which is binding on all EU Member States, defines participation in the activities of a terrorist group to include 'supplying information or material resources, or... funding its activities in any way, with knowledge of the fact that such participation will contribute to the criminal activities of the terrorist group'.

The UK has expanded this so that not only 'knowledge' that the support will contribute to terrorist activity, but also 'having reasonable cause to suspect' that this is the case, is enough to attract criminal responsibility.7 In Australia the intent required is lower, with being 'reckless' as to whether the funds will be used to facilitate or engage in a terrorist act considered a crime.8 In the US, no knowledge or intention to support terrorism *per se* is required if support is knowingly provided to a designated Foreign Terrorist Organization (FTO).

It is worth looking at US law in this area in more detail, as this is by far the law with the greatest potential adverse impact on humanitarian organis-ations. The two most relevant regimes in the US are the sanctions regime, implemented by the Office of Foreign Assets Control (OFAC), and the Material Support Statute in US criminal law. Under the International Emergency Economic Powers Act (IEEPA) of 1977, the President may block resources to designated entities in wartime or if a national emergency is declared 'to deal with any unusual and extraordinary threat, which has its source in whole or substantial part outside the United States, to the national security, foreign policy, or economy of the United States'.

Resources which may not be blocked include 'donations ... of articles, such as food, clothing, and medicine, intended to be used to relieve human suffering', although this can be overridden in three cases: where making such an exception would 'seriously impair [the President's] ability to deal with [the] national emergency'; where the donations 'are in response to coercion against the proposed recipient or donor'; and where they 'would endanger Armed Forces of the United States which are engaged in hostilities or are in a situation where imminent involvement in hostilities is clearly indicated by the circumstances'.

The list of individuals and organisations subject to sanctions under the IEEPA, known as Specially Designated Nationals, is maintained by OFAC. OFAC can licence private entities to engage in prohibited transactions in sanctioned countries (*e.g.* Iran) or in countries where designated groups are located (*e.g.* Somalia).9 Violations of OFAC sanctions are subject to both civil and criminal penalties, with the latter increasing in 2007 to a maximum fine of $1 million or up to 20 years in prison.

After 9/11, US President George W. Bush used his powers under the IEEPA in Executive Order 13,224, entitled 'Blocking Property and Prohibiting transactions With Persons Who Commit, Threaten to Commit, or Support Terrorism'. Terrorism is defined in the Executive Order as involving 'a violent act or an act dangerous to human life, property, or infrastructure' which appears to be intended either 'to intimidate or coerce a civilian population... to influence the policy of a government by intimidation or coercion; or... to affect the conduct of a government by mass destruction, assassination, kidnapping, or hostage-taking'. Section 4 of the Order overrides the humanitarian exception in the IEEPA on the grounds that allowing donations of food, medicine and so on would not only impair the President's ability to deal with the emergency but would also endanger armed forces on the ground. Alongside the OFAC-run sanctions regime, the US criminal code prohibits a range of terrorist activities, including the provision of material support or resources to terrorism, and these crimes can be prosecuted in the US even when committed abroad. The scope of these prohibitions was broadened after 9/11 by the USA PATRIOT Act.10 The code distinguishes between providing material support to terrorists generally and to designated FTOs in particular.11 The former requires that the support or resources be given 'knowing or intending that they are to be used in preparation for, or in carrying out' a terrorist act, whilst this is not necessary in the case of support to a listed FTO.

It suffices for the provider to know either that the organisation is a designated terrorist group or that it has engaged or is engaging in terrorist activity; no knowledge or intent that the support or resources given will be used for terrorist purposes is required.12Material support or resources include the provision of 'any property, tangible or zintangible, or service, including currency or monetary instruments or financial securities, financial services, lodging, training, expert advice or assistance, safe houses, false documentation or identification, communications equipment, facilities, weapons, lethal substances, explosives, personnel (one or more individuals who may be or include oneself), and transportation, except medicine or religious materials'. When first defined in the criminal law,13 material support excluded 'humanitarian assistance to persons not directly involved in [terrorist] violations'. This was amended to the current, narrower exception for medicine and religious materials in the wake of the Oklahoma City bombing in April 1995.14 The definition of terrorism in the statute closely resembles that in Executive Order 13,224.

The scope of this humanitarian exception has been explored in a number of lawsuits in the US. Prosecutions so far are notable for primarily targeting Islamic organisations and individuals who are allegedly ideologically linked to a proscribed group.15 In 2008, the Holy Land Foundation for Relief and Development, then the largest Islamic charity in the US, was found guilty of supporting Hamas through its contributions to West Bank zakat committees. The charity was dissolved and its Directors received sentences of up to 65 years in prison (the case is currently under appeal).16 In an associated civil case brought against the Holy Land Foundation by a victim of Hamas, the court examined the scope of the humanitarian exception, in particular the exclusion of medicine from the definition of material support.

It considered the theoretical case of 'medical (or other innocent) assistance by nongovernmental organizations such as the Red Cross and Doctors Without Borders' to injured Hamas fighters, and confirmed that this would fall within the terms of the exception. In the court's non-binding interpretation,17 even if Doctors Without Borders/Médecins Sans Frontières (MSF) knew that it was treating Hamas fighters, it would not be liable for contributing to terrorism:

It would be helping not a terrorist group but individual patients, and, consistent with the Hippocratic Oath, with no questions asked about the patients' moral virtue... The same thing would be true if a hospital unaffiliated with Hamas but located in Gaza City solicited donations.18However, in two criminal cases concerning individual doctors ideologically affiliated with Al-Qaeda, rather than humanitarian organisations, the doctors were convicted of supporting terrorism by providing medical treatment to members of a proscribed group (the cases are US v. Shah and US v. Farhane).19 The humanitarian exception was interpreted narrowly in these cases as including the provision of medicine only, and not the provision of medical treatment, which draws upon medical expertise.

However, a significant factor in each case was the stated commitment of the defendants to the goals of Al-Qaeda, and the judgments suggest that a different conclusion could be reached in the case of independent humanitarian organisations not acting under the 'direction or control of a designated foreign terrorist organization'.20 In its well-publicised 2010 judgement in Holder v. The Humanitarian Law Project (HLP), the US Supreme Court authoritatively clarified that the intention of the provider of support to a designated FTO is irrelevant, as long as the provider knows of the terrorist nature of that organisation, as defined by US law.

This case was not a prosecution but a challenge to the constitutionality of the Material Support Statute initiated by the HLP, five other organisations and two US citizens, and the judgement is particularly significant because it issues from the Supreme Court, the highest legal authority in the US. The particular forms of support considered by the court case were training, expert advice or assistance, services and personnel provided by the HLP to the Kurdish Workers' Party (PKK) and the Liberation Tigers of Tamil Eelam (LTTE), and the innocent intentions of the HLP were not in dispute. The court found that even 'material support meant to promote peaceable, lawful conduct can be diverted to advance terrorism in multiple ways'.21

DONOR FUNDING

A number of states and inter-governmental funding bodies have introduced clauses into grant agreements and procedures into relationships with humanitarian organisations to comply with counter-terrorism laws and policy objectives. NGOs or NPOs (Not for Profit Organisations) were identified as a potential conduit for terrorist financing soon after the events of 9/11. In October 2001, the inter-governmental Financial Action Task Force (FATF) expanded its remit beyond money-laundering to specifically include the funding of terrorism, and issued eight Special Recommendations on terrorist financing, including better regulation of NPOs. Greater regulation also stems from concern among donor officials about their possible individual liability and the reputational hazards for the governments they serve if their partners are deemed to be providing resources or funds to designated individuals or groups.

USAID has taken a number of steps designed to prevent diversion of its funds to terrorist organisations. In March 2002 it began including a clause in grant agreements reminding applicants of the ban on transactions with organisations on the list of Specially Designated Nationals. From December 2002 USAID has also required all grantees to certify that funds do not assist terrorist activity, and has introduced a 'Partner Vetting System'. This is intended to 'ensure USAID funds and USAID-funded activities are not purposefully or inadvertently used to provide support to entities or individuals deemed to be a risk to national security', and requires information on implementing partners to be sent to USAID headquarters.22 The UK Department for International Development (DFID)'s funding agreements include a clause requiring recipients of funding to not in any way provide direct support to a listed organisation.

The EU first tried to address this issue by recommending best practices to member states and developing a code of conduct for NPOs. However, the experience of recipients of ECHO funding in certain sensitive contexts suggests that lately more restrictive contractual terms have been introduced. AusAID requires grantees to use their best endeavours to ensure that their funds 'do not provide direct or indirect support or resources to organisations and individuals associated with terrorism', and to inform AusAID immediately if 'the Organisation discovers any link whatsoever with any organisation or individual listed by the Australian government as associated with terrorism'.23 Although the explanatory notes say that 'the obligation to notify AusAID does not ... confer an active intelligence gathering responsibility',24 this may be perceived differently in the field.

COUNTER-TERRORISM : SECURING A NETWORK SOCIETY— MODES OF PREVENTION

Indicating that no acts of cyber terrorism have occurred, does not necessarily imply that the potential cyber terrorist threat should not be addressed. Irwin Cotler argues that the nature of security legislation, particularly in regards to terrorism, is preventative rather than reactive– that it is necessary to stop acts of terrorism, including cyber terrorism, before they occur. While the extent and scope of preventative approaches should be questioned, the following portion of this chapter examines current and potential legal and political mechanisms at various scales for combating the threat of cyber terrorism.

EXISTING DOMESTIC LAW

Canadian domestic legal mechanisms are insufficient for addressing terrorism, and especially cyber terrorism. The transnational nature of the threat, severely limits the utility of federal or sub-federal law. Of particular interest here is the lack of geographic restrictions on acts of cyber terrorism. Not only can cyber terrorism occur from outside the territorial boundaries of the state, but acts can originate from numerous foreign states simultaneously. Therefore, domestic mechanisms such as the U.S., terrorism watch lists are either inadequate or inefficient.

The dilemma rests on the rise of the network society and increasing dependence on information and computer technologies for the production of everyday life. Additionally, considerations of national sovereignty and issues of jurisdiction emerge when investigating or prosecuting transnational criminal acts. The same can be said for addressing cyber terrorism. While Canadian security legislation, such as the *Anti-Terrorism Act* (ATA), addresses acts of terrorism against Canadian citizens abroad, it cannot take legal action against cyber terrorism without the consent of the foreign government from which the cyber terrorist act originated. National sovereignty remains enforced and universal jurisdiction is currently non-existent. As such, existing domestic legal mechanisms are insufficient.

BILATERAL AGREEMENTS

Bilateral agreements may not be feasible due to the mobility and deployability of cyber terrorism, as well as bureaucratic impracticability. First, cost-effectiveness, the global extension of computer technologies and lack of geographic restrictions suggests that cyber terrorist attacks can originate in almost any country. Second, with over 200 countries enjoying access to the Internet and related communications technologies, bilateral agreements are bureaucratically unfeasible. As such, governments must approach the issue at the international scale. Whereas Canada's *Securing an Open Society* is a national strategy, securing a network society requires approaching the issue transnationally.

International Agreements I : Combating Terrorism

Common international platforms are required to address the terrorist threat, and there are two components of international agreements worth considering: international law and policy harmonisation. International law originating within international, multilateral institutions can most successfully address cyber terrorism. While there has been disagreement over whether a universal definition of terrorism can be ascertained, the United Nations has successfully issued international legislation concerning weapons of terrorism, and regarding supporters of terrorism.

Multilateral institutions are particularly crucial because of the variegated definitions of terrorism and the legitimacy that comes from agreements among several states in an open and transparent forum. The legislating of any international law on cyber terrorism should consider three factors. First, a definition of what constitutes a cyber terrorist act should be established. Distinctions can and should be made between acts of cyber terrorism and acts of cyber dissent or hacktivism. Second, a designation of what actions are required for a legal response should be determined. This includes whether a target should be notified before retribution for a cyber terrorist act is executed, and under what circumstances. Third, the agreement should promote transnational cooperation. National interests should be compromised to the minimal extent possible when addressing the attribution of cyber terrorist attacks and subsequent potential retribution. Policy harmonisation is a consequence of common international platforms. International requirements for the legislating of domestic policies on cyber terrorism increase domestic and international security and transnational cooperation.

An instructive example, addressed specifically at terrorism, is *UN Security Council Resolution 1373*. A second example is the *Council of Europe Convention on Cyber -Crime*. Signed by Canada in 2001, this treaty is "the first-ever international treaty to address criminal law and procedural aspects of various types of criminal behaviour directed against computer systems, networks or data and other types of similar misuse". While not addressed specifically at cyber terrorism, the cyber crime treaty requires states to criminalise certain forms of abuse of computer systems and certain crimes when they are committed using computer systems. The treaty also supports international cooperation to detect, investigate and prosecute these criminal offences, as well as to collect electronic evidence of any criminal offence.

However, the *Convention on Cyber-Crime* does not include key elements of the terrorism definition. Specifically, it does not refer to political, ideological or religious motivations or objectives. Therefore, current international legal mechanisms are insufficient in addressing the cyber terrorist threat and new agreements must be established. The secondary danger is the collection of data by governments from commercial actors. This activity lacks transparency and accomplishes an "end-run around the checks otherwise applicable when government seeks personal information". Information-gathering requires governmental regulation, oversight and transparency, a feature not common in the commercial harvesting of personal data.

International Agreements II: Addressing the Causes of Terrorism

International agreements on combating terrorism necessarily require complementing initiatives on other issues that are perceived to be causes of individuals and groups turning to terrorist methods. The process of determining the causes of terrorism deserves much longer treatment than this chapter can provide. However, international policies directed at the alleviation of poverty, war, repression and other forms of social, political and economic exploitation should be a counterpart of any counter-terrorism campaign. Information and communications technologies can assist in this process by extending the ability of governments to understand which regions require aid and to the development of a transnationally scaled civil society that seeks to drive marginalised individuals away from destructive forms of political action.

TECHNOLOGY-DRIVEN SURVEILLANCE AND INTELLIGENCE

There are two methods of defending against cyber terrorism: passive defence and active defence. Passive defence is another name for target hardening, involving the use of technologies such as firewalls or cryptography to protect information technology assets and the data stored within. A considerable part of the problem is the combination of demands for large-scale connectivity and access, as well as the massive number of owners, operators and users of these systems and networks.

As Goodman argues, "the domain of actors in cyber space is much larger and more diversified than is the case with more traditional security issues." Analyses of private sector products and systems indicate that software quality assurance is problematic. Defective or poorly-designed products rushed to market without adequate concern for security raise many questions about whether regulation will be necessary. Additionally, in both the public and private sectors, the many legacy systems still in use were not designed with security in mind. Even presently, security is often perceived to be in conflict with design criteria focusing on accessibility and data throughput. Security is commonly identified with reduced efficiency and impaired functionality. Active defence seeks to determine the identity of the attacker and possibly initiate a counter-attack. One form of active defence, discussed here, is computer-driven surveillance. An effective response to the threat of terrorism and cyber terrorism requires international cooperation, but such cooperation must be reinforced with transnational surveillance mechanisms. Technology-driven intelligence gathering methods can be more effective and less intrusive than traditional forms of surveillance and intervention. As such, while the following portion provides an analysis of the legal and political implications of new technology in counter-terrorism efforts. While there are currently no global surveillance systems with the full participation of all countries, two more limited types of systems are presently in operation: domestic systems and transnational systems.

Domestic systems, such as the FBI surveillance system known as Carnivore, are inward-looking. While domestic systems may be more comprehensive than transnational systems, the former does not infringe upon the national sovereignty rights of foreign countries, not does it violate the jurisdiction of foreign intelligence and security services. As such, neither bilateral nor international agreements are necessary for the legal functioning of domestic surveillance systems.

Transnational systems are a different breed altogether. These systems, such as ECHELON, are both inward-looking and outward-looking. Transnational systems are of a controversial nature due to a perceived lack of respect for national sovereignty rights and issues of jurisdiction. While transnational agreements or understandings are necessary for the functioning of transnational surveillance systems, such arrangements are often mired in secrecy. The features of transnational surveillance systems dictate that the types of transnational or international agreements are necessary for their legal operation.

ECHELON TRANSNATIONAL SURVEILLANCE SYSTEM

The ECHELON surveillance system began its current phase of development in 1971 as a component of the post-WWII UK/USA intelligence cooperation and information-sharing alliance. Using electronic-intercept stations and space satellites, the purpose of ECHELON is generally signals intelligence (SIGINT), and specifically communications intelligence (COMINT). The transnational surveillance system additionally has the capability to acquire other forms of intelligence and information. ECHELON captures military, political and diplomatic communications traffic from across the globe, though recent events have indicated that the system is also being used for economic purposes.

ECHELON is not designed to eavesdrop on specific individuals. Instead, the surveillance system works on the basis of automated analysis. Messages and conversations are filtered though a computer system called Dictionary which detects keywords and phrases– a method of processing information is known as "data-mining." Five countries currently participate in the ECHELON system, providing global coverage through intercept ground stations and space-based satellites. Australia and its Defence Signals Directorate (DSD) monitors Indochina, Indonesia and Southern China.

The Government Communications Security Bureau (GCSB) of New Zealand covers the Western Pacific region. The United Kingdom's Government Communications Headquarters (GCHQ) monitors Europe, Africa and Russian territory west of the Urals. The National Security Agency (NSA) in the United States, possessing the most advanced and comprehensive surveillance infrastructure, covers Latin America, and Asia, as well as Asiatic Russia and northern China. Canada's Communications Security Establishment (CSE) monitors northern portions of the former Soviet Union, embassies around the world and central and southern parts of the Americas. Commentators argue that the nature of cyber terrorism demands that transnational surveillance systems be implemented to compliment international agreements, and that while legal issues and concerns over ECHELON in its current form will invariable arise, the basic transnational approach behind ECHELON is sound. The remainder of this chapter examines these legal dilemmas and explores some of the ways that surveillance systems such as ECHELON may gain increased or decreased legitimacy.

Technological Intervention in the Age of Terrorism

Addressing matters of privacy and surveillance inevitably results in debates concerning oversight and the balancing of rights and security.

The following portion of this stage discusses these issues in five parts:

1. The proportionality test,
2. The existence of a right to privacy in the Canadian context,
3. The nature of automated surveillance; and an analytical section on "veil of ignorance",
4. The balancing act between the right to privacy and security; and
5. A proposal to remedy the problem of oversight.

THE PROPORTIONALITY TEST OR OAKES TEST

Derived from The Queen v. Oakes, the "Oakes test" considers S.1 of the Charter, which provides that:

- The *Canadian Charter of Rights and Freedoms* guarantees the rights and freedoms set out in it subject only to such *reasonable limits* prescribed by law as can be *demonstrably justified* in a free and democratic society.

In other words, the rights and freedoms under the *Charter* can be violated if the violation is reasonable and justifiable. The Supreme Court of Canada has defined a test for determining whether a violation is reasonable and justifiable. This test, referred to as the "*Oakes test*" or proportionality test, has two components: sufficient importance and proportionality. First, the government must demonstrate that its objective is sufficiently pressing and substantial to warrant the violation of a right or freedom. Second, the party invoking s.1 must show the means to be reasonable and demonstrably justified.

Proportionality itself has three requirements:

1. The measures must be fair and not arbitrary (the means chosen to limit rights and freedoms must be rationally connected to the objective);
2. There must be a minimal impairment of rights in achieving the objective; and
3. The detriments of the violation must not outweigh its benefits.

The *Oakes test* was further solidified in Canadian law after *Dagenais v. CBC*.

THE RIGHT TO PRIVACY

While not expressed explicitly in the Charter of Rights and Freedoms, the right to privacy has been interpreted through the Supreme Court of Canada's purposive approach to s.8 of the Charter, which provides that:

- Section 8. Everyone has the right to be secure against unreasonable search or seizure

Through precedence in case law, the right to a reasonable expectation of privacy has been demonstrated in Canadian law. As La Forest J. stated in *R. v. Dyment*, "the restraints imposed on government to pry into the lives of the citizen go to the essence of a democratic state". Historically, privacy was associated with private property, whose possession protected against intruders. "If the rights of private property were respected, and the curtains of the home were pulled, the King's agents could watch from a distance but would have no way of finding out what was going on inside". However, technological developments diminished the protections provided by property rights, and new interpretations of law or new legislation were required. As a result, the Supreme Court of Canada (SCC) has indicated that s.8 of the *Charter of Rights and Freedoms* provides for the right to a reasonable expectation of privacy.

Canadian case law has identified three different types of privacy:

1. Personal;
2. Territorial; and
3. Informational.

Personal privacy includes the protection of bodily integrity, as indicated in *R. v. Golden* and in *R. v. Stillman*. Territorial privacy includes the protection of privacy in the home, being the place where the most intimate and private activities are likely to take place. As per Cory J., in *R. v. Silveira*, "[t]here is no place on earth where persons can have a greater expectation of privacy than within their 'dwelling-house'". Other forms of territorial privacy include: in the perimeter space around the home, in commercial space, in private cars, in a school, and in prison. Territorial privacy is used as an analytical tool for evaluating the reasonableness of a person's expectation of privacy.

Much more controversial than personal privacy and territorial privacy is informational privacy, defined as "the claim of individuals, groups, or institutions to determine for themselves when, how, and to what extent information about them is communicated to others". The existence and lawfulness of a right to a reasonable expectation of informational privacy has been indicated in *R. v. S.A.B.* and in *R. v. Law*.

The "reasonable" nature of the expectation of privacy is derived from two factors:

1. The *Oakes test*; and
2. The "totality of the circumstances" test.

First, the expectation of privacy can be violated if the objective is reasonable and demonstrably justified. The *Oakes test* demands that two requirements be met before the violation of a right or freedom can occur: sufficient importance of the objective, and proportionality between the limiting measure and the objective. Second the reasonable expectation of privacy is subject to the "totality of the circumstances" test set out by Cory J. in *R. v. Edwards*. Briefly, this test asks two questions: Did the respondent have a reasonable expectation of privacy? And if there was a reasonable expectation of privacy in this case, was it violated by police conduct? These questions must be specifically tailored, depending on facts of the case.

Thus the expectation of privacy can "reasonably" be violated:

- If the objective and means of the violation is in accordance with s.1 of the *Charter*; and
- If there is either no reasonable expectation of privacy, or if a reasonable expectation of privacy was violated by the lawful conduct of law enforcement.

A potential third factor affecting the "reasonable" nature of the expectation of privacy is s.33 of the *Charter*, though the relevance of the non-withstanding clause would depend on the nature of the violating legislation. Nonetheless, the development of case law suggests that Canada is either progressing towards or already situated at a position in which the right to privacy in constitutionally protected, but subject to the context of the crisis or emergency at hand.

AUTOMATED SURVEILLANCE AND THE "VEIL OF IGNORANCE"

The nature of ECHELON and other electronic surveillance systems is such that information is automatically filtered by computer systems. ECHELON is not designed to eavesdrop on specific individuals. Instead, the surveillance system works on the basis of automated analysis. Messages and conversations are filtered though a computer system called Dictionary which detects keywords and phrases.

This structure is analogous to John Rawls' conception of a "veil of ignorance." While those developing the surveillance system are not completely disinterested, automated analysis removes personal biases that pervade other forms of intelligence gathering. Automated systems, while not immune from subjectivity due to their construction by humans, are more capable of eliminating the discrimination often witnessed in human intelligence (HUMINT) or in law enforcement.

The use of computer-based keyword and phrase analysis results in amplified complexities and increased difficulties in manipulating the system. Currently, electronic surveillance systems are the most objective components of the intelligence apparatus. However, the analysis of electronically-gathered information is the realm in which increased subjectivity and bias come into play. As such the issue concerns how the data is analysed rather than how information is collected.

BALANCING THE RIGHT TO PRIVACY AND SECURITY

Taking into consideration the threat of cyber terrorism, the preventative nature of law, the reasonable expectation of privacy and the automated nature of transnational surveillance, the "*Oakes test*" can be employed in analysing the balance between the privacy and security. When situating the risk in relation to national security, a tangible threat of cyber terrorism is non-existent, yet a potential threat remains. In the post-9/11 security environment, increasingly driven by information technology, preventative measures are necessary for the maintenance of security. The potential number of casualties resulting from a cyber terrorist attack on critical infrastructure, or government systems is sufficient to warrant a limitation on the right to privacy. Therefore the first requirement of the "*Oakes test*" is satisfied. In the second component of the "*Oakes test,*" the rational connection requirement is satisfied due to the transnational nature of cyber terrorism. Transnational surveillance is a prerequisite for any success derived from international agreements. However the issue becomes more problematic when considering the final two requirements: proportionality between the effects of the violation and the objective; and the minimal impairment of rights. This complexity is the result of the secretive nature of the ECHELON system. To what extent does ECHELON eavesdrop on the global communication networks? Who has ultimate control over the intelligence acquired? What restrictions exist on access to and operationalisation of the intelligence collected? These questions are of significant importance in analysing the balance between rights and security.

Without a deeper understanding on the functioning of the ECHELON surveillance system, the application of the "*Oakes test*" cannot be fully realised. However, a consideration of the automated nature of analysis in combination with an appreciation of the potential threat posed by terrorism and cyber terrorism may be sufficient to establish that a balance between rights and security in the utilisation of ECHELON can be achieved. If further information on the functioning of ECHELON is unavailable for logistical or security reasons, oversight mechanisms will increase confidence in the stability, legality and efficiency of the ECHELON surveillance system. A potential issue, though outside the scope of this chapter, is the prospective balance required between transnational privacy and international security. While citizens may tolerate domestic surveillance within reasonable limits, it remains to be seen whether surveillance by a foreign government will be as acceptable.

OVERSIGHT

The problematic of oversight, prevalent and reoccurring in historical analyses of Canadian security services, is further complicated when considering

ECHELON, due to the system's transnational nature. The issue of oversight can be considered in both a Canadian context and a transnational context. The Canadian contribution to the ECHELON surveillance system is through the Communications Security Establishment (CSE). This presents a problem for oversight. While security and/or intelligence agencies such as the Royal Canadian Mounted Police (RCMP) and the Canadian Security and Intelligence Service (CSIS) are regulated and restricted by the *RCMP Act* and *CSIS Act*, respectively, the CSE has no specific legislation governing or guiding its actions. While privacy and oversight are present in numerous forms of legislation in other fields, such as the *Personal Information Protection and Electronic Documents Act*, the *Privacy Act*, the *Telecommunications Act*, and the *Competition Act*, the CSE has very little evidence of its existence outside of Orders-in-Council and a headquarters on Heron Road in Ottawa, Ontario. The CSE ultimately reports to the Minister of National Defence and is not subject to the oversight mechanisms in place for other agencies.

As such, domestic oversight of Canada's participation in the ECHELON system is generally absent. In the transnational context, oversight becomes additionally complex. While international cooperation in addressing cyber terrorism is already perceived as a monumental task, the development of transnational oversight mechanisms for the ECHELON surveillance system seems almost impossible. And yet, the completion of such a task is necessary to establish confidence in the balance between rights and security. Four types of oversight are worth briefly considering here: governmental oversight, judicial oversight, public oversight, and civilian oversight. Governmental oversight is possible through internal watchdogs. This is a relatively common occurrence in national governments, however here it is recommended that an independent organisation outside the government be responsible for oversight (due to its transnational nature and to prevent any conflict of interest). Judicial oversight is a potential solution, though no international court suitable to addressing this issue currently exists. Both the International Criminal Court (ICC) and the International Court of Justice (ICJ) have mandates outside the scope of assessing transnational surveillance systems.

However, if the participating members of the ECHELON system establish themselves as an international institution or agency, approaching the ICJ becomes a possibility. Public oversight, through the media for example, is impractical due to the confidential nature of the intelligence collected. Civilian oversight, similar to SIRC, is potentially the most feasible and the most effective form of oversight currently available. While the process of establishing transnational oversight mechanisms is not within the scope of this chapter, the issue must be considered before an analysis of the ECHELON surveillance system under the framework of the "*Oakes test*" can be completed.

5

Terrorism in India and National Security

BROAD DEFINITIONS OF TERRORISM

Many of POTA's aws stemmed from its broad text. While all laws may be susceptible to abuse, anti-terror legislation in particular invites it by placing permissive language in the hands of zealous law enforcement officers. The USA PATRIOT Act, like POTA, defines terrorism crimes broadly, but POTA's definitions are even less precise. POTA defined terrorism as any violence "with intent to threaten the unity, integrity, security or sovereignty of India or to strike terror in the people or any section of the people." Moreover, the law imposed a minimum five-year sentence on "[w]hoever conspires or attempts to commit, or advocates, abets, advises or incites or knowingly facilitates the commission of, a terrorist act or any act preparatory to a terrorist act...."

Particularly troublesome were the words "advocates" and "incites," for they implicated issues of free speech and political expression. The same problems arose under section 21 of POTA, which made it an offence for one to "invite support for a terrorist organization" or "address a meeting for the purpose of encouraging support for a terrorist organization...." POTA did more, however, than create broad new crimes under the rubric of terrorism. Like the PATRIOT Act, POTA defined terrorist acts in generalized terms that encompassed ordinary cases of murder, robbery, theft, and comparable offenses. Thus, its violators could have been subject to improperly severe penalties and overzealous law enforcement officials attempting to circumvent constitutionally-mandated procedural safeguards.

SWEEPING POWERS OF ARREST AND DETENTION

POTA's broad definitions of terrorist offenses were especially problematic in light of its modified arrest and detention procedures and special terrorism courts. Section 49(2) of POTA allowed police to detain a suspect for up to 180 days without a formal charge, far exceeding the limit under ordinary Indian criminal law. Although the Indian Constitution requires police to promptly inform a person of the grounds for his or her detention and to provide the "earliest opportunity to make a representation" before a magistrate, and Indian case law identifies a speedy trial as "an integral and essential part of the fundamental right to life and liberty enshrined in [the Constitution]," POTA managed to dramatically undermine these safeguards against the arbitrary and punitive detention of innocents.

Stringent bail procedures further frustrated the rights of the accused. The POTA court could postpone bail petitions for a year. Furthermore, if the prosecutor opposed bail, the court could not release the accused without "grounds for believing that he is not guilty...." This provision reversed the presumption of innocence at the bail hearing and effectively granted the prosecutor a veto of the bail application. The presumption of guilt extended even further beyond the bail procedures. In effect, POTA mandated a presumption of guilt for those accused of terrorist activities, if the accused unlawfully possessed arms or explosives or if his or her fingerprints were found at the scene of the alleged offence.

APPEAL AND REVIEW

POTA did, however, have some safeguards. Either party could appeal a bail ruling or verdict from a Special Court to a bench of two judges of the High Court of the same jurisdiction. On appeal, a court could review both issues of fact and law. No guidelines existed, however, as to who the reviewing judge would be.

Even more problematic was the non-reviewability of orders by the Special Court passed at the interlocutory stage. The central government initially defended POTA as being safe from abuse because it entrusted only senior law enforcement and judicial functionaries with the most extensive investigative and adjudicative authority. Because POTA operated at the state level, however, state governments wielded tremendous power over state law enforcement officials, regardless of their seniority.

In a cursory attempt to check this power, legislators provided for a central review committee with some oversight authority. Although POTA's text provided for a review committee, an absence of interpretive guidelines led to considerable confusion. The government's initial interpretation limited the provision's application to the primarily advisory review of certain surveillance procedures and the designation of terrorist groups. Only after reports of widespread POTA abuses proliferated throughout India did the central government select certain cases for further review. A formal amendment in December 2003 gave the review committee the ability to review prima facie cases and made its decisions binding on POTA courts. Still, much ambiguity remained, and the central review committee continued to lack both resources and timelines.

THE TERRORIST AND DISRUPTIVE ACTIVITIES ACT

Criminal laws explicitly designed to combat "terrorism" were enacted during the 1980s in response to an extended period of violence in Punjab. Political grievances between Sikhs in Punjab and the central government had accumulated for years without meaningful resolution. During the Emergency, leaders of the Akali Dal, a leading Sikh political party, were among Indira Gandhi's sharpest critics, and after the 1977 elections the party joined the Janata-led government that assumed power. After Gandhi and the Congress Party returned to power in 1980, extensive negotiations for several years between the central government and the Akali Dal failed to resolve their differences.

In the meantime, both civil disobedience and violence in Punjab escalated sharply, including attacks by militant Sikhs against Hindu and moderate Sikh politicians and civilians and communal violence between Hindus and Sikhs. After negotiations with the Akali Dal broke down, the government banned several Sikh organizations in 1982. Members of some of the banned militant groups soon sought refuge in Amritsar in the complex of Sikhism's holiest site, the Harmandir Sahib, which quickly became the main base of operations for the heavily-armed militants. In June 1984, the central government imposed a curfew and deployed the military throughout Punjab as part of "Operation Bluestar," an operation involving a massive offensive by the army and central paramilitary forces against militants in the Harmandir Sahib complex.

The overwhelming use of force caused tremendous death and destruction. Unofficial estimates place the numbers of civilians killed in the thousands, including priests, pilgrims, and temple employees and their family members. The offensive also caused extensive damage to the temple complex itself. Many thousands more were detained throughout the state in the aftermath of the offensive. Journalists and advocates have extensively documented evidence of human rights violations by the security forces, including many arbitrary killings of Sikh civilians.

In October 1984, Indira Gandhi was assassinated by two Sikh bodyguards, and in the aftermath of her death, thousands of Sikhs were killed and tens of thousands displaced in targeted violence. In the aftermath of Operation Bluestar and the massive post-assassination violence, many Sikhs were outraged and alienated, including many who had not previously supported the militants. Militant demands intensified, and as efforts to reach a political resolution failed, both militant violence and draconian government responses escalated dramatically throughout the rest of the decade and into the early 1990s. Even before Operation Bluestar, the government relied significantly upon its emergency and preventive detention powers in responding to the Punjab situation.

The government extensively used the NSA throughout the early 1980s, and in October 1983, the government dismissed the Punjab state government and imposed President's Rule. The government also amended the NSA in early 1984 to permit it to be used more aggressively in Punjab, extending the maximum period of detention from one year to two years, extending the deadline for referral to an Advisory Board from three months to four-and-a-half months, and permitting the government to dispense with Advisory Board review under certain circumstances.

The central government again imposed President's Rule in Punjab in 1987, and amended the Constitution to expand the grounds for declaring a national state of emergency to include "internal disturbance" in Punjab. Punjab remained under President's Rule until 1992. In addition to using these emergency powers, the government also enacted new non-emergency laws that defined acts of terrorism as substantive criminal offenses. In early 1984, Parliament enacted the Terrorist Affected Areas Act, which established special courts to adjudicate certain "scheduled offenses" related to terrorism in areas designated by the central government, for specified time periods, as "terrorist affected."

The statute required the special courts to hold proceedings in camera unless the prosecutor requested otherwise, and authorized the courts to take measures to keep witness identities secret upon a request by either the prosecutor or the witnesses themselves. The TAAA also instituted a stringent bail standard under which an individual accused of a scheduled offence could not be released if the prosecutor opposed release, absent reasonable grounds to believe the accused was not guilty, and extended the time during which an individual may be detained pending investigation from 90 days to one year.

Most of these provisions were incorporated into the more sweeping Terrorist and Disruptive Activities Act of 1985, which was enacted in the wake of Indira Gandhi's assassination. Unlike the TAAA, which deemed certain existing substantive offenses terrorist-related only if they were committed in specific geographic areas designated for limited periods of time as "terrorist affected," TADA explicitly defined a series of new, substantive terrorism-related offenses of general applicability, which could be prosecuted by state governments throughout the country without any central government designation that the area in which the offence took place was "terrorist affected."

At one level, this may have been desirable, for as Jaswant Singh noted during the 1980s, the singling out of Punjab for emergency treatment may have contributed to the "psychological isolation of [that] beleaguered state." At the same time, enactment of a powerful, nationwide antiterrorism law without sufficient safeguards to constrain its misuse and ensure national uniformity in its application led to human rights abuses and disparate patterns of enforcement throughout the country.

TADA's principal provisions made it a crime to:

- Commit a "terrorist act,"

- Conspire, attempt to commit, advocate, abet, advise or incite, or knowingly facilitate the commission of a terrorist act or "any act preparatory to a terrorist act,"
- "Harbour or conceal, or attempt to harbour or conceal any person knowing that such person is a terrorist," or
- Hold property that has been "derived or obtained from commission of any terrorist act" or that "has been acquired through the terrorist funds."

The statute also made it a crime to commit any "disruptive activity," defined as any act, speech, or conduct that, "through any other media or in any other manner whatsoever," either

- "Questions, disrupts, or is intended to disrupt, whether directly or indirectly, the sovereignty and territorial integrity of India," or
- "Is intended to bring about or supports any claim, whether directly or indirectly, for the cession of any part of India or the secession of any part of India from the Union."

The procedural rules under TADA departed from the ordinary rules of evidence and criminal procedure in several respects. While ordinary law precludes admissibility of any confessions made to police officers, TADA provided instead that confessions to police officers could be admitted as substantive evidence as long as the officer's rank was superintendent or higher; the confession was recorded in writing, audio, or video; and the confession was voluntary. The stringent bail and pretrial detention provisions and the special procedural rules for the special courts under the TAAA also were included under TADA. Human rights advocates sharply criticized the antiterrorism practices of the central and state governments in Punjab and elsewhere throughout the late 1980s and early 1990s.

In Punjab, much of this criticism focused on the practices of the police, paramilitary, and armed forces, drawing attention to the many thousands of civilian deaths and extensive evidence that the security forces engaged in arbitrary arrests and detentions, extortion, torture, extrajudicial killings, and thousands of disappearances. As in other parts of India, extrajudicial killings in Punjab frequently took the form of "false encounters," a longstanding, well-documented practice by which the police simply execute someone extrajudicially and then falsely claim that the killing took place in response to an attack.

However, laws such as TADA also have been a focal point of these criticisms, since they purported to provide both the legal and symbolic authority for many of these rights violations. Critics frequently noted the facial inconsistency of many of TADA's provisions with human rights norms under international law and the Constitution.

Considerable evidence suggests that in its application, TADA's sweeping powers were predominantly used not to prosecute and punish actual terrorists, but rather as a tool that enabled pervasive use of preventive detention and a variety of abuses by the police, including extortion and torture. In Punjab, advocates extensively documented evidence that thousands of individuals, virtually all of them Sikh, had been arbitrarily arrested under TADA and detained for prolonged periods without being told the charges against them. The availability of TADA's provisions as a means of coercion also helped facilitate many of the other well-documented human rights violations by the police.

Frequently, the Punjab police would eschew use of the ordinary criminal laws when TADA's more powerful provisions also were available. But human rights violations associated with TADA were not limited to Punjab. To the contrary, police often committed similar abuses even in states that lacked the acknowledged problem of political violence found in Punjab. For example, of the 67,507 individuals detained under TADA as of August 1994, 19,263 of them were in Gujarat – even more than in Punjab, and in a state without any significant terrorism problem. As in Punjab, advocates presented considerable evidence that in other states TADA was similarly used to facilitate extortion, illegal arrests and detentions, torture, and other human rights violations.

While the precise contours of this pattern varied from state to state, depending on the local social and political context, TADA's provisions consistently were used in an arbitrary and discriminatory manner to target political opponents, religious minorities, or Dalits and other lower caste groups, or to prosecute ordinary criminal offenses with no connection to terrorism. Statistics documenting detention and conviction rates under TADA provided further evidence suggesting the law's misuse. While precise numbers have varied, the overall picture is clear and consistent: large numbers of individuals were detained under TADA, but only a miniscule fraction of them were ultimately convicted of anything.

Statistics reported by the government in October 1993 showed that only 0.81 percent of the 52,268 individual detained under TADA since its enactment had been convicted. In Punjab, the conviction rate was even lower: only 0.37 percent of the 14,557 individuals detained under TADA in Punjab had been convicted. In August 1994 the Minister of State for Home Affairs reported that of the 67,059 individuals reported to have been detained under TADA since its enactment, only 8,000 individuals had been tried, of whom 725 individuals were convicted.

Other government statistics suggested that by mid-1994, 76,036 individuals had been detained under TADA, of whom only one percent had been convicted. For individuals arrested under ordinary criminal laws, by contrast, the conviction rate in 1991 was 47.8 percent. Together with qualitative evidence concerning TADA's application, these data suggest that TADA functioned more as a tool to enable preventive detention and police abuse than as a meaningful and effective criminal law.

Indeed, in 1987 the Punjab director-general of police implicitly conceded that the police frequently used TADA primarily as a preventive detention law, describing a common practice by which the police would first detain at least some individuals for the maximum two years available under the NSA's preventive detention authority before then charging and detaining the same individuals under TADA, in order to "keep them in custody for another year or two."

Even when the laws were not used sequentially, TADA's onerous pretrial detention and bail provisions made it almost impossible for defendants to obtain release if the prosecution opposed bail. The Supreme Court of India ultimately upheld the constitutionality of TADA in almost all respects, although it did seek to rein in its potential misuse by requiring relatively modest safeguards. However, political opposition to the law and the manner in which it was applied continued, and by the early 1990s, the overall level of violence had declined sharply in Punjab, the state which originally had been the impetus for TADA's enactment.

TADA contained a sunset provision requiring Parliament to reconsider and renew the legislation every two years, and by the mid-1990s political pressure had mounted on Parliament not to renew the Act when it expired. In February 1995, the chairperson of the NHRC wrote a letter to all members of Parliament urging them not to renew TADA. Even the Supreme Court of India, in upholding TADA's constitutionality, noted with concern the "sheer misuse and abuse of the Act by the police."

When TADA came up for renewal, the Congress-led government ultimately lacked support to renew the law and it was permitted to lapse in May 1995. Despite TADA's lapse, the law cast a long shadow for years to come. Cases initiated while TADA was in force were not automatically dismissed upon its lapse, and the central and state governments still have authority – to this day – to institute new cases based on allegations arising from the period when TADA was in effect. As of 1996, over 14,000 TADA cases were still pending, and by 1999, almost 5,000 trials under TADA remained to be completed and over 1,300 cases were still being investigated.

While many of the accused in these cases were released on bail, many remained in detention for years. According to government statistics, at the time of TADA's lapse approximately 6,000 individuals were in detention under TADA, and as of 1997, the number of TADA detainees still was approximately 1,500.

Today, the number of TADA detainees appears to be fewer, but some cases instituted under the law are still pending, with defendants continuing to await trial before TADA's special courts. Evidence suggests that in some instances wholly new proceedings under TADA have been instituted through fraudulent backdating of factual allegations.

THE PREVENTION OF TERRORISM ACT OF 2002 AND THE AFTERMATH OF ITS REPEAL

Just as successive governments in the late 1970s had difficulty letting go of the extraordinary powers conferred by MISA, both the Congress-led government in 1995 and the Bharatiya Janata Party-led government elected in 1999 had difficulty relinquishing the authority conferred by TADA. In 1995, almost immediately after permitting TADA to lapse, the Congress-led government introduced the Criminal Law Amendment Bill, which would have reenacted many of the same provisions found in TADA.

The Human Rights Committee noted concerns over the proposal when reviewing India's periodic report under the ICCPR in 1997. No action ultimately was taken on the bill. In 1999, the Law Commission of India undertook a study at the request of the new BJP-led government to determine whether new antiterrorism legislation was necessary. The Commission responded by proposing a new Prevention of Terrorism Bill based largely on the Criminal Law Amendment Bill of 1995. Throughout 2000 and 2001, the government sought to enact a new antiterrorism law based on this proposal, explicitly invoking antiterrorism laws in the United States and the United Kingdom to justify its proposal.

These efforts were met with vigourous resistance not only from Indian human rights advocates, but also from the NHRC, opposition parties including the Congress Party, and even some of the BJP's coalition partners. Opponents cited the abuses that occurred under TADA, fearing that the new proposal's virtually identical provisions would result in similar abuses and would be similarly ineffective in combating terrorism. As in other countries, however, the terrorist attacks on September 11, 2001, affected the political dynamics in India.

Within days, the Prime Minister asserted that India needed to review its "hobbled laws" and "dilatory procedures." Within weeks, the government ushered its preexisting proposal into law as an ordinance, the Prevention of Terrorism Ordinance, temporarily deferring full parliamentary consideration of the proposal. In the midst of the debate over the proposed bill, the government's proposal gained further momentum from two significant terrorist attacks – an attack on the legislative assembly complex in the state of Jammu & Kashmir in October 2001 and an assault on the Indian Parliament building in Delhi in December 2001. The debate over the proposed legislation was highly charged.

Soon after POTO was promulgated, the Home Minister asserted that POTO's opponents "would be wittingly or unwittingly pleasing the terrorists by blocking it in Parliament." Despite vigourous opposition, Parliament ultimately affirmed the government's ordinance, enacting the Prevention of Terrorism Act into law in March 2002, during an extraordinary joint session of both houses of Parliament. POTA quickly became highly controversial for many of the same reasons that made TADA controversial years earlier, and as a result, the law became a significant political issue during the election campaign in May 2004. When the Congress-led coalition won that election, it proceeded to fulfill its pledge to repeal POTA, given its "gross misuse," and to ensure instead that "existing laws are enforced strictly." While human rights advocates have commended the new government for repealing POTA and thereby eliminating several of the statute's more troubling features, several important concerns remain even in the aftermath of POTA's formal repeal. First, POTA continues to apply to many individuals notwithstanding its formal repeal.

Like both the Rowlatt Act, which preserved orders issued under the lapsed Defence of India Act of 1915, and TADA, which continued to be applied throughout the country long after its formal repeal, the repeal of POTA was not made fully retroactive. In contrast to the experience under TADA, however, the government more aggressively sought to cabin the extent to which POTA would continue to apply long after repeal by:

- Prohibiting any court from taking jurisdiction of new POTA cases any later than one year following repeal, and
- Requiring each case to be reviewed by a central POTA "review committee" before permitting any pending POTA investigation or prosecution to proceed.

The review committees also were required to complete their review within one year after repeal. Second, when the new government repealed POTA, it simultaneously reenacted and thereby preserved several of its provisions as amendments to the Unlawful Activities Act of 1967.

These provisions continue to raise some of the same human rights issues that arose under POTA. Moreover, several states already have laws conferring authority similar to that available under POTA, and some state governments have suggested that they will enact new laws to provide additional antiterrorism authority. While laws on the same subject by the central government, such as UAPA and its 2004 amendments, have supremacy under the Indian Constitution, the existence of these state laws nevertheless means that the same human rights concerns arising under POTA might well arise in those particular states.

Third, the issue of special, national antiterrorism legislation has remained a controversial issue. Opposition parties continue to criticize the government for repealing POTA and periodically propose that it be reenacted, often most sharply in the immediate aftermath of significant terrorist incidents. Indeed, not long before POTA was repealed, a government commission considering broader reforms to the criminal justice system proposed that many of POTA's provisions be extended to all criminal cases. Just as MISA's provisions were reenacted in the form of the NSA, and TADA's provisions were reenacted in the form of POTA, it is not out of the question that proposals will eventually emerge to reenact

POTA's repealed provisions in some future antiterrorism or criminal law. The discussion that follows therefore considers the human rights issues arising under both POTA and the amendments to UAPA, since the provisions in POTA that have been incorporated into UAPA continue to apply prospectively to all Indian citizens. In addition, the provisions in POTA that have been repealed continue to apply directly to many individuals, under POTA's savings clause, and have support from a number of political leaders who advocate their reenactment.

Definitions of "Terrorist Acts" and "Terrorist Organizations"

While governments and the United Nations have extensively legislated against "terrorism" and "terrorist acts," defining these terms precisely has been a major challenge. Most governments, including the United States, have found workable and consistent definitions of "terrorism" elusive, and with POTA the Indian government has continued to struggle with the same issues.

The result is a set of open-ended definitions that fail to give sufficient notice of what conduct is being criminalized and are susceptible to arbitrary and discriminatory application. POTA's substantive provisions expand upon the similar provisions in TADA and may be placed into three broad categories.

First, POTA directly criminalizes:

- Commission of a "terrorist act,"
- Conspiring, attempting to commit, advocating, abetting, advising or inciting, or knowingly facilitating the commission of a terrorist act or "any act preparatory to a terrorist act,"
- "Voluntarily harbour[ing] or conceal[ing], or attempt[ing] to harbour or conceal any person knowing that such person is a terrorist,"
- "Possession of any proceeds of terrorism," and
- Knowingly holding any property that has been "derived or obtained from commission of any terrorist act" or that "has been acquired through the terrorist funds" Like TADA, the statute defines "terrorist act" to include:
  - Any one of several enumerated acts of violence if committed "with intent to strike terror in the people or any section of the people" or with intent to "threaten the unity, integrity, security and sovereignty of India" or
  - Commission of any act "resulting in loss of human life or grievous injury to any person," or causing "significant damage to any property," if the defendant is a member of, or voluntarily aids or promotes the objects, of an association declared unlawful under UAPA and in possession of unlicensed firearms, ammunition, explosives, or other instruments or substances "capable of causing mass destruction."

Many of these core offenses in POTA duplicate provisions found in TADA and, as such, raise the same concerns. While human rights advocates praised the government for excluding TADA's vague provisions criminalizing "disruptive activities," POTA's definition of "terrorist act" remains vague and overly broad.

The definition broadly encompasses many ordinary criminal law offenses with little relationship to terrorist activity, creating tremendous potential for arbitrary or selective application. Several provisions fail to specify the mental state required for conviction, raising the same concerns of adequate notice identified by the Supreme Court in its review of similar provisions under TADA. As such, POTA's definition may run afoul of the principle of legality, a non-derogable obligation under the ICCPR that requires the law to define criminal offenses before they are committed and with "sufficient precision" to prevent arbitrary enforcement. The open-ended nature of these provisions has enabled violations of the rights to equality and to freedom of association and expression by facilitating selective enforcement on the basis of religion, caste, tribal status, and political opinion, and prosecution for activities solely involving speech and association. Second, POTA goes beyond TADA's original provisions to target several forms of association with terrorism.

The law authorizes the government to ban any "terrorist organisation" and criminalizes a host of actions associated with these banned entities, including:

- "Belonging or professing to belong to a terrorist organization," unless the defendant can prove (a) "that the organization was not declared as a terrorist organization at the time when he became or began to profess to be a member" and (b) "that he has not taken part in the activities of the organization at any time" since its having been banned by the government, "invit[ing] support" for a terrorist organization, not limited to the provision of money or other property, arranging or managing, or assisting in arranging or managing, a meeting that the defendant knows is (a) to support or further a terrorist organization's activities or (b) to be addressed by a person who belongs to a terrorist Organization, raising, receiving, or providing money or other property when either intending or having "reasonable cause to suspect" it will be used "for the purposes of terrorism."

The statute does not define "terrorist organisation" in substantive terms, providing instead that:

- The central government may designate and ban a "terrorist organisation" if it believes that entity is "involved in terrorism," and
- An organization shall be deemed to be "involved in terrorism" if it commits or participates in acts of terrorism, prepares for terrorism, promotes or encourages terrorism, or is otherwise involved in terrorism.

While the definition of "terrorist act" provides some interpretive guidance, the statute defines no additional substantive criteria to guide the government's determinations, and does not provide for judicial review of those decisions.

The statute confuses matters further by defining a separate criminal offence, for membership in a "terrorist gang or a terrorist organisation, which is involved in terrorist acts," which relies upon a completely different definition of "terrorist organisation" – namely, any "organisation which is concerned or involved with terrorism," apparently without regard to whether the organization has been officially banned by the government. To the extent that these provisions fail to specify the requisite intent to establish criminality or define any criteria for designating an association to be a "terrorist organisation" – much less to define those criteria with clarity – they, too, fail to satisfy the principle of legality.

As written, these provisions criminalize mere "membership," "belonging," or "professing" to belong to an association deemed to be involved in terrorism without either defining those terms substantively or requiring the accused to have knowledge of the organization's activities. The provisions directly target protected speech and associational activities, and their application has in fact infringed upon these rights under the Constitution and the ICCPR. Third, POTA defines a handful of other offenses deemed terrorismrelated.

The statute criminalizes violent threats, wrongful restraints or confinements, or "any other unlawful act with the said intent" against any person who is a witness or "in whom such witness may be interested," although by failing to define what the "said intent" in this provision actually means, this vague provision also is susceptible to arbitrary application. In addition, POTA criminalizes unauthorized possession of certain categories of arms and ammunition in a "notified area" – defined as any area that the state government so designates, without any substantive criteria to guide that determination – and unauthorized possession of a broad range of other specifically identified weapons and hazardous substances in any area, whether "notified" or not.

Finally, POTA enhances the penalties for several other criminal law offenses if committed "with intent to aid any terrorist." The UAPA amendments retain most of POTA's substantive terrorism-related offenses without significant modification. POTA's provisions permitting the government to designate "terrorist organisations" have been retained with only two changes.

First, the amendments supplemented POTA's existing provisions by authorizing the central government to designate as a "terrorist organisation" any entity that has been designated as such by the U.N. Security Council. Second, the amendments explicitly require an individual liable for an offence related to membership in a designated "terrorist organisation" to intend to support the organization's activities. However, the law continues to provide limited substantive criteria to guide the government's designations and no opportunity for judicial review – which is particularly anomalous given that under the existing provisions of UAPA, designations of "unlawful associations" are guided by statutory definitions and are subject to full review by a tribunal which has the powers of a civil court.

Pretrial Investigation and Detention Procedures

Like TADA, POTA relaxes many of the ordinary procedural rules that otherwise would apply during pretrial investigations and, at the same time, establishes substantive and procedural requirements for bail that are much more stringent than the standards under ordinary law. After the police initially produce an accused individual before a magistrate, the magistrate may then remand the individual to police custody for up to 30 days, rather than fifteen days, and thereafter may order judicial custody for up to 90 days. The POTA special court may order additional detention in judicial custody for up to 180 days if the prosecutor informs the court that the additional time is necessary to complete the investigation. The availability of this extended period of detention in judicial custody thereby extends the period within which the police must file a charge sheet to as long as 180 days, rather than the 90 days provided for under ordinary law.

While POTA requires the police to inform individuals of their right to counsel upon arrest and to permit the accused to meet with counsel during the course of the interrogation, the law provides explicitly that the accused is not entitled to have counsel present "throughout the period of interrogation." This failure to ensure access to counsel throughout the period of detention is inconsistent with the ICCPR. As under TADA, the substantive bail standard under POTA presents a nearly insurmountable burden.

If the prosecutor opposes bail, then for one year the court only may release the accused if there are reasonable grounds to believe that the accused is not guilty of the alleged offence and not likely to commit any offence while on bail. But since the charge sheet itself need not be filed for up to 180 days after the accused has been detained, the two provisions together effectively permit the prosecutor, rather than the court, to determine whether an individual will remain in detention. If the prosecutor opposes bail before the charge sheet is filed, the accused will have trouble showing grounds supporting their innocence since they will know neither the allegations against them nor the basis for the prosecutor's opposition.

Even after the accused receives notice of the prosecution's allegations when the charge sheet is filed, the standard for bail under POTA remains exceedingly high, in effect requiring the defendant to show that the prosecution lacks any substantial basis for its charges. These provisions are among the most severe in POTA and the most clearly inconsistent with the ICCPR. According to the Supreme Court, POTA affords the prosecution greater latitude in pretrial investigation and detention because POTA offenses "are more complex" than ordinary criminal offenses and therefore demand greater time to fully investigate. However, the possibility that continued detention might be necessary in a complex investigation does not justify a blanket rule making bail a virtual impossibility, since the normal, case-by-case bail standard fully accounts for that possibility when circumstances warrant.

By contrast, POTA's bail provisions permit prosecutors – at their discretion, and without making any evidentiary showing – to reverse the general rule under the ICCPR that accused individuals awaiting trial should not remain in custody pending trial unless necessary to ensure the accused's appearance. Taken together with the provisions providing the government with up to six months to file a charge sheet, POTA's bail provisions fail to ensure that individuals are given prompt notice of the charges against them or that they be tried within a reasonable period of time or released from custody.

The bail standard deprives the accused of meaningful judicial review of their custody, and undermines the presumption of innocence guaranteed by the ICCPR, since it requires the accused to provide reasonable grounds to establish their innocence – before any trial has taken place, and in many cases before a charge sheet even has been filed – in order to obtain bail. The UAPA amendments temper these human rights concerns by eliminating POTA's stringent bail standard and extended time limits for pretrial investigations. While the restoration of the normal bail standard constitutes a step forward, the period of time before an individual must be charged under ordinary law – 90 days – remains quite lengthy.

Still, the repeal of POTA's bail and detention provisions eliminates a key incentive for the government to charge individuals under POTA for offenses that more appropriately should be charged under ordinary criminal laws and restores to the court, rather than the prosecutor, ultimate responsibility to determine whether an accused individual should remain in custody.

Admissibility of Confessions to Police Officers

Like TADA, POTA makes confessions to police officers admissible as substantive evidence, reversing the normal rule that confessions to police officers are flatly inadmissible. This provision is of tremendous importance, especially since the Supreme Court has made clear that a voluntary and truthful confession–which, in ordinary criminal cases, must be given before a magistrate– can be sufficient to sustain conviction without any further corroboration.

For confessions to police officers to be admissible under POTA, several statutory criteria must be satisfied, most of which codify the procedural requirements imposed by the Supreme Court in upholding the analogous provisions in TADA. The officer must not be lower in rank than superintendent of police and must advise the accused in writing that they are not compelled to make any confession and that any statement may be used against them. If the individual chooses to remain silent, the officer may not compel or induce any confession. The confession also must be recorded, either in writing or by audio or video, in an "atmosphere free from threat or inducement" and in the same language in which the individual has given the statement. The individual must be produced, and the recorded confession presented, before a magistrate within 48 hours, at which time the magistrate must record any additional statement the individual wishes to make and obtain their signature or thumbprint.

Finally, if there is any complaint of torture, the individual must be given a medical examination and, thereafter, sent to judicial custody. As with TADA, the Supreme Court upheld POTA's provisions authorizing confessions to police officers against constitutional challenge. While POTA is silent on whether confessions obtained under these provisions may be used to prosecute non-POTA offenses, whether charged together with the POTA violation or in a separate prosecution, the Supreme Court resolved a similar ambiguity under TADA in favour of permitting such confessions to be admitted in non-TADA offenses.

As commentators have noted, permitting such confessions to be admitted in ordinary criminal cases creates a risk that the police might circumvent the ordinary law prohibition on the admissibility of confessions to the police by initially investigating an individual for an alleged violation of POTA, obtaining a confession under its provisions, and then using that confession to obtain a conviction for a non-POTA offence for which such confessions ordinarily cannot be used.

The UAPA amendments eliminate POTA's rules authorizing confessions to police officers, which, along with the rules governing bail and pretrial investigations, were among the provisions in POTA that most troubled advocates as facilitating violations of the rights to be free from torture, cruel, inhuman, or degrading treatment or punishment, and compelled self-incrimination.

While neither the Constitution nor international law *per se* requires the preclusion of voluntary confessions to the police, advocates have raised concerns that given the extensive, longstanding, and widely acknowledged problems in India with police torture and other violations of fundamental rights, relaxing the traditional rule increases the likelihood of torture, coerced confessions, and other abuses in violation of international human rights norms.

Indeed, the government seems to recognize that the important underlying issue is not the admissibility of confessions as such, but rather the need to ensure that the police respect human rights – in addition to repealing the police confessions provision of POTA, the government also has undertaken a serious effort to fundamentally reform the police in India.

Special Courts and Procedural Rules

Like TADA, POTA authorizes the central and state governments to establish "special courts" to adjudicate offenses punishable under the statute. These courts, which essentially function as fast-track sessions courts with a special set of procedural rules, may be established by either the central or state governments to adjudicate a single case, a category or group of cases, or cases arising from particular geographic areas, and are presided over by sitting sessions judges appointed by the central government or, if applicable, the state governments with concurrence of the Chief Justice of that state's High Court. When trying an offence arising under POTA, a special court may also try any "connected" offenses, and the central government, rather than the court itself, has "final" authority to determine the court's jurisdiction. The modified procedural rules governing cases before the special courts are essentially the same that applied before TADA's "designated courts." POTA affords the special courts discretion to conduct proceedings wherever they deem "expedient or desirable," including potentially prejudicial or intimidating locations such as the prison facility where the accused is detained.

Upon an application by the prosecutor or a witness, or on its own motion, the court may conduct its proceedings in camera or take other steps to keep the witnesses' identities secret so long as it records its reasons in writing. The court also may try the accused in absentia and record the evidence of witnesses, subject to the right of the accused to recall witnesses for cross-examination. While the Supreme Court has sustained these witness identity procedures in both TADA and POTA against constitutional attack, it also has expressed concern that accused persons may be "put to disadvantage to effective cross-examining and exposing the previous conduct and character of the witnesses." The use of special courts, and the procedural rules that apply in their proceedings, infringes upon judicial independence and violates the right to a fair trial guaranteed by both the Constitution and the ICCPR. Structurally, the very use of special courts in this context might be inherently prejudicial to anyone charged, at least absent mechanisms to minimize the potential prejudice. Permitting the executive to constitute and appoint judges to the special courts and to determine their jurisdiction creates the risk of political influence over particular cases and violates the principles of judicial independence and separation of powers guaranteed by both the Constitution and international law.

This encroachment upon judicial independence is particularly pernicious in antiterrorism cases, which are more likely to be politically charged than others. As one Indian lawyer has argued based on his experiences representing individuals accused under POTA, "[a] Judge of the Special Court firmly believes that he is a one-man army against terrorism.... The Special Judge convinces himself so much that he is on an anti-terrorist mission that he refuses to see anything else." While an equally prejudicial sense of being on an antiterrorism mission certainly could develop with a generalist judge presiding over a single terrorism-related case, the manner in which the POTA special courts are constituted exacerbates the risk.

The rules available in the special courts are in tension with the rights to be tried in a public hearing before an impartial tribunal, to be present during one's trial, and to examine the state's witnesses against the accused. Moreover, the procedures for the protection of witnesses are not evenhanded. While the prosecution or its witnesses may seek protection of their identities from the court, the defendant does not have the right to seek protection of its witnesses – even though defence witnesses themselves might be just as likely to fear intimidation or coercion by the police as prosecution witnesses might be to fear intimidation by the defendant.

The UAPA amendments temper the potential infringement of these provisions upon judicial independence by eliminating the special courts altogether, providing instead that alleged violations of the terrorism-related offenses in UAPA shall be tried in the same courts as any other criminal offenses, without any special executive control over jurisdiction or judicial administration. The amendments also eliminate the ability of the courts to try defendants in absentia. However, the amendments retain for the regular courts the discretion to hold in camera proceedings, potentially in prejudicial settings, or take other steps to protect the identity of prosecution witnesses, but not defence witnesses. To this extent, the UAPA amendments raise the same concerns as POTA itself about potential violations of the right to fair trial.

Adverse Inferences and Presumptions of Guilt

POTA also permits the court to draw adverse inferences against the accused, and in some circumstances affords state governments broad, unilateral power to create presumptions of involvement with terrorist activities. The statute authorizes the police to request an order from a magistrate to obtain bodily samples from anyone accused under POTA, but without explicitly requiring the police to establish that they have obtained informed consent from the accused.

Rather, for the sample to be admissible, the police need only testify that the individual provided it voluntarily, and if the individual refuses to provide it, POTA requires the special court to draw an adverse inference. POTA also requires the court to draw an adverse inference in prosecutions for commission of "terrorist acts" if:

- Arms, explosives, or other specified substances are recovered from the accused, and there is reason to believe similar items were used in the offence, or
- The accused's fingerprints are found at the site of the offence or on anything used in connection with the offence.

In prosecutions for conspiring or attempting to commit a terrorist act, or for advocating, abetting, advising, inciting, or knowingly facilitating the commission of a terrorist act, the court must draw an adverse inference if the prosecution proves that the accused provided financial assistance to a person with knowledge that they are accused or reasonably suspected of an offence under POTA. Two of POTA's criminal provisions permit state governments to presume involvement in terrorist activity in the absence of any individualized basis.

First, if a state government designates a particular region as a "notified area," then any offence in that area involving unauthorized possession of arms or ammunition in violation of the Arms Act of 1959 will, irrefutably, constitute a violation of POTA as well. While this provision does not technically reverse the burden of proof, it confers sweeping power upon state governments to arbitrarily charge alleged violators of the Arms Act as "terrorists" instead, without any criteria to guide the state government's decision either to designate notified areas or to prosecute offenses under POTA rather than the Arms Act.

Indeed, the government of Tamil Nadu went so far as to designate the entire state a notified area, and since the statute does not require the government's designation to be supported with any reasons, it offered none. While the Supreme Court reversed this determination on the ground that the state government had failed actually to exercise any discretion by "applying its mind" to the decision, the court did not disturb the state's underlying authority to designate notified areas at whim. Second, POTA's provision criminalizing an individual's knowing, active membership in an entity designated as a "terrorist organisation" similarly presumes mere membership in such an organization is sufficient to constitute a terrorist offence unless the individual proves that:

- The organization was not banned at the time he became a member and
- He has not taken part in the organization's activities since it had been banned.

The UAPA amendments retain this burden-shifting aspect of the offence for membership in a designated "terrorist organization," but repeal the rest of these provisions, which undermine the presumption of innocence protected by the Constitution and the ICCPR.

Accused individuals might refuse to give a bodily sample for any number of innocent reasons. Moreover, given widespread concerns in India about the police, arms and other items might be found in the possession of accused individuals, or their fingerprints discovered at the scene of a crime, for reasons that are either:

- Completely innocent, or
- Completely nefarious, but not their doing.

Judicial and Administrative Oversight

Actions taken under POTA are subject to limited judicial and administrative scrutiny. Final judgements, sentences, and orders of the special courts may be appealed to the High Courts on issues of both fact and law, and while most interlocutory orders are not appealable, orders granting or denying bail may be appealed to the High Courts.

However, most other decisions under POTA are not subject to judicial review. Instead, POTA authorizes the central and state governments to establish administrative "review committees," which consist of three members appointed by the central or state governments themselves and whose chair must be a current or former High Court judge. As originally enacted, POTA formally defined only two responsibilities for the review committees – review of the central government's designations of entities as "terrorist organizations" and review of orders authorizing interception of electronic communication.

Neither function is directly related to individual prosecutions, and POTA did not specify other functions for the committees to perform. However, after concerns emerged about misuse of POTA, the central government constituted a review committee in 2003 to assess how the law was being applied in particular states and make findings and recommendations for improvement.

In the aftermath of that evaluation, the government attempted to strengthen oversight of POTA's implementation in late 2003 by amending the law to permit any "aggrieved party" to seek review by a central or state review committee of whether a prima facie case exists for a particular prosecution. If the review committee was to determine that no prima facie case exists, then the proceedings would be deemed withdrawn.

These decisions were binding. The amendment provided no further criteria for the exercise of this review authority, no procedural rules, and no time limits for decisions. Prominent Indian lawyers, including Rajeev Dhawan and Fali Nariman, dismissed this iteration of the administrative review mechanism as a "gimmick," arguing that the review committees had not been conferred with enough power to exercise meaningful oversight over the states and that the fundamental problem was permitting the states to arrest and charge individuals under POTA at all. Perhaps confirming these criticisms, very few POTA accused – by one count, only 39 out of 514, or 7 percent – actually filed complaints with the review committees before the law's repeal. Moreover, states have consistently resisted efforts to constrain their discretion.

In the months immediately after POTA's enactment, some states lagged even in merely coordinating with and reporting to the central government on how the law was being implemented. After the central government strengthened the power of the central POTA review committee, several states resisted central authority even more vigourously. While the repeal of POTA does not apply retroactively, the repeal statute strengthened the review committee mechanism to mandate central review of all investigations and prosecutions pending at the time of POTA's repeal.

Under this scheme, a central government review committee was required to review each pending prosecution under POTA – regardless of whether the accused had affirmatively sought review – to independently determine whether a prima facie case for prosecution exists and, if not, to automatically deem the case withdrawn and any investigation closed. The review committees themselves have afforded defendants great latitude in their proceedings, permitting representation by counsel (appointed counsel, if necessary) and submission of whatever information they deem appropriate, without regard to formal rules of evidence, to refute the government's claim that a prima case exists for prosecution.

Conceptually, the use of this administrative review mechanism is a promising innovation insofar as it attempts to interpose an independent check on the highly politicized prosecutorial discretion exercised by state governments. Such a mechanism permits the central government to avoid the extreme option of imposing President's Rule, which has proven highly susceptible to misuse for many years and frequently would be disproportionately intrusive, since it displaces state governance altogether, rather than merely exercising control over a particular prosecution. However, states have continued to vigourously resist and challenge the legality of this review mechanism, and the ultimate validity and effectiveness of the central review committees remains unclear.

While the review committees themselves have moved aggressively and seriously to consider whether pending prosecutions under POTA should go forward, in some instances the central government has hesitated to implement recommendations by the committees as a result of the legal and political uncertainty caused by the states' resistance. Moreover, these sorts of review mechanisms may place an onerous burden upon defendants and their lawyers to persuade the government to withdraw cases that never should have been instituted in the first place. Many detainees are not aware of their right to seek review of the charges against them, especially given their limited access to counsel. And because counsel themselves have limited resources to litigate on behalf of their clients, administrative review might not be vigourously pursued even if the detainee does have meaningful access to counsel.

Indeed, the Rowlatt Act provided even greater judicial oversight of prosecutorial decisions, since the government was required – before a special court even was constituted, rather than after the accused was arrested and charged – to forward its allegations to the Chief Justice of the High Court, who could request further information before determining whether appointment of a special court was justified. While it may be desirable, in the interests of justice and nationwide uniformity, to create mechanisms short of President's Rule for the central government to monitor and oversee specific prosecutorial decisions, it may be appropriate to consider more efficient and effective means of doing so before individuals are subject to the coercive power of arrest, detention, and prosecution.

VIOLENCE IN THE NORTHEAST

The Northeast accounted for highest percentage of violence during the year at 40.36. Armed violence and terrorism continues to dominate the various insurgencies of the Northeast with Manipur emerging as the most violent state followed by Assam and Nagaland. While no particularly new terror tactic was visible in any of the states, a further intensification of the already-in-use terror tactics resulted in an increase in violence that severely disrupted normal life in most states.

ASSAM

In Assam, terrorism in 2008 was marked by increased violence perpetrated by smaller groups in the southern hilly districts even while the main insurgent group, United Liberation Front of Asom (ULFA), continued to further weaken as the year progressed.

Profile of Violence

Terrorism-related violence recorded a climb down from last year albeit remaining high as compared to previous years. Casualties among civilians were much higher than that among security forces and militants, indicating the deepening of ethnic tensions in the state. Among the numerous militant groups indulging in violence in Assam, the most active during the year were the Karbi Longri NC Hills Liberation Front (KLNLF), the Jewel Garlosa faction of Dima Halam Daogah (DHD-G) and National Democratic Front of Bodoland (NDFB) whereas the ULFA carried out a number of minor lowintensity attacks through the year.

Strategies and Tactics

Attack on Infrastructure

Security personnel and employees of development projects and construction companies, particularly those associated with the East-West railway corridor and gauge conversion projects in the North Cachar Hills district, came under heavy attack by the DHD (G), commonly known as Black Widow (BW) militants. Their daring attacks include indiscriminate firing on a special passenger train traveling between Migrandisa and Haflong, the district headquarter of the NC Hills carrying 22 railway engineering staff and 10 Railway Protection Special Force (RPSF) personnel. By attacking road and railway construction, this group that reportedly has only over 200 cadres seems to be using violent methods to clearly lay down its own control over the NC hills in pursuance of its objective of establishing a separate state of Dimaraji for the Dimasa tribe. With alleged backing of the NSCNIM, the effectiveness of the outfit cannot be taken lightly.

Attack on Civilians

Two kinds of attack on civilians were prevalent in Assam: general and targeted. The general attack on civilians was carried out mainly through bomb blasts in public places including market places, passenger trains and public parks. Most of the blasts were low intensity, causing minor damages and inflicting injuries rather than casualties and are suspected to have been carried out by ULFA and the KLNLF. However, the state also suffered from its worst terror incident on 30 October with thirteen coordinated blasts that rocked different parts of the state, killing as many as 84 people.

While a new group by the name of Islamic Security Force of Indian Mujahideen (ISFIM) claimed responsibility for the blasts, investigations are still on; the police are not ruling out the possibility of the involvement of Bangladesh-based terrorist group Harkat-ul-Jihad-e-Islam (HuJI-B) based on the discovery of RDX used in the blasts. Targeted killing of civilians was carried out mainly through attacks on Hindi-speaking people that began in 2007 with a series of attacks on migrant workers. The attacks were carried out mostly in the Karbi Anglong district by the KLNLF claiming to represent the interests if the Karbi people.

However, the attacks remained few and spaced out mainly because of counterinsurgency operations that resulted in the surrender of as many as 34 KLNLF cadres thereby posing a question mark on the strength of the outfit.

Rift in ULFA

In a significant development, a section of ULFA's 28 battalion (Alpha and Charlie companies) declared a unilateral ceasefire on 24 June with the objective of entering into negotiations with the government to address their grievances. This created a rift between the walk-away 'moderate' faction and the outfit's central leadership that continues to reject negotiating with the government based on deep distrust of the latter's sincerity.

Despite the large scale surrendering of ULFA cadres in the past two years, this is the first time that its central leadership has been openly challenged. With the weakening of two out of four companies of the outfit's most dreaded battalion, the outfit remained largely subdued in the following months. In the coming days, the possibility of a factional conflict between the two factions cannot be ruled out.

Implication

In Assam, the use of terrorism by smaller militant outfits has further complicated the security dynamics in the state even as the weakening of ULFA is being seen as a positive sign. This confirms two significant facts, that the weakening of the ULFA has neither destroyed wholly the terror infrastructure in the state nor has it dissipated the aspiration among the Assamese for greater autonomy. On the contrary, the emergence of militant groups on ethnic grounds is being seen as providing a fertile ground for radical jihadi outfits sponsored by Bangladesh and Pakistan.

MANIPUR

Profile of Violence

Violence spiraled in the state in 2008 with a 20 percent increase in terrorism-related casualties. Notably, the casualties among militants were much higher than those among security forces and civilians. Violence and terrorism in the state were marked by encounters with the security forces and factional strife between various militant groups that together accounted for the high casualty among militants; extortion, abductions, bomb explosions, killing of non-locals and surrendered militants (although very few) were collectively responsible for perpetrating a state of fear. The main militant groups active through the year were the valley-based groups including the People's Revolutionary Party of Kangleipak (PREPAK), Military Council faction of the Kangleipak Communist Party Military Council (KCP), United National Liberation Front (UNLF), People's Liberation Army (PLA) and the Kanglei Yawol Kanna Lup (KYKL), whereas the hill-based Kuki groups are currently under the ceasefire agreement signed with the central government in August 2005.

Strategies and Tactics

Attack on Security Forces

Casualties among security forces recorded a decline of 67.5 percent as per provisional data recorded by the South Asia Terrorism Portal. This directly follows a decline in the number of ambushes laid on security forces this year as compared to past years, indicating a strategic decision on part of militant groups to not attack security forces. Moreover, the few incidents of attacks carried out were against the paramilitary forces instead of the state police.

Attack on Political Authorities

Low intensity attacks were carried out against political authorities including Members of Legislative Assembly (MLA) and panchayat leaders. Attacks on the residences of Congress MLA Bijoy Koijam in Imphal West district and MLA K Meghachandra at Wangkhem are few such examples.

Bomb Explosions

Bomb Explosions in Manipur increased from 31 in 2007 to at least 60 in 2008 as per provisional data of the South Asia Terrorism Portal. Of these, 60 percent were unspecified while the PREPAK and the KCP-Military Council claimed responsibility for seven blasts each. Majority of these blasts took place in public areas including high security areas like the rear headquarters of 20 Assam Rifles and the Manipur Police commando complex (bomb blast on 21 October killing 18 persons) and the Manipur Assembly Complex (8 March 2008).

Militant Decrees

The most common method used by militant groups to exercise their power remained the issue of decrees. While the KYKL reiterated its decree on 31 January 2008 of using Meetei Mayek language on signboards of shops, offices and institutions in the four valley districts of Imphal West, Imphal East, Bishnupur and Thoubal, the PLA 'banned' the export of rice or paddy outside Manipur with effect from 12 December 2008, to discourage the cultivation of cash crops, and the UNLF imposed a ban on petty non-local traders and artisans settling in or penetrating local villages in August 2008.

Extortion and Abductions

Extortion of money remains the dominant revenue source for most militant groups of Manipur. Places of worship, educational institutions, human rights organizations, hospitals and commercial establishments continue to suffer from extortion demands. As a result, many educational institutions like the Jawahar Navodaya School at Umathel in the Thoubal district (in July) and two government colleges in Imphal (in September) and hospitals were forced to shut down. Between January and July 2008, at least four schools were forced to close down. Cases of abductions were also high in the state with the Imphal Free Press recording as many as 45 in the first sixand- a-half months itself. Abduction cases were highest among the engineers particularly those working in government departments, although a majority of them were either released unharmed or rescued.

Recruitment of Children

According to the Manipur state government, a new trend emerging in the state is the recruitment and training of children by militant outfits, particularly the PREPAK. As many as 30 children were found missing, believed to have been abducted from across the state by militant groups of which 22 were abducted between June and July 2008. As a measure to prevent child abduction, the Manipur state government, at the behest of the national security forces operating in the state, issued a direction in August 2008, requiring children to be accompanied by their parents when they are in a public place. While the absence of even a single complaint by parents of missing children reflects the fear among the people against militants, security analysts point out that this step would cost the militants a great deal and could indeed become the turning point for the insurgency for this has already incited the people to revolt against the militants. The question whether this is a sign of desperation by the militant group or of further consolidation still remains?

Implications

Among states in the Northeast, Manipur emerged as the most violent with incidents of violence taking place almost on a daily basis. Despite the heavy presence of security forces and a high policepopulation ratio, activities of militant groups have further intensified and spread to all nine districts of the state. A common thread running through the use of various tactics is attacks against representatives of the central government, be it paramilitary forces or employees of central government schemes in a bid to oppose their authority in the state and assert their autonomy. In addition, the crackdown by the state also intensified the turf war between the militant groups in an attempt to retain their areas of influence. The coming days are likely to witness an intensification of this trajectory as security forces continue their hunt for militants.

NAGALAND

Civilian and militant fatalities have increased dramatically over the past few years whereas that among the security forces has remained more or less constant. This can be largely attributed to the intensification of the internecine clashes between Naga insurgent groups with the formation of the Nationalist Socialist Council of Nagaland-Unification (NSCN-U) in November 2007 in addition to the traditional groups, the NSCN-Isak-Muivah (NSCN-IM) and the NSCN-Khaplang (NSCN-K). The NSCN-U mostly targeted the IM cadres, tilting the balance of the turf war in favour of the K faction with whom it is believed to have certain strategic ties.

Through the year, the NSCN-U displayed tremendous firepower by carrying out a number of lethal attacks against IM cadres, provoking an equally lethal response from the NSCN-IM. Violence between the two groups was marked by encounters, clashes, abductions and killings. In particular, a number of military cadres of the two groups were targeted by the other. The months of May to July witnessed the highest killings primarily because of the decision of the government to establish designated camps of the NSCN-U and NSCN-K (Khehoi village) in close proximity to the existing camp of the NSCN-IM (Camp Hebron) around the town of Dimapur. This explains why Dimapur remained the hotbed of internecine clashes, although the desire to control areas around Dimapur also stems from the commercial viability and prospects of the town that provides control over the flow of goods to other parts of the state. With regards to civilian casualties, most of them were caught in cross fire between the warring factions.

However, the NSCN-U faction attributed a part of the casualties to the targeting of the Tangkhul community that forms the backbone of the NSCN-IM. The state also witnessed a number of abductions through the year. Apart from cadres of different factions, a number of traders, businessmen, and youth also became victims of abductions partly as part of the struggle against non-locals and partly for ransom purposes. According to one estimate, the state witnessed 35 cases of abduction and kidnapping and 65 cases of extortions till November 2008 as against 19 and 59 cases respectively in the previous year. This resulted in a number of non-Naga entrepreneurs fleeing from Dimapur.

COUNTERING THE THREAT OF TERRORISM AFTER THE ATTACKS

While there has been debate on collaborations between the private sector and the government to strengthen security measures, the most important fallout nevertheless of the Mumbai attacks has been to generate a shared sense of vulnerability among the business community and the Indian government.

- Strong reaction by Indian business community condemning the attacks.
- Debate on the need for working together with government. *E.g.* Indian hotels like the Taj Mahal Hotel in Mumbai have arranged new security arrangements themselves without government assistance. At the same time, business leaders have stressed on the need of the government to strengthen security in public places.
- Indian business community is now a shareholder in prevention of future terrorist attacks against Indian interests: Mr Rajeev Chandrashekhar, *FICCI President,* said "It is time we all join this debate on terrorism and demand stronger and firmer leadership and approach to this threat of terrorism, including better laws." He said the Indian business has so far been "mute and very detached from this debate on terrorism and tougher approach to terrorism and terrorists, including anti-terror laws".
- Result of the attacks has been the generation of a shared sense of vulnerability between the business community and the Indian government paving the way for potential public private partnerships to counter the threat of terrorism.

There was a limited impact of the attacks. The most vulnerable sectors-were the Airlines, Hospitality and Tourism. Business tourism especially was affected to a certain extent in the short term. However, overall the attacks haven't changed the 'India growth story' that investors find so alluring and the country remains a standout among emerging markets for its large middle class, thriving service sector and low export dependency.

SECURITY LEGISLATION AND FREE MARKET 'TERRORISM'

With the onset of neo-liberal globalisation, "public purpose" and "public interest" is increasingly sought to be served through private corporate interests to whom the State is willing to entrust all natural and livelihood resources. This has not only sharpened the lines of conflict between large parts of people, especially the poor and indigenous people, who depend on common natural resources for their livelihood but also intensified it. The direct and sometimes violent resistance to the State and its private allies seeking to take over natural resources and sources of livelihood is perceived as a challenge to the legitimacy of the Nation State itself.

These challenges and resistance movements are criminalised or delegitimised as 'law and order' problems or 'national security threats' and organisations and individuals involved in resistance movements dubbed 'anti-national' or 'terrorist'. This opens the door for their repression, legalised through a spate of repressive laws and practices. Clinching evidence of this is the fact that by late March 2003 the state of Jharkhand was infamous for having the largest number of arrests under POTA.

Jharkhand is not a state where there is an armed conflict raging like in Jammu and Kashmir or other parts of India, it is however a state populated predominantly with indigenous people and is home to some of the richest natural resources in the form of forests, water and minerals. The past decade has witnessed an increasingly intense conflict, sometimes also violent, between indigenous peoples' organisations on the one hand and the state and its private allies on the other with the former struggling to retain control over their natural resources, habitat and sources of livelihood. No sooner was POTA introduced that the Government of Jharkhand began affecting a series of arrests, which crossed the 680 mark by April 2003.

A large number of those arrested were indigenous people or those who supported the resistance movement. Following exposure in the media and protests by civil liberties organisations more than 80 cases were subsequently dropped. For the people struggling to protect their livelihoods from State and corporate interest, POTA is another addition to the existing arsenal of laws that are regularly used and invoked against them to break their resistance. At the national level, India is witnessing the redefinition of freedom as a level playing field and the role of the State from one of welfare to one of enhancing wealth. More insidious is the redefinition of democracy as the rule of the majority. A natural concomitant of this is the redefinition of national security so that any movement or people that challenge the economic system, the market or majoritarianism become threats to national security. A system and a market that cannot tolerate the poor and the weak is to be protected by special 'security' legislation, as brute force can be the only answer to rebellion - democratic or otherwise. Any other solution would entail concessions that the system is unwilling and unable to make for its own survival.

WHOSE NATION? 'TERRORISM AS THE MILITANCY OF MINORITIES?

Another important dimension that needs stressing is the frequent confabulation of the militancy of ethnic and religious minorities with terrorism. The Law Commission of India's 173rd report on the Prevention of Terrorism Bill 2000 rationalised the need for a draconian anti-terrorist legislation citing increasing militancy of secessionist movements in Jammu and Kashmir and the North-East.

The same report also noted that such a law was required to deal with religious militancy, which according to the Law Commission first raised its head with the 1993 bomb blasts in Mumbai. The Commission clearly did not view events of the 1992 mosque demolition in Ayodhya and the widespread violence engineered by militant Hindu nationalist organisations prior to preceding the demolition as religious militancy. The Annual Reports of the Union Home Ministry are very instructive in this regard.

Terrorism is discussed primarily in terms of Pakistan, Islamic fundamentalism or the activities of the armed radical left-wing organisations *i.e.* Naxalites. There is however, little discussion in the Annual Reports of the Union Home Ministry on issues such as communal harmony and the incendiary politics or violent activities of militant Hindu fundamentalist nationalist forces. It is only Islamic fundamentalism is seen as a grave threat to national security. It is this thinking that apparently gets translated into policy and eventually takes the form of laws that cannot but be repressive. Clinching evidence of this is the selective use of POTA in the case of the violence in Gujarat early last year. In the days following the torching of a train in which 59 people, many of them Hindu pilgrims, were killed, over 2000 Muslims were killed and hundreds of women raped and Muslim businesses and houses looted and burnt etc.

As of today the Gujarat Government has charged over 120 Muslims under POTA in the train burning incident. The same Government or the Central Government has not taken any meaningful steps to bring to justice any of the accused in the massacre that followed. Indeed the Gujarat Government and leaders of the ruling BJP branded the attack on the train terrorism, while they characterised the massacres that followed as 'natural' or 'spontaneous' reactions, exposing beyond doubt the political and communal expediency of invoking terrorism. A cursory analysis of 32 organisations listed as terrorist organisations and therefore proscribed under POTA, for instance, illustrates this point. Of the organisations, 4 are organisations related to the movement for an independent Sikh homeland, 9 organisations are Islamic in character, 11 are organisations of various ethnic minority groups from the North-East and 2 are radical left wing organisations. Another is the Liberation Tigers of Tamil Eelam (LTTE) which does not function in India and 2 are organisations that support the cause espoused by the LTTE.

The latest to be added to the list is an organisation of Nepalis living in India, in no way concerned with the Indian State. What does a ban under POTA represent? Though the stated purpose of bans, whether under the Unlawful Activities Prevention Act or POTA or other State enactments is to target criminal activities of such organisations, in effect they result in a ban on the politics of these organisations.

On the other hand militant Hindu organisations like the RSS, Bajrang Dal, Shiv Sena etc that have supported, instigated and engineered large scale violence are not branded terrorist organisations. So terrorists according to POTA essentially tend to be Sikhs, Muslims, Bodos, Tripuris and other ethnic minorities and of course the dalits and the poor. Terrorism as defined by the Indian State today seems to be really the militancy of minorities, religious or ethnic.

2008 ASSAM BOMBINGS

The 2008 Assam bombings occurred on October 30, 2008, before noon in markets in Guwahati city and the surrounding area of western Assam. Reports indicated as many as eighteen bombs went off, causing at least 77 deaths and 470 injuries.

BOMB ATTACKS

Union Minister Shakeel Ahmed confirmed 10 blasts took place, however, reports did indicate the number could have been as high as eighteen. The blasts ripped apart Guwahati, Barpeta, Bongaigaon and Kokrajhar. The explosions in Guwahati ripped through Pan Bazar, Fancy Bazar and Ganeshguri, which were crowded with shoppers and office goers. Three blasts occurred in Kokrajhar, with another possible grenade explosion; two in Bongaigaon and one in Barpeta. Indian media outlets pointed out that the blasts took place just after the Diwali holidays making the blasts even more unexpected and adding to a toll count. The bomb at Ganeshguri was planted in a car and took place about 100 meters from Chief Minister of Assam Tarun Gogoi's official residence. In Guwahati, 41 people were killed; in Kokrajhar, 21; and in Barpeta, 15. On November 2, four more succumbed to their injuries here. Three died at Gauhati Medical College Hospital, while another died at the Basistha Army Hospital. Twentry others were also in a critical condition. Police officials added that huge amounts of explosives like RDX or other plastic explosives, like C4, have been used as a fire erupted immediately following the blasts. Timers were also speculated to have been used to execute the blasts, which were seen with timing almost to perfection as the blasts took place within a short span of 15 minutes. It was further speculated, after investigations were initiated, that motor bikes may have been used. However, Assam police chief RN Mathur also said most of the bombs were "planted in cars." In addition to the immediate casualty toll seven more people succumbed to their injuries overnight.

Immediate Consequences

- Immediately following the attack the Government of Assam issued a high alert and called out paramilitary forces to control a potentially volatile situation. Security was also increased in the Jalpaiguri district following the blasts. The police and Sima Suraksha Bal (Border Security Force) were said to be keeping a joint vigilance along the Bangladesh border. The superintendent of police, Jalpaiguri, Manoj Varma, said that police had been instructed to keep a round the clock vigilance over important public places in the district.
- Following the blasts, angry crowds clashed with police in some areas of Guwahati. Some people were injured in the clash and, at one point, police had to fire in the air to disperse an angry mob. It was also reported on the television media that mobs were hampering efforts by police and the fire brigade to clean up after the blasts. The mobs were seen attacking police and fire equipment. A curfew had been imposed in Guwahati and some other cities of Assam following the serial bomb blasts.
- It was also reported that members of the Assamese diaspora trying to contact relatives following the blasts faced jammed telephone networks, making it impossible to get information out of the region.
- Gauhati Medical College and Hospital where the victims are being treated has reported acute shortage of blood. The Health Minister Himanta Biswa Sarmah has urged the people to donate blood. Asom Gana Parishad has directed the party cadres to donate blood. Several NGOs and volunteers of social organisations have come forward to donate blood and provide help to family members of the injured and those who have lost their lives.
- In response to the Tarun Gogoi government's alleged failure to protect Assam, a motley crowd attempted to storm into the state secretariat with two charred bodies from the blasts as hundreds more took to the streets in protest. The mob, shouting slogans like "Tarun Gogoi murdabad", was stopped at the gates of the seat of government by the security staff. They also demanded that "Gogoi come out and

see what your failure to protect the people has caused. It has killed innocent people."

Follow Up

On the same day a convoy of police cars in Assam came under fire from rebels resulting in seven police and three civilian casualties.

Consequences

A spontaneous bandh, total shut down, was observed the next day at Kokrajhar on a call given by the Vishva Hindu Parishad (VHP), the Bharatiya Janata Party (BJP), and the Bajrang Dal, while schools and educational institutions also remained closed in Guwahati. Only a few shops in the capital were opened and vehicular traffic was thin with most people choosing to stay indoors. BJP leader L. K. Advani, who arrived in Assam on the same morning, visited the blast site near the Deputy Commissioner's office, where he also faced a group of angry lawyers who shouted slogans saying "Advani go back." He also visited the Gauhati Medical College and Hospital and met the injured. The Union Home Minister Shivraj Patil, who was arrived later in the day, visited Kokrajhar and Barpeta. He also held a high-level meeting at the Lokopriyo Gopinath Bordoloi International Airport in the evening. Attendance in commercial areas where offices are located was thin, and in many areas shops and business establishments, particularly those in and around the blast sites remained closed.

Few public transport were seen plying on the roads in the morning. The opposition Asom Gana Parishad observed a Black Day with all its leaders and cadres sporting black badges. Lawyers from both Gauhati High Court and the Sessions Court in Guwahati abstained from work and held protests outside the court premises. A curfew was again clamped on the worst-hit Ganeshguri in the afternoon, after the initial curfew was relaxed the previous evening, as an angry mob braved tight security in the presence of the city SS and went on a rampage. The police then resorted to firing blanks, injuring at least five people in the ensuing melee. The leader of the opposition and former Deputy Prime Minister Advani visited the spot just minutes before the disturbance. On November 1 the prime minister was set to visit his home constitency to take the stock of the situation after the blasts.

He would meet the Assam Governor Shiv Charan Mathur and Chief Minister Tarun Gogoi, as well as visit the Gauhati Medical College and Hospital to see the injured in the blasts. As a result of this blast, the biggest in Assamese history, CM Gogoi moved to recruit 4,000 more police personnel in all ranks to augment the strength of the police force to over 65,000 before the end of the year as part of Assam's counter-terrorism plan. He added the necessity of such a move was predicated by having experienced 605 bomb blasts in the least eight years, each of which caused significant devastation to life and property. He added that police and other security personnel had also recovered or defused more than 5,000 bombs and grenades.

INVESTIGATION

The Union home secretary, Madhukar Gupta, said a team of National Security Guards experts from New Delhi also visited the blast sites at Ganeshguri, the deputy commissioner's office and Fancy Bazaar. When asked about the nature of the explosives, he said forensic experts were already examining the blasts sites. In regards to more paramilitary forces, saying there were already enough forces already deployed, he added: "As suggested, retain them for some more time and probably not deploy them on poll duties (in six states)." A high-level team consisting of senior Home Ministry officials also visited Assam to make an on-the-spot assessment of the situation arising out blasts. Police said they had picked up about a dozen suspects for interrogation within the first 24 hours.

An official in the police department said: "We are making good headway in our investigations and should be able to zero in on the people or groups involved in the serial bombings." Two persons from Nagaon district were arrested in connection with the attacks. Asib Mohammed Nizami and Zulfikar Ali were the owners of two vehicles in which the bombs were planted in the Ganeshguri area of Guwahati and Bongaigaon. On November 1, the army told the Prime Minister that it had previously intercepted a message from Calcutta one week before the incident that said: "Attack Guwahati." The army told the PM that had known about the impending terror strikes in the western Assam towns for six weeks and had tried to prevent them. Lt. Gen. B.S. Jaswal, of the GOC 4 Corps, told the PM the army had received "non-specific" information on September 17 about possible strikes in Guwahati, Barpeta Road and Kokrajhar.

CM Gogoi, who heads Assam's unified command that includes the army, corroborated the message with Singh. In admitting such knowledge he added that the government did not anticipate the scale of the blasts. The government then also formed a special team, headed by the inspector-general of police (special task force), R. Chandranathan, to probe the blasts and issue a report within 30 days. Evidence emerged that a hit-team of the National Democratic Front of Bodoland (NDFB) executed the bombings in Assam. This undermined earlier claims of HuJI responsibility. Police were quoted as saying a text message sent to a local television station claiming responsibility for the bombings on behalf of the hitherto unknown Islamic Security Force-Indian Mujahideen turned out to be a hoax.

Assam police investigators determined that two of the three Maruti 800s used as bombs were purchased by NDFB activists less than six weeks prior to the attacks. Interrogation of suspects linked to the fabrication of the car-bombs led investigators to believe that there were orders to initiate the operation by the NDFB founder-chief, Rajan Daimary, as early as September. Daimary, believed to shuttle between Bangkok, Manila and Singapore, is said to have authorised the attacks to signal a frustration with the lack of progress in talks between the NDFB and the Indian government. Following this, the Indian government decided to clamp down on the organization and other regional outfits. A ban on the NDFB, set to expire in 2008, was extended by two years. The Cabinet Committee on Security also decided to re-impose a ban on the outlawed ULFA, Hynniewtrep National Liberation Council (HNLC), however it spared the ANVC.

On November 12, a Bhutanese man who lives in Nepal and fought against the monarchy was arrested for aiding the Assam attacks. Tenzing G. Zangpo, a senior leader of the Druk National Congress (DNC), a formation by Bhutanese exiles in Nepal, was picked up with the "home secretary" of the NDFB, Sabin Boro, from a rented house at Japorigog in Guwahati. An unknown source was quoted as saying, "After interrogation, both of them were arrested this morning on the charge of being part of the conspiracy behind October 30 blasts." The arrest attention from Bangladesh based forces to Bhutan for the first time since the probe was initiated. Police said the DNC claimed to be a political outfit opposing the alleged discrimination of Bhutanese people of Nepali origin by the monarchy since the 1990s.

PERPETRATORS

Union Minister Shakil Ahmed hinted that communal riots in Assam for the preceding several days could be inter-linked to the attacks. He said that the politics of hate was a plausible reason behind the attacks. Though the Assam government said it was too early to reach a conclusion on the perpetrators, Assam's Health Minister Himanta Biswa Sarma said: "It is very early to make a conclusion but ULFA has a history of triggering serial blasts."

To corroborate this speculation the intelligence officials said the separatist ULFA was responsible for the blasts. This follows most fighters in one of the ULFA's elite strike battalion having previously announced a ceasefire with the government, with the security services have used the lull to attack and killed many other ULFA fighters in the weeks preceding. A faction that did not agree to the ceasefire was said to be responsible for the blasts. Assam police chief R N Mathur added that "So the Ulfa is striking back in a massive way by taking on soft targets. No other group can trigger so many blasts in so many places in such a coordinated fashion."

REACTIONS

Central Reactions

Leader of the opposition, L. K. Advani, used the blasts to lambaste the ruling UPA-led government. He said: "I believe that these blasts are symbolic of the sense of insecurity in the country. This also proves the total failure of the government in combating terrorism", adding that it was likely that illegal Bangladeshi migrants in Assam, with an increasing influx of such immigrants, could be involved in the blasts. The next day he came out again blaming illegal infiltration from Bangladesh as the main reason for the breeding of terrorism in Assam saying "I blame the state and the central government for the blasts in Assam."

He continued to question the PM, "I ask the prime minister, who is elected from Assam, what his government has done after the Supreme Court's landmark judgment on the IMDT (Illegal Migrants Determination by Tribunals) Act indicting the Government of India for having colluded with external aggression. The government only incorporated all those provisions in the struck down IMDT in the Foreigners Act, which the Supreme Court declared as unconstitutional." He also visited blast sites and met injured victims at the hospitals. Union Minister of State for Home, Shriprakash Jaiswal, also condemned the blasts and added: "The blasts will have no impact on the forthcoming Assembly elections in Mizoram.

The Home Ministry has asked for a report on the serial blasts from the Assam government." He claimed that due to the sincere efforts of the ruling central coalition government, incidents of terror in the northeastern sister states had gone down by as much as 50 per cent in the last four years. The prime minister also strongly condemning the blasts and added that his government would take all possible steps to bring the perpetrators of the attack to justice. Along with the UPA chairperson, Sonia Gandhi, were set to visit Assam on November 1.

The day before Union Home Minister, Shivraj Patil, also arrived in Assam and visited blast sites in Kokrajhar and Guwahati, as well as holding a security meeting with the chief minister, and senior police and administrative officials. He said: "We shall nab the culprits involved in the blasts. Investigations are on and we should be able to come out with something concrete." Former Indian prime minister Atal Behari Vajpayee hinted at a call for greater national unity and what he termed a collective war on terror after the blasts.

PAN-INDIAN REACTIONS

The Jharkhand government also came out strongly condemning the serial blasts, while having summoned a cabinet meeting in Ranchi for the next day to discuss the security situation in his region. Deputy Chief Minister, Sudhir Mahto, described the act as one of "cowardice" and said the state machinery had been alerted in Jharkhand following the incident. He added that he expressed confidence that the UPA government at the centre would initiate all necessary steps to rein in anti-national elements who are bent upon weakening the prevailing peace and tranquility, while appealing to the central government to provide adequate compensation to the family members of the victims. While he also denied the fact that the militant activities were on the rise in the country at large during the rule of the UPA government, he expressed concern over the recent revelation that Hindu militants' were involved in the Malegaon incident.

He said this by alluding to the fact that vested interests were keen on dividing the country by creating panic. Vigilance was also stepped up along the West Bengal border with Assam following the blasts. Additional security forces were rushed to assist in combing operations to track down those responsible for the blasts attempting to flee from Assam through the border with north Bengal. State's Home Secretary, Ashok Mohan Chakavarty, said an alert had been sounded across West Bengal, with security tightened in the captail city. Further security arrangements were under review, particularly in the border districts where check-posts have been set up. A senior police official in West Bengal said: "A special alert has been sounded in the region.

Vehicles passing through the border with Assam are being checked." He added that surveillance had also been considerably tightened at West Bengal's international borders with Nepal, Bangladesh and Bhutan. Uttar Pradesh Chief Minister, Mayawati, also strongly condemned the serial blasts, while demanding that the Prime Minister take effective measures to ensure that such incidents are not repeated.

INTERNATIONAL REACTIONS

U.N Secretary-General Ban Ki-moon, who was in India at the time of the attack, issued a statement via a spokesman expressing his deep sorrow and sympathy to the government and people of India for the loss of life and destruction caused by the attacks. He also stated that he "strongly condemns this act of terrorism in its targeting of civilians", also declaring that there can be absolutely no justification for such indiscriminate violence. Russian President Dmitry Medvedev resolutely condemned the deadly blasts dubbing them as an "inhuman and monstrous" crime which cannot have any justification. In a message to Indian President Pratibha Patil and Prime Minister Singh, he expressed his indignation at the "barbarous" act and called for strict punishment for those responsible. He said: "I learnt with deep indignation about the series of coordinated terrorist acts in Assam, which led to the deaths of scores of innocent people.

Such inhuman and monstrous in cruelty crime have no justification. Terrorists guilty of committing this barbarous act must be severely punished." The Russian Foreign Ministry also said: "The Foreign Ministry of Russia resolutely condemns the acts of terrorists. They have no and cannot have any justification. The criminals must be severely punished for their acts." Bangladesh also strongly condemned the attack. Foreign adviser Iftekhar Ahmed

Chowdhury term the attack an act of "cowardly terrorism." Adding: "We strongly condemn the bomb blast in the North Eastern India that led to so many deaths and injuries. It is a cowardly act of terrorism. Violence cannot be a tool for achievement of political objectives."

ASSAM INSURGENCY AND THE DISINTEGRATION OF CIVIL SOCIETY

This paper proposes to focus more on the 'decline' of the United Liberation Front of Asom and less on either its emergence in 1979 or its development through the 1980s. While I have had earlier occasion of dealing with ULFA's emergence and development, I have written almost nothing till date on its much-touted 'decline' in the 1990s.

The monograph I wrote in 1994 covered the period between 1979 and 1991 and only briefly hinted at some of the very early signs of its disintegration. My otherwise longish essay on ULFA written for a Bengali journal in 1999 was not only published much later but also meant for a limited audience. Although right from the days of the monograph's publication, many scholars—both from India and abroad, have joined issue with me, I have not felt sufficiently provoked to respond to them. My Bengali essay sought to put across the argument that ULFA has brought to the fore a unique political critique, which its adversaries will find difficult to simply wish away or for that matter, wipe out by force and coercion. If ULFA *appears to have* deserted the critique it had produced and so fervently brought to the fore over the years, its adversaries have squarely to be blamed for making it desert what once was so dear to it.

As the critique deserts itself, ULFA does not make itself felt any longer through the power of a discourse. It is thus *forced* to clutch on to various non-discursive forms of power. The political critique *per se* has not lost its validity. It has only outlived one of its most powerful agents. In many ways, this paper is a continuation of the same argument. But it marks a departure on at least two counts: First, my earlier paper took a romantic view of the political critique or the discourse that ULFA produced and brought to the fore.

The critique in question is not something that can be deserted and left in the cold in this manner or, for that matter, be subsequently reactivated and represented by any other political force at its own sweet will. The critique does not so much require the mediation of an agent to articulate it, but very much a conjunction of forces within which it gains its currency. The conjunction of forces gives it a site where it articulates and circulates itself—a site where the terms of the critique are debated, exchanged and transacted—in short, acquire its meanings and thereby produces and reproduces itself. We describe this site as a discourse. This paper, in short, proposes to move away from an agent-centric view of the critique to a view that focuses on what Foucault calls, 'the relations peculiar to a discourse'. The agent-centric view only indulges in what I prefer to call 'a blame game'. My Bengali essay was not altogether free from this game. Analyses on ULFA today seem to have approached a blind alley within this context: On the one hand, commentators like, Jaideep Saikia accuse ULFA of having provoked the government into 'a counter-insurgent over-reaction'. As he argues: Counter-insurgency measures by the state are mostly stimulus responses. This is true primarily for the State of Assam where counter-insurgency operation has largely been limited to a military option.

Very few cases have been recorded whereby the government forces… have taken a proactive role in order to neutralize ULFA. Referring to the extraordinarily high and rising level of political violence in the State, Harin Mahanta, on the other hand argues, "the government that has decided to answer the reason only through gun has given birth to terrorism." Even as late as in 1998, Mukul Mahanta argues that if 'muscle power has gained in importance' it is the Indian army that has 'taught' it.

In other words, if ULFA has turned 'terrorist' it is the government that has pushed it in this direction. The problem with the agent-centric view of discourse is that it has the inherent tendency of finding fault with either of the adversaries involved in a conflict situation.

Second, the irony is that there is nobody to celebrate the 'decline' of ULFA. This degeneration does not give the ULFA's adversaries any reason whatsoever to celebrate. Even a very rough estimate made by official agencies suggests that more than 500 security force personnel lost their lives in course of their encounters with the militants in Assam during the 1990s. Moreover, the people by now have become used to the huge presence of security forces—especially troops all over the State. As Wasbir Hussain observes: Today, the Army has lost its psychological edge due to its prolonged use in internal security duties, because the people see the troops everywhere, in the towns and cities, guarding bridges on the national highways, patrolling rivers, checking vehicles and so on.

Some of the country's top policemen, with enviable records of successfully handling insurgencies—whether in the northeast or in the northwest are also aware of the limits of counter-insurgency operations. As a scholar argues in a somewhat general vein: "… there is a latent awareness in many of those directly engaged in fighting terrorism that state violence has its limits and by itself cannot solve the problem of terrorism." On the other hand, what is trumpeted as widespread public disenchantment with ULFA also involves many complexities. It is true that there have been reports of ULFA cadres being beaten and subsequently turned over to the security forces by villagers in upper Assam. Examples of a cross-section of people taking out processions against alleged 'ULFA atrocities' are by no means rare. But ULFA's loss of public sympathy does not seem to signify any gain for the Indian state. As Udayon Misra observes:

The excesses committed by the State alienated it further from the people and its moral authority was severely eroded. The collapse of the moral authority of the State actually helped the proponents of *Swadhin Asom*. Consequently, though there may have been a noticeable decline in public sympathy for ULFA's recent activities, people by and large seem to be against any kind of 'stern' action being taken against them. *Prantik*—an Assamese biweekly, had conducted an opinion poll amongst its readers drawn from as many as 19 districts of Assam and parts of Arunachal Pradesh on the eve of the Legislative Assembly elections in May 2001.

The respondents, among the many other segments of the reading public covered by the Survey, included a disproportionately large section of middle-class professionals. While 60 per cent of respondents believed that 'terrorism of the militants' would be an issue in the then approaching elections in Assam, only six per cent actually asked for 'stern measures' against them. In the writings of such analysts as Jaideep Saikia, the fact of erosion of public sympathy is blown out of proportions, often at the expense of ignoring this dilemma that characterizes the public psyche in contemporary Assam. My Bengali essay indicated, but paid only inadequate attention to, this dilemma.

This dilemma to my mind is extremely significant: First of all, its presence demonstrates that the critique implicit in ULFA's theoretical and political practice is still not dead or fully destroyed. What I call the critique is, according to Jaideep Saikia, 'adequate for the purpose of examining the genesis of the movement'. If one assumes now that ULFA 'began to careen out of control', does this necessarily mean that the critique has lost its adequacy? The fact that an organization has supposedly deserted the 'cause' that it had once so steadfastly upheld and brought to the fore does not imply that the 'cause' has been realised or rejected, or that it has, consequently, lost all its relevance for the society.

Further, the ULFA's course of development and decline also points to the continuing necessity of nurturing and developing the critique through such social and political institutions that are essential for the development of the cause, and certainly not through the kind of violence that the insurgents and counter-insurgents are found to have unleashed and perpetrated against each other.

The ensemble of institutions that helps the critique and the discourse enveloping it is called 'civil society'. It is at this point that we choose to pitch in our plea for a vibrant civil society in Assam. Unfortunately, the decline of ULFA has also been accompanied by a certain disintegration of civil society institutions in Assam. Accordingly, this paper is divided into three rather unequal parts: In the first part, we propose to examine the reported decline of ULFA. The second part takes us back to what we describe as ULFA's critique, and it seeks to draw attention to some of the questions posed by the critique relating to nationalism in Assam that are considered crucial, but that nevertheless seem to remain unresolved. The third part takes note of the factors that are responsible for the disintegration of civil society institutions in Assam.

THE 26/11 ATTACKS: INITIAL REACTIONS AND RESPONSES

The facts of the 26/11 attacks have become common knowledge. On the evening of November 26, 2008, 10 terrorists launched coordinated attacks on multiple targets in Mumbai, India's largest city and financial capital. Among the targets were two luxury hotels and a café frequented by Mumbai's business elite and by international tourists, a Jewish Centre, and a major railway station.

Over the ensuing 60 hours, the attackers killed more than 160 people and wounded hundreds of others before the Mumbai Police, aided by National Security Guard commando forces arriving from New Delhi, brought the situation under control. In the process, nine of the terrorists were killed and one captured. The 26/11 attacks on Mumbai left many Indians with a weary feeling of déjà vu, after years of terrorist attacks on civilian targets imputed to Pakistan-based militant groups. If the default assumption for Americans is that any major attack must be the work of Al Qaeda, the default Indian hypothesis, based on history and geo-politics, has been that Pakistan did it.

While tempers flared in Mumbai and some politicians gave voice to their suspicions about a Pakistani role in 26/11, India's senior leaders were guarded in their initial public statements and actions. This judicious stance was doubtless buttressed by pleas from the United States, United Kingdom, and other friendly governments to avoid fanning tensions with Pakistan.

In addition, India's leaders were mindful of the weakness of the new civilian government in Pakistan relative to the powerful Army and reluctant at first to push the civilian side.Another possible reason for the initial caution shown by India's leadership was uncertainty about whether local citizens might have been responsible for the attacks. Previously sceptical that Indian Muslims at home or abroad would mount attacks triggered by ideology rather than local grievances, some Indian counter-terrorism experts had concluded by 2008 that their country confronted a growing internal challenge from groups such as the 'Indian Mujahideen' that were both Indian and inspired by "global jihadism."

Seeking to discourage any terrorist impulses in their communities and to underline the latters' loyalty to the Indian state, numerous Indian Muslim religious leaders took public stands against terrorism even before 26/11.While Indian officials asserted after 26/11 that all options for responding to the attacks were still on the table, their list probably did not include repeating New Delhi's ultimately-costly reaction to the December 13, 2001, militant attack on India's Parliament. At the time of that attack, Indian officials were still reeling from a devastating militant assault two months earlier on the Jammu and Kashmir (J&K) State Assembly in Srinagar.

They reportedly were frustrated by Deputy Secretary of State Richard Armitage's single-minded emphasis, when he visited New Delhi, on India keeping the peace with Pakistan — a formulation that seemed to equate India, a victim of terrorism, with the font of terrorism next door.Furious after the December attack at the involvement again of two Pakistan-based groups that had long been part of the Pakistan Army's proxy war against India — the Lashkar-e- Tayyeba (LeT) and Jaish-e-Mohammad (JeM) — India deployed troops to the frontiers with Pakistan starting in late December 2001.

Islamabad's quick response in kind left India with an unpalatable choice between mounting attacks that could quickly lead to all-out war and withdrawing its forces with no tangible gains.Post-mortems of these events led the Indian military to adopt and disclose a new plan for rapid offensive mobilisation, the "Cold Start" doctrine,viewed by some as a deterrent to rash moves by Pakistan. Although differing in many respects from 9/11, 26/11 similarly sparked public criticism of government performance and demands for improvements of government abilities at all levels to forewarn of, and to prevent, attacks — not just to respond to, and investigate, them.

The Indian public was said to be especially angry about the failure of officials to act on intelligence warnings in advance of 26/11 and to stop the attackers more rapidly. In India, as in the United States after 9/11, reform proposals zeroed in immediately on communication and coordination problems among federal, state, and local authorities. In India's case, the fact that policing is constitutionally defined as a "state subject" poses some unique challenges to improving coordination. Even so, barely three weeks after 26/11, India's Congress-led coalition government announced an overhaul of the national security system, including establishment of a national investigative agency to coordinate with state and local law enforcement and oversee the modernisation of police forces and improvements in coastal security.

Many more changes were subsequently outlined by P. Chidambaram in his new post-26/11 capacity as Home Minister. In addition, New Delhi — concerned anew about India's air and naval surveillance capabilities, after the undetected arrival by sea of the 26/11 attackers from Pakistan — reportedly stepped up purchases of radars and early-warning systems from Israel.Analysis of India's post-26/11 institutional reforms and security acquisitions is beyond the scope of this chapter, however.The 26/11 attacks evoked déjà vu feelings of a different sort among senior officials in the Bush Administration. For them, too, the salient reference point was the December 13, 2001, assault on India's Parliament by militants based in Pakistan. Enmeshed in responding to 9/11, these officials barely had a chance to focus on the string of militant attacks in India that preceded the December 13 assault. As the Americans saw it, while the assault on India's Parliament had fortunately failed in its objectives, it had brought the two nuclear powers unacceptably close to war and undercut US efforts to keep Pakistani troops focussed on counter-terrorism operations on the border with Afghanistan in support of Operation Enduring Freedom.

The 2008 attacks in Mumbai seemed again to have targeted an important symbol of India's rising power — this time, the country's financial centre. Once again, war seemed disquietingly possible.As in 2001-02, any moves towards war between India and Pakistan would put US operations in Afghanistan at risk. As the 2008 attacks unfolded, US officials — particularly those at the US Embassy, New Delhi, and the US Consultate in Mumbai — focussed on the immediate threat to American lives in Mumbai. For most of the US public, the November 2008 attacks in Mumbai — broadcast live on national television for days — seemed to come from nowhere.

The high profile of 26/11 for Americans caused a few in the broader Washington defence community initially to suppose that the 26/11 terrorist attacks must be the worst ever in India and, therefore, must pose an unprecedented risk of an Indo-Pakistani War, with escalation to nuclear use.Many South Asia specialists in the United States saw the 26/11 attacks as a continuation of a longstanding pattern — but a pattern that carried a variety of risks. Reflecting India's long-term view of the issue, veteran Indian counter-terrorism expert B. Raman pointed out, in his year-end retrospective on 2008 terrorism in India, that the Mumbai attacks, although terrible, were by no means the most lethal in the country's history; indeed, even counting 26/11, 2008 was not India's most "terrorism-hit" year.Rather, the uniqueness of these attacks in Mumbai lay in the fact that Westerners, including Americans, were specifically targeted.

The attacks on 26/11 occurred just as President-elect Obama was preparing to announce his national security team in preparation for taking office eight weeks later, on January 20 (2009.) Obama's initial post-26/11 public message of sympathy for India consequently was delivered by a spokesman for his transition team.

Thus, in the weeks before the Presidential inauguration, it was outgoing Secretary of State Condoleezza Rice who, with the initial evidence uncovered by the investigation of 26/11 in hand, shuttled from Washington to New Delhi to urge restraint towards Pakistan, and to Islamabad, to press Pakistan to cooperate in the Indian investigation of the 26/11 attacks.Rice was accompanied by Chairman of the Joint Chiefs Admiral Mike Mullen on one trip; Deputy Secretary John Negroponte followed up with a separate visit days later.

In her discussions with New Delhi, Rice reportedly drew on rapport she had established with Indian officials over the preceding years and on trust earned by the Bush Administration while working on the bilateral nuclear deal with India, a deal intended to signal India's unique importance to Washington.Although dwarfed by Indian casualties in Mumbai, particularly from the attack on the train station, the fact of American deaths guaranteed significant involvement by US law enforcement officials in the investigation. As the attacks were winding down, the Indian press reported that the United States was rushing Federal Bureau of Intelligence (FBI) investigators and forensic scientists to Mumbai to "coordinate…about the planning and evidence collected on the attacks."As described subsequently in testimony by an FBI official before the US Congress, "The FBI objective was to assist the Indian government with its investigation, determine who was responsible for the deaths of Americans in the attacks, uncover any possible US nexus to the attacks and any other related threats to US citizens or interests abroad, and share intelligence and other lessons learned with rest of the US intelligence and law enforcement communities."

Additional FBI personnel were sent to Mumbai in mid-December to assist in the onthe- scene investigation, while "FBI HQ and FBI LA established 24/7 command posts to support the FBI team in Mumbai.

These command posts also helped to process information obtained from the investigation and related interviews, as well as process tactical and strategic analysis to define the overall intelligence picture."The interrogation by Mumbai Police of the lone attacker who was captured alive quickly led to the identification of two known leaders of the Pakistan-based militant LeT, who evidently had stage-managed the attack from different Pakistani cities.FBI investigators on the scene reportedly likewise concluded in December 2008 that the 26/11 attacks were the work of LeT.There was "no doubt" that the attacks originated in Pakistan, Rice asserted publicly on December 7.

Thus, as 2008 and the Bush Administration drew to a close, US and Indian diplomacy and investigative efforts on 26/11 were in tune; Indian observers were uncertain about what to expect of the incoming Obama team, however. One Indian strategic analyst, K. Subrahmanyam, hoped that the new President would be willing to countenance a "showdown" with Pakistan "unless Pakistan is prepared to mend its ways."Others worried that India was about to experience a de facto demotion by the incoming Obama Administration.

International Relations Professor Amitabh Mattoo of Jawaharlal Nehru University in New Delhi, for example, expected a "more sophisticated, less benign treatment under Obama; he surmised that India 'won't get the kind of carte blanche you got with the Bush administration…..I don't think the wow factor is going to be there."Having briefly examined the 26/11 attacks and their immediate implications for Washington and New Delhi, we turn now to the pre- 26/11 record of US-India counter-terrorism cooperation and the patterns it revealed.

THE MUMBAI ATTACKS

In January 2008 India nationals Fahim Ansari and Sabuddin Shaikh handed over rough target maps to the "Lashkar-e-Taiba" (LeT) leadership. This was fed into five Garmin Rino GPS sets procured by the LeT. Fake Indian (Hindu) identity cards were prepared for ten terrorists (in five "buddy pairs") who were taught the Hindi spoken in Mumbai. To hide their communication, the LeT booked an account in October 2008 with Callphonex, a New Jersey (USA) VOIP service provider and obtained different cell numbers in an Indian fictitious name as a VOIP re-seller. Separate numbers were obtained for two way communications (handler to terrorists and terrorists to handler). Payments were made from different locations including Pakistan and Italy. Fictitious e-mail ID created by them was traced subsequently to ten IP addresses in Lahore, Chicago, Kuwait, Koroliov (Russia) and Rawalpindi.

This was used for communication with Callphonex and also with an Indian TV channel claiming themselves as "Deccan Mujahideen". One IP address - that of Sajid Iftikar - was traced to "Special Communication Organization", Rawalpindi, which was suspected to be a government organization. An inflatable rubber dinghy was procured with a Yamaha outboard engine by "Business and Engineering Trends", Lahore. Five cell phone handsets used by terrorists and abandoned in Mumbai were found procured from Nokia, in Dongguan, China by different addresses in Pakistan. Live hand grenades recovered from dead terrorists had "Arges" mark traced to the "Wah Nobel Company" located near Islamabad. The fully trained terrorists left Pakistani waters on November 23 in a Pakistani vessel "al-Husaini". Each was armed with a AK-47 rifle with 240 bullets, 10 grenades, one 7.62 pistol with 14 rounds, a Nokia cell phone, a RDX laden IED (Improvised explosive device) and dry fruits. The group had a satellite phone. On entering Indian waters off Saurashtra coast they hijacked an Indian vessel *M.V.Kuber* with five crew members. Four of them were led away in al-Husaini and reportedly killed. One was taken to Mumbai coast as a guide, until the last four nautical miles, and then killed.

They then inflated the rubber boat with a foot pump, transferred all equipment and abandoned the *Kuber* with the dead sailor, and reached the Mumbai shoreline around 8:30pm on November 26. On landing in the thickly populated Machimar Nagar (Fishermens Colony) opposite Badhwar Railway Officers quarters, they split themselves into five groups and went towards target areas. Some hired taxis while one team walked up to the Chabad House through narrow bye-lanes. All were guided by GPS instruments. Targets were: Leopold Café, Taj Palace Hotel, Chabad House, Railway Terminal and Oberon/Trident Hotel. The Chabad House terrorists were the last to fall at about 4:00 pm on November 29 while the two terrorists in the Oberoi-Trident lasted until that morning.

The two terrorists who attacked the railway terminal tried to escape through a narrow lane into Cama Hospital where they killed seven and hijacked a senior police officers vehicle after killing nine, including three senior police officers, around midnight of November 26 and 27. However soon thereafter they were finally intercepted by a police road block on "Marine Drive". One terrorist was killed while the other was taken alive. He was Ajmal Kasab, the lone Pakistani terrorist who was caught alive, faced trial and was sentenced to death on May 6, 2010.

As far as can be ascertained this was the first time terrorist handlers actively guided attacks from Pakistan through cell phones with numbers appearing from European countries. Also almost certainly for the first time, the terrorist handlers were helped by a visual media broadcasting minute to minute details on attacks at different spots, casualties, persons who were trapped, public panic and all other operational details. Policemen who saw visuals of their top leaders dying in ambush including an Inspector General in charge of the State anti-terrorist squad conveyed to the Enquiry Team that it seriously demoralized the entire force which was engaged in combat operations for 68 hours. Further and significant public panic also resulted from several bombs going off in different parts of the city. The terrorists had planted bombs in unsuspecting taxis which took them to target spots which later blew up in different parts of the city. Bombs planted in the Taj hotel, the Oberoi-Trident and Chabad House, exploded causing great damage. Rumours that started to spread claimed 60 terrorists had invaded the city.

STRATEGIC FAILURES OF GOVERNMENT MACHINERY

Even though central agencies received a series of intelligence alerts from 2006 that the LeT was training teams for sea borne commando attacks on multiple targets including luxury hotels in Mumbai they did not lead to capacity building by the local police in Maharashtra state. No efforts were made to strengthen sea patrolling. In the Indian system, the State Police were responsible for guarding 12 nautical miles from shore line, the Defence Ministrys Coast Guards from 12 to 200 nautical miles and the rest is the responsibility of the Navy.

Owing to several reasons the state of Maharashtra, which has 720 kilometers of coast line, could not set up satisfactory coastal security. The Central Government also failed to order the Coast Guards to keep vigilance despite generating terror alerts since 2006. Special anti-terrorist squads created in Maharashtra to confront terrorists in the wake of earlier bomb attacks also proved inadequate. The terrorists used "area clearing weapons" like grenades against which the local police had no suitable equipment to counter.

Prior to the attacks the central and state governments neglected "open source intelligence" on such attacks. They failed to verify press reports that a suspected LeT vessel with terrorists was intercepted in March 2007 off the Mumbai coast by the Coast Guards. Similarly the Mumbai police failed to analyze capacity building by the terrorist groups concerned and their implications for Mumbais own security following the Kabul Serena Hotel attack (January 2008) or Islamabad Marriot attack (September 2008). The governments response was also let down by the time it took (almost 11 hours) for the National Security Guards (NSG), the specially trained commando force to counter terrorist attacks, to arrive at the scene since they had to be flown from a location near New Delhi. By the time they arrived most of the killings and arson had already taken place.

The Army and Navy contingents who were deployed in the interim to help the local police proved ineffective in resisting the heavily armed and well trained terrorists. Even the NSG only managed to clear the last of the terrorists in the afternoon of November 29. The local police, although poorly equipped and took heavy casualties in the process, contributed most to containing the damage by avoiding the violence from spilling beyond the target spots. Its officers even ventured inside the narrow labyrinths of luxury hotels to keep terrorists at bay although they could not match the terrorists skill.

A constitutional provision of division of power between the Union and the states is partly responsible for the poor preparedness of State Police forces. The primary responsibility for internal security affecting the 1.3 billion Indian people is with the civil police numbering about 1 million working under 28 state governments and seven Union territories. The Seventh Schedule of Indian Constitution provides for distribution of powers wherein "police" and "public order" is the states responsibility. States have been reluctant to dilute this. The deployment of police is a prerogative of state governments and the Union government, as such, has no authority to order the deployment of police. Unlike other countries India has no law on "federal crime. Consequently terrorism even emanating from outside international borders is considered as crimes to be investigated only by state police. Training and deployment of state police are left to individual states. The quality of police training and preparedness thus differ from state to state. The Mumbai incident confirms long standing experience that this is a key weakness in Indias anti-terrorist capacity.

Inexperience of local authorities also contributed to their failure in handling an attack on the scale of the Mumbai assaults. Ambulance services failed while fire engines ran out of water. Police vehicles had to be used to ferry the injured to hospitals and also as escorts for fire engines trying to replenish their water. Instead of having one centralized Operations Room, different sets of supervisory officials met in different "Control Rooms". The experience underlined the need to have an overall "Operational Incident Manager" to take charge of the situation.

PRESENT FEATURES OF JEHADI TERRORISM IN SOUTH ASIA AND INTER-STATE LINKS

Educated Indian Jehadi recruits continue to have links with others including like minded extremists abroad as revealed by the terrorists arrested in

September 2010 for the February 13, 2010 Pune (Maharashtra) "German Bakery" IED attack which killed 17 and injured 56. Footprints of the Indian Mujahideen (IM) and the LeT were clearly visible proving James Kitfields premonition in 2006.

The attack architecture was prepared in a remote town, Udgir, 590 kilometers from Mumbai in a small "Cyber Café owned by Mirza Himayat Baig. The 3 kilogram RDX bomb assembled here was carried all the way from Udgir to Pune (380Km) on a public bus! They also wanted to attack a major Indian Army camp in Deolali (Nashik District adjoining Pune District) to avenge the Malegaon Bomb attack on September 28, 2008 by a Hindu extremist group. The main terrorists were trained by the LeT in Pakistan and had used Bangladesh and Nepal for clandestine cross border journeys.

Mirza Himayat Baig revealed that he received training in Colombo, a hitherto unknown training center, in "Daura-e-aam" (Basic combat course) and "Daura-e-Khaas" (3 months advanced combat course). Colombo was preferred since Pakistan-Nepal or Pakistan-Bangladesh routes have been kept under close surveillance since November 26. He also said that terrorists preferred operating in small modules to prevent detection. Another terrorist Sheikh Hussain Fareed alias "Bilal" who lived as a Hindu in Nashik District said that he was indoctrinated in Qatar in 2007 while working as a mechanic. Bilal was then sent to Dubai and Iran to meet with LeT leadership. He said that Gulf countries continued to be key recruiting areas for Indian youths. Some fringe organizations representing "marginalized sections" of Indian society with avowed political agenda were found instigating extremist activities clandestinely. Abdul Nasser Madani of Kerala State, leader of the Islamic Sevak Sangh (Islamic Service Society-ISS) and later of Peoples Democratic Party (PDP) when ISS was banned in 1992 was accused in the 1998 Coimbatore serial bomb blasts killing 60.

After his acquittal in 2007 he was wooed by Kerala State political parties to garner Muslim votes. However he was again arrested in 2010 for inciting LeT terrorists responsible for several bomb blasts including the 2008 Bangalore serial bombing cases. Similarly some activists of the Popular Front of India (PFI) were accused of chopping off the right hand of Mr. Joseph, a Kerala College professor on July 4 2010, for alleged blasphemy in preparing a College question paper.

"MEGA CITIES": A BIG PROBLEM IN DEVELOPING COUNTRIES

South Asian cities are "Endless Cities" with nightmarish logistical problems for law and order even in normal times. Indias Central Urban Development Ministrys "Expert Committee" has said that the projected slum population in or around major Indian cities would go up from the present 75.26 million to 93.06 million in 2011. Lop sided urban development in most major cities has created honey comb residential structures on narrow streets causing traffic snarls, water scarcity and a host of other problems. Mumbai, which had a population of 7 million in 1975, has 14 million now. Including its satellite cities it is 19 million. The entire population is confined to a land area of 604 square kilometers, with 54 per cent living in slums occupying only 6 per cent of the land area. Seven million travel daily by suburban trains while the volume of daily traffic by bus is four million. Flash riots take place if daily transit trains are delayed. Even in ordinary times emergency vehicles have grave difficulties in reaching trouble spots promptly.

SECURITY CHALLENGES FOR INDIA

India is very sure that terrorist activities of Pakistan will extend far beyond the confines of J&K and will cover all parts of the country. There is credible information of ongoing plans of terrorist groups in Pakistan to carry out fresh attacks. Hence India needs to be prepared for encountering more sophisticated technologies and enhanced capabilities of all terrorist groups operating out of Pakistan. India has been emphasizing at international level the need for combating terrorism and called for global action to counter terrorism and enactment of various political and economical sanctions against state responsible for sponsoring terrorism across international borders.

However due to political and military interest of super powers like USA and China in and around Pakistan nothing much has been done to control rogue activities of Pakistan. India has to fight this war alone by strengthening its military, police and paramilitary forces and at the same time garner international support for combating terrorism. There is also a need to keep Pakistan politically engaged on bilateral conflict issues, so that Pakistan is motivated to reduce/stop their support for terrorist groups operating out of Pakistan. This three prong strategy will ultimately reduce cross border terrorism in India.

If India wants to assert itself globally in international politics and power game, it must control such misadventures from Pakistan. India is a growing nation and in few years from now it will be an international power to reckon with, for which it must concentrate in economic, trade, infrastructure and agriculture development, but at same time keep Pakistan under check and well humored.

REASONS FOR CROSS BORDER TERRORISM

India is emerging as economically and military strong nation in both continental Asia as well as the Indian Ocean region. In the present scenario, India faces a great threat from all the countries with which it has borders, in one or the other form. The form of threat varies from pure military to a combination of military and non-military. Today India faces more security threat from Pakistan than any of its neighbours, because of multiple conflicts since 1947 partition on issues like J&K, water sharing, Sir Creek etc. Pakistan has not accepted regional supremacy of India and undertaken many military and terrorist actions to destabilise India since independence.

The dynamic nature of the problems concerning management of borders is brought out by manner in which the sensitivity of the India- Pakistan, Indo-Bhutan and India- Bangladesh borders have changed over a period of time. These borders, which have been open, were once peaceful and trouble-free. However, with the increasing activities of the Inter Services Intelligence (ISI) in Pakistan and frequent movement of militants in other States, the nature of the borders has changed completely.

The Pakistan is resorting to Cross border terrorism, to covertly bringing pressure to bear on India across the border through violence, so as keep it engaged in proxy wars, divert its resources from other development and garner support of Muslim community in India for creating separate Muslim state and finally to degrade India's conventional superiority through a process of strategic fatigue.

TERRORISM TRENDS IN INDIA

India is one of the most terrorism-afflicted countries in the world. The U.S. State Department's 2007 *Country Report on Terrorism*, released in April 2008, states that terrorists, separatists, and extremists killed more than 2,300 people in India in 2007.As one of the world's most ethnically, linguistically, and religiously diverse countries, India has dealt with numerous separatist and insurgent movements over the past 30 years, including a Sikh uprising in the state of Punjab in the 1980s, a Muslim separatist movement in the state of Jammu and Kashmir from 1989 to the present, and various ethnic separatist movements in the northeastern states. Another challenge facing the Indian government is a leftist extremist movement (Maoist and Naxalite) that is spreading in the rural areas of eastern and central India.The late November attacks in Mumbai follow the 1993 bombings of the Mumbai stock exchange, which killed more than 250, and the July 2006 attacks on Mumbai commuter trains and railway stations that left 180 dead.

These most recent attacks differed from previous assaults in that they lasted over a period of three days, with the attackers holing up inside hotels and a Jewish center where they fought Indian commandos to the death with assault rifles and grenades. Indian authorities say that one of the surviving November attackers is a member of a Pakistan-based group, Lashkar-e- Tayyiba (LET). The LET was listed as a Foreign Terrorist Organization (FTO) by the U.S. State Department in 2001 following its involvement in an attack on the Indian parliament that led to a sixmonth Indo–Pakistani military standoff.

Although Islamabad officially banned it in 2002, the LET continues to operate in Pakistan unimpeded. Its leaders move about the country freely, raising funds and recruiting young Pakistani men for jihad. Its headquarters are located in a town outside of Lahore, and the group played a major role in providing humanitarian assistance to victims of the 2005 Pakistan earthquake. Although focused primarily on waging jihad in Kashmir, the LET has married its objectives with al-Qaeda's virulent pan-Islamic, anti-West agenda and signed Osama bin Laden's 1998 edict calling for attacks on Americans and Israelis. The LET has included in its objectives the institution of Islamic rule over all parts of India. Under pressure from the U.S., Pakistan over the weekend raided an LET camp in Pakistani Kashmir and detained several of the group's leaders. There is increasing concern in India about the threat posed by homegrown Islamist extremists who are linking domestic grievances to pan-Islamic agendas.Since May, India has suffered at least eight major attacks inside the country with a death toll of more than 400. A group identifying itself as the Indian Mujahideen (IM) has claimed responsibility for some of the most recent attacks, usually through e-mail messages sent just before or after the attacks.

Indian terrorism experts have not yet determined whether IM is a single organization or a united front of several autonomous groups. The IM claimed credit for the May 13, 2008, bomb blasts that exploded at crowded markets in the city of Jaipur and for similar attacks in Ahmedabad in July, in New Delhi in September, and in the cities of Varnasi, Faizabad, and Lucknow in the state of Uttar Pradesh on November 23, 2007.

A group identifying itself as ISF-IM claimed responsibility for the October 30, 2008, serial blasts in Assam in northeast India that left 75 dead. Local police believe the initials may stand for Indian Security Force–Indian Mujahideen. Another group that has often been associated with the recent attacks is the Students Islamic Movement of India (SIMI). SIMI was formed in April 1977 at the Aligarh University in Uttar Pradesh with a mission to revive Islam in India and transform the country into an Islamic state. It built its organization from networks of the Jamaat-e-Islami's student wing.

One year after the destruction of the Babri Mosque by Hindu zealots in December 1992, SIMI-linked operatives carried out terrorist strikes across India. In a 1996 statement, a SIMI leader declared that since democracy and secularism had failed to protect Muslims in India, the sole option was to struggle for the Caliphate.

After 9/11, SIMI members held demonstrations in support of Osama bin Laden, prompting the Indian government to ban the organization. Analysts believe that SIMI may have about 400 full-time activists and 20,000 regular members and that its operatives cooperate with the LET and the Harakat ul-Jihad Islami (HUJ/I), based in both Pakistan and Bangladesh. What has been most surprising to the Indian authorities and public is that many of the individuals arrested for involvement in the recent attacks are young men (under the age of 35) with good educations and lucrative, prestigious occupations, such as Web designers, doctors, and engineers.

The IM's top leader, Mohammed Subhan Qureshi, is a highly trained computer specialist. The Indian authorities have found that these men are often motivated through the Internet or through terrorist groups based in Pakistan. The new homegrown terrorists are apparently inspired by al-Qaeda's jihadi ideology and by local grievances. The groups formed to carry out the attacks are loose conglomerations, and it is still unclear whether there is an overarching commanding element directing the different cells. Raman says that there has been a "mushroom-like growth of jihadi terrorist organizations throughout India— self-radicalized, self-motivated, motivated by local grievances but having invisible connectivity with a single source orchestrating them."

INDIA'S RESPONSE

The increasing number of terrorist incidents in the country is forcing India to re-examine the government's approach to terrorism prevention. Following strong public criticism of the government's handling of the Mumbai attacks, Prime Minister Manmohan Singh vowed to overhaul India's counterterrorism efforts. The Indian government had also announced new security measures in September following Prime Minister Singh's admission that there were gaps in intelligence related to the recent spate of bombings. The Indian cabinet approved proposals to hire 7,000 additional policemen in New Delhi; install closed circuit televisions in busy areas; and create a research wing to investigate terrorist threats in the country's internal intelligence service, the Intelligence Bureau (IB). Singh was quoted as saying that the "issue is really one of examining the efficacy of the totality of the systems and the mechanisms that we have to deal with terrorist incidents." He went on to note that "the role of Pakistan-based terrorists cannot be minimized but the involvement of local elements in recent blasts adds a new dimension to the terrorist threat."

Indian terrorism analysts have made several suggestions for improving India's ability to prevent further attacks, such as increasing police levels and improving their effectiveness and streamlining the criminal justice system. There are currently 1.2 million police officers in India and 1 million paramilitary officers, which amounts to about 126 security personnel for every 100,000 people. In Western countries, the number of security personnel per 100,000 people ranges from 250 to 500. The Indian government may also decide to take a page from the British book by focusing more on improving relations between the local police and Muslim communities to prevent further radicalization of youth.

Many observers have raised the issue of lack of coordination among the various Indian investigative and intelligence organizations operating across the country as a major impediment to improving terrorism prevention. They note a reluctance, even refusal, to share information among the intelligence and security agencies. One renowned Indian terrorism analyst has cited the Indian government's failure to develop a national database on crime and terrorism despite a mandate to do so in 2001 as an indicator of government inaction to rectify shortcomings in the system.

Several Indian government organizations currently conduct intelligence activities related to countering terrorism:

- The Intelligence Bureau (IB) handles domestic intelligence operations and reports to the Home Ministry, which oversees all national police, paramilitaries, and domestic intelligence gathering.
- The IB oversees an interagency counterterrorism center similar to the CIA's National Counterterrorism Center that analyzes intelligence flowing in from different organizations and coordinates follow-up actions. Observers say that its work is inhibited by lack of staffing and resources.
- The Research and Analysis Wing handles external intelligence and reports to India's national security adviser. The National Technical Research Organization, which focuses on collecting technical intelligence, is part of RAW.
- Paramilitary organizations like the Central Reserve Police Force and Border Security Forces maintain their own intelligence wings to deal with counterinsurgency efforts in Jammu and Kashmir and elsewhere. The Director General of Military Intelligence (DGMI) also has a network of field offices and posts in border areas that collect intelligence on terrorist activities. India created a Defence Intelligence Agency (DIA) in 2002 to increase coordination of the various intelligence activities of the different military services.
- The Central Bureau of Investigation (CBI) is responsible for a variety of criminal and national security investigative matters. The CBI's powers and functions are limited to specific crimes based on the Delhi Special Police Establishment Act of 1946, and the organization is prohibited from initiating investigations until it is given consent from the state government.

Another controversial issue has been whether to revive more stringent anti-terrorism legislation. The political opposition, the Bharatiya Janata Party (BJP), has criticized India's government, led by the Congress Party, for its 2004 decision to repeal the Prevention of Terrorism Act (POTA). POTA, passed in 2002, expanded the government's powers to combat terrorism through measures like the ability to keep suspected terrorists in custody indefinitely without bringing them to trial. Leaders of the Congress Party argued that the legislation was misused to settle political scores and to harass Muslims.

MUSLIM GRIEVANCES

Indian terrorism experts and government officials increasingly acknowledge that alienation among Indian Muslim communities is contributing to the problem of homegrown terrorism. (Virtually all reports about the November 2008 attacks in Mumbai indicated that they were not generated in the Indian Muslim community.) They have further noted that increased prosperity in the country has not necessarily led to increased integration among various religious communities. Indian Finance Minister Palaniappan Chidambaram recently said that "the divide between Hindus and Muslims is taking new and dangerous forms" and noted a growing sense of alienation among India's Muslims.

Perpetrators of some of the recent terrorist attacks were apparently motivated by speeches that focused on perceived wrongs against the Muslim community in India, such as the demolition of the Babri Mosque by Hindu zealots in 1992 and communal riots in Gujarat in 2002 that led to the killing of at least 1,000 Muslims. Muslims account for nearly 150 million of India's 1.1 billion people.

While a minority in India, the Muslim community is the world's third largest, after those in Indonesia and Pakistan. To explore the level of disaffection in the Muslim community and seek ways to address the issue, Prime Minister Singh established a high-level committee in 2005 to prepare a report on the social, economic, and educational status of Muslims in India. The report, named the Sachar Committee Report after the chairman of the Committee, Justice Rajindar Sachar, was released in November 2006.

It found that India's Muslims lag behind the rest of the Indian population in literacy, employment rates, and income and that there has been a general decline in the socioeconomic conditions of Muslims in India. The report offered recommendations to ensure equity and equality of opportunity for Muslims, especially in employment and education.

One of the follow-up actions the government has initiated includes establishment of the National Minorities Development and Finance Corporation (NMDFC) by Finance Minister Chidambaram. There have been numerous complaints that the government is moving too slowly in following up on the report's other proposals, however.

INTERNAL SECURITY IN INDIA

India was partitioned in the backdrop of large-scale communal riots, but the partition of the country on religious lines, without taking into consideration its multiple identities, instead of bringing the communal tensions down, in fact, worsened the situation.

The two-nation theory created Pakistan, and it still survives on this theory. Pakistan finds it difficult to accept the reality that India continues to be a democratic, plural, multi-religious society and that India today has more Muslim citizens than Pakistan. The Government of Pakistan has taken upon itself the responsibility of not only protecting its own citizens, but also the Indian Muslims.

The power structure in theocratic Pakistan, dominated by the army, the feudal landlords, the bureaucracy and the religious leaders has been able to retain its hold over the levers of power by playing the anti- India and Islamic cards. Pakistan plays the Islamic card in its foreign policy also. It misses no opportunity to club India as an anti-Islamic country where Muslims are not safe. The continuing tensions between India and Pakistan have a direct bearing on the internal situation in India. They have further complicated the internal security situation. The management of internal security, therefore, assumes great importance. If the internal security issues are tackled effectively, subversion by the external forces to that extent becomes more difficult. Unfortunately, the rise of contentious politics based on sectarian, ethnic, linguistic or other divisive criteria, is primarily responsible for the many communal and secessionist movements flourishing in India. The presence of hostile neighbours enables the internal conflicts to get external support, which includes money, arms and sanctuaries. The vested interests exploit these conditions to pursue their own agenda.

In a well-established political system and a developed economy, conflicts between the various group identities are kept under check as in due course they get assimilated into the national identity. But that has not happened in India as yet, where the wounds of the partition and the colonial rule have still not fully healed. Moreover, the dependence on the government by a large section of our people for their very survival sharpens these conflicts among them. The democratic institutions and the state structures are still not strong enough to fully harmonise these conflicts in a peaceful manner. Violence erupts when conflicting interests cannot be consensually reconciled. The hostile external forces, taking advantage of this situation through subversive propaganda, further accentuate these conflicts. They give material and ideological support to aggravate this sense of grievance to such an extent that a small minority are willing to become tools in their hands to subvert the stability and security of the country.

In addition, a number of secessionist and the so-called revolutionary movements are operating in India today. Their goal could be to overthrow the government and bring about revolutionary changes in the structure and functioning of the state, or even secession from the Indian Union. Ever since independence, India has been facing all types of violent conflicts based on religion, caste, language, ethnicity and regional loyalties. Political insecurity further compounds the problem. Preoccupied with the problem of survival, the governments in some of the most affected states are not looking at the problem from a long-term perspective. They have bought temporary peace by compromising with the subversive forces.

Such shortsighted policies can have disastrous consequences in the long run. Instead of effectively dealing with them in the initial stages when the problem is manageable, they have allowed these anti-national forces to take roots and spread their tentacles far and wide. When a state government is unable to effectively deal with them, instead of strengthening the state police machinery, it rushes to the Centre to hand over its responsibility at the first sign of any serious trouble. It is not surprising that in these states some sections of the police have actually joined hands with the subversive forces against the central forces.

"If you cannot fight them, join them". Finding themselves at the mercy of these subversive forces, the people tend to change sides and start supporting them instead of supporting the security forces. It would be wrong to assume that all those supporting, directly or indirectly, these forces are sympathetic to their ideology. Far from it! For most of them, preoccupied with the daily battle of survival, this is the obvious choice, because the police are unable to protect them. Polarisation on caste and religious lines can further reduce the credibility of the police in the minds of the people.

The police-politician-criminal nexus can embolden the criminal elements. Their activities can create an environment of lawlessness, where influential and rich people violate the law with impunity. The police is not the only component of the criminal justice system that has suffered because of this nexus. In fact, the entire criminal justice system is under strain. Not all crimes are being registered and those registered are not being properly investigated; and even out of those charge-sheeted, very few are ending in conviction. The conviction rate in case of heinous crimes is steadily falling. In some North-Eastern states it has reached almost zero level, where the police have stopped even submitting the charge sheets in the insurgency-related cases.

When the fear of legal punishment disappears, organised crime finds it convenient to spread its tentacles. The crime syndicates are finding the new communication and information technology very useful. Extortion and payment of the so-called 'protection money' is more widespread than we would like to believe. Direct extortion from the government funds runs into hundreds of crores of rupees. Many of the insurgent and militant groups are not driven by ideology, but by sheer greed. Money power is a bigger motivating factor than ideology.

Vested interests have developed around these groups with active connivance of corrupt politicians, police officers and civil servants. Some politicians even take their assistance during election times. They have to return their favours when they come to power. This mutually beneficial relationship has seriously damaged the quality of governance in the interior areas. The real losers are the people. The development process gets seriously hampered in a violent environment. When large development funds are siphoned out by this unholy alliance between the criminal and corrupt forces, even the delivery of the most basic services like water, power, health care, education and communications becomes a stupendous task. A vicious circle starts. The deprived and the marginalised sections of the society, unable to survive in the present system, get alienated.

The militant and extremist forces thrive in this environment. The rise of Left extremism is more due to these compulsions than on ideological grounds. There are media reports about the carving out of a corridor by the Left extremist forces from Nepal to Tamil Nadu. Even if there is no truth in these reports, the involvement of hostile external forces in support of the Left extremist forces to destabilise the country cannot be ruled out.

The mushrooming of armed 'Senas' on caste and ethnic lines in some parts of the country is a direct consequence of the polarisation of the society. This phenomenon has also affected the police and the administration in general. Loss of public confidence in the capacity of the state to protect their life and property is the primary cause of this dangerous development. Far from controlling them, a politicised and partisan police actually encourages this development. The tensions in some parts of the country, especially in the tribal areas, due to a perceived threat to their identity is not new, but the rise of so many violent movements is a relatively recent development. In the border states these movements become secessionist because of the support they receive from the hostile neighbouring states.

The rise of fundamentalist forces is posing the most serious threat to India's security. Fired with religious zeal these forces have created an entirely new situation. The intelligence agencies in our neighbourhood and the organisations, like Al Qaida, and Jaish-e-Mohammad, are encouraging the so-called 'Jehadis' to enter India from outside.

After first targeting the border states they have now spread deep inside the country. These bands of fanatics are not only indulging in subversive activities, but are spreading the virus of fundamentalism among the Indian Muslims. The break-up of the Indian Union continues to be the main goal of Pakistan's domestic and foreign policy. Easy availability of deadly weapons with the subversive groups operating in India has created new dangers for India's security.

With the 'Golden Crescent', and the 'Golden Triangle' in India's neighbourhood, drug trafficking poses yet another threat to our security. Drug syndicates are generating huge funds, a part of which is being used to give financial support to some of these subversive groups. The intelligence agencies like the ISI are recruiting a number of 'carriers' in drug trafficking as their agents. These agencies provide legal immunity for their criminal activities in their own country in addition to giving them financial and logistical support. Internal security challenges are not confined to any one area, but the North-East, Jammu and Kashmir, and the areas afflicted by Left extremism deserve special mention.

NORTH-EAST

The Naga leadership under Z.A. Phizo had challenged their integration into the Indian Union even before India became independent in 1947. The Naga insurgency started way back in the early 1950s. Since then the insurgencies in this region have multiplied and spread to many new areas. In this extremely diverse and strategically sensitive region, there are different reasons for the ethnic upsurges and insurgencies in different states. Some seek secession from the Indian Union, some others seek separate states and yet others greater autonomy within the existing state. The number of such insurgent groups could reach three-digit figures.

In Manipur alone, more than twenty-five groups are operating. Thousands have died in the insurgency-related violence. Insurgencies have seriously affected the economic life of the region. The whole developmental process is seriously hampered because of this unending violence. One can imagine the plight of the people who are already living on the margin. What to talk of getting a share of the fruits of development, they are deprived even of the most basic services. Unfortunately, unlike Jammu & Kashmir, these violent movements do not stir much response in national consciousness. Even serious incidents of violence hardly find any mention in the so-called mainstream media.

The geo-strategic importance of the North-East is not sufficiently appreciated even in the security establishment. All the states in the North-East share an international border with other countries and the seven North-Eastern states are linked to the rest of the country only by a narrow strip of land. The lack of physical, cultural and emotional links has encouraged a feeling of alienation, which is being exploited by the nottoo- friendly neighbours to pursue their own agenda. They are giving support and sanctuaries to many of these groups to use them as leverage against a much bigger and more powerful neighbour.

The roots of these many insurgencies in the North-East lie deep in its history and its geography. But, it would be wrong to treat it as one homogeneous region with common problems, or social systems and customs. Even physiographically, the region can be divided into three broad areas — hills, plateaus, and plains. The many ethnic groups, speaking many different languages and dialects, who inhabit this remote part of the country consider themselves as separate people with little in common with the people in the rest of the country. The lack of physical, cultural and emotional links has encouraged this feeling of separation.

The partition of the country seriously dislocated the old system of communications with serious demographic consequences. At the heart of the problem, however, is the new political consciousness and an urge for asserting their identity, especially among the fiercely independent tribal communities. The partition left the entire region land-locked, and even the old road, railway and river-waterway links with the rest of the country were severed, because they all passed through East Pakistan (now Bangladesh). The new rail link via North Bengal is circuitous and too long and expensive for easy access to the region.

The air link is not only expensive, but also unreliable due to climatic conditions. The people have to bear enormous additional transport cost for all their supplies. Another intractable problem is created by the influx of migrants from East Pakistan and now continuing from Bangladesh. In the beginning it was confined to the Hindus leaving East Pakistan due to insecure conditions, but later, because of intense population pressure even Muslims started migrating. The fear that immigrant population will one day dominate them is keeping many of the insurgent and secessionist movements alive.

The terrain in this region is eminently suitable for insurgency. The hilly terrain and dense forests provide convenient hiding places to mount ambushes on the moving convoys of the security forces. Large parts of the interior areas have little or no police presence. The insurgent groups virtually control the administration in these areas. After attacking the security force they can easily disappear into the local population. Because of deprivation and alienation, a large section of the people tend to be sympathetic to the members of these groups. It is the alienation of the people that has sustained insurgency all these years, though logistic support and sanctuaries provided by the neighbouring states play a vital role in sustaining them. The dispersion of ethnic groups across the international boundaries has profoundly influenced the nature of political conflicts. However, it needs to be emphasised that internal-external linkages originate with the failure of the domestic political and administrative system in coping with the internal conflicts.

Secessionist leaders often adopt alternative strategies to achieve their goal. They keep on changing their tactics and demands according to the ground situation. The intensity of the conflict depends very much on how strong the public support is. Ethnicity can become an important dimension of internal conflict when it becomes intertwined with other social, political and economic issues. As conflicting groups go from one crisis to the next, they learn by experience to raise their demands to increase their bargaining power. Political changes that offer new opportunities for personal gain and extending their influence can spark violent conflicts. Even though most of them are conscious of the fact that secession is not a viable option, they keep on raising this demand to bring together the various contending conflicts on one platform. Making common cause against the Indian state is how many of these groups with conflicting ideologies cooperate with each other in their fight against the Indian state. The *United Liberation Front of Assam* (ULFA) was born out of the demand to throw out the migrants from Bangladesh, and yet its top leaders are today finding sanctuary in that country.

The South Asian countries have more in common with India than with other countries in the region. They do not even have a common boundary with each other. But this reality has not made them friendlier towards India. History and geography have encouraged negative sentiments rather than positive sentiments about India in these countries. The big powers too have not hesitated to fish in troubled waters. Till the 1970s, China was directly supporting the insurgencies in the North-East. Strategically, politically and economically the North-East is the most sensitive part of the country and should receive the serious attention it deserves.

The ongoing dialogue between the government and the NSCN (IM) is a positive development, but it is going to take a long and torturous route. The NSCN (IM)'s claim on the Naga-inhabited areas in the neighbouring states has created serious complications. The riots in Manipur in 2001 following the extension of the ceasefire to the areas beyond the boundaries of Nagaland are a pointer to the difficult road ahead. The situation in Assam has shown some signs of improvement, but large-scale extortion by the ULFA and other groups is posing serious problems. The NLFT and the ATTF continue to be active in Tripura.

They have sanctuaries in Bangladesh. Mizoram is quiet, but there are problems between the Mizos and the Chakmas, and the Mizos and the Reangs. Thousands of Reang refugees from Mizoram are staying in camps in Tripura. In spite of many rounds of negotiations between the Mizoram government and the representatives of the Reangs, so far no solution appears to be in sight. The unending internecine feud between the NSCN (IM) and the NSCN (K) has spilled over from Nagaland to the neighbouring states and even to Myanmar. A number of Meitie and Kuki groups have sanctuaries in the Chin Hills in Myanmar. The ULFA and the Bodo groups have sanctuaries in the forests of Bhutan. There are unconfirmed reports of some sort of tie-up between the ULFA and the LTTE. A number of groups have also come up in Meghalaya and Arunachal Pradesh. Many experts have called the Naga insurgencies as the mother of all insurgencies in the North-East. The level of violence, however, in this explosive region continues to be high in spite of the fact that the ceasefire agreement with the NSCN (IM) has been in place since 1997. This only goes to show how difficult the road to peace is going to be in this trouble-torn region.

It is truism to say that it is not only a law and order problem. It has many other dimensions. No strategy will succeed unless it strikes a right balance between political, economic and security measures. There is need for closer co-ordination among the policymakers. Ideally, there is need for a consensus among the major political parties. The pursuit of narrow political agenda can be exploited by the subversive groups. Many political leaders in this region indulge in double-speak. They mouth nationalist slogans in Delhi but have no hesitation in making strong anti-national statements and collaborating with the insurgent groups in the state. Nor do they have any reservation in changing parties. They frequently hop from one political party to another. In Manipur some politicians have changed sides as many as six times in a year. A chief minister changed his party three times in one month, and his coalition partners three times in 48 hours. A party label has very little meaning. Money and muscle power with active support of the insurgent groups play a key role in the elections.

Most of these states are not financially viable. They hardly collect any revenue and depend almost entirely on the Union government for financial support. This has caused lack of responsibility in incurring public expenditure. For example, Manipur has created a huge bureaucratic structure with a workforce of almost 100,000 on its pay roll. Over 80 per cent of its total revenue (both Plan and non-Plan) is spent on payment of salaries and pensions. Extortion by the insurgent groups, the leakage's of huge funds through corrupt practices leave very little for development. And they conveniently put the blame on the Centre for not giving them adequate funds. Through years of neglect this potentially rich region is today the most backward, almost primitive, part of our country. In these appalling conditions an alienated population becomes an easy target for the secessionist propaganda.

JAMMU & KASHMIR

The problem has been with us since independence even though Pakistan has no legal case. The ruler of this erstwhile princely state decided to accede to India. The Independence Act it was for the rulers of the princely states to decide to join India or Pakistan. Pakistan has been disputing the legality of the accession signed by the then J&K ruler, Maharaja Hari Singh. The initial hesitation of the Maharaja to accede to either India or Pakistan and the unilateral Indian offer to find out the wishes of the people of the state has given Pakistan an excuse to challenge the legality of the accession. It has been doing everything for the last 56 years to grab this state. It has not been able to achieve its objective through wars with India.

So, it has started a proxy war since 1989. Waging of a proxy war fits into the Pakistani designs of bleeding India. Unfortunately, the weaknesses of the state and of the administrative systems have provided Pakistan with opportunities to fish in troubled waters. More interested in perpetuating their rule than governing the state, its rulers have been exploiting regional and religious differences. Anti-national forces thrived in this environment and Pakistan has missed no opportunity to support and encourage them. Over the years it has succeeded in building a pro- Pakistan base in the state. Frustrated in their efforts to gain power through democratic means, some politicians joined the anti-India front, more to put pressure on the Indian government than on ideological grounds. In a state, where the overwhelming population was against communal politics at the time of partition, the fundamentalist forces have managed to penetrate into the secular polity. The many serious problems of the people have to be addressed. It is not a coincidence that Pakistan's efforts to destabilise the situation in the state received some success only when our own political mismanagement provided it with an opportunity to intervene, as in 1965 and again in 1989. One of Pakistan's main aims is to divide the polity on communal lines.

The attitude of the Pakistani military government is unlikely to change in the near future. But that does not mean that Pakistan should be allowed to set the Kashmir agenda. Moves will have to be made on all fronts to regain the initiative on both political and diplomatic fronts. The proposals made in the announcements by the Cabinet Committee on Security on October 22 are steps in the right direction, but the ground situation does not justify over-optimism. There are likely to be many ups and downs on this long torturous road to peace in Jammu and Kashmir.

LEFT EXTREMISM

Making a beginning in Naxalbari in West Bengal and Telengana in Andhra Pradesh in the 1970s, the movement has since spread to many states: Bihar, Jharkhand, Madhya Pradesh, Chhattisgarh and Orissa. The root cause for the rise in Left extremism is the inability of the states to address the many genuine grievances of the people. The gap between the unrealistic expectations, fuelled by populist rhetoric, and their actual fulfilment has increased and not decreased over the years. The younger generation is no longer willing to put up passively with injustice and humiliation without a fight. The bitterness of the angry young man against the prevailing unjust socio-economic system is spilling over. The older generation is not unsympathetic to them.

An educational system which produces unemployable young boys and girls has not helped. Pressure on land has made the task of survival on agriculture more difficult. A callous district administration, especially in the rural areas, a clogged judicial system and feudal attitudes have compounded the problem. The land disputes have multiplied, but the land records and the judicial system to settle them is in disarray. There is a sense of frustration and anger. The most prominent among the groups, that have mushroomed in the recent years, are the People's War Group (PWG) and the Marxist Communist Centre (MCC). But it is not ideology and revolutionary zeal that is driving them. For many, joining these groups is the only way to survive. Their main activity is extortion. Huge funds amounting to hundreds of crores of rupees are being extorted by them. What they cannot get through legitimate means they obtain through arms and explosives. Their tactics are no different from the insurgents and terrorists. Create terror and extort money. They are, however, not secessionists. Their aim is to overthrow what they call an unjust socio-economic system. But they are in no hurry to achieve their ideological aims as long as they can extort enough money. Corrupt politicians, policemen and civil servants have made their own adjustments with these groups. A live-and-let live attitude is mutually beneficial to all of them. Who knows how much money goes to the extremists and how much goes to the others. The real sufferers are the very people for whom the extremists are waging this war against the state.

In public perception a government that is unable to discharge all its responsibilities is more likely to respond when the demand is loud, organised and backed by acts of violence. The many progressive, wellintentioned legislations are not being implemented effectively and sometimes have done more harm than good by creating more bitterness and frustration, *e.g.*, the Minimum Wages Act. The marginal and deprived sections of the society are the worst hit. Social and economic factors are important, but even more important are religion and identity. The secessionist movement in J&K is politically motivated, but its ideological base is built around religious funda-mentalism. Fired by religious fervour, the young recruits have no hesitation in attacking ruthlessly what they consider the decayed political and moral order, which they perceive as hedonistic. Once the instruments of governance are discredited, it is not too difficult to justify their destruction as in J&K, the North-East or in the states afflicted by Left extremism. In another sense, however, the aim of all these movements is no different from the aim of legitimate political movements. They too seek to acquire power, measured in terms of exercising influence or control over the people and acquisition of wealth for them is the source of all power. Extortion, therefore, becomes an essential part of their strategy. Their goal and strategy could change during the course of the movement. In the initial stages some of them may only demand economic and political justice or more autonomy in the existing political system, like the Bodos in Assam, but they can take a more extremist stand and demand secession in the later stages.

Effective steps to reduce ethnic and social inequalities, disparities in educational and employment opportunities, and for creating an effective machinery for the redressal of public grievance, are absolutely essential to improve the environment in which extremist violence flourishes. Steps to reduce economic deprivation and improve the delivery of essential services can erode the base of public support on which the extremist movements survive. It is relatively easier to find solutions to seemingly intractable political problems, like in J&K, in an environment where people are by and large satisfied with the functioning of the government agencies and are not deprived of essential services. More than anything else, it is the economic policies that would ultimately determine the future of these movements. A thriving economy, which gives hope and opportunity to the people, is more likely to defeat all types of extremist movements than any other strategy. The need for a well co-ordinated security apparatus can hardly be overemphasised. It should include the police, the paramilitary forces, the army and the intelligence agencies. A composite force on the lines of the National Security Guards (NSG) should be organised in all the states, even in those states where the internal security situation is not so serious. It is easier to deal with the problems at the initial stages, than later, when the state police is no longer able to cope with them. But in the states where the situation has gone beyond their control, the Centre, as laid down in the Constitution, is duty-bound to intervene, notwithstanding the fact that law and order is under the State List. The Union government is charged with the responsibility of protecting the states from internal disturbances under Article 353 of the Constitution, even though law and order comes under List-II, the State List. The Union government can issue directions to the state under Articles 257-258. Action for non-compliance of the directions from the Union government can be taken under Article 365. A state government can be dismissed under Article 356, if a situation arises in which the administration of the state cannot be carried on in accordance with the provisions of the Constitution. A national emergency can be declared under Article 352.

But, even if the Centre decides to intervene, the state's role cannot be minimised. The primary responsibility to deal with the security challenges must rest with the state governments. A situation should not be allowed to develop where the state government washes its hands off, or its forces instead of cooperating with the central forces, actually work against them. The many internal security challenges can be met effectively only with full cooperation between the central and the state governments. The police, the paramilitary forces, the army and all the intelligence agencies must act in close co-ordination. The hostile foreign forces can and will take advantage of the internal situation to destabilise the country in pursuit of their own agenda. All serious internal security problems: communal and sectarian violence, organised crime, drug-trafficking, labour and students' unrest, political violence and even economic crimes, if not checked effectively can develop an external dimension. There is an urgent need to make the police and the paramilitary forces more professional. The emphasis has to shift from 'more numbers' to 'more professionally trained forces'.

The internal security problems should not be treated as merely law and order problems. They have to be dealt with comprehensively in all their dimensions and at all levels — political, economic and social. They are all interlinked. At times, the required measures will conflict with each other. Going too far in one direction could be counter-productive. The security requirements have to be met, but that does not mean giving the security agencies a free hand. Striking the right balance is the key to success in meeting these challenges effectively. We need a comprehensive security policy that will be implemented effectively at all levels.

6

Narcoterrorism and Security

INTRODUCTION

On a quiet Sunday morning in Colombia, a Catholic priest delivers a sermon to a congregation in a small church. As he does so, members of the Fuerzas Armadas Revolucionarias de Colombia (FARC) surround the church, enter it, and lock the doors. FARC members kill the priest by cutting his throat. Moreover, they cut out the 6-month-old fetus from a young woman, killing both. They videotape this massacre and leave the tape as a warning to residents not to cooperate with government efforts to combat coca cultivation—a source of hundreds of millions of dollars to the FARC who tax cultivation, processing, and transport as a means of financing their terror operations.

In Afghanistan, a senior narcotics trafficker named Haji Bashir Noorzai similarly taxed opium production. He generated millions of dollars in profit and used a portion of his profits to purchase weapons, improvised explosive devices, and other materials that he provided to representatives of the Taliban, al Qaeda, and other terrorists. Congressional testimony revealed that Noorzai provided a least $28 million directly to al Qaeda in 2003. Over the past several years, Colombian-based groups such as the FARC, the Autodefensas Unidas de Colombia, and Ej´ercito de Liberaci ´ on Nacional have waged a brutal campaign of terror against the Colombian people by financing their efforts through taxation of coca cultivation. Individuals and groups in Afghanistan, Southeast Asia, and Russia similarly tax the growth, processing, transport, and sale of illicit drugs to finance terror, criminal, and other covert activities.

The profits are used to purchase weapons, safe houses, transportation, and information. Most ominously, terrorists and other criminal organizations increasingly rely upon the methods of moving drugs across national and regional boundaries as a means to move individuals, weapons, and precursors. Narcoterrorism exists in two forms: First, it exists wherever the profits from drug trafficking—its cultivation, processing, transport, or eventual sale and use—are used to pay for politically motivated terrorist activity; and second, it exists whenever drug traffickers use terrorist acts, such as assassination, bombing, extortion, and other threats, to hinder or otherwise contest acts of sovereignty, including law enforcement.

Most often, narcoterrorism thrives in parts of the world where the state is either ineffective or nonexistent. For example, narcoterrorism thrived in Colombia until that country's government, with the support of the United States and other nations, began efforts to establish sovereignty and combat drug trafficking. In response to these efforts, these criminal groups threatened coca farmers with death, kidnapping, and extortion if they did not continue to produce coca for processing and shipment. Colombian officials who oppose their efforts are also threatened, killed, or otherwise intimidated.

In the Balkans and central Asia, criminal and terrorist groups use drug trafficking tactics, techniques, and procedures (often with the active, paid assistance of drug trafficking organizations) to move weapons, people, money, and information throughout the regions. As a result, groups are able to pay volunteers and move weapons, people, and other material throughout the region (weapons and terrorist transport to and from Georgia's Pankisi Gorge is an example) via routes and established methods that are clandestine and time-proven. In Southeast Asia, groups have encouraged drug cultivation and trafficking to generate profits to pay for terrorist activity. Jemaah Islamiah, for example, derives significant proceeds from and methamphetamine consumption by U.S., Australian, and other Western citizens.

These proceeds are used, in part, to fund its activities in Southeast Asia and support terrorist organizations there. Finally, and perhaps of most concern to U.S. policymakers, drug trafficking organizations in Mexico, the Caribbean, and other Latin American countries are known to provide transport, for a price, to non-Latins seeking illegal entry into the United States. Many of these individuals seek entry for criminal or, potentially, terrorist activity. The existence of time-proven, clandestine access into the United States is a continuing threat to homeland defence and security since these access providers seek to kill or injure American citizens (through drug trafficking) and will provide support for the right price.

International and governmental responses to these worldwide threats have been tepid for several reasons. First, many do not understand the nature of the threat. Traditional threats to national sovereignty and regional stability have been viewed as state action (that is, state-on-state aggression). This traditional view considers narcotics-related activity as exclusively criminal in nature. Second, some view the threat of narcotics-funded terrorism as someone else's problem. These views ignore the fact that this threat is a multinational or transnational one. Third, many governmental and international bodies lack the will to confront this threat individually or as a collective group.

Thus, the narcotics-funded terrorist threat to Colombia is seen as a Colombian problem, rather than a regional or hemispheric one. Finally, some governments lack the capability to address the threat even when they recognize the danger. In these cases, they either ignore the challenge or seek, unsuccessfully, regional or international assistance. Narcoterrorism, however, is starting to receive attention from U.S. officials and the international community.

Prior to September 11, 2001, conventional wisdom failed to appreciate not only the nature and danger of transnational threats such as terrorism but also the need to identify and combat the lifeblood of these threats: the money that finances it. Narcotics trafficking was viewed as a purely criminal and social problem, not as a source of funding and method of covert movement for terrorist activity.

Soon after 9/11, U.S. leaders began to call for increased attention and effort to combat terrorist financing, including drug trafficking. For example, former U.S.

Drug Enforcement Agency (DEA) Administrator Asa Hutchinson called on the U.S. Government to combat drug trafficking since it funded the Taliban. Soon after, President George W. Bush similarly drew attention to the need to combat narcoterrorism as a part of the larger war on terror. While many outside the Department of Defence (DOD) have opined on this issue, few understand the nature and potential of the threat.

As a result, U.S. policies, and the necessary coordination with U.S. agencies, are not as effective as possible. For instance, U.S. Southern Command, the DOD component with the most experience in fighting transnational threats such as narcoterrorism, has not been called upon to provide guidance or other assistance to U.S. Central Command, whose area of responsibility includes states in Central Asia. As a result, understanding of the nature of the threat is limited and the ability to work closely with other U.S. and international agencies to combat narcoterrorism is minimal at best.

As a preliminary matter, however, one must identify terms and assumptions in order to assess the ability of U.S. agencies to combat the problem. What is narcoterrorism and why should it be of concern? This stage identifies what narcoterrorism is, differentiates it from purely criminal narcotics trafficking and terrorism, and discusses the potential that it has to support terrorism and the proliferation of weapons of mass destruction (WMD).

NARCOTERRORISM AS AN ISSUE OF U.S. POLICY

Narcoterrorism is not a novel concept or issue. For decades, many have referred to it, but U.S. leaders began to use the term only after September 11, 2001. Narcoterrorism, commentators conclude, was first coined as a term of art in 1983 by former Peruvian President Bela ´ unde Terry to describe attacks by Sendero Luminoso and others upon Peruvian counternarcotics police.

Since 9/11, U.S. leaders now describe narcoterrorism as acts that support terrorist activity and provide financing and other support to terrorist organizations. Part of the problem lies in the fact that some U.S. agencies—with the authority and resources to combat potential domestic and international narcoterrorism—either define the term in limited ways or fail to identify it at all. Thus, the United States will continue to face difficult obstacles in delineating and defeating this threat because responsible agencies lack even a common concept of the problem, much less a coordinated strategy.

The DEA, for example, defines narcoterrorism as:

- A subset of terrorism, in which terrorist groups, or associated individuals, participate directly or indirectly in the cultivation, manufacture, transportation, or distribution of controlled substances and the monies derived from these activities. Further, narco-terrorism may be characterized by the participation of groups or associated individuals in taxing, providing security for, otherwise aiding and abetting drug trafficking endeavors in an effort to further, or fund, terrorist activities.

This definition, however, is largely limited to the context of drug law enforcement. It fails to identify the diplomatic, commercial (particularly maritime), intelligence, military, and other equities needed to combat the threat. Moreover, this definition is perhaps the broadest among U.S. agencies and fails to address key parts that other responsible agencies' efforts are required. On the other hand, DOD defines narcoterrorism in an even more limited (and, from an operational perspective, limiting) manner.

According to Joint Publication 1–02, DOD Dictionary of Military and Associated Terms, narcoterrorism is:

- Terrorism conducted to further the aims of drug traffickers. It may include assassinations, extortion, hijackings, bombings and kidnappings directed against judges, prosecutors, elected officials, or law enforcement agents, and general disruption of a legitimate government to divert attention from drug operations.

Clearly, this definition maintains the distinction between violence-related drug trafficking and other transnational threats, including narcoterrorism. It fails to acknowledge, though, the past, present, and future ability of the drug trade, first, to finance operations by those not necessarily involved in drug trafficking (that is, those who tax the cultivation, processing, shipment, or sale of drugs); and second, most glaringly, to transport terrorists, arms, money, and WMD through established, covert logistical networks.

For the purposes of this stage, therefore, basic principles of economics are instructive. Assume that if one can transport a product—radios, cars, food, or other commerce—from point A to point B, then that capability is of value. Americans spend millions (if not billions) of dollars each year for the delivery of food, personal services, and other items. This assumption is axiomatic. Further assume that if one can transport a product covertly (across borders and without notice to law enforcement, security, or regulatory authorities), then that capability increases in value. Again, this principle is axiomatic.

The ability to move drugs covertly and across local, national, regional, and international borders has been a lucrative commodity. The better the track record of undetected movement, the more is the value of that service. Thus, the international drug transport industry presents an additional threat to U.S. domestic and international security. The industry is a logistical system that moves drugs, arms, terrorists, and WMD at any time. This is not just a potential capability.

In fact, many nations are encountering this development. In early 2004, for example, European law enforcement, while reviewing entry documents for passengers on board a train leaving Russia and traveling west, found an individual carrying a large container marked "radioactive," which contained weapons-grade uranium. The individual was carrying the uranium on orders from a Russian drug trafficker who was paid to transport the uranium into Europe.

The Colombian navy has interdicted numerous diesel-fueled submarines carrying hundreds of millions of dollars of cocaine to the United States. The traffickers purchased at least one submarine, investigations found, from members of the Russian mafia. Afghan, Tajik, and other southwest Asian drug traffickers who deliver Afghan-produced opium to Russia have increased their profits by offering their capability to those who wish to move things and people out of Russia.

The traffickers either offer new contracts for this return delivery service or, if they themselves want a Russian product, barter or sell the drugs in exchange. Items transported out of Russia and south towards Afghanistan have included arms, individuals, money, and WMD precursors. Thus, it would be accurate to describe narcoterrorism as more than just a means to generate funds for terror and a description of the violence committed by drug traffickers. A discussion of narcoterrorism must also recognize and address its logistical network.

Perhaps the following definition, then, is appropriate: Narcoterrorism refers to the transnational threat that:

- Generates revenue for terrorist activity by taxing all facets of the drug trade (cultivation, processing, shipment, or sale)
- Challenges national and international sovereignty through acts of violence, corruption, and intimidation to create or maintain ungoverned space within which drug trafficking and other illicit activity may flourish
- Moves any illicit product from one point to another.

HOMELAND SECURITY

The Department of Homeland Security (DHS) is so overburdened with priority missions such as securing U.S. air transport, borders, and providing support to first responders that it has not had the time, resources, or staffing to consider and implement policy designed to detect and defeat narcoterrorist threats to the United States. Recognizing that challenge, however, does not excuse the lack of any central guidance for an agency that controls over 80 per cent of the U.S. law enforcement resources whose primary mission is to protect our borders from covert entry.

The Homeland Security Act of 2002, which created DHS, unsuccessfully tried to place all Federal law enforcement agencies responsible for securing U.S. borders from covert entry into one department. Congress also suggested (rather than required) that DHS pool its operational and intelligence collection assets with other U.S. assets into a Joint Interagency Task Force for Homeland Security.

Unfortunately, the Congress failed to create a department office responsible for DHS-wide policy development. As a result, Homeland Security has not promulgated policy, including common definitional policy, that would align the policies, programmes, and budgets of the respective components. Congress also created the DHS Office of Counternarcotics. Unfortunately, the official named to lead this office is also tasked with responsibilities within the Office of National Drug Control Policy, serves as the U.S. Interdiction Coordinator, and maintains no staff. The position, as currently authorized and organized, lacks the ability to institute meaningful change.

DEPARTMENT OF DEFENCE

For years, DOD resisted any involvement in activity, whether foreign or domestic, that countered transnational threats such as narcoterrorism. This cultural and institutional resistance is based on legitimate concerns and an ignorance of these threats to international, as well as U.S. national and domestic security. Counterterrorism has never been a concept that the conventional U.S. military has understood, fully accepted as a "military mission," trained for, or practiced. The Armed Forces fought the creation of Special Forces and other unconventional, special, or low-intensity conflict that the world now faces.

Indeed, DOD opposed efforts to create an organization within the Office of the Secretary of Defence that would advise him on all matters (for example, special operations, counterterrorism, counternarcotics, U.S. territorial security, stability, and information operations) until Congress forced its creation as part of the Goldwater Nichols DOD Reorganization Act of 1986. The Assistant Secretary of Defence for Special Operations and Low Intensity Conflict, the official in charge of that office and principal advisor to the Secretary on those issues, however, remained vacant until the summer of 2003—almost 2 years after 9/11. Again, some of the resistance within DOD to address counternarcoterrorism and other transnational threats is valid.

In a democratic society, the military should not have a significant role in domestic issues such as illegal drug use, domestic terrorism, and immigration control. As far back as the nineteenth century, U.S. law has prohibited military involvement in domestic law enforcement. While notable exceptions do exist, such as for providing limited support to domestic counterdrug law enforcement, domestic nuclear terrorism, and specific support for national security events such as the Super Bowl and political conventions, the U.S. military continues to perform strictly limited domestic missions, even after 9/11.

The resistance lacks validity, however, in terms of supporting U.S. and international partners in combating transnational threats. Partner nation intelligence and military forces and international and U.S. law enforcement agencies lack the necessary resources, training, and, most notably, command, control, communication, and intelligence, which are so necessary to prevent and defeat narcoterrorism and other transnational threats to our friends and the U.S. homeland.

Thus, DOD is called upon to use its unique resources and capabilities to address this problem in a holistic manner. Changes to DOD policies and authorities since 9/11 reflect the beginning, hopefully, of this change and recognition that the U.S. military must identify and defeat the narcoterrorist threat to defend the homeland from a variety of dangers that will utilize the logistical network to gain entry to the United States.

In 2003, the Bush administration requested congressional authority to expand its support to Colombia from the limited counterdrug support that it provided pursuant to Colombia's Plan Colombia. The administration requested the authority to use counterdrug resources, mainly provided by the Departments of State and Defence, to assist Colombian efforts to fight narcoterrorism, rather than the limited counterdrug role originally intended. The administration requested and received authorization and appropriations to continue support, through DOD, State, and the CIA, for Colombian counternarcoterrorism until 2006. On October 3, 2003, DOD Deputy Secretary Paul Wolfowitz instituted a long-awaited policy that attempted to address the transnational threat of narcoterrorism. It also recognized the danger to the United States by the threat's logistical network. While it is directed to all parts of DOD, including its regional (for example, U.S. Central Command) and functional (for example, U.S Special Operations Command) commands and intelligence organs, including the National Security Agency and Defence Intelligence Agency, passive resistance to the policy shift remains.

First, the DOD policy expressly recognizes the links between drug trafficking and terrorism and recognition that activities traditionally separated from military missions should cross jurisdictions when appropriate. Moreover, the policy's most important, and perhaps most subtle, shift was to define DOD counterdrug activities.

The term is consistent with the purpose of congressional appropriation and provides the necessary flexibility to address narcoterrorist and other transnational threats in a timely, efficient, and coordinated manner:

- The term "counterdrug activities" includes those measures taken to detect, interdict, disrupt, or curtail any activity that is reasonably related to narcotics trafficking. This includes, but is not limited to, measures taken to detect, interdict, disrupt or curtail activities related to substances, materiel, weapons, or resources used to finance, support, secure, cultivate, process or transport illegal drugs.

Thus, as a matter of policy, DOD recognized all three prongs of narcoterrorism: the act of funding terror; the use of violence to create instability necessary to support drug trafficking; and the logistical network that moves drugs and other things across U.S. and international borders.

NATIONAL DRUG CONTROL FRAMEWORK

CONVENTION ADHERENCE

India is a signatory to all three UN drug control conventions, namely, the Single Convention on Narcotic Drugs 1961 (as amended by the 1972 Protocol), the Convention on Psychotropic Substances 1971 and the United Nations Convention against Illicit Traffic in Narcotic Drugs and Psychotropic Substances, 1988.

Legislation

The broad legislative policy on narcotic drugs and psychotropic substances is contained in the three Central Acts.

These are:

- Drugs and Cosmetics Act, 1940,
- The Narcotics Drugs and Psychotropic Substances Act, 1985 (NDPS Act, 1985), and
- The Prevention of Illicit Traffic in Narcotic Drugs and Psychotropic Substances Act, 1988.

Amendment to the NDPS Act

The NDPS Act 1985 was amended with effect from 2nd October 2001. The amendments now incorporated in the Act have brought about significant changes in the penal structure under the NDPS Act 1985 as they have made financial investigations and the forfeiture of illegally acquired property more purposeful. In addition, provisions have been included for new investigative techniques and for removing certain practical difficulties faced by the investigating officers.

The amendments are:

- *Graded Punishments*: The amended Act grades punishment into three categories depending on the quantity of drugs seized and also provides for judicial discretion as far as the severity of punishment is concerned. Violations relating to small quantities now attract imprisonment of up to six months or fine or both. Violations in respect of commercial quantities continue to attract a minimum prison sentence of 10 years, which may extend to 20 years and shall also involve a fine of not less than ₹100,000 (approx. US$2,100) that may extend to ₹200,000 (approximately US$4,200). Any violations involving quantities of drugs more than prescribed the small quantities but less than commercial quantities shall be punishable with rigorous imprisonment for a term, which may extend to 10 years and with fine.
- *Financial Investigations Made Easier*: The property of a drug offender can, after the amendments be frozen as soon as he is arrested, without waiting for conviction or completion of full period of preventive detention.
- *Money Laundering Becomes an Offence*: The laundering of illegally acquired property has been made an offence under the Narcotics Act.
- *Removal of Difficulties in Compliance*: The provisions of Section 50 of the NDPS Act, non compliance of which has resulted in a large number of acquittals, have been made more flexible to cater to the real life situations where it is not practicable to take the person to be searched to the nearest Gazetted Officer or Magistrate without the possibilities of the suspect parting with the drugs.
- *Controlled Deliveries*: Further to facilitate complete investigations and to neutralize the entire syndicate involved in drug trafficking, a provision has been made for the movement of seized drugs from one place to another within and outside the country under controlled conditions.
- *Ambit of Sections 41 & 42 Enlarged to include Controlled Substances and Financial Investigations*: The provisions of search, seizure etc. under sections 41 & 42 shall now be applicable for cases relating to financial investigations and controlled substance as well.

The NDPS (Regulation of Controlled Substances) Order, 1993

While the NDPS Act 1985 contains provisions for the control of precursor chemicals, in 1993, the government of India promulgated the NDPS (Regulation of Controlled Substances) Order, which sets out the detailed rules and procedures governing the manufacture, distribution, trade, import, extort, etc. of specified 'controlled substances'. Presently five substances namely, acetic anhydride, anthranilic acid, N-acetylanthranilic acid, ephedrine and pseudo-ephedrine have been notified for controls under this order. In addition controls are also exercised on imports/ exports of a few other chemicals. Together, the 2001 amendments and the 1993 order constitute substantive compliance with the asset forfeiture and precursor control provisions of the 1988 Convention.

The Prevention of Illicit Traffic in Narcotic Drugs and Psychotropic Substances Act

The Prevention of Illicit Traffic in Narcotic Drugs and Psychotropic Substances Act is a preventive detention law. Persons who indulge in drug trafficking can be detained through an executive order passed by designated authorities. The Joint Secretary (Revenue) in the central government is empowered to issue such detention orders. Similarly, relevant authorities are also designated to act in this capacity by the state governments.

Institutions

The Department of Revenue in the Ministry of Finance has the nodal co-ordination role as administrators of the NDPS Act, 1985 and the Prevention of Illicit Traffic in Narcotic Drugs and Psychotropic Substances Act, 1988. The Ministry of Social Justice and Empowerment is responsible for implementing the drug demand reduction programme in the country, mainly through support to NGOs. The nodal agency dealing with drug trafficking is the Narcotics Control Bureau (NCB) located in the Ministry of Home Affairs.

However, officers of the Central Bureau of Narcotics, the Directorate of Revenue Intelligence, Customs, Central Excise, Border Security Force, the Coast Guard and the Police authorities of State governments are also empowered to take action against drug trafficking under the provisions of the NDPS Act, 1985. The nodal agency for drug demand reduction is the Ministry for Social Justice and Empowerment (MSJE) that implements its programmes mainly by supporting NGOs all over the country. The health, treatment and hospitalisation facilities are the responsibility of the Ministry of Health and the Health Departments of the States and Union Territories.

National Policy

National policy on Narcotic Drugs and Psychotropic Substances is based on Article 47 of the Directive Principles of State Policy, Constitution of India, where the 'Duty of the State [is] to raise the level of nutrition and the standard of living and to improve public health'. It directs, inter alia, that the "...the State shall endeavour to bring about prohibition of the consumption, except for medicinal purposes, of intoxicating drinks and of drugs which are injurious to health". The government's policy on the subject which flows from the above said constitutional provision is also guided by the international conventions on the subject, mentioned under 'Conventions adherence' above. However, India does not have a national drug control policy or an apex organization in respect of drug control. The NDPS Act, 1985 lays down the focus and direction of drug control strategy in the country. This Act made an express provision for constituting a Central Authority for the purpose of exercising the powers and functions of the central government under the Act.

In exercise of the powers, the "Narcotics Control Bureau (NCB)" was constituted with Headquarters in Delhi on 17th March 1986. Though the master plan has not been formally adopted, many of its provisions have been absorbed into subsequent National Five-Year Plans.

LICIT CONTROL (DRUGS AND PRECURSORS)

Licit Control

Licit opium cultivation in India is supervised by the CBN headed by the Narcotics Commissioner. An elaborate control system has been designed to ensure that all opium produced in India is duly accounted for and to prevent its diversion to illicit channels. The main elements of the system are licensing control, with the prescription of Minimum Qualifying Yields (MQY), and government monopoly of purchasing. Strict monitoring measures, including stepping-up test measurements and checking of Preliminary Weighment Registers, have been introduced. The entire licensed harvested crop is procured by CBN, and is processed in its two opium and alkaloid factories at Neemuch and Ghazipur.

Precursors

India has an advanced and large chemical industry which manufactures and uses a wide range of chemicals for legitimate purposes. Some of these chemicals are also precursors or essential chemicals frequently used by the illicit drug industry and are, therefore, susceptible to diversion. India produces 15 precursor chemicals, including acetic anhydride, ephedrine, pseudo-ephedrine, anthranilic acid and N-acetylanthranilic acid. The chemical and pharmaceutical industry manufactures, uses and exports many of the precursors of the 1988 UN Convention. India is a signatory to all the three UN Conventions. It exercises control over precursors under three different laws as follows:

Controls under the NDPS (Regulation of Controlled Substances) Order, 1993

This order issued under Section 9A of the NDPS Act, 1985 requires the manufacturers, distributors, sellers, importers, exporters and consumers of controlled substances to maintain records and file quarterly returns with the Narcotics Control Bureau. It also requires any loss or disappearance of the controlled substance to be reported to the Director General, NCB.

Precursors Covered

Acetic anhydride, Anthranilic acid, N-acetyl anthranilic acid, Ephedrine and Pseudoephedrine. Enforcement agency: Narcotics Control Bureau for scrutinizing returns. For violations, any officer empowered under NDPS Act can take action.

Controls Imposed under the EXIM Policy

The EXIM policy (export-import policy) framed under the Foreign Trade (Development and Regulation) Act, 1992 imposes restrictions on the import and export of goods. Export of seven precursors is subject to a No Objection Certificate and import of three precursors is restricted.

Precursors Covered

Export of Acetic anhydride, Ephedrine, Pseudoephedrine, Methyl-ethyl-Ketone, Phenyl-2- Propanone,3,4 methyl-enedioxyphenyl-2-propanone and Potassium permanganate requires a No Objection Certificate from the Narcotics Commissioner. The import of acetic anhydride, ephedrine and pseudoephedrine is restricted in India.

Enforcement Agency

Narcotics Commissioner issues NOC for exports and licences for import of precursors whose import is restricted by the Director General of Foreign Trade.

Controls under Section 11 of the Customs Act 1962

The goods specified under this section are subject to intensive checks in the specified areas by the customs officers. The Government of India has notified acetic anhydride as a specified substance under this section within an area of 100 km. along the Indo –Myanmar border and 50 km. along the Indo Pak border. Broadly, the special measures under this section require all persons who own, possess or control the specified substance to maintain records and notify the Customs officers of the details of quantities held and transported.

SUPPLY REDUCTION

An effective statutory and administrative framework has been set up in India to combat drug trafficking. India complies with the regulations under the various United Nations Conventions and co-operates with countries in the region in supply reduction and law enforcement efforts. India is also signatory to the SAARC Convention on Narcotic Drugs and Psychotropic Substances. The detection and eradication of illicit drug crops is a law enforcement priority.

At the operational level, India's drug law enforcement strategy is coordinated by the NCB and is focused upon:

- combating trafficking through appropriate intelligence, interdiction and investigative initiatives;
- Eradicating illicit drug crops;
- Preventing leakage from licit opium crop;
- Implementing a regime of domestic and international trade controls over select precursor chemicals; and
- Increasingly targeting assets derived from drug trafficking for confiscation and forfeiture.

DEMAND REDUCTION

The Ministry of Social Justice and Empowerment has developed a strategy for Drug Demand Reduction in India. The strategy is based on the conviction that a co-ordinated response of government and non-government organisations is more effective for drug abuse prevention. This is being achieved through the Scheme for Prohibition and Drug Abuse Prevention wherein funds are released to voluntary organisations for setting up/maintenance of counselling and awareness centres.

The Ministry is supporting 369 NGOs running 459 (counselling, awareness and de-addiction cum rehabilitation centres). Every year on average in excess of 300,000 addicts register at these centres. The health, treatment and hospitalisation facilities are the responsibility of the Ministry of Health of the States/Union Territories. MSJE has drawn up a three-pronged demand-reduction strategy based on the approach that drug abuse is a psycho-socio-medical problem that can be handled through community-based interventions.

The three components are:

1. Building awareness and educating people about ill effects of drug abuse.
2. Dealing with addicts through a programme of motivation, counselling, treatment, follow-up and social reintegration.
3. Imparting drug abuse prevention rehabilitation training to volunteers having in view to build up and educated a cadre of drug abuse control operators.

The strategy involves the training of volunteers in drug abuse prevention and rehabilitation and is based on the conviction that a coordinated response of government and nongovernment organisations is more effective for drug abuse prevention. This is achieved through the Scheme for Prohibition and Drug Abuse Prevention wherein funds are released to voluntary organisations for setting up/maintenance of counselling and awareness centres, deaddiction-cum-rehabilitation centres, de-addiction camps and for preventive awareness programmes, workplace prevention programme and training of service providers. The national demand reduction strategy formulated by MSJE is complementary to the national master plan drawn up in 1994.

In order to counteract the demand for dependence-producing drugs, the Scheme for Prohibition and Drug Abuse Prevention, being launched since the Seventh Five Year Plan as a Central plan Scheme, has been reviewed, restructured and titled "Scheme for Prevention of Alcoholism and Substance (Drugs) Abuse". The revised Scheme was implemented from 1st April 1999 in the light of the approach and objectives envisaged for Ninth Five Year Plan. The Scheme is implemented through registered Societies/ Trusts/ Companies or the Organisations/Institutions by providing financial assistance to the extent of 90% of the total approved expenditure and in case of the north eastern states, Sikkim, Jammu and Kashmir it is 95%.

These organizations are financially assisted for setting up and maintaining counselling and awareness centres and treatment-cum-rehabilitation centres and for organizing de-addiction camps, Awareness programmes and manpower development. The Ministry of Social Justice and Empowerment is also in the process of drafting its National policy and study for Drug Demand Reduction in India.

The National Youth Policy 2003 recognizes the vulnerability of young people to substance abuse, STDs and HIV/ AIDS and considers these issues as a priority. The Policy, therefore, advocates a two-pronged approach of education and awareness for prevention and proper treatment and counselling for cure and rehabilitation. It further enjoins that information in respect of the reproductive health system should form part of the educational curriculum.

The Policy also stresses the need for establishment of adolescent clinics in large hospitals and similar projects in rural areas to address the health needs of young adults. The department of Youth Affairs and Sports, through the National Service Scheme, and the NYKs through their volunteers, carry out awareness generation on drug abuse and AIDS. NSS volunteers, (Urban Student Youth), concentrate on the integrated development of adopted villages and slums, and NYK carry out their activities in rural India. No specific policy on drug abuse control has been drawn up as yet in the Health Ministry.

The National Health Policy 2002 does not specifically mention drug use as a component or concern. The programme of the National AIDS Control Organisation (NACO), Ministry of Health and Family Welfare recognises that injecting drug use is also one of the major causes for the spread of HIV/AIDS in the country. The NACO's policy document recognises harm minimization measures such as exchange of syringes and needles, peer education, community outreach, access to health services and oral drug substitution, as the appropriate strategy to prevent HIV among injecting drug users, although the policy further recognises that in India the harm-reduction approach is yet to find wider acceptability because of ethical and moral considerations.

An analysis of national policies pertaining to drug use and HIV/AIDS found that there was no signal from government that HIV/AIDS prevention will be established as a central element of all drug treatment programmes. Although it had become a part of the draft National AIDS Prevention and Control Policy by then, harm minimisation was not a part of national drug control policy and strategy. Many drug treatment agencies did not consider HIV intervention as an urgent issue.

Several key informants expressed the view that the injecting epidemic that arose in Manipur was substantially influenced by the adoption of harsh anti-drug policies at that time–the so-called "police model." Instances were cited where severe law enforcement resulted in an acute shortage of heroin, prompting many heroin users to shift to injectable buprenorphine, (which, being licit, is relatively easily accessible). The same analysis also noted that there was also no clear policy on opioid substitution treatment in India. Many government officers were reported to believe incorrectly that UNDCP (now UNODC) was non-supportive of substitution treatment and several NGO representatives expressed the view that this policy stance was hindering progressive policy reform in India.

MONEY LAUNDERING CONTROL MEASURES

The Narcotic Drugs and Psychotropic Substances Act, 1985 contains provisions for tracing, freezing and forfeiting the properties of drug traffickers, their relatives and associates. It provides for tracing, identifying, freezing, seizing and forfeiting of illicitly acquired properties of drug traffickers, their relatives and associates. The definition of "relatives" is quite comprehensive and thus includes all the relatives in whose names traffickers might place drug money.

The offence of acquiring properties illicitly under the provision of this act is punishable with imprisonment of 10–15 years or more. A quasi-judicial authority entitled the 'Competent Authority' who also decides on whether the frozen properties should be forfeited must confirm the freezing order. While freezing and seizing are techniques of temporary restraint, the process of forfeiture is a process that transfers the title of ownership to the government. The properties can be forfeited only after the person is either convicted or has been detained under PITNDPS Act.

One interesting aspect of the law is that the burden of proving that the property is not illegally acquired rests on the charged person. Only properties earned during the previous six years can be frozen and forfeited under this law. The President of India has signed the Prevention of Money Laundering Act 2002. The Act has ten Chapters.

In Chapter II money laundering is defined as an offence punishable with imprisonment for a term which shall not be less than three years but which may be extended to seven years. Chapter III Attachment, Adjudication and Confiscation refers to the attachment of property involved in money laundering, Adjudicating Authorities and the Management of Properties confiscated. Chapter IV spells out the obligations of banking companies, financial institutions and intermediaries. Chapter V explains summonses, searches and seizures. Chapter VI through to Chapter X goes into administrative details regarding the appellate Tribunal, special courts, authorities, reciprocal arrangements for assistance in certain matters and procedure for attachment and confiscation of property and Miscellaneous.

Other Laws

In addition, certain other laws namely:

- The Benami Transactions (Prohibition) Act 1988,
- The Income Tax Act 1961,
- The Foreign Exchange Regulation Act (FERA) 1973 and
- The Smugglers and Foreign Exchange Manipulators (Forfeiture of Property) Act, 1976, also contain provisions for countering money laundering to some extent.

The current legislation provides for a holistic approach to matters that perpetuate or result in money laundering. The Foreign Exchange Regulations Act, 1973 (FERA) has been repealed and is replaced by Foreign Exchange Management Act (FEMA). The Directorate of Enforcement is the enforcement authority for the control of crimes relating to money laundering.

INTERNATIONAL COOPERATION

India has hosted an international, regional and bilateral exchange programme under the aegis of UNODC, SAARC, system, ICPO-INTERPOL and Colombo Plan Bureau. Particularly noteworthy are India's contributions in the fields of precursor control and demand reduction. India has entered into bilateral agreements with a number of countries on matters relating to combating trafficking in narcotic drugs, psychotropic substances and precursor chemicals. To date, India has entered into bilateral agreements with several countries including USA, Mauritius, Afghanistan, Russia, Myanmar, Zambia, the UAE, Bulgaria, Egypt, China, Italy, Turkey.

These agreements relate to:

- Exchange of information/experience of operational, technical and general nature;
- Assistance in joint investigations, identification and destruction of illegal drug processing sites/laboratories;
- Control over precursor chemicals;
- Prevention of money laundering;
- Training and measures to reduce demand through prevention; and

- Treatment and public awareness activities.

The Government is a signatory to the 1990 SAARC Convention on Narcotic Drugs and Psychotropic Substances. The UNODC Regional Office for South Asia is located in New Delhi.

DRUG POLICY IN INDIA

INTRODUCTION

Contemporary international drug policy seeks to control both the demand and supply of drugs through the criminalisation of production, trafficking and use. Furthermore, adherence to the United Nations drug control conventions ensures that most nation states adopt a similar prohibition-oriented approach when formulating national drug control legislation.

Recent research suggests that this can be problematic in some Asian countries where longstanding cultural sanctions already existed for drug use; particularly those involving psychoactive plant products such as cannabis and opium. With its focus on India, this briefing paper examines the impact of the punitive approach towards drugs in those societies and communities that have traditionally exerted socio-cultural controls over the use of mind-altering substances.

The discussion highlights the unintentional but often harmful consequences of such drug control policies. In framing the discussion of this topic, it is important to note that the socio-cultural context of traditional drug use within many Asian countries means that experiencing an altered state of consciousness is only a part of the drug taking experience and not the ultimate goal of users. Indeed, norms controlling excessive and regular drug use have customarily governed socially and culturally accepted consumption of native mind-altering substances.

While such traditional use management strategies vary across Asian countries, it is possible to identify similarities that exist between these approaches to drug use and contemporary interventions that collectively fall within the so-called harm reduction paradigm. The defining feature of harm reduction programmes is their focus on the prevention of harm rather than the prevention of drug use itself.

It can be argued, therefore, that as signatories to the 1961 UN Single Convention on Narcotic Drugs, many Asian countries have been required to move away from longstanding approaches to control customary drug use. In many respects, there has been a subsequent shift from traditional drug use management to an emphasis on eradicating all drug use and trade. The implementation of law-enforcement-dominated policies has generated a tense relationship between contemporary legislation and culturally ingrained drug use patterns and associated management strategies.

This situation is compounded by changing patterns of drug use within India. This is the result of a number of interrelated factors; the rising popularity of new non-traditional forms of drug use introduced via tourism; urbanization; and leakage from illicit drug production in the region. Indeed, evidence suggests that changes in policy may have contributed to increases in the use of harder forms of drugs and more harmful modes of consumption, notably drug injecting.

Such a change in user behaviour is particularly significant given the role played by injecting drug use in the transmission of HIV/AIDS and other blood borne infections. The management of this issue has become a cause for concern within the field of drug demand reduction and has serious implications for the development realities of many Asian countries.

HISTORY

The use of the cannabis plant for a variety of purposes has long existed in India, a fact also noted for many other countries of Asia. Its use for medicinal reasons, as well as its mind altering capacity, is significant. Cannabis has been used along with other ingredients to treat rheumatism, migraine, malaria and cholera; to relieve fluxes; facilitate surgical operations; to relax nerves; restore appetite; for general well-being; and it is also considered beneficial for the functioning of the heart and liver. Additionally, the cannabis plant provides food grain, oil seed and fibre for manufacture of fibrous products in select parts of India.

The practice of using cannabis to alter consciousness and as part of religious and shamanistic rituals has also existed in India for centuries. For example, the drug has a strong religious association as a gift from Lord Shiva to his followers. Opium has also been used for socio-cultural reasons in different parts of the country with medicinal use being more prevalent than cultural use, like that seen among the Rajputs in Rajasthan and Gujarat. Prior to the introduction of contemporary drug control legislation, a system for procuring opium and cannabis through legal outlets existed.

However, drug control initiatives put in place procedures that made it difficult to obtain these substances. Legislation in 1985 and 2001 include provisions for medical use, but there has been a trend not only to reduce the quantity released by the government, but also to tighten up procedural regulations for obtaining the drugs by traditional medicinal practitioners. The resulting inability to source sufficient licit opium and cannabis for traditional use has forced such practitioners to make purchases from the expanding illegal market.

SOCIO-CULTURAL CONTROLS

Until the 1980s cannabis consumption does not appear to have been regarded as an issue of major social concern in India, with little or no official mention of excessive use. Prevalent socio-cultural regulations with regard to the form of use, mode of consumption, context of use and profile of users, ensured a system of use management that limited drug use within the country. For instance, norms restricted the use of cannabis and opium to the adult male population.

In the case of cannabis, this is a pattern documented in a number of countries including Cambodia, Vietnam, Thailand, Laos, China, Nepal and Pakistan. Even among the male adult population, there were restrictions on the context for consumption, with sanctioned use often linked or limited to specific religious and social occasions. In India and Nepal, the use of cannabis appears to be linked to religious festivals like Shivaratri, Krishna Ashtami and participation in bhajan sessions.

Indeed, occasions like Holi, 'the festival of colours,' are not complete without the sharing of bhang - a drink made with cannabis. At such select occasions, women and youngsters were permitted to use bhang and other items made from cannabis, including snacks, sweets and curry. Opium is also offered at the harvest festival in a ceremony called akha teej, intended to strengthen family marital clan bonds and put aside old feuds. It is this specification regarding the profile of users and a desire for cultural confirmation that ensured the existence of mechanisms to control drug use.

The provision made for women and children to consume cannabis products in select cultural contexts and in specified forms indicates a strong cultural acceptance for cannabis within India. Norms reaffirmed the cultural dimension of cannabis use and probably prevented excessive non-cultural use of cannabis. As noted earlier, the adherence to cultural norms on sanctioned use emerged from a strong association of cannabis with Lord Shiva.

For example, Sadhus of various sects who primarily worship Lord Shiva make use of the drug for strengthening their concentration and spiritual search. Prior to smoking cannabis, the sadhus praise their Lord and take it in his name, a pattern of consumption seen also among lay followers. During Shivaratri, the distribution of cannabis drink and other products is perceived as a way to strengthen the association with the Lord. It is likely that such a relationship played a major role in restricting its use within India and Nepal, despite easy availability and local cultivation.

The drug's connection to Shivaratri almost certainly limited its use beyond the ceremonial context. Unlike cannabis, opium does not appear to have any significant religious associations, but even here the link between cultural identity and the consumption of opium acted as a strong mechanism to restrict consumption of the drug in excess. Studies conducted into opium use in Rajasthan and Gujarat indicate strong links between cultural and caste membership, and use of the drug. An opium drink can be used to greet guests to social functions that include marriage celebrations, sealing a business deal or mourning the demise of a relative. In this case, culture permits opium consumption in the male adult population but, unlike with cannabis, there is no specific cultural sanction for women and youngsters to use the substance except for medicinal purposes. Such sanctioned cultural use, and its occasion or context, produces a situation within which a drug's mind-altering properties are not the sole focus of the practice. For example, in consumption during a celebration or get together, songs and social interaction form the binding force for consuming the substance.

Consumption of bhang during Holi calls for community participation from the decision to prepare the drink, through to making it, and finally its consumption in a group setting. The pattern of consumption for smoking cannabis and opium also restricts drug use, because as a group activity the users only inhale a few times from the pipe.

Moreover, smoking the pipe is but a part of social interaction and not the sole activity of the group. Sharing the drug is also not the result of any economic consideration as is sometimes seen in the case of heroin.

NARCOTICS DRUGS AND PSYCHOTROPIC SUBSTANCES ACT 1985

Prior to the present drug control legislation, the focus of Indian drug policies was control of the drug trade and the collection of revenues through licensed sales. The change in policy direction had much to do with India's international commitments. As a signatory to the UN 1961 Single Convention, India, like many other nations, was obliged to eradicate culturally ingrained patterns of drug use, including those involving cannabis and opium. Indian delegations at the UN had long objected to a proposed policy of international cannabis prohibition, but had "made little headway against the massive," predominantly Western and US-led, "anticannabis bloc.". Yet, in order to gain widespread acceptance, the final draft of the Single Convention included transitional reservations allowing socalled grace periods for phasing out traditional drug use. This meant that the "quasi-medical use" of opium had to be abolished within 15 years of the Convention coming into force.

Similarly, the non-medical or non-scientific use of cannabis was to be discontinued as soon as possible, "but in any case within 25 years" from the date the convention came into force. Referring to cannabis, one expert has commented that it was a rather optimistic timetable when "matched against three thousand years of use by untold millions".

In political terms, any moves to phase out cultural drug use within India were problematic, since it was difficult for any party in power to tamper with popular religious and cultural feelings concerning the use of opium and cannabis. Consequently, mindful of international obligations regarding the UN grace period and the political sensitivity of the issue within the country, the NDPS Act was quietly put on to the statute books with little national debate.

The only provision for non-medical cultural use within the 1985 Act was that drinks made from cannabis leaves were to be sanctioned. As such, the legislation made many traditional forms of drug use a criminal act that could be punishable by imprisonment.

Some of the significant measures taken under the NDPS Act include:

- For the consumption of substances such as narcotic drugs or psychotropic substances or any other substance specified by the Central Government, the punishment is imprisonment for a term, which may be extended to one year, or a fine, which may extend to twenty thousand rupees, or both.
- In the case of consumption of cannabis products other than bhang, imprisonment may be for a term of six months, or a fine which may extend to ten thousand rupees, or both.
- The quantity specified for various substances that could lead to arrest for trading in drugs was not very large. For example, 250 milligrams of heroin, five grams of opium, five grams of charas or hashish, 500 grams of ganja and 25 milligrams of cocaine.

Evidence suggests that, in largely ignoring the sociocultural context of traditional drug use, the NDPS Act led to a significant increase in the arrests of low-level drug users. Arrests under the Act in 2001 totalled 16,315, of which around 76 per cent (12,400) were prosecuted and 28 per cent (4,568) convicted.

A study undertaken in the same year in Tihar jail provides an insight into the make-up of such figures. Interviews with 1,910 individuals arrested under the NDPS Act (1985) indicated that around 325 (17 per cent) were arrested under Section 27. This refers to the possession of small quantities of drugs meant for personal consumption. While the law has provision for such arrestees to seek treatment instead of serving a sentence, the provision is rarely utilised. Research also shows that many of those arrested on drug charges spent years in jail before their cases came up for hearing.

This was a result of the notoriously slow pace of the Indian judicial system. In some instances, it has meant that those caught with small quantities of drugs were eventually acquitted after spending years behind bars. Beyond concerns about the obvious injustice of such cases, prolonged prison time for low level drug offenders also raises the issue of recruitment by criminal groups. A recent study on organised crime in Mumbai suggests that prisons in India, as in many other parts of the world, are ideal places for orienting vulnerable individuals into the world of crime.

CHANGES IN PATTERNS OF DRUG USE

The convergence of a number of important structural changes, at both national and international levels, around the time of the NDPS Act, impacted on longstanding patterns of drug use within India. Research suggests that tourism has contributed to a diversification of drug use patterns. In the mid and late 1970s, exposure to other cultures in both Nepal and India produced new forms of drug taking behaviour. Since the early 1980s, most major Indian cities have been introduced to new "foreign" drugs such as heroin.

The interaction of young Indians with tourists has also facilitated an alteration in the relationships they later form with those drugs traditionally consumed. This is seen in all parts of the country, although the process is more gradual in rural areas. Such a rural-urban split can be explained by the impact of urbanization upon traditional patterns of drug use and management. Put simply, urban communities do not tend to adhere to traditions to the same degree as those in rural areas.

Furthermore, the relatively easy availability of a "foreign" drug like heroin, in comparison to opium, within the urban setting contributed to a shift in the drug of choice. As such, data from 16,942 drug users as part of the Drug Abuse Monitoring System reveal that, other than alcohol, there is significant variation in drug use patterns between urban and rural areas. With regard to heroin, for example, 14.9 per cent of users were from urban areas with nearly half that figure (7.9 per cent) being from rural areas.

The shift to heroin is also more likely to take place in urban settings that fall along the illicit heroin trafficking routes from South West and South East Asia. Indeed, the illicit drug trade has a significant, although complex, impact on drug use patterns within many parts of India. Shifts from opium to heroin use can be seen to depend on a number of inter-related factors. These include proximity to areas of illegal cultivation and processing, traditional regional drug use patterns and geographic accessibility. For example, there is illicit poppy cultivation in the North Eastern state of Arunachal Pradesh. Nonetheless, in a state with a history of cultural opium use and, due to the densely forested nature of the terrain, limited connectivity with the surrounding areas, drug use is limited to opium. In other parts of North East India, circumstances are different, however. The combination of the easy availability of heroin from Myanmar and absence of cultural use of opium in these regions resulted in the emergence of heroin use. In the states of Madhya Pradesh, Rajasthan and Uttar Pradesh there is a history of cultural opium use with the demand long supplied by diversion from licit cultivation. A study in Rajasthan in 1989 indicated that drug use was largely limited to opium and cannabis. Nonetheless, recent research shows that in the mid-1990s there was a shift from traditional drugs to heroin.

It is significant that this change took place at a time when there was an increase in the illicit heroin traffic to India from Afghanistan via Pakistan. Evidence suggests that the new legislation exacerbated the problems arising from such structural changes. For example, far from reaching its goal of eradicating drug use, enforcement of the NDPS Act appears to have inadvertently facilitated a shift to harder forms of drugs and riskier modes of consumption. The impact of the legislative changes was initially felt in urban areas in the 1990s, especially the major cities. As a result of the factors discussed above, hard drugs seem to have found a niche in many cities. An official study showed that of those drug users seeking treatment, significant numbers were using heroin, opium and the narcotic analgesic, propoxyphene.

Another study among opiate users in fourteen sites across India indicated the primary substance of abuse was heroin followed by buprenorphine, a synthetic opiate. From the total sample of 4,648 drug users, around 43 per cent had injected drugs at some time. In many cases, the drug of choice was buprenorphine followed by heroin and propoxyphene. Among the injectors around 51 per cent in Amritsar were found to have shared needles at some time, with 15 per cent from Hyderabad, New Delhi, Dimapur, Trivandrum and Chennai reporting the same practice.

The conditions for widespread transmission of HIV and other infections through drug use are therefore increasingly present in India. It is possible to see that the shift in patterns of use is not only from traditional drugs to derivative drugs but also to synthetic products as well. A 2004 study on the illicit Indian drug trade indicated that increasing controls over poppy straw used in the preparation of opium drinks is creating a shift towards synthetic opiates.

This is a dangerous trend considering that the morphine content in poppy straw is very low. Given the cultural acceptance of cannabis and opium, monitoring of the drug of initiation among users can be a useful process in identifying changing patterns of drug use across the country. For example, the 2002 Ministry of Social Justice and Empowerment Rapid Assessment Study revealed that within the majority of fourteen study sites respondents cited cannabis (40 per cent) followed by alcohol (33 per cent) to be dominant drugs of initiation.

However, in Dimapur, a city from North Eastern region, for around 34 per cent of the sample the first drug of abuse was propoxyphene, followed by heroin for 30 per cent. The profile of drugs users is another area that has undergone significant changes. Traditional users were predominantly from the male adult population. Data collected from fourteen study sites in the Rapid Assessment Study indicate that after legislative measures were put in place to criminalise drug use, the age of initiation to drug use fell.

The Study showed the mean age to be nineteen and below, with around 52 per cent of the users in the sample starting to use drugs between the ages of 16 and 20 years. Socio-cultural mechanisms also traditionally ensured that drug use by women within India was limited. There now appears to be a shift in this pattern. Drug use among women is often hidden with available data being based on random sampling of identified drug users. Nonetheless, data collected from 75 drug users in Mumbai, Delhi and Aizwal indicated the main substances of abuse to be heroin, propoxyphene, alcohol, minor tranquilisers and cough syrup.

Around 40 per cent were injecting drug users with 49.3 per cent of the sample aged between 21 and 30 years old. In Aizwal, a larger proportion of the drug users were between 15 and 20 years old. The consequences of an erosion of the traditional gender based restrictions on drug use also include negative secondary impacts. Of the seventy-five women within Pratima Murthy's 2002 study, 45.3 per cent derived their main source of income from sex work and drug dealing. In combination with the high incidence of injecting drug use, this reality clearly has serious implications for the management of HIV/AIDS and other blood borne infections.

DRUGS AND DEVELOPMENT

The traditional approach to development has been to stimulate economic growth through investment in infrastructure, support for institution building and promotion of economic reform. These measures to generate economic growth are designed to increase incomes generally, with the population and government having more material resources with which to meet their needs.

In addition, development programmes have also frequently incorporated a basic needs strategy that emphasizes the putting into place of governmental programmes to ensure elementary hygiene, clean drinking water, primary health care, education and literacy. Economic growth and basic needs strategies have been pursued simultaneously by a number of development assistance organizations at the national and international level.

Historically, drug control and drug abuse considerations were not often viewed as issues of primary concern for development planners, even in the context of programmes following a basic needs strategy. This is because many development assistance programmes were devoted either to promoting economic growth or to some aspect of basic needs of the population related to, inter alia, health or education. To some extent, there has been limited recognition that drug-related issues should be taken into account, particularly when an entire country or a specific region of a country has an influential illicit drug industry. The importance of production of illicit drugs to an economy will vary significantly from country to country. As noted earlier, income from the drug trade is exorbitant in some nations. Speaking of Colombia, a country expert estimates that businessmen of the illegal drugs industry would have "huge combined drug and capital income relative to the size of the country's economy". He further states that "between 1976 and 1986 gross private fixed investment ranged from $1.6 to $3.7 billion and averaged $2.8 billion, figures that clearly indicate that the illegal businessmen had the capacity to invest in Colombia an amount as large as what official data attributes to the whole private sector of the country".

This view of the impact of the drug trade is not atypical. The United States Office of Technology Assessment has found that in Bolivia, the coca economy annually generates as much foreign exchange as all other exports combined. It has also found that a significant number of persons are employed in the coca economy: 7 per cent of the labour force in 1990, although this figure is significantly less than the 20 per cent estimated to have been employed in coca in the late 1980s.

The economic costs of drug abuse can be categorized as direct and indirect. Direct costs involve increased costs of police, courts, military, treatment programmes, welfare payments to drug addicts and their families, as well as increased security measures by businesses. Indirect economic costs include the displacement of legal industries; diminished control over the economy; spending money for drugs and inappropriate use of money gained from drug sales; and fiscal problems related to the inability to tax the drug economy. Concerning displacement of legal industries due to the cocaine trade, commentators have found that the cocaine industry in a developing country" can create such a high inflow of foreign exchange that dollars become cheap relative to the local currency. This reduces the competitiveness of local products in both foreign and domestic markets". Diminished control over an economy occurs in several ways. Because money generated by illicit activities does not normally enter into the formal economic process of a country, macroeconomic planning is not possible for these funds.

Hence, a source of serious error is introduced into estimates of national income and expenditure. In speaking of the need for improved information on the illegal sector, a country expert has concluded that "large financial flows are not accounted for and the enormous sums generated by the opiate industry fail to show up in investment rates. This allows a general conclusion that most investment has been unproductive and used for speculative purposes.

However, an increasing part of the GNP is produced outside official accounts and thus outside intervention possibilities. This inevitably contributes to skewed macro-planning". Moreover, control over expenditures is reduced when governments have to devote resources to protect the financial and banking systems against subversion through additional banking regulation, increased reporting and other anti-money-laundering measures.

It has also been found that the poor often spend a greater percentage of their income on drugs than middle- or upper-income persons, and at a much greater cost to their families. A country expert 9 on Pakistan has found that the "bulk of consumer expenditures on heroin are made by lower income groups, while the income generated by the heroin industry mainly flows to upper and middle income groups ".

The poorest 20 per cent of the population represent nearly one-half of the drug abusers, primarily heroin addicts, according to the National Survey of Drug Abuse. The lowest income groups are most frequently represented; the highest income groups are somewhat below them; and the middle income group have the least number of drug users in Pakistan. Drug traffickers, however, do not normally put their illicit profits into productive enterprises. Nor is employment in the illicit drugs industry a significant means of putting money back into the community.

According to this expert, the drug industry provides employment for less than 1 per cent of the labour force of Pakistan. A very important indirect cost of the drug industry is a result of the fact that governments are not able to tax it. In such a case, governments have no choice but to increase taxes on those who can be expected to pay. However, the externalities of the drug industry, *i.e.* the hidden economic and social costs of illicit drug production and trafficking, cannot be charged back to those involved.

They are, therefore, an added burden to the law-abiding population. Experts consider cocaine a good example of market failure, a situation where markets encourage behaviour that is unprofitable for society and discourage behaviour that is better for development: "Market failure occurs when there is a difference between the costs of an action for an individual and the cost of that action for society.

In the case of cocaine, market failure occurs -the market encourages cocaine production even though it may be bad for society -because the roughly 5% to 15% of the national population involved in the cocaine industry do not bear many of the costs they impose on society". This situation of market failure applies not only to cocaine production and trafficking but also to the production and sales of other illicit drugs.

HOW CAN ALTERNATIVE DEVELOPMENT BE CHARACTERIZED

According to one commentator, "Alternative development is an approach to policy formulation and implementation that takes into account the economic and social structures that influence illicit drug supply. This approach recognizes that in order to achieve long-run success it is necessary to integrate into the social mainstream peasants, producers and traffickers". The aim, therefore, is to combine development for drug abuse prevention and control with broader, mainstream development efforts. Alternative development programmes assist governments in finding alternative socioeconomic strategies and extending them to farmers engaged in the production of drug-producing crops that the governments want to eliminate.

These programmes "may also serve to ease, and thus help encourage, the transition of an entire country from an economic dependency on narcotics production and/or trafficking to a non-narcotics based development strategy". As broad as these programmes are, there is no single approach to alternative development suited to all countries where it may be used. Each country needs a carefully tailored strategy to fit its situation. Alternative development differs from mainstream development in that it not only indicates a process of change to strengthen the legal economy but also sets an additional goal, directing change so as to prevent or exclude illicit activities. As a response to rural poor people living in isolated areas producing plants for drugs, infrastructure development is necessary. By itself, however, increasing the infrastructure is not sufficient for successful alternative development. What happens after an area is opened by infrastructure development depends on measures designed to suppress drug production and use and enhance productivity and sustainable income for rural households.

Access to productive resources means access to inputs, markets and services. These latter objectives are frequently accomplished with coordinated agricultural development, including sustainable production, marketing and social measures that respond to potential or actual drug problems. Also normally required are credit facilities, extension services, training and information provided to farmers and campesinos. Hence, infrastructure development should be followed up by comprehensive programmes that provide projects tailored to specific needs of communities.

NECESSARY COMPONENTS AND IMPLEMENTATION

Why would a farmer grow an alternative crop knowing he will be paid less than he can get for opium, coca or cannabis? Narco-traffickers have huge profits and the flexibility to pay much more than competing buyers can pay for licit crops. On purely economic grounds, it is possible that farmers cannot make as much money, crop for crop, for coffee, fruit, nuts or other commodities as they can from cannabis, opium or coca.

The question turns on the issue of what the farmer wants and whether he sees the question solely in terms of immediate money. Hopes for realistic drug abuse control approaches to alternative development depend on the answers to this question. This recurring issue arises in rural development, where it is not always evident whether economic factors alone, or other social, moral or religious considerations, influence the behaviour of farmers, peasants and campesinos.

The rationale for alternative development involves several considerations. The first is to see the financial side of crop production as involving more than single isolated payments for drug crops as opposed to the security and stability of potential non-drug crop income over several years. By experience, farmers have their own perceptions of the risks involved. They weigh intuitively the known and potential risks and gains of one course of action, growing poppies, coca or cannabis, against the known and potential risks and gains of growing alternative crops.

What has been the experience of farmers with payments for drug crops over several seasons? How likely is it that zealous police will rip up plants or put natural predator insects in his fields to destroy crops? Non-economic concerns may also be relevant. Is the farmer afraid that his sons or daughters may become involved in the illicit drug trade or prostitution? Does he or his family have ethical or religious concerns about growing drug crops? Is he under pressure to grow these crops from criminal organizations?

In some cases, realistic planning for alternative development needs information on the views of individual farmer and how they, in fact, weigh prospects for gain from legitimate crops promoted by alternative development strategies versus drug crops. The crucial issue is the motivation of farmers and community leaders, as well as civil and military figures and government authorities. If relatively modest income is enough for these persons and they can obtain it through alternative development programmes, then the higher income of poppies or coca may not be sufficiently attractive to offset additional risks. The closed and limited market for selling illicit drugs needs to be turned to the advantage of drug control personnel and against dealers. It may be helpful to regard the farmer or campesino as a private investor who is probably risk-averse and whose primary concern is to have a decent life for himself and his family.

The self-interest of all those concerned should be assessed as part of feasibility planning in alternative development programmes since it can bring valuable insights to understanding the process of change. Alternative development programmes in rural areas may also have literacy, vocational training and health components. The combined expertise of different national and international development assistance agencies should be used to plan and implement components of integrated programmes, capitalizing on the strengths of each organization.

The combined efforts of these agencies, particularly at the international level, increase the likelihood that high-priority targets, such as women and children, will be reached. Alternative development as a strategy applies especially to producing areas where a government has access and influence, along with a political commitment, to make changes. Mobilization of resources is required and collaboration of provincial, national and international agencies is a prerequisite. Short-term aims must be distinguished from long-term goals. The outcome of such projects should be assessed in terms of measurable progress, not achievement of perfection or complete solutions.

As described in the UNDCP technical information paper, recurrence of production in zones where it had been eliminated, emergence of illicit cultivation in neighbouring zones within or across national borders and opportunistic expansion of production in new areas by criminals-all of these are to be expected. Sustainability of progress in alternative development will increase with experience, given the necessary political, financial and organizational commitments. Drug risks will remain, however: "Experience shows that without the continuation of development activities, there is an increased risk of return to illicit crops as long as there remain disparities between the former drug areas and similar areas which are more developed".

DRUG ABUSE PROBLEMS: LOSING GROUND

Over the last 30 years, awareness of illicit drugs, access to them and their abuse have dramatically increased. Despite major gaps in information, increases in the abuse of major dependenceproducing drugs are reflected in reports from official and unofficial sources. Reports from the United Nations, observations of experts, studies of crime, education, work and health - all point to serious problems in developing and industrialized countries.

Although systematic quantification of problems is not available, there is general agreement that populations at highest risk are those in the age range most needed for productive work. Other groups of people, however, are involved in substance abuse, such as street children in developing countries as well as youth elsewhere who misuse volatile solvents, thinners and marijuana. Reports from the United Nations and other sources indicate increases in drug abuse and harmful consequences in most parts of the world.

Substance-related deaths have been estimated at nearly 5 million annually for alcohol and tobacco and 200,000 annually for injecting drug abusers. Life years lost through disability related to drug dependence have been estimated for 1990 at 39.3 million years worldwide for males and 13.3 million years for females. Aggregate worldwide estimates of the burden of drug-related diseases, lost job time and the costs of other associated conditions are not available.

Due to the fact that many drug-impacted conditions were not included in this brief compilation, it is clear that figures cited here for mortality, morbidity, disability or impairment are not only incomplete but are also underestimates of the real impact of addictive disorders. Patterns of abuse in different countries show enormous variation, including different drugs abused, individuals who take drugs, various settings and a range of impacts.

A problem of major concern is the consumption of drugs in areas producing opium/heroin, coca/cocaine and cannabis. Another way of expressing this problem is in terms of a shift in consumption from developed to developing countries. To the extent that producers of these drugs are themselves regular users, they represent a permanent market: their own pattern of drug abuse ties them closely to future illicit production. This situation now exists in Pakistan, several Latin American countries and other parts of the world as well.

Compulsive or regular consumption guarantees continued production. These producers become victims of their own "success". Production and illicit traffic in opium/heroin, coca/cocaine or cannabis appear extremely high whether assessments are based on official estimates or the opinions of independent experts. Since 1989, estimates of opium production have been between 3,000 and 4,000 tonnes per year. Coca leaf, produced in fewer countries than opium, has increased since 1988, from just below 295,000 tonnes of leaf to slightly over 330,000 tonnes. While these are not precise totals of world production, they do indicate the magnitude of world supply, a first step in understanding the supply-demand equation. The magnitude should be considered in the context of commodities that may not be very large in volume but have enormously high value and unit costs. Production of both opium and coca take place in the developing world where favourable growing conditions, remoteness from the law and cheap labour are available.

Control of precursors and chemicals essential for production of illicit drugs has become increasingly difficult with more movement of people, more porous national boundaries and, in many countries, reduced government authority. Extremely high profit margins provide cash to hire new waves of couriers, finance insurgent movements, buy political protection and give financial support to terrorists. The world of illicit drug dealing is harsh and ruthlessly competitive, with marginal and incompetent dealers often eliminated by rival gangs or police action.

In sum, illicit supply and demand for drugs have surged with enormous profits for a few and modest incomes provided to others. Increased morbidity and mortality and associated family, educational and employment problems due to drug abuse are pervasive. Measures to prevent and control drug abuse are weak and the knowledge base on which these measures rest is even weaker. While it is possible that this dire picture may improve, further deterioration is more likely.

LACK OF PRODUCTIVE EMPLOYMENT AND IMPACT ON THE WORKPLACE

The workplace is part of the community, reflecting its strengths and weaknesses. With an estimated 30 per cent of the world's labour force not productively employed and young people seeking jobs faster than they are created, the ranks of the unemployed, and their problems, continue to increase. Drug abuse occurs frequently in the same age groups as those without productive work, increasing the vulnerability of this segment of the population to social problems. Drug abuse represents difficult problems for employers because they are under competitive pressure to increase output.

At the same time, these employers must respond to critical human resource issues to continue in business. Illicit drugs as well as alcohol and tobacco create significant problems in the workplace, according to recent studies and reports. Prescription drug problems, *i.e.* legal drugs used in unwise fashion or with unexpected results, are a major concern to employers, workers and enterprise representatives. Work tasks that require higher level judgement, constant attention, immediate memory and fine motor skills are easily disrupted by drugs.

Safety-sensitive jobs with immediate responsibility for the welfare of others are particularly vulnerable to drug impairment. Illicit and licit drugs may increase response time, disrupt fine motor skills and cause mood changes. Cocaine and other stimulants have the potential to induce compulsive use, disrupting work and family life. Drug abusers have more absenteeism, accidents on the job, medical claims and lost productivity than non-users. The high costs of drug abuse can be reduced by careful pre-employment appraisal, supervision on the job, periodic prevention efforts and occasional interventions as required.

IMPLICATIONS OF RURAL AND URBAN POVERTY

Although rural and urban poor are alike in that they must constantly seek the essentials of daily living, they have basically different kinds of involvement in drug problems. Rural poverty is more related to the supply of illicit drugs and urban poverty is more related to both dealing and demand. Illicit growth provides income for farmers willing to take risks for the higher gain than obtained from licit crops.

Because of the size of the shadow economy created by illicit drug money, the absorption of drugs and drug money into the fabric of society and the degree of dependence of many social and economic sectors on this relatively new income, drugs have a social significance far beyond that reflected in statistics on production, consumption or impact. Persons with marginal incomes often spend money on drugs, alcohol or tobacco instead of food, clothes and shelter. With dependence-producing drugs, sporadic use may deteriorate into regular or compulsive use, reinforcing consumption and guaranteeing a market for the supplier. When suppliers become compulsive or regular abusers, illicit growth and supply-demand patterns are more difficult to change. Poverty may change perspective so that immediate money with a risk is preferable to stable but delayed income with less risk. Development programmes should examine the behaviour of farmers and peasants, however, to determine their economic motivations rather than make assumptions about their behaviour based on theory or impressions. Reasonable assurance of a modest income over a long timespan from licit crops may be sufficient to motivate farmers to participate in alternative development programmes.

The urban poor do not have the opportunities for crop production as do the poor in remote rural areas. Urban dwellers are, however, exposed to more varieties of abuse and are more vulnerable to taking up jobs in the illicit distribution system. More negative role models and opportunities to make illicit money are found among urban than rural poor.

MARGINALIZATION

Due to its highly varied nature in different sociocultural contexts, drug abuse may be seen as normative, marginal, deviant or criminal behaviour.

Processes of marginalization apply to the behaviour of governments and communities as well as people. Large numbers of people are migrating from rural poverty to urban squalor, creating shanty towns where serious housing, health, and education problems are bred. Young people especially are vulnerable to drug abuse, especially abuse of cheap solvents, volatile substances and marijuana.

Drug subcultures rapidly develop, teaching young persons drug practices. Persons who are identified as drug abusers become more difficult to reintegrate back into the larger community. Indifference or denial to the plight of those with substance abuse disorders, whether practised by individuals, communities or governments, are common. How to avoid stereotyping and stigmatizing persons with drug problems is problematic. A start can be made by separating drug using behaviour from the person, rejecting the illegal behaviour but accepting the person for his or her human potential to follow a different path.

In the remote areas of developing countries, no authority may be present to represent the rule of law. Tribal, religious, ethnic or other groups may control a region relatively independent of national policies. In many countries, social and political institutions appear weaker now than decades ago. In extreme cases, these institutions appear under siege, having lost legitimacy and stability. When governments lose contact with people and control of the economic process, civil society is weakened. Civil frustration, violence, terrorism and corruption create conditions ripe for illicit drug growth, production and abuse and vice versa. Drugs, delinquency and crime are related in many ways.

In some cases, drug abuse may lead to crime; in others, criminal behaviour precedes drug abuse. The broader impact of drug abuse and crime may increase tension and other deviance, placing additional burdens on institutions such as the family. Drug-related crimes and terrorism cause instability and overload police, courts and prisons. Given sufficient size, drug problems may marginalize governments and institutions as well as people. In extreme cases, these problems may lead to parallel governments, where drug czars exercise enormous personal and financial power.

FUTURE CHALLENGES

With neither a single cause nor a simple cure, drug abuse and its many related problems continue to increase in many regions of the world. Problems related to the abuse of drugs are severe in some parts of both the developing and the industrialized world: disease, accidents, deaths, crime, lowered productivity and many other problems are frequently reported. Not adequately monitored, drug abuse acts as a brake on human and social development and cannot be separated from endemic problems of disease, poverty, joblessness and violence. Varying widely between countries, illicit drug use and related problems reflect several characteristics: sales of drugs are usually highly profitable and they are easily marketed commodities. Also, they have powerful effects on the brain and behaviour, influencing a wide range of human activities. Progress in the field of drug abuse prevention depends on several factors. First, our strategies to response to drug problems should begin with the people, communities and institutions involved.

People should be considered as the heart of the problem and the beginning of any solution. This principle will obviously take different forms in rural and urban areas and also be influenced by class distinctions. Secondly, alternative development strategies for rural areas should respond to the conditions found in target areas, which will differ according to the communities involved. Thirdly, as in rural settings, urban drug problems also need an individualized assessment and response, building on the strengths found on site.

To succeed, urban and rural interventions need a series of support mechanisms and long-term planning. To be effective, both need the support of the local community and a base in public policy. The concentration of drug money in the hands of a small number of persons is as important as its size. Further, people who become rich from illicit drugs, however they spend money, are not publicly accountable. The accumulation of huge sums outside the official governmental and economic structures threatens the stability of government, economic institutions and civil society.

Further, the illicit activity that produces these sums generates enormous social costs in governance, health care, crime control and integrity of public institutions and officials. Whether the resulting social costs of drug abuse and its problems are greater than any benefits of illicit funds, basic principles of social justice require that these funds not be considered the same as legitimately earned money.

By any reasoning, such illicit funds cannot be considered simply another example of the redistribution of wealth by an unsanctioned, alternate market. AIDS has changed the nature and impact of drug abuse.

In the illicit drug scene, the HIV virus is spread in two primary ways: first, contaminated needles or syringes are shared; secondly, infected injecting drug abusers may travel widely. Although heterosexual transmission is the major cause of AIDS in many countries, drug injection is widely practised and high concentrations of seropositive drug injectors exist in Africa, Asia and Latin America. Recent evidence shows that "in cities such as Bangkok and Edinburgh and in the Indian state of Manipur, HIV seroprevalence among drug users has risen from 0 to 40 per cent within two years or less".

Persons between 15 and 45 are frequently the victims of AIDS, with most deaths occurring so far, at least in Africa, among skilled workers. A growing population of young orphans and dependent, older family members will be severely affected socially and economically.

NARCOTICS-SMALL ARMS LINKAGE

Though the "cascading phenomenon" wherein the initial supplies have been controlled or funnelled through state agencies to arm non-state actors and groups, has not come to light in the north east region, there has been a massive interplay of both criminal and insurgent activities with a substantial arms base. The detection of exact linkage is further constrained by the absence of necessary databases, automation, communications and collection management necessary to improve the intelligence contribution. With the intent of developing pre-movement tactical information, detection and monitoring mission must be emphasised early by identifying the overall structure that led to the movement of narcotics.

However, this has been true equally of other countries more seriously affected by drug trafficking. J F Holden-Rhodes mentions that "one of the most difficult and continuing problems was the lack of a database to support the analysis effort. Initially, it was thought that the necessary information was held in law enforcement community files. Early examination revealed that the data contained material on US citizens which made receiving and storing it in the DIA an illegal act." Almost every state in the north-east is affected by insurgent activities.

Many parts of the northeast have been declared as "disturbed areas" under the Armed Forces Act 1958. There is an array of insurgent outfits, many of whom have emerged very recently. A brief idea about various insurgent groups and terrorist organisations operating in the region. There are a number of common features among these groups, beginning with their varied political demands starting from statehood within the constitution of India to re-demarcation of interstate borders to the expulsion of "foreigners" and outsiders.

A number of them are fighting against the Union of India and have been demanding secession from the Indian Union, some of them since preindependence times. Since most of them are well equipped in sophisticated weaponry they seldom hesitate to resort to violence particularly against the state armed forces. This violence is sometimes extended also against a particular community or a group leading to arson, destruction and mass killings.

Many of these groups are said to have been working in close co-ordination with each other within and outside the north-east. A more notable phenomenon is their links with extraterritorial forces including China and the ISI of Pakistan. The leadership of many of these outfits is known but untraceable as they are stationed outside India, in Bangladesh, Bhutan and Thailand. Many of them have resorted to large scale extraction of money from both the government and private agencies. Some of them have even been practising what they call tax collection. Most of them have been boycotting all the regular democratic processes in the respective states including the state assembly and general elections.

There are quite a few of them who have come over-ground and participated in the negotiating process. Some have even surrendered and thereafter joined mainstream political movements. There is a large quantity of modern and sophisticated small arms including AK47s and M16s in circulation in the north-east region, and generally in the hands of these insurgent groups and other non-state actors.

Many believe that unless these insurgent groups resort to smuggling and drug trafficking, they could not have mobilised resources for purchase of weapons and maintenance of their cadres. The other possible sources could be extortion or supply by inimical foreign agencies. In order to substantiate this latter contention examples are provided of the links between extraterritorial forces and insurgent groups.

As a Times of India report indicated "ULFA received arms training from Kachin Liberation Army which operates from Myanmar and later from both factions of NSCN. They have been in contact with the Bangladeshi army, Pakistan's ISI and the LTTE." But since these activities have been sustained for so many years with a lot of vicissitudes in the material situation, the major role of these external sources in funding the insurgents could be largely discounted.

It is believed that a subnationalist movement led by the ULFA gets at least 10-15% of its funds from the illegal narcotics trade. In fact, many of the prominent insurgent groups such as UNLF, NSCN and PLA have been vociferously campaigning against the drug addicts and the drug traffickers particularly in Manipur and Nagaland.

It was the PLA which imposed prohibition in January 1990, with the government announcing the prohibition immediately after.

- Their anti-drug campaign appears to be serious because they have been shooting hundreds of drug addicts and peddlers in the region in the recent years. The UNLF and PLA would first 'warn' the addicts, peddlers and traffickers to give up consumption or selling it. If their warning is ignored, the extremists would shoot them below the thigh or in the leg. The underground activists published names of drug addicts or the peddlers soon after they had 'punished' them. Their intelligence network, monitoring of persons who took heroin or sold the narcotics was far better than that of the government agencies... In fact, there has been a mass movement against drug addiction and alcoholism in the region particularly in Manipur and Nagaland... The drive launched against these social evils by underground activists was more effective than those adopted by other agencies. The armed extremists would enter the house of drug addicts or peddlers and explain to them the worst effect drug addiction or alcoholism would have on society and warn them not to take narcotics. The extremists even threatened parents if they did not keep their addicted children either at drug de-addiction centres or in jails. If the underground warnings were not heeded the extremists would 'punish' them by shooting them.

In the north-eastern region, arrests of local drug dealers are not very common or frequent. There has been occasional bursts of activity such as when several small packets of heroin were seized in Mizoram and the border was temporarily closed on the Mizoram side. Thereafter it was a return to normal. Likewise, arrests at the Myanmar border town of Tamu are not very common, even though Tamu is a major transhipment point.

In geographical areas where the presence of drug traffickers and terrorists coincided, a convergence of interests occurred for the purpose of confronting a common enemy, which was the state. However, the Indian policy of neutrality in the case of Myanmar affairs, has so far kept terrorism and drug trafficking as two separate phenomena in the region. The other part of the story is quite damning. The arms—running through the sea off the Andamans to the north-east has come to light in recent years. Apparently many of these illegal arms consignments including AK series rifles, rocket propelled grenades, night vision fitted rifles and hand grenades originating in the Far East, were meant to go to the Myanmar rebels fighting the military regime in Yangon, but are increasingly being diverted to insurgent groups in the north east including the ULFA and the NSCN.

All these arms are brought to Cox's Bazaar in Bangladesh and consignments are broken up into small caches to be carried by three different routes. A part of it goes to the Chin rebels and the rest to the north-east. This has largely gone against the counter-insurgency operations in the north-east for which over 25,000 troops are deployed at a maintenance cost close to ₹100 crore a year.

The importance of this arms-import-route was confirmed by the successful tri-service interception named "Operation Leech" on the high seas off the Andamans conducted in February 1998. "In that operation, security forces killed six gun-runners, arrested 73 others and seized a huge consignment of arms, including 140 AK47 series rifles and assorted ammunition.

The end users of this particular consignment were mainly three major groups two in the north-east and one in Myanmar— the banned NSCN, the All Tripura Tiger Force and the Chin National Army in Myanmar." The narcotics and illegal arms import connections were confirmed again in May 1998, when defence forces intercepted two more Thai trawlers near Narcodam island and seized a 50kg consignment of heroin along with an unspecified number of guns and assorted weapons.

In fact, much of this heroin was meant for European and American destinations which prompted the Narcotics Control Bureau of the USA to seek support from the Defence Services headquarters to check the flow of narcotics.

The Bhutan-Nepal area is also fast emerging as another route for the illegal trafficking of narcotics; this is confirmed by a number of big seizures in the recent past. It includes 5.25kg of cannabis seized by the Bhutanese police from the Bhutanese who were working for a Nepal-based gang in Phuentsholing.

THE OPPORTUNITIES OF A NEW AGE

In recent years, an unfortunate but perhaps inevitable underbelly of globalization has emerged to reveal increasingly adaptive individuals and groups with malevolent associations and agendas. While long the scourge of international society, a fresh crop of non-state criminal actors such as terrorists, organized criminals, pirates, and valueless international entrepreneurs in the arms and slave trade are assaulting states the world over. Many, if not all, of these powerful groups are armed with new and improved technological advances and opportunities peculiar to this age. As a result, a conundrum has arisen for international civilized society: how to counteract these transnational, non-state enemies and still remain cohesive and cooperative in the interests of international order.

At the heart of the problem, these menaces are increasingly weakening the relatively concordant spirit between states, while simultaneously strengthening their stranglehold on host nations. Meanwhile, states squabble over legal, political, and economic measures adequate to combat terrorists and criminals. One of the more sinister activities that non-state criminal actors excel in is the smuggling and trafficking of any number of goods, services, and people. While much of this illicit trade brings great misery and sorrow to many, so too does it provide jobs and buoys up sagging economies, often blending seamlessly into busy commerce.

It is this problematic dichotomy that has led to nothing short of a strategic quandary for leaders of fledgling democracies. The so-called losers of globalization are finding it tricky to survive in an increasingly competitive and interconnected world. Leaders now have to respond to citizen demands for prosperity. When it comes to the source of critical revenues, if looking the other way means vast amounts of foreign exchange will flow into the country, even if the activities involved are criminal, governments may find themselves bending to their need for political survival first and international public opinion second. Beyond this problem, the globalized world has become so complex that it may be impossible to distinguish between the various roles and relations of the actors.

States may harbor terrorists, mafia bosses may govern states, terrorists may be voted into office, criminal enterprise may be funding terrorists, and terror tactics may be used by criminals. This situation could create an atmosphere of near global anarchy. It is hardly surprising that, along with every other non-state actor, terrorists and organized crime groups have capitalized on this chaos to delve into myriad schemes for survival and prosperity.

Smuggling and trafficking, now more than ever, are booming industries. Left untended, the consequences will be long lasting and detrimental to both economic and political stability of entire regions. Borne of this realization, states have intensified cooperative multilateral and bilateral initiatives to become a unified force in the battle against international thugs and thieves. Yet there is still work to do.

To cope effectively with these complex and dangerous threats, the United States needs to tackle six significant challenges:

1. Understand the true nature of the problem
2. Resolve bureaucratic inefficiencies
3. Deal more effectively with root causes
4. Improve intelligence and law enforcement sharing
5. Close the security gaps between military, law-enforcement, and intelligence authorities in situations where their competencies overlap
6. Engage in a more comprehensive threat assessment

It is the intent of this book to address this overall need and to connect the dots between seemingly disparate threats. Examining smuggling and trafficking gives a unique perspective of the underbelly of global commerce. It further provides a glimpse of the true challenges of this era. For their part, policymakers would be well served to view national security as a continuum where there are gradations of threats that must be dealt with by all of the tools in the government's toolkit. This would mean taking new approaches to deal effectively with matters that no longer fall neatly into either the law enforcement or the defence domains exclusively.

The challenge for the U.S. Government is to address threats such as smuggling and trafficking and to formulate working relationships among agencies that meet the new reality. The terrorist attacks of September 11 only underscore the urgency of this task. Few people would have been able to predict that— in a century in which technology dominates—terrorists would use some unconventional ideas combined with very simple means to wreak significant havoc.

Nor would they have imagined the complexity of the criminal schemes and the extent of the power that organized criminal groups have developed. Combating such unpredictable behaviour will require a revolutionary examination of how the world is viewed, combined with some unconventional and innovative means on the part of the U.S. Government to counteract these menaces.

THE NEW WORLD

With the end of the Cold War and the increasing globalization of the economy, many people expected an era of peace and sustained global wellbeing to be the hallmark of the twenty-first century. The new century, however, took an unexpected turn: greater disparity of wealth and opportunity around the globe, regional instability and conflict, and the threatened failure of many states all contributed to a surprising number of transnational threats to the security of many, if not most, nations. In the United States, as policymakers were muddling their way into the global century, they often gingerly sidestepped looming issues, such as those brewing in Afghanistan and Rwanda, preferring to remain at a careful distance from unsavory situations to avoid more disasters such as Mogadishu in 1992. Arguably, this cautious detachment gradually developed into a "gap in understanding" and overall incomprehension of the magnitude of the problems that face the world. The extent to which the gap saturates the U.S. policy community and hampers the ability of many government agencies to analyse and address threats to national security correctly and adequately is a problem of immense proportions.

Issues and threats tend to be analysed and treated discretely, without seeing, or understanding, the connections between them and the fluid nature of the problems they pose. Since September 11, a great deal of catch-up in this field has transpired. Indeed, a near avalanche of bewildering and often contradictory information on terrorists and their networks has emerged. Experts and hacks alike have sifted through and analysed every available detail of terrorists' financial records, their modus operandi, childhood backgrounds, mental and emotional states of mind, religious upbringing, criminal lives, socioeconomic status, and so forth, looking for clues to answer a rather simple question: Why do they hate us?

While sociologists and psychiatrists continue to ponder the answer to this question, what is more important is to sweep aside the detritus of these studies and reveal what is being said about power and the way that has changed. That is, power has somehow morphed from something that was possessed and located within institutions to an ephemeral phenomenon wielded by individuals and arranged in rather confusing collectives of influences and pressures.

These collectives appear in varying stages of organization but are most often manifested in quasi-hierarchical yet loosely coordinated clusters of relations between primarily non-state actors. That they have all seemingly materialized from thin air in a few short decades is nothing short of alarming to conventional war fighters and traditional brokers of influence and authority in Washington, London, Paris, and, presumably, Moscow—all of whom are accustomed to the rule-laden second strike nuclear chess game of the Cold War. Yet, despite this blizzard of new information on terrorism, foreign policy has since September 11 reflected a chronic reliance on outdated and misguided conceptions of the threats to national security, driving it inexorably off course to flounder on the rocks of any number of Third World states such as Iraq. Of course, for others who follow trends in organized crime and other transnational threats, these problems have been looming for generations and, to them, the fall of the Berlin Wall was the signal that every international villain with ambition and ability would soon be vying for power in the new global disorder.

Almost 5 years after September 11, the policy gaps that mirror these gaps in understanding are slowly being closed. From the perspective of U.S. policymakers, the attacks of September 11 were a nasty jolt that irrevocably altered the perception of what and who threatens global stability. Errant individuals of indeterminate origins, loosely knit gangs of determined killers, small bands of criminal clans with extensive international connections and numerous other combinations of non-state actors, many of whom possess state-like capabilities, are proving to be elusive, sophisticated, and deadly enemies, not only in the war on terror but also for the stability of many sovereign states in a number of regions.

The actions of these groups have generated a host of problems in the economic, political, and social realms in every region where they operate, hijacking entire governments through corruption and extortion campaigns, visiting violence and terror on local populations, and distorting local economies until they are dependent on, and monopolized by, criminal enterprise. Power in the international arena has transformed from a tool of national influence to a dispersed mechanism that borders on near anarchy in any number of areas and that falls beyond the grasp of states to manage. Much of this may be attributable to globalization, which has brought with it the good, the bad, and the ugly. Along with the rapid movements of people, money, and information have come the criminals, terrorists, and thugs who cross international frontiers undetected, who peddle human beings, who sell weapons intended for mass murder, who conduct illicit monetary transactions in mere minutes, and who may carry disease and death in a suitcase. By exporting capitalism and democracy to the world, the West did not envision that free trade would be twisted by rogues who understand that the new world order is less orderly and more anarchical than before.

Indeed, the anarchy that is perpetuated by the international free market has afforded villains more opportunity and maneuverability than at almost any time since the Treaties of Westphalia. Today, prowess is measured by guile and stealth, the ability to suborn and to distort, and the ability to buy and sell any merchandise for which there is a market. No longer can domestic security or even law and order, be conceptualized as something distinct from national security and international armed conflict.

There has been a fundamental shift in the international strategic environment, and criminal actors with ideological purpose now threaten the national security of states. Meeting this challenge will require changing the approaches of both law enforcement and the national security establishment. Both currently sit at opposite ends of the security continuum in many countries.

Closing the gap between them must occur if global terrorism and organized criminal activity is to be successfully combated.

SMUGGLING AND TRAFFICKING AS SECURITY THREATS

Most smuggling activities may not appear as overly menacing in relation to wars, genocide, and other atrocities that the world continues to witness. Indeed, if one were to consider the intrastate smuggling of cigarettes within the United States, it might appear to deprive state authorities of tax revenue, which people often find amusing. What is not amusing is that even cigarette smuggling has a sinister side. For example, Hezbollah ran a complex cigarette-smuggling scheme in North Carolina from 1996 until the summer of 2000, when 18 members of the ring were apprehended.

Among other things, proceeds from this scheme purchased night-vision goggles, cameras and scopes, surveying equipment, global positioning systems, mine and metal detection equipment, video equipment, advanced aircraft analysis and design software, laptop computers, stun guns, radios, mining, drilling and blasting equipment, radars, ultrasonic dog repellers, and laser range finders. Other forms of smuggling and trafficking are more egregious still.

Human trafficking, which often means slavery, has long been considered a legacy banished centuries ago. However, today both of these anachronisms have managed to reappear and flourish. Trafficking in human life not only is increasing in frequency but also continues to exact a terrible toll on its victims, stripping them of liberty and visiting upon them humiliation, suffering, torture, and other outrageous violations of human rights. It is the fastest growing criminal enterprise in the world, which only shows how dispensable human life remains in an era of globalization and democratization.

In almost every region of the world, human trafficking has become a more attractive business prospect than other forms of smuggling and trafficking because it does not require technical expertise or a distribution network as do other highly profitable enterprises, such as narcotics and smuggling of military hardware. Furthermore, in many countries, the penalties for trafficking in persons are significantly lower than they are for narcotics. Malaysia, for example, provides the death penalty for drug trafficking—but has a maximum penalty of 15 years for human trafficking. Much of this trade involves the abduction or fraudulent recruitment of women and children for the purposes of the sex industry, domestic servitude, and sweatshop labour.

This tends to raise a plethora of gender issues, making it a problem that is almost taboo for some cultures to tackle and one to which others pay too little attention because of gender stereotyping. The traffic in illicit drugs is also a grave threat to international security. The illegal narcotics business is estimated to be the second largest industry in the world, meeting the demand of between 3 and 4 per cent of the world's population. The obscene profits that flow from the illicit drug trade rival the gross national product of many countries. Moreover, these profits are sufficient to undermine legitimate commerce and a nation's balance of payments and monetary system, as well as to jeopardize international bank cooperation. The drugs that end up on the streets undermine social order, contribute to diseases, spark poverty for many, and often lead to the breakdown of justice systems. The profits from the traffic of illicit narcotics have enabled drug traffickers to become increasingly adept at suborning, undermining, and threatening entire governments and, thereby, not only elude law enforcement efforts but also conduct their activities with relative impunity.

Moreover, drug trafficking activity is more than ever what former U.S. Drug Czar William Bennett termed a "clear and present danger to the national security of the United States," if not the world. This danger increases exponentially as many of the most powerful terrorist groups are now engaging in drug trafficking to fund terrorist operations. Meanwhile, the traffic in small arms amounts to somewhere between $1 billion and $4 billion per year and contributes to seemingly intractable and bloody conflicts that have continued unchecked for decades.

The spread of arms is a catalyst for further and more intense conflict in regions such as sub-Saharan Africa where protracted ethnic strife has spread from within single states to inundate entire regions in genocidal rampages. The arms are often circulated from one war zone to another, stoking conflicts wherever they arise. With mass killing comes stymied economic growth, the spread of disease, mass starvation, mass migrations, and the use of child soldiers.

The tragedy in Darfur is only the latest in generations of wars fueled by small arms trafficking. The trafficking in higher-end arms, such as nuclear, biological, or chemical weapons, has far-reaching and nightmarish consequences. In terms of nuclear smuggling, availability of materials and the intentions of the end user dictate the nature of the threat. While great fear is generated by the chance that a nuclear weapon will be smuggled into the wrong hands, the probability is low. More probable scenarios are the smuggling of nuclear materials or components used to make weapons.

In 2003, the smuggling network of the infamous "godfather" of Pakistan's nuclear weapon's programme, A.Q. Khan, was revealed to have been selling nuclear components to Libya, which led to speculation of other similar marketplaces such as North Korea, Iran, Iraq, and Syria. Whether all the components were to land in the hands of state authorities is another question altogether. Biological weapons contain living or viral organisms, or the toxins produced by them, to kill or incapacitate.

Some toxins cause death within minutes or hours, while bacteria and viruses usually require an incubation period of at least 24 hours before symptoms appear. Chemical weapons include nerve and cyanide gases and more plebian toxic industrial chemicals such as chlorine. The proliferation of both chemical and biological weapons has increased since the termination of chemical/biological programme in a number of countries, most significantly in some of the client states of the former Soviet Union. It is unknown precisely what chemical or biological agents terrorist groups may have in their possession. The al Qaeda videotapes documenting the testing of poison gas on three dogs confirmed that the group had been experimenting with chemical weapons. The use of sarin gas in the Tokyo subway in 1995 by Aum Shinrikyo, killing twelve and leaving approximately 5,000 with damaged health, demonstrates that this kind of attack could be easily repeated in virtually any major city. The traffic in other commodities represent large criminal enterprises the world over. The trade in the now notorious "blood diamonds" has been well documented as a funding source for such deliberate bloodbaths in places as Sierra Leone, Liberia, Angola, Guinea, and the Democratic Republic of Congo.

In Sierra Leone, the country's 10-year civil war was significantly fueled by the smuggling of diamonds. In a bid for control of the country's rich diamond fields, the Revolutionary United Front rebel group waged a brutal campaign against the government. Employing a combination of guerrilla, criminal, and terror tactics, they systematically murdered, tortured, and mutilated tens of thousands of civilians to win the advantage. To fund their campaign, the rebels traded in illegally mined diamonds, often dumping them below fair market value.

The diamonds were subsequently smuggled to international diamond markets in places such as Antwerp, Belgium, to be sold at unseemly profits. Al Qaeda has also been involved in smuggling diamonds as a way of moving money to fund operations around the world. Along with gold, which can be melted down, diamonds are practically untraceable and can be readily sold for cash just about anywhere.

Moreover, due to the increasingly successful interdiction of illegal monetary transactions by law enforcement, terrorists and criminal groups have been driven further underground or towards more sophisticated methods for moving their money.

The underground money exchange system in South Asia has been used extensively, as have other alternate specie such as gold and diamonds. Gems are easy to hide, generally maintain their value, and are untraceable for the most part. Gold is often used by hawaladars to balance accounts. Its origins are also untraceable because it can be smelted, made into jewelry, and reconstituted in a variety of forms. Gold is probably more easily manipulated than are gems because it can be deposited on account without a transaction report. There has always been incentive for just about everyone in society to be complicit in such illegal trade: from consumers who prefer the better/lower priced goods, to smugglers who make a large profit, to middlemen and authorities with their propensity for bribery and corruption. Even in countries such as the United

Kingdom and the United States, consumers save money when and where they can. In the United Kingdom, it is estimated that approximately one-third of the cigarettes smoked are imported illegally. Smuggling in counterfeit goods has exploded in recent years. In June 2006, trade representatives from the European Union met with U.S. trade representatives to intensify efforts across the Atlantic to stop counterfeit goods trafficking. The overwhelming majority of these goods are consumer luxury items, such as Gucci handbags, Rolex watches, and Louis Vuitton luggage.

A sobering statistic is that along with the seemingly harmless counterfeiting of luxury items there has been an egregious global trade in counterfeit pharmaceuticals: an estimated 10 per cent of all the medicines traded globally are counterfeit. For instance, criminal groups have exploited the market for a drug based on the Chinese plant Artemesinin.

It is the only drug left available that resists the malaria parasite. To realise windfall profits, criminals have diluted the drug to the point that it is inevitable that the parasite will soon be able to resist Artemesinin. In a world where malaria accounts for some 350 to 500 million malaria illnesses annually—of which more than a million end in death—this is not simply a trade in counterfeit snake-oil remedies; it is trade in human misery and poses a potential catastrophic transnational health threat.

7

Terrorism, Cyber Surveillance and National Security

INTRODUCTION

The modern concept of "national security" and the electronic digital computer are roughly the same age, both products of World War II. ENIAC, the world's first digital electronic computer, went into service at the University of Pennsylvania in 1946. The U.S., government's Central Intelligence Agency and National Security Agency were launched a year later, authorised by the National Security Act. Until relatively recently, national security and computers enjoyed a symbiotic relationship, too.

Until the mid-1960s, perhaps even later, the chief U.S., government agencies responsible for national security were also the chief catalysts and funders for computer research, and also the largest customers of the computer industry. Indeed, the appearance of the digital computer even shaped the strategy of national security in the United States, as more and more national security planning became dependent on computer-based models using techniques of systems analysis and operations research.

One might even argue that this symbiotic relationship between computers and national security is the primary bearer and symbol of U.S., power in the latter half of the twentieth century, even more so than nuclear weapons. Computer technology is still important to national security, perhaps of paramount importance. Without computers, modern arsenals and "battle management" and communications would be impossible. The future appears to belong to so-called "smart" weapons, complex systems of command and control, telecommunications, satellites, electronic surveillance, and split-second information processing. The end of the Cold War has appeared to speed up the process of integrating advanced computers into weapons and command systems, rather than slow it down.

The United States' overwhelming superiority in information technologies is the key to its superpower status for the foreseeable future. But a new phenomenon is the threat to national security posed by networked computers, particularly through the Internet. This is accompanied by more than a small amount of irony, as the Internet was, for decades, a project of the U.S., Department of Defence.

For a long time, during the period when the Internet was used almost exclusively by scientists, engineers, academics, and a handful of military personnel, the Internet was viewed by experts mainly as a benign and interesting research project, one with modest and limited application to national security objectives. But in the 1990s, and especially in the past two to three years, the Internet has increasingly been regarded by national security officials as a new playing field for international conflict, a new medium in which national security will take on new forms, and one in which the U.S., government agencies responsible for national security have a growing stake. High officials of the CIA, the National Security Agency, the FBI, the White House, and other, less well-known agencies now believe that the Internet is a "critical national asset" that requires their attention and protection.

This may signal a new era in the development of the Internet, equal in importance to its commercial potential. In fact, the commercial use of the Internet may be influenced by national security controversies as much as by consumer response to new Internet applications. This chapter will review this controversy, looking first at the history of the Internet's relationship to national security, then providing an overview of the new landscape now that the Internet is increasingly embedded in "critical national infrastructure." The concept of "infowar," or "cyberwar," will be described, along with the attendant difficulties of assessing computer-based threats to national assets. Finally, the chapter will offer some thoughts on what this new phenomenon might mean for the future development of the Internet, what strategies policymakers and technology experts should consider, and what dangers lie ahead for democracy and public policy.

CYBER TERRORISM

As a result of globalisation, computerisation and the emergence of a network society, numerous authors have argued that cyber terrorism is becoming increasingly attractive to terrorists for several reasons. First, cyber terrorism is generally perceived to be more cost-effective than traditional terrorist methods. Typical computers and phone or broadband internet connections are generally much cheaper and easier to acquire than traditional types of weaponry, such as explosives and military-grade vehicles. Cyber terrorist attacks also do not result in the attacker's death, as is the case with suicide bombers, and as is potentially the case in traditional acts of terrorism.

Second, cyber terrorism possesses a certain amount of anonymity not found in more traditional forms of terrorism. The global extension of computer technologies in post-industrial societies has facilitated terrorist mobility and deployability. As such, it has become increasingly difficult for security agencies to determine the real identities of the terrorists. This complex obstacle is further enhanced by the lack of customs, borders or checkpoints within cyber space. While the fact remains that all Internet traffic passes through at least one of thirteen central servers that act as the foundation of the World Wide Web, the sheer amount of information transferred creates considerable challenges for data analysis and effective intelligence collection.

Third, the quantity and quality of targets increases as society moves towards further dependence on information technologies. The multiplicity of potential targets is already enormous, ranging from government military systems to civilian economic and scientific networks.

Fourth, cyber terrorism removes or reduces the requirement for geographical proximity to the target. This virtually eliminates the traditional requirements for physical and psychological training to avoid capture, and risk of mortality. The ability to conduct cyber terrorism remotely is a key factor in the transnational nature of committing terrorist acts and in recruiting new members.

Fifth, cyber terrorism can potentially have a direct affect on a larger number of people than traditional terrorist methods, thereby generating widespread effects and increasing awareness of particular causes. While a suicide bomber may destroy a building, killing the tens or hundreds of individuals inside, a cyber terrorist attack on a waste-management or energy system has the potential to kill or injure thousands, if not millions of people.

IS THERE A REAL THREAT

It should be emphasised that no single cyber terrorist attack has been recorded – that is, categorised as such. This begs the question of whether cyber terrorism is a real threat. Current discussions revolve around military systems, intelligence networks, government systems and critical infrastructure. First, suggestions have been put forth that cyber terrorists could compromise military systems, such as a nuclear missile launch facility, and either launch a missile or disable the entire system.

Currently, the cyber terrorism threat of this type is non-existent. Government statements indicate that major military systems, such as the Canadian Department of National Defence, the Pentagon, and nuclear launch facilities, are "air-gapped". That is, they are not physically connected to external networks such as the Internet. The implied conclusion is that computer network attacks would be ineffective against these types of military networks.

However, during a U.S., military exercise conducted by the National Security Agency (NSA), attackers using tools available on the Internet were able to gain access to several key U.S., systems. While the details remain classified, the report on the exercise concluded that military infrastructure could be disrupted and troop deployments could be hindered. Most security and intelligence systems are also protected in the same way as military infrastructure.

The Canadian Security and Intelligence Service (CSIS), the Central Intelligence Agency (CIA) and the Federal Bureau of Investigation (FBI) all utilise stand-alone networks. Martin Libicki, a defence analyst at the National Defence University and RAND Corporation, indicates that this is partially rooted in the general paranoia that exists within intelligence agencies, and that such paranoia is a sound governing principle when considering cyber security. Like most military systems, security and intelligence systems in their current form are shielded from computer attack. More general government systems, in both the United States and in Canada, are further protected by the development of proprietary systems, unique to each branch of government. While this has often led to difficulties in cooperation between agencies, it has also provided protection in that only a select few individuals understand the systems well enough to violate them. In an ironic twist, inefficiency breeds security.

While government systems may be connected to external networks, such as the Internet, the proprietary nature of current computer applications in combination with screening processes for new employees ensures a relatively high level of security from the cyber terrorist threat. Critical infrastructure consists of less-protected secondary targets, such as power grids, oil pipelines, water-treatment and waste-management systems. Particularly in the United States, most of these systems are privatised and are not currently as of much a concern as military or government systems. As such, critical infrastructure systems are less secure than military, intelligence or government systems.

Concerns over the susceptibility of U.S., critical infrastructure are significant to Canadians due to the numerous connections between Canadian and U.S., systems. Additionally, 85 per cent of Canada's critical infrastructure is owned by stake holders other than the federal government. However, while critical infrastructure is possibly more vulnerable to cyber terrorism, it is still quite secure. These systems are under constant threat from natural disasters such as hurricanes, floods or tornados, and company employees are trained to act in emergency scenarios.

Nonetheless, as a consequence of openness to external networks and lower security thresholds, a cyber terrorist threat to critical infrastructure does exist. Cyber attacks differ from traditional emergencies and natural disasters in that they can be directed and concentrated at specific weak points in a computer network. Attackers were also able to gain access to power grid and emergency systems, resulting in service disruptions. Currently, it seems as though the greatest threat to the aforementioned systems comes not from cyber terrorism, but from two other factors: insider action and deregulation. Insiders possess specialised knowledge that is difficult, if not impossible, for outsiders to acquire. Disgruntled staff or vengeance-seeking former employees may possess both the resolve and the means to wreak havoc on internal computer and information systems. For example, in 2000, a disgruntled consultant hacked into a waste management control system and let loose millions of gallons of raw sewage on the town. While this potential problem may be alleviated through comprehensive employee screening processes, such security measures may be decreasingly feasible as a result of deregulation.

Second, deregulation potentially leads to an increased risk of cyber terrorism. An amplified focus on profitability has forced utility companies and other critical infrastructure businesses to move increasing proportions of their operations to the Internet in search of greater efficiency and lower costs. This may result in further risk and exposure to cyber terrorist threats.

Growing cross-border interdependency will play an increasingly important role in the vulnerability of vital networks. For example, strong links between Canadian and U.S., critical infrastructure were demonstrated during the 2003 Canada-U.S., blackout, in which a transformer station in Cleveland malfunctioned, causing power outages affecting 40 million people in Canada and the north-western United States.

In sum, despite current concerns over the vulnerabilities of military, security and intelligence, government and critical infrastructure systems, the nature of these systems currently suggests that such concerns are generally unfounded, though a potential threat is present. While dangers to critical infrastructure systems exist, in the form of insider action and deregulation, a "digital Pearl Harbour" has yet to occur.

AN EXAGGERATED THREAT

The relatively insignificant threat of a cyber terrorist attack brings forth the question of why the threat is exaggerated. The reasons behind this are four-fold. First, as Dorothy E. Denning, a professor of computer science speaking before the U.S., House Armed Services Committee, has observed, "cyber terrorism and cyber attacks are sexy right now. It's novel, original, it captures people's imagination".

As such, the concept of cyber terrorism has symbolic power that creates compelling and frightening scenarios, influencing perceptions and contributing to the remaining three reasons below. In addition to the symbolic impact of cyber terrorism, the mass media frequently fail to distinguish between hacktivism and cyber terrorism, often exaggerating the threat of the latter. The two are not analogous. Additionally, misunderstandings between computer crime and cyber terrorism have also surfaced. Ambiguity about the very meaning of "cyber terrorism" has confused the public and given rise to many misrepresentations.

Third, there is a general fear of the unknown. Despite the advent of Third Wave society, many people, including most lawmakers and government officials, still do not fully understand and therefore tend to fear both computer technology and terrorism. As a result, psychological distress and the desire for self-preservation increase the likelihood of accepting unnecessary measures to combat an exaggerated threat.

Fourth, some groups are eager to exploit this ignorance. National security officials are inclined to take measures to increase their presence and influence in government, while the computer technology industry, still recovering from the collapse of the high-tech bubble, seeks to regain its economic foothold.

Any response to a cyber terrorist threat requires enhanced technology, training and maintenance. Some politicians have "played the role of prophets of doom", purposely stoking fears of cyber terrorism, whether out of genuine conviction or from a desire to create public anxiety in order to advance a political agenda. While the potential threat of cyber terrorism is currently exaggerated, many analysts predict an increase in the actual threat. Looking at the various trends in military transformation, technological innovation and terrorist sophistication, the threat of cyber terrorism and computer-based attacks in expected to increase in the future for three principal reasons. First, the next generation of terrorists is now growing up in an increasingly digital world, alongside or integrated into post-industrial society, and will therefore be progressively more proficient in the use of information and computer technologies.

An example of recent activity, though not classified as cyber terrorism, is *Titan Rain,* the name given to a series of attacks against the U.S., since, 2003, in which the networks at Lockheed martin and NASA were infiltrated. Second, cyber terrorism may also become more attractive as the real and virtual worlds become more closely coupled. Increasing demands for efficiency and interoperability in critical infrastructure, government systems and potentially intelligence systems will ultimately result in elevated degrees of exposure to outside networks, and therefore cyber terrorist attacks. For example, the push by the U.S., military towards the network-centric warfare doctrine has resulted in new attempts at military transformation and integration.

The Global Information Grid, which seeks to encompass the end-to-end set of information capabilities, is a primary example. In terms of supervisory control and data acquisition (SCADA) systems, they are no longer only on stand-alone networks – connections between SCADA systems via the Internet are perceived as better for business. While SCADA systems are solely for the management and supervision of critical infrastructure (such as power-grid systems), their intentional or unintentional misuse can still cause damage. During a no-notice exercise performed by the U.S., Department of Defence, operators at a power management station were fooled by manipulated SCADA data into taking actions that would have damaged the system. Third, success in the "war on terror" on the traditional battlefield may result in terrorists turning increasingly towards unconventional weapons such as cyber terrorism. The cost-effectiveness (in both human and economic terms), anonymity, abundance of critical targets and geographical freedom provide several incentives for terrorists to experiment with this new method. As such, while the current conjecture regarding the cyber terrorist threat is exaggerated, the expected increase in cyber terrorist activity demands that legal and technological remedies be explored.

FEDERAL GOVERNMENT EFFORTS TO ADDRESS CYBER TERRORISM

A number of U.S. government organizations appear to monitor terrorist websites and conduct a variety of activities aimed at countering them. Given the sensitivity of federal government Programmes responsible for monitoring and infiltrating websites suspected of supporting terrorismrelated activities, much of the information regarding the organizations and their specific activities is deemed classified or law enforcement-sensitive and is not publicly available. The information listed below represents a sampling of what has been publicly discussed about some of the federal government organizations responsible for monitoring and infiltrating jihadist websites.

It should be noted that the actions associated with the organizations listed below could be conducted by employees of the federal government or by civilian contract personnel.

- *Central Intelligence Agency (CIA)*: development, surveillance, and analysis of websites, commonly referred to as honey pots, for purposes of attracting existing and potential jihadists searching for forums to discuss terrorism-related activities.
- *National Security Agency (NSA)*: surveillance of websites and rendering them inaccessible.
- *Department of Defence (DOD):* surveillance of websites focused on discussions of perceived vulnerabilities of overseas U.S. military facilities or operational capabilities and disabling those that present a threat to operations.
- *Department of Justice (DOJ)*: development of polices and guidelines for creating, interacting within, surveilling, and rendering inaccessible websites created by individuals wishing to use the Internet as a forum for inciting or planning terrorism-related activities.
- *Federal Bureau of Investigation (FBI)*: monitoring of websites and analysis of information for purposes of determining possible terrorist plans and threats to U.S. security interests.
- *Department of Homeland Security (DHS)*: monitoring of websites and

analysis of information for purposes of determining possible threats to the homeland.

Numerous other federal government organizations have cyber security responsibilities focused on policy development, public awareness campaigns, and intergovernmental and private sector coordination efforts. Information gleaned from the agencies may at times be used to help inform and advise non-federal government entities responsible for safeguarding a geographic area or activity that has been discussed in an online jihadist forum.

FEDERAL GOVERNMENT MONITORING AND RESPONSE

A number of reasons exist that may provide justification for the federal government to monitor websites owned, operated, or frequented by individuals suspected of supporting international jihadist activity that pose a threat to U.S. security interests.

Such websites may be used for purposes of spreading propaganda, recruiting new members or enticing existing participants, communicating plans counter to U.S. interests, or facilitating terrorist-related activities. Quite often the jihadist websites are the first indicators of extreme elements of the jihadist community identifying a controversial issue for purposes of inciting action harmful to U.S. interests. For example, a recent controversy in the United States about a proposed burning of copies of the Quran on the ninth anniversary of the September 11, 2001, attacks led to increased chatter on international jihadist websites. The FBI reportedly disseminated an intelligence bulletin specifically noting online threats to the pastor and church planning to conduct this event and more general threats to U.S. global interests. When assessing whether to monitor, infiltrate, or shut down a Web site suspected of inciting participants to take harmful actions against U.S. security interests, numerous competing interests should be considered. First, the federal government would determine whether the Web site is owned by a U.S. corporation and whether U.S. citizens may be participating in the Internet forum. Such a determination is necessary to ensure that proper procedures are adhered to with respect to upholding the rights afforded by the U.S. Constitution's First and Fourth Amendments, in particular.

Second, once it is confirmed that a suspected jihadist Web site is being used to facilitate terrorism-related activities, the national security community may consider the short- and long-term implications of a variety of operational responses. Options include permanently or temporarily shutting down the Web site, passively monitoring the Web site for intelligence-gathering purposes, or covertly engaging the members of the forum with the desire to elicit additional information for purposes of thwarting a potential terrorism-related activity and/or building a stronger criminal case. Different agencies may weigh each option differently, creating a need to achieve interagency consensus prior to action.

DOD has been considering establishing a computer network monitoring database for government and private networks. Organizations would provide information on a voluntary basis, and the data collected would be shared with all participants. However, privacy concerns and questions of DOD's proper role in federal cyber security make the implementation of such a Programme unlikely in the current political climate.

A memorandum of agreement signed in October 2010 between DHS and DOD represents an effort to increase coordination of operations and plans to protect civilian critical infrastructure as well as military networks. The partnership could be used as a means through which DOD would have a greater role in defending privately owned critical infrastructure using the EINSTEIN 2 and 3 network monitoring systems developed by DHS.

COUNTERPROPAGANDA

In common parlance and in media reporting, the terms "strategic communications," "public diplomacy," "global engagement," "information operations," and "propaganda" are often used interchangeably. This confusion in terms makes it difficult to determine exactly what sorts of programmatic activities are being discussed. There is no overarching definition of strategic communications for the federal government.

DOD has defined strategic communication as "focused United States Government efforts to understand and engage key audiences to create, strengthen, or preserve conditions favorable for the advancement of United States government interests, policies, and objectives through the use of coordinated Programmes, plans, themes, messages, and products synchronised with the actions of all instruments of national power." This term, as defined, describes a U.S. government-wide process, not an organizational structure, capability, or discrete activity within DOD or any other government agency.

As prescribed by the 2009 National Framework for Strategic Communication, the Deputy National Security Advisor for Strategic Communications (DNSA/SC) serves as the National Security Advisor's principal advisor for strategic communications. The Senior Director for Global Engagement (SDGE) is the principal deputy to the DNSA/SC.

Together, they are responsible for ensuring that

- The message-value and communicative impact of actions are considered during decision-making by the National Security Council (NSC) and Homeland Security Council (HSC);
- The mechanisms to promote strategic communication are in place within the National Security Staff (NSS); and
- Similar mechanisms are developed across the interagency.

The DNSA/SC and SDGE are also responsible for guiding and coordinating interagency deliberate communication and engagement efforts, and they execute this responsibility through the NSS Directorate for Global Engagement (NSS/GE) and through the Interagency Policy Committee (IPC) on Strategic Communication. Public Diplomacy (PD) within the State Department is led by the Under Secretary for Public Diplomacy and Public Affairs.

The Department of State distinguishes between Public Affairs (PA), which includes outreach to domestic publics, and PD—which seeks to promote the national interest of the United States through understanding, engaging, informing, and influencing foreign publics, and by promoting mutual understanding between the people of the United States and people from other nations around the world. In DOD, strategic communication-related activities are primarily supported by the integration of three capabilities: Information Operations (IO), and, primarily within IO, Psychological Operations (PSYOP), Public Affairs (PA), and Defence Support to Public Diplomacy (DSPD). Military Diplomacy (MD) and Visual Information (VI) also support strategic communicationsrelated activities.

DOD sees strategic communications as a process to synchronise efforts that:

- Improve U.S. credibility and legitimacy;
- Weaken an adversary's credibility and legitimacy;
- Convince selected audiences to take specific actions that support U.S. or international objectives;
- Cause a competitor or adversary to take (or refrain from taking) specific actions.

Many DOD activities support the State Department's public diplomacy efforts and objectives, which in turn support national objectives. DOD refers to these activities as "Defence Support to Public Diplomacy" (DSPD). Although some reports warn of social media's potential misuse by terrorists, government policies are evolving to embrace the use of tools such as Facebook and Twitter as a means of strategic communications and public diplomacy. On the one hand, social media tools such as Twitter and Facebook can be used by terrorist groups to expand networks and exchange real-time information, enabling operatives to organise and act quickly. These tools can not only spread propaganda, but can also host embedded malicious software in links and applications that can corrupt an unsuspecting user's electronic device.

Based on these security concerns, several services and offices within DOD had banned certain social networking sites from access on their unclassified networks. However, the federal government has begun to embrace using these same tools to allow free access to information, spread democratic values and ideas, and combat the misinformation spread by terrorist groups' media campaigns. In February 2010, DOD issued a directive-type memo (DTM) outlining the department's new social media policy, citing Internet-based capabilities including social networking services as integral to operations.

This policy is due to expire in March 2011; reportedly, there are no plans to develop a replacement policy, nor plans to fill the top positions that were instrumental in creating the social media policy. Some fear that the recent WikiLeaks issue may push the pendulum back Towards more restricted access to Internet-based capabilities and less information sharing between organizations.

Others note that, to date, much of the activity conducted under the current policy has been one-sided, focused on using social network tools to gather information about others, including potential adversaries, rather than to send messages outward in order to shape the information environment. Reportedly, the U.S. Air Force and U.S. Central Command have been developing deceptive identities on the Internet in order to infiltrate chat rooms and other social media using a special software. The U.S., Air Force software contract states that it shall be used to target adversarial sites worldwide without detection, and spokesmen for the U.S. Central Command have stated that it shall not be used to target law-abiding American citizens. Critics of these Programmes point to the potential loss of credibility, a tenet of successful information operations, using the former Office of Strategic Influence (OSI) as an example. Reports that the OSI was planting false news stories into foreign newspapers to gain support for the war in Iraq led many—including the Public Affairs Office—to question the legality of such activity. The OSI was subsequently disestablished.

DEPARTMENT OF DEFENCE OFFENSIVE RESPONSE

Information operations do not refer exclusively to messaging and content; another integrated capability within this area is computer network operations (CNO), which includes cyberattack capabilities, cyber espionage and exploitation, and cyber Defence. The Joint Functional Command Component—Network Warfare (JFCC-NW) and the JFCC—Space and Global Strike (JFCC-SGS) have responsibility for overall DOD cyber security, while the Joint Task Force—Global Network Operations (JTF-GNO) and the Joint Information Operations Warfare Center (JIOWC) both have direct responsibility for Defence against cyberattack.

The DOD focal point for coordinating military information operations is the JIOWC. The JTF-GNO defends the DOD Global Information Grid, while the JIOWC assists combatant commands with an integrated approach to information operations. These include operations security, military information support operations (formerly psychological operations), military deception, and electronic warfare. Many of the specific Programmes under the JIOWC's purview are classified.

The JIOWC also coordinates computer network operations and network warfare with the JTF-GNO and with JFCC-NW. These latter two organizational activities are to fall under the responsibility of the newly formed U.S. Cyber

Command (USCYBERCOM), a sub-unified command under U.S. Strategic Command (USSTRATCOM). The commander of USCYBERCOM, General Keith Alexander, also serves as the director of NSA.

Traditionally, the NSA mission has been information assurance for national security systems and signals intelligence, and gathering information about potential threats under the Foreign Intelligence Surveillance Act (FISA). The dual-hatted nature of this appointment places this intelligence function alongside the offensive operations command. Information security and cyberwarfare planners in the Pentagon have noted both in doctrine and in informal channels that a good offensive cyber operations capability is the best Defence.

For this reason, USCYBERCOM has integrated the military's defensive computer network operations components with its offensive arm under one joint command. Many of USCYBERCOM's capabilities are unknown, due to the classified nature of offensive cyber operations. There have also been questions in the executive branch and in Congress about what authorities they operate under and how oversight is to be conducted.

A question-and-answer exchange from the Senate Armed Services Committee revealed that DOD had not included cyber operations in its quarterly report on clandestine military activities. Michael Vickers, the nominee for Undersecretary of Defence for Intelligence, reportedly told the committee that those quarterly reporting requirements related only to human intelligence. How USCYBERCOM relates to NSA and how both relate to the private sector, which owns most of the U.S. telecommunications infrastructure, has been a continued subject of discussions.

On the defensive side, although USCYBERCOM is developing plans to defend the.mil domain, there is still no unified federal response policy for coordinating offensive cyber operations at the national level. Yet DOD has been working with DHS and the National Cyber security and Communications Integration Center through Cyberstorm and other exercises to map out a National Cyber Incident Response Plan, which gives a structure for how the federal government might respond in the event of a major cyberattack. At a Reserve Officers Association conference, USCYBERCOM Chief of Staff Major General David Senty said that the sub-unified command might take the lead in defending the nation's military networks as a "supported command" prior to "turning things over" to U.S. Northern Command.

FEDERAL GOVERNMENT CHALLENGES AND IMPLICATIONS

Although organizations, policies, and plans exist to counter violent extremists' use of the Internet, implementation may be hampered by several factors. Laws may be interpreted by some agencies to prohibit certain activities, and in some cases agencies may have competing equities at stake.

Legislative and policy authority may be given to organizations that lack the technical capability to fulfill a mission, while entities with the capacity to address cyber attacks may be legally constrained from doing so due to privacy or civil liberties concerns. There may be tensions between the Global Internet Freedom Initiative as highlighted by Secretary of State Hillary Clinton and overall counterterrorism objectives. Additionally, the lack of clarity in definitions related to information operations and terrorism may lead to institutional questions such as which agency has the lead for federal government coordination or independent oversight.

INSTITUTIONAL CONSTRAINTS

Some argue that the effectiveness of the U.S. government's strategic communications, information operations, and global engagement Programmes is still hampered by the U.S. Information and Educational Exchange Act of 1948, also known as the Smith-Mundt Act. The law directs that information about the United States and its policies intended for foreign audiences "shall not be disseminated within the United States, its territories, or possessions."

Amendments to the Smith-Mundt Act in 1972 and 1998 further clarified the legal obligations of the government's public diplomacy apparatus, and several presidential directives, including NSPD-16 in July 2002, have set up specific structures and procedures as well as further legal restrictions regarding U.S. public diplomacy and information operations. Some say that these policies have created an unnecessary "firewall" between domestic and foreign audiences, limiting what information the United States produces and distributes to counter extremists in cyberspace for fear of "blow-back" to its own citizens. Cyberspace as a global domain does not recognise territorial boundaries, making it difficult to target a specific geographic region. Some argue that this has effectively created a ban on all government "propaganda," a term that carries with it negative historical connotations, although the term is neither defined nor mentioned in the law itself.

Some critics argue that the law does not prevent government propagandizing, but rather has been consistently misinterpreted. Others maintain that the Smith-Mundt provisions may prevent undue government manipulation of citizens and are a necessary protection. In addition to questions over what constitutes propaganda and the applicability of Smith-Mundt, confusion over "information operations" Programmes has led some to question their budgetary process and management within DOD.

Often confused with Information Operations as a whole, PSYOP refers to influence activities specifically intended "to induce or reinforce foreign attitudes and Behaviour in a manner favorable to U.S. objectives." While PSYOP is focused at audiences abroad, it is supported by the public affairs function. The Public Affairs Office (PAO) is the entity responsible for working with media outlets both domestic and foreign, to "inform" rather than to "influence." Given the public's and government's aversion to the term "propaganda" and particularly military activities that might be described as such, DOD has changed military lexicon from PSYOP to Military Information Support Operations (MISO). The Secretary of Defence approved the name change in June 2010 following a recommendation from the Defence Senior Leadership Council. Some argue that the name change elevates the importance of information support to military operations for commanders in the field, while others point to the traditional career field of PSYOP as a source of pride among its servicemembers. A January 2011 memorandum issued by DOD acknowledges the heightened strategic emphasis on countering violent extremism and transnational, global networks through effective strategic communications and information operations. The memo outlines organizational changes that are designed to facilitate better Programme integration and coordination to meet these challenges.

The new construct places the JIOWC under the Joint Staff in all but its electronic warfare coordinating function, which shall still remain the purview of USSTRATCOM. The memo also describes new requirements for resource managers to capture the costs of MISO and to develop standardised budget methodologies for SC and IO capabilities and activities. This is in response to congressional concerns over what constitutes an "information operation" and how much federal money is spent on what has been perceived as military propaganda. The Department of Defence Appropriations Acts for FY2002 through FY2010 provide that, "No part of any appropriation contained in this Act shall be used for publicity or propaganda purposes not authorised by the Congress."

Title 10 of the *United States Code*, Section 167, authorises combatant commanders to conduct psychological operations as part of clandestine special operations campaigns in support of military missions. However, Title 10 does not define PSYOP, nor does it clarify DOD's authority to conduct information operations versus propaganda. Some private U.S. citizens have attempted to work outside of these institutional constraints. For instance, inspired by 9/11, Montana resident Shannen Rossmiller has been using the Internet to glean information about potential terrorist suspects and their plans.

This information, which she has shared with federal intelligence agencies, has led to the arrests of a Washington state National Guardsman, convicted in 2004 of attempted espionage for plans to transmit U.S. military armor information through the Internet, and a Pennsylvania man who prosecutors say sought to blow up oil installations in the United States. As a self-taught private citizen, Ms. Rossmiller can operate outside of the institutional constraints that may bind federal employees. Rita Katz of Search for International Terrorist Entities (SITE Institute) performs similar activities, funneling intelligence mined from online extremist chat rooms to government officials without having to go through the sometimes onerous and time-consuming official channels. The intelligence agencies have not discussed publicly the nature of the information shared, nor how it was used.

INTELLIGENCE GAIN/LOSS CALCULUS

Tensions between a website's purported intelligence value and operational threat level can determine the particular capabilities used to thwart the site. For example, a "honey pot" jihadist Web site reportedly was designed by the CIA and Saudi Arabian government to attract and monitor terrorist activities. The information collected from the site was used by intelligence analysts to track the operational plans of jihadists, leading to arrests before the planned attacks could be executed. However, the Web site also was reportedly being used to transmit operational plans for jihadists entering Iraq to conduct attacks on U.S. troops. Debates between representatives of the NSA, CIA, DOD, DNI, and NSC led to a determination that the threat to troops in theater was greater than the intelligence value gained from monitoring the Web site, and a computer network team from the JTF-GNO ultimately dismantled it. This case raised questions of whether computer network attacks on a Web site are a covert operation or a traditional military activity, and under what authority they are conducted.

It also illustrated the risk of collateral damage that an interconnected, networked world represents, as the operation to target and dismantle the honey pot inadvertently disrupted servers in Saudi Arabia, Germany, and Texas. Also, some point to the potential futility of offensively attacking websites, as a dismantled site may be easily relocated to another server. The 2010 National Security Strategy mentions the importance of the Internet for commerce and for disseminating information, and the importance of cyber security in protecting national security assets, but does not appear to present a strategy specifically for combating violent extremism on the Internet.

FOUNDATIONS OF INTERNET SURVEILLANCE STUDIES

Since, Michel Foucault has published his book Surveiller et punir in French in 1975 and in English in 1977, the amount of literature on surveillance has increased enormously and represents a diffuse and complex field of research. Lyon stresses: "Michel Foucault's celebrated, and contentious, historical studies of surveillance and discipline had appeared that mainstream social theorists began to take surveillance seriously in its own right". David Murakami Wood emphasises that "for Surveillance Studies, Foucault is a foundational thinker and his work on the development of the modern subject, in particular Surveillir et Punir, remains a touchstone for this nascent trans-disciplinary field".

Foucault's book Discipline and Punish is cited more than 17 thousand times. Foucault is one of the most important historians and philosophers of the 20th century with wide influence in different disciplines. The overall aim of this part is to elucidate how Internet surveillance is defined in the existing literature, what commonalties and differences of various notions of online surveillance exist, and what advantages and disadvantages such definitions have. For doing so, Foucault's understanding of surveillance and the idea of the panopticon are introduced.

For analysing the existing literature on a more abstract level and identifying advantages and disadvantages, it is essential to discuss commonalties and differences and to find certain typologies. Finally, subsection four gives a summary, discusses how different notions deal with Internet surveillance in the modern economy and makes clear if there is a gap in the existing literature.

FOUCAULT'S NOTION OF SURVEILLANCE AND THE PANOPTICON

Foucault analyses surveillance in the context of the emergence of disciplinary societies. He stresses an evolution from feudal societies of torture, to reformed societies of punishment, and on to modern disciplinary societies. In the age of torture, arbitrary penalties and public spectacles of the scaffold took place in order to exterminate bodies. Afterwards, in the age of punishment, defendants were punished and exterminated. In the age of disciplines, direct violence has been replaced with softer forms of power in order to discipline, control, and normalise people in respect of drilling docile bodies and "political puppets".

For Foucault, Jeremy Bentham's panopticon is a symbol for modern disciplinary society. "On the whole, therefore, one can speak of the formation of a disciplinary society in this movement that stretches from the enclosed disciplines, a sort of social 'quarantine', to an indefinitely generalisable mechanism of 'panopticism'". The panopticon is an ideal architectural figure of modern disciplinary power. It exists of an annular building divided in different cells and a huge tower with windows in the middle. Prisoners, workers, pupils, as well as patients stay in the cells and a supervisor occupies the middle tower.

The architecture allows the supervisor to observe all individuals in the cells without being seen. Not every inmate is observed at every moment, but no one knows if she or he is monitored. Observation is possible anytime. As a result, everyone acts as if kept under surveillance all the time – individuals discipline themselves out of fear of surveillance. The panopticon creates a consciousness of permanent visibility as a form of power, where no bars, chains, and heavy locks are necessary for domination any more. Foucault finally asks: "Is it surprising that prisons resemble factories, schools, barracks, hospitals, which all resemble prisons?" In summary, Foucault analyses surveillance in the context of the emergence of modern disciplinary societies. He understands disciplines as forms of operational power relations and technologies of domination in order to discipline, control, and normalise people.

For Foucault, the panopticon is an ideal symbol of modern surveillance societies. Foucault's understanding of surveillance and the panopticon allows to distinguish panoptic and non-panoptic approaches of defining Internet surveillance that can be used for constructing a typology of existing surveillance literature and for discussing commonalties and differences of definitions of Internet surveillance: The task of the following two subsections is to give a representative, but still eclectic overview about different definitions of online surveillance.

NON-PANOPTIC NOTIONS OF INTERNET SURVEILLANCE

Lyon understands the "world wide web of surveillance" as a neutral concept that identifies positive consequences such as protection and security as well as negative consequences such as control. Computerisation of surveillance makes bureaucratic administration easier and surveillance in cyberspace permits "greater efficiency and speed, and may well result in increased benefits for citizens and consumers, who experience them as enhancing their comfort, convenience, and safety".

Nevertheless, Lyon says that the nation-state and the capitalist workplace are the main sites of surveillance on the Internet and argues that surveillance technologies such as the Internet reinforce asymmetrical power relations on an extensive and intensive level. "So surveillance spreads, becoming constantly more routine, more intensive and extensive, driven by economic, bureaucratic and now technological forces". The Internet has become a multi-billion dollar industry, because it is primarily corporations that are interested in collecting, analysing and assessing a huge amount of personal consumer data in order to target personalised advertisement. Similarly to Lyon's notion of Internet surveillance that assumes there are enabling and constraining effects, Seumas Miller and John Weckert articulate advantages and disadvantages of being monitored. Their paper examines monitoring at the workplace in general and observing of e-mail and the Internet usage in particular. Although the authors claim that privacy is a moral right and criticise existing approaches that stress benefits of workplace monitoring for both employers and employees, they argue that "surveillance and monitoring can be justified in some circumstances" and reason: "The proposition must be rejected that the extent and nature of the enjoyment of rights to individual privacy is something to be determined by the most powerful forces of the day, be they market or bureaucratic forces."

For Anders Albrechtslund, positive aspects of being under surveillance are worth mentioning and he argues that online surveillance also empowers the users, constructs subjectivity, and is playful. Internet surveillance as social and participatory act involves mutuality and sharing. Hille Koskela emphasises individuals' active role in the context of surveillance in general and online surveillance in particular. For instance, reality shows are based on viewer participation, mobile phones with cameras create an active subject, and home webcams generate new subjectivities. Koskela wants to analyse "the other side of surveillance", which has resistant and liberating elements. "Webcams can also be argued to contribute to the 'demo-cratisation' of surveillance".

In addition, Koskela argues that webcams have an empowering role and that the active role of individuals with surveillance equipment shows that the lines of control are blurred. In conclusion, non-panoptic notions of Internet surveillance either use a neutral concept that assumes there are enabling effects such as protection and security as well as constraining effects such as control or a positive concept that identifies comical, playful, amusing, and even enjoyable characteristics of surveillance and where everyone has the opportunity to surveil. In addition, these approaches tend to reject the proposition that surveillance mechanisms are dominated by political and economic actors and see monitoring not necessarily as annoying and disturbing. In non-panoptic notions, Internet surveillance is understood as a useful and effective management tool and as fair methods and procedures of monitoring individuals online. Now, we move on to panoptic notions of Internet surveillance.

PANOPTIC NOTIONS OF INTERNET SURVEILLANCE

Based on a diagrammatic understanding of panoptic surveillance, Greg Elmer predominantly understands the Internet as a powerful space of economic surveillance. "The Internet is first mapped, through indexical search engines, and then diagnosed, via 'spiders' and 'cookies', to actively monitor, survey, solicit and subsequently profile users' online behaviour". Corporations map consumer profiles including demographic and psychographic data in order to target advertising and to accumulate profit. Likewise, in The Internet Galaxy, Manuel Castells describes the Internet not only as a space full of opportunities, but also as a technology of control, which has primarily emerged from the interests of economic and political actors such as corporations and state institutions. He argues that these institutions make use of such technologies in order to locate individual users.

State institutions such as governments and corporations like Microsoft and Google use special surveillance technologies that allow the monitoring of online behaviour in one central database:

- Surveillance technologies... often rely on identification technologies to be able to locate the individual user ... These technologies operate their controls under two basic conditions. First, the controllers know the codes of the network, the controlled do not. Software is confidential, and proprietary, and cannot be modified except by its

> owner. Once on the network, the average user is the prisoner of an architecture he or she does not know. Secondly, controls are exercised on the basis of a space de fined on the network, for instance, the network around an Internet service provider, or the intra-network in a company, a university, or a government agency.

Castells understands the rise of the Internet as an emergence of a powerful electronic surveillance system and concludes: "If this system of surveillance and control of the Internet develops fully, as suggested, not be able to do as we please. We may have no liberty, and no place to hide". Castells considers, just like Foucault, surveillance to be negative and centralised and being connected to control and power. Hence, although Castells does not refer to the concept of the panopticon directly, his contribution to online surveillance can be considered as being a panoptic notion of Internet surveillance.

Michael Levi and David Wall emphasise the new politics of surveillance in a post 9/11 European information society and the increase of the panoptic power of the EU member states mediated through surveillance techniques such as identity/entitlement cards, asylum seekers' smartcards, data sharing schemes, and smart passports in order to create a suspect population. Wall analyses the growth of surveillant Internet technologies in the information society. He draws on Foucault's understanding of panoptic power relations and distinguishes between personal and mass surveillance. For Wall, the Internet as a multidirectional information flow has brought new opportunities for individuals in the context of surveillance.

Techniques such as spyware, spam spider bots, and cookies allow a synoptic effect where the surveilled can surveil the surveillers. The Internet is not simply a 'super', 'virtual' or 'electronic' Panopticon: an extension of Foucault's conceptualisation of Bentham's prison design – 'seeing without being seen', as has become the conventional wisdom. It is important to emphasise that Internet information flows are simultaneously panoptic and synoptic – not only can the few watch the many, but the many can watch the few. Wall argues that the balance between personal surveillance on the one hand and mass surveillance on the other hand is "rarely even" and lists powerful corporations such as DoubleClick and Engage that are able to undertake largescale surveillance. In addition, he emphasises the growth of surveillance and privacy threats as tradeable commodities in information capitalism and presents an empirical case study of the spam industry such as e-mail list compilation and unsolicited bulk e-mails. Joseph Turow speaks about marketing and consumer surveillance in the digital age of media.

He stresses that online media are interested in collecting data about their audience in order to sell these data to advertisers. In a next step, the advertisers use these data in order to increase the efficiency of marketing. Furthermore, customer relationship management constructs audiences and produces a surveillance-driven culture, where consumers understand surveillance as a cost-benefit calculation and willing to the data collection of media and advertisers. Turow's understanding of surveillance can be seen in the context of Foucault's notion of panoptic surveillance. He considers, just like Foucault, surveillance to be negative and centralised and being connected to discipline, control, and power. Similarly to Foucault, Turow stresses that surveillance is predominately undertaken by powerful institutions such as corporations.

Also interesting in this context is the national survey of Internet privacy and institutional trust by Joseph Turow and Michael Hennessy. In 2003, they undertook 1200 quantitative telephone interviews in the United States with adults (18 years and older), who go online at home. The authors tried to analyse what US citizens think about institutional surveillance and conclude "that a substantial percentage of Internet users believe that major corporate or government institutions will both help them to protect information privacy and take that privacy away by disclosing information to other parties without permission". Mark Andrejevic wants to offer an alternative approach of online privacy in the era of new media.

Andrejevic studies the economic surveillance of interactive media such as interactive TV and Google's business model of free wireless Internet access and analyses interactive surveillance in the digital enclosure: "the model of enclosure traces the relationship between a material, spatial process – the construction of networked, interactive environments – and the private expropriation of information". The author argues that Foucault's approach of the panopticon is suitable in order to study surveillance and hierarchical power asymmetries in the online economy and speaks about a "digital form of disciplinary panopticism". Andrejevic argues that just like workplace surveillance rationalised production in the era of scientific management, online surveillance rationalises and stimulates consumption, produces customised commodities and the crucial capital of the economy. "Viewers are monitored so advertisers can be ensured that this work is being done as fiefciently as possible. Ratings, in this context, are informational commodities that generate value because they help to rationalise the viewing process". Also in the context of economic surveillance, John Edward Campbell and Matt Carlson revisit Foucault's idea of the panopticon as well as Gandy's notion of the panoptic sort.

CYBER SECURITY: A PROBLEM OF NATIONAL IMPORTANCE

TRUSTING SYSTEMS IN A DANGEROUS WORLD

The Nation's information technology (IT) infrastructure, still evolving from U.S., technological innovations such as the personal computer and the Internet, today is a vast fabric of computers – from supercomputers to handheld devices – and interconnected networks enabling high-speed communications, information access, advanced computation, transactions, and automated processes relied upon in every sector of society. Because much of this infrastructure connects one way or another to the Internet, it embodies the Internet's original structural attributes of openness, inventiveness, and the assumption of goodwill.

These signature attributes have made the U.S., IT infrastructure an irresistible target for vandals and criminals worldwide. The PITAC believes that terrorists will inevitably follow suit, taking advantage of vulnerabilities including some that the Nation has not yet clearly recognised or addressed. The computers that manage critical U.S., facilities, infrastructures, and essential services can be targeted to set off system wide failures, and these computers frequently are accessible from virtually anywhere in the world via the Internet.

THE INFORMATION TECHNOLOGY INFRASTRUCTURE IS 'CRITICAL'

Most Americans see and use the components of the IT infrastructure – mainly desktop computers connected to the Internet – that enable e-mail, instant messaging, exchange and downloading of sound and images, online shopping, information searches, interactive games, and even telephony.

Americans also work with the information technologies that drive day-to-day operations in industry and government and are relied upon by organisations large and small for a range of functions including design, manufacturing, inventory, sales, payroll, information storage and retrieval, education and training, and research and development. In fact, economists credit successful applications of information technologies throughout the economy for the spectacular gains in U.S., productivity over the last decade.

Less visible, and certainly less well understood, is the fact that these technologies – computers, mass storage devices, high-speed networks and network components such as routers and switches, systems and applications software, embedded and wireless devices, and the Internet itself – are now also essential to virtually all of the Nation's critical infrastructures. Computing systems control the management of power plants, dams, the North American power grid, air traffic control systems, food and energy distribution, and the financial system, to name only some.

The reliance of these sensitive physical installations and processes on the IT infrastructure makes that infrastructure itself critical and in the national interest to safeguard. The electric power generation industry, for example, relies on a range of IT systems and capabilities.

As in other industries, power companies implement business management systems for administrative and information services. But the power industry uses much more information technology. It relies on supervisory control and data acquisition (SCADA) systems to collect information about system operation, help regulate and control power generation, optimise power production, respond to changing power demands and system parameters, control distribution, and coordinate among the various generation and storage facilities within a power company system. Increasingly, SCADA systems are also used to integrate electric companies into regional or national power grids to optimise power production, minimize production and distribution costs, and provide backup services. This requires a private network that often includes links to the Internet. A cyber attack that disables key Internet nodes could disrupt the power network's communications. And if an entity within the private network is compromised, an attacker could gain direct control of the SCADA systems and their data and operation.

Today, the Internet also is used to manage essential services provided by business and government, such as electronic financial transactions, law enforcement dispatch and support, emergency response and community alerts, and military communications. Banks, for example, rely on extensive distributed Internet and information services, both for customer interaction and in inter-bank operations. To assure reliability and security of its most sensitive systems, the banking industry, like the power industry, uses private networks and is vulnerable to cyber attacks that cripple Internet nodes and/or result in unauthorised access to data and services. Such shared Internet links, for example, enabled the "Slammer" worm to disable a major bank's ATM system and an airline's computer system, even though they were not directly connected to the Internet.

During a national emergency, it is imperative that the Nation's communications infrastructure be available for emergency response coordination. Today, that vital infrastructure is vulnerable to a variety of denial of service attacks, including the release of simple viruses and worms that can disrupt Internet communications as well as more sophisticated attacks in which modems from compromised servers are used to flood key parts of the telephone network.

The latter example demonstrates how vulnerability in one system (e.g., the Internet) can be exploited to attack a totally separate system (e.g., the telephone network). These examples illustrate how computing and computer communications have become integral to virtually every domain of activity in the U.S., today. Those systems are interconnected and interdependent in highly complex ways, which are often surprisingly fragile.

UBIQUITOUS INTERCONNECTIVITY = WIDESPREAD VULNERABILITY

The Internet – now a global network of networks linking more than 300 million computers worldwide – was designed in a spirit of trust. Neither the protocols for neither network communication nor the software governing computing systems (nodes) connected to the network were architected to operate in an environment in which they are under attack. Indeed, the protocols used by the Internet today are derived from the protocols that were developed in the 1960s for the Federal government's experimental ARPANET. Only a few researchers used ARPANET and they were trusted to do no harm. The civilian networks, such as NSFNET, that developed from ARPANET into the Internet likewise did not incorporate security technologies at the system software or network protocol levels. Ubiquitous interconnectedness – first exhibited by the Internet and further extended in local area networks, wide area networks, and wireless and hybrid networks – has generated whole new industries, rejuvenated productivity in older ones, and opened new avenues for discourse and education and an unprecedented era of collaborative science and engineering discovery worldwide. That is indeed good news. The bad news is that ubiquitous interconnectivity provides the primary conduit for exploiting vulnerabilities on a widespread basis. Despite efforts in recent years to add security components to computing systems, networks, and software, the acts of a hostile party – whether a terrorist, an adversary nation, organised crime, or a mischievous hacker – can propagate far and wide, with damaging effects on a national or international scale.

For example:

- In the past several years, worms such as Code Red, which defaces World Wide Web sites and/or launches distributed denial of service (DDoS) attacks, and Slammer, which severely degraded the Bank of America's ATM network in January 2003, have caused damage estimated in the billions of dollars.
- The Department of Defence responded to the Code Red worm by disconnecting its unclassified network (NIPRnet) from the Internet to protect it from infection. This protective measure disabled the Army Corps of Engineers' control of the locks on the Mississippi River, since, the NIPRnet was used to transmit commands to the locks through the Internet.
- By using a laptop computer and radio transmitter, a former contractor for an overseas wastewater system was able to assume command of hundreds of control systems that manage sewage and drinking water. Over a period of two months, hundreds of thousands of gallons of putrid sludge were intentionally released from the wastewater system.
- Many businesses are now being attacked by cyber extortionists who demand payment in return for not attacking the businesses' Web presence. Seventeen percent of the 100 companies surveyed in a 2004 poll by Carnegie Mellon University-*Information Week* reported being the target of some form of cyber extortion.
- Identity theft is a rapidly increasing problem for Internet users. One of the simplest methods of stealing a user's identity is known as

"phishing," a technique that uses fake e-mail messages and fraudulent Web sites to fool recipients into divulging personal financial data. Consumers Union estimates that 1 per cent of U.S., households fell victim to such attacks at a cost of $400 million in the first half of 2004.

SOFTWARE IS A MAJOR VULNERABILITY

Network connectivity provides "door-to-door" transportation for attackers, but vulnerabilities in the software residing in computers substantially compound the cyber security problem. As the PITAC noted in a 1999 report, the software development methods that have been the norm fail to provide the high-quality, reliable, and secure software that the IT infrastructure requires. Software development is not yet a science or a rigorous discipline, and the development process by and large is not controlled to minimize the vulnerabilities that attackers exploit. Today, as with cancer, vulnerable software can be invaded and modified to cause damage to previously healthy software, and infected software can replicate itself and be carried across networks to cause damage in other systems.

Like cancer, these damaging processes may be invisible to the lay person even though experts recognise that their threat is growing. And as in cancer, both preventive actions and research are critical, the former to minimize damage today and the latter to establish a foundation of knowledge and capabilities that will assist the cyber security professionals of tomorrow reduce risk and minimize damage for the long term. Vulnerabilities in software that are introduced by mistake or poor practices are a serious problem today. In the future, the Nation may face an even more challenging problem as adversaries – both foreign and domestic – become increasingly sophisticated in their ability to insert malicious code into critical software.

ATTACKS AND VULNERABILITIES ARE GROWING RAPIDLY

Today, the threat clearly is growing. Most indicators and studies of the frequency, impact, scope, and cost of cyber security incidents – among both organisations and individuals – point to continuously increasing levels and varieties of attacks. The data show that the total number of attacks – including viruses, worms, cyber fraud, and insider attacks in corporations – is rising by over 20 percent annually, with many types of attacks doubling in number.

For example, 83 percent of financial service organisations experienced compromised systems in 2003, more than double the percentage in 2001. Moreover, the reported level of security incidents almost certainly understates the actual level. There are few incentives – but strong disincentives – for large organisations to report incidents in a public forum. Targets of cyber attacks typically are concerned that widespread disclosure of their victimisation could shake public confidence in their operations, not to mention attract other attackers. Technology-oriented indicators clearly reflect the rapid growth in the rate of cyber attacks. For example, ICSA Labs reports that the monthly percentage of personal computers infected by a virus has grown from 1 percent in 1996 to over 10 percent in 2003.

From January to June of 2004, the rate at which new hosts were compromised and incorporated into "bot armies" rose from well under 2,000 a day to more than 30,000 a day. When compromised hosts are incorporated into bot armies, they can be used as platforms for launching denial of service attacks against a given target or to distribute "spam" e-mail without the knowledge or consent of the owners or operators. Trends within large organisations are also disturbing. For example, the percentage of organisations that experienced virus disasters (defined as those with more than 25 simultaneous infections or with major impact from infection) has grown nearly every year over the last decade, with 92 percent of organisations reporting such incidents during 2003. Symantec reports that 40 percent of the networks controlled by the Fortune 100 companies were exploited to originate hostile worm traffic, despite the fact that these companies have taken a variety of protective measures.

The cost, downtime, and days to recover from significant virus events have also trended upward for each of the past nine years. Meanwhile, the number of identified system and network vulnerabilities has also risen. The Computer Emergency Response Team Coordination Center (CERT/CC) at Carnegie Mellon University reports that 3,780 new electronic vulnerabilities were published in 2004, more than a 20-fold increase from 1995.

Once published, most of the details of vulnerabilities are available for miscreants to begin attacking or developing attack tools and techniques, thus forcing users and organisations to scramble to assure that their defences are adequate. The Symantec security threat report notes that in the first half of 2004, for example, the average time between the public disclosure of vulnerability and the release of an associated exploit was 5.8 days, substantially reduced from the months estimated in prior years. In fact, many IT system designs continue to incorporate characteristics that make these systems vulnerable to attack. In some instances, system designs may be pushing the state of the art, so their vulnerabilities may not be understood until they are deployed.

In other instances, vulnerabilities may be designed into systems because the developers lack technical knowledge or fail to execute best practices. In this brief report, PITAC can point to only a few examples to provide the reader with a sense of the vulnerabilities of IT systems. But it is clear that without action, IT vulnerabilities will become more severe, as computers, cell phones, and embedded systems proliferate globally and as expanding "always-on" high-speed or broadband connections enable attacks to propagate more rapidly and with more force than the occasionally connected low-bandwidth modems that were the norm until recently.

ENDLESS PATCHING IS NOT THE ANSWER

A broad consensus among computer scientists is emerging that the approach of patching and retrofitting networks, computing systems, and software to "add" security and reliability may be necessary in the short run but is inadequate for addressing the Nation's cyber security needs.

As computer security expert and PITAC member Eugene Spafford testified before the House Science Committee:

- Security cannot be easily or adequately added on after the fact and this greatly complicates our overall mission. The software and hardware being deployed today have been designed by individuals with little or no security training, using unsafe methods, and then poorly tested. This is being added to the fault-ridden infrastructure already in place and operated by personnel with insufficient awareness of the risks. Therefore, none of us should be surprised if we continue to see a rise in break-ins, defacements, and viruses in the years to come.

Granted, our IT infrastructure may be less secure right now than it could be if all known security best practices were applied everywhere. But Professor Spafford's comment suggests that, even if all best practices were fully in place, in the absence of any fundamental new approaches we would still endlessly be patching and "plugging holes in the dike."

FUNDAMENTALLY NEW SECURITY MODELS, METHODS NEEDED

We urgently need to expand our focus on short-term patching to also include longer-term development of new methods for designing and engineering secure systems. Addressing cyber security for the longer term requires a vigourous ongoing programme of fundamental research to explore the science and develop the technologies necessary to design security into computing and networking systems and software from the ground up.

Fundamental research is characterised by its potential for broad, rather than specific, application and includes farsighted, high-payoff research that provides the basis for technological progress. The vast majority of cyber security research conducted to date has been based on the concept of perimeter defence.

In this model, what is "inside" an information system or network is protected from an "outside" attacker who tries to penetrate it to gain access to or control its data and system resources. However, once the perimeter is breached (whether by virtue of a technical weakness such as a software vulnerability or an operational weakness such as an employee being bribed or tricked to reveal a password), the attacker has entirely free rein and can compromise every system connected in a network with not much more effort than is required to compromise only one.

This weakness of the perimeter defence strategy has become painfully clear. But it is not the only problem with the model. The distinction between "outside" and "inside" breaks down amid the proliferation of wireless and embedded technologies connected to networks and the increasing complexity of networked "systems of systems." One element of a more realistic model for cyber security may be a principle of mutual suspicion: Every component of a system or network is always suspicious of every other component and access to data and other resources must be constantly reauthorised. More generally, cyber security would be an integral part of the design process for any large, complex system or network. Security add-ons will always be necessary to fix some security problems, but ultimately there is no substitute for systemwide end-to-end security that is minimally intrusive.

CENTRAL ROLE FOR FEDERAL R&D

"The National Strategy to Secure Cyberspace" states that the private sector has the most important role to play in cyber security. The PITAC agrees with this conclusion as it pertains to relatively short-term efforts to improve the security of today's systems and networks. But the Federal government has a vital, irreplaceable role to play as well. As at earlier stages of the digital revolution, Federal investment in fundamental research is required to fill the pipeline with new concepts, technologies, infrastructure prototypes, and trained personnel needed for the private sector to accomplish its cyber security mission.

The Government can also promote technology transfer mechanisms that accelerate adoption of these new technologies by industry, in part by supporting the development of performance metrics, models, datasets, and test beds so that new products and best practices can be evaluated. Federally sponsored fundamental research is a unique national investment in the production of new knowledge that can be broadly used across all sectors of society for the common good. Such research takes place primarily in universities and national laboratories.

As for-profit entities, companies typically focus on short-term results or proprietary research that can provide near-term competitive advantage. It is the mission of research universities to take the long-term view of a problem. Unclassified research performed in universities and national laboratories has the added benefit of creating trained talent in the field, as university graduates obtain employment in industry, universities, and government. University graduates who pursue advanced degrees in IT become the new generation of research leaders; other graduates frequently become involved in start-up companies, which have historically played critical roles in the IT industry.

Research at universities also accelerates changes in the education of new college graduates, as researchers rapidly move new ideas into undergraduate courses and textbooks. Fundamental research focuses on problems of extraordinary difficulty and complexity that often require a number of years to solve. The Federal government has long played a central role in supporting fundamental research in information technology. The results of this research lie at the heart of many of today's billion-dollar information technology industries – industries that are transforming our lives, driving our economy, and enhancing our security.

Fundamental research is a "public good" – hence, the role of the Federal government in supporting it. The result of a highly effective interplay of Federally supported fundamental research, industry-supported applied research, and industry product development: The United States today is the world leader in information technology. An expanded portfolio of Federal cyber security R&D efforts is required because today we simply do not know how to model, design, and build systems incorporating integral security attributes such as mutual suspicion – or any other fundamental security innovations.

In addition, we face substantial new challenges from the constant stream of emerging technologies. For example, we do not fully understand the security ramifications of networks of embedded devices. In that context, a principle of mutual suspicion would have to consider controlled access to the sub-networks, the information stores, the devices that are interconnected, and the computing and communication resources of a given network. In our current methods of software development, security is simply one more incremental requirement further burdening an already cumbersome, slow, and expensive process.

The add-on approach will not address our fundamental need for far-sighted advances in systems and software technologies that provide innovative new approaches to the problem of security. We urge a rethinking of the Federal investment balance between military/intelligence and civilian cyber security R&D. In part, this is because the military and intelligence communities rely on the commercial Internet and commercial providers of computing systems and software for the bulk of their own operations.

It is only through fundamental research in civilian cyber security that we can hope to address the strategic and pervasive vulnerabilities of our national IT infrastructure. We also underscore the importance of technology transfer because new concepts do not appear in products automatically. For this to happen, IT vendors must build into their products and services new security functionalities. But vendors respond to what users demand, and it is only recently that most users – corporations, government agencies, and individual users – have begun to care about cyber security.

In the absence of significant demand for cyber security, IT vendors have mostly chosen to add new features for which customers are willing to pay.

(Ironically, the addition of new features and added complexity often leads to the introduction of more security vulnerabilities.) This market-driven bias away from cyber security is the "valley of death" for cyber security noted by many analysts.

R&D may provide the knowledge and the proof of operational feasibility, but in the absence of customer demand for the security that may be provided, vendors have little incentive to include new security technologies in their products.

A NOTE ON NON-TECHNOLOGY ASPECTS OF CYBER SECURITY

PITAC recognises that the development of technologies to counteract vulnerabilities or – better yet – designs that avoid vulnerabilities in the first place, constitute only one component, although arguably the most important component, of effective cyber security. We briefly point here to several facets of cyber security that require societal attention but are not addressed in this report.

Domestic and International Law Enforcement

A hostile party using an Internet-connected computer thousands of miles away can attack an Internet connected computer in the United States as easily as if he or she were next door. It is often difficult to identify the perpetrator of such an attack, and even when a perpetrator is identified, criminal prosecution across national boundaries is problematic.

Education

We need to educate citizens that if they are going to use the Internet, they need to continually maintain and update the security on their systems so that they cannot be compromised, for example, to become agents in a DDoS attack or for "spam" distribution. We also need to educate corporations and organisations in best practices for effective security management. For example, some large organisations now have a policy that all systems in their purview must meet strict security guidelines. Automated updates are sent to all computers and servers on the internal network, and no new system is allowed online until it conforms to the security policy.

Information Security

Information security refers to measures taken to protect or preserve information on a network as well as the network itself. Thus it also involves physical security, personnel security, criminal law and investigation, economics, and other issues. These factors need to be included in the curriculum for cyber security practitioners, and supporting law and technologies need to be made available.

THE FUTURE OF CYBER CRIME ACTIVITY

During an eight day period in August of 2003, three separate worms cost the U.S. economy close to two billion dollars in lost production. Later that summer, the east coast of the United States experienced a massive blackout that might have been exacerbated by a worm called Blaster. Robert Cringley believed that same year that "the cost to society of identity theft is in the range of $4-5 billion per year and may be even higher." With the convergence of organised crime and technically savvy cyber criminals, the growing fear of cyberterrorism, the inability to understand security from major software vendors and the slow footedness of the government, the future seems to point to an Internet that is not only vulnerable to major attacks, but also infested with scams, thieves, and ever increasing opportunities for exploitation. Although inherently difficult to predict trends within the field of technology, there are some eventualities that seem certain, like the growth of extortion and fraud though the Internet. These difficulties will of course result in new responses that better protect customers and force criminals into new realms. Although it is a hackneyed expression, the Internet is still in the Wild West stages. It is important to remember, though, that the Wild West eventually turned into suburbia after successful methods were found to control and police criminals, making their life extremely difficult. An examination of some of the potentialities will help to illustrate how the Internet and cyber crime can be envisioned, at least in the near term future.

FUTURE TRENDS IN CYBER CRIME ACTIVITY

The pace at which cyber crime is growing is one of the most disturbing trends. Valerie McNiven, a U.S. Treasury Advisor, has proclaimed "last year was the first year that proceeds from cyber crime were greater than proceeds from the sale of illegal drugs, and that was, I believe, over $105 billion." She further added that "cyber crime is moving at such a high speed that law enforcement cannot catch up with it." It seems clear that the issue will only become worse in the next few years, now that professionals have realised the potential windfalls if exploited properly. Recently, there has been significant discussion over the amalgamation of organised criminals and cyber crime. Such a pairing indeed forebodes an ill omen for the near term future.

With most of the criminal groups operating out of eastern Europe, Russia and Asia, where laws and enforcement are scanty, there seems little hope in containing and neutralising the threat through traditional means. Phil Williams, a visiting scientist at CERT, summarised the issue succinctly. "The Internet provides both channels and targets for crime and enables them to be exploited for considerable gain with a very low level of risk. For organised crime it is difficult to ask for more." The result that can then be expected will be an increase in sophisticated phishing attacks and other means for identity theft that may be two pronged. For example, using call centers to notify "customers" ahead of time of some issue, and then following up with e-mails that request personal information. These types of social engineering attacks can be very damaging and have had a long history of success within cyber crime and fraud related transgressions.

The Internet makes it even easier since a degree of authority can be imparted with official looking e-mails and fraudulent web sites that mimic their legitimate counterparts exactly. In the past, such social engineering relied on interpersonal skills like gaining trust. Now, the same idea has been transferred to technology, which can be done with greater ease by a wider group of people. Another aspect of fraud will result from the aggregation of personal information in many third party data centers, making them valuable targets to infiltrate. It is not hard to imagine criminals using data mining techniques to find the most gullible consumers, or tailoring phishing e-mails for specific people based on their medical, financial or personal history. Identify theft will also move in more automated directions. For example, botnets will become vehicles not just for denial of service attacks and spam, but also as giant search platforms for finding personal information, like credit cards and social security numbers.

Controllers of the botnets will then receive payment to run queries on their "database." With professional criminals managing the money laundering and organisation of such schemes, it begs to ask where will all the technical know-how come from in order to perform cyber crime? Unfortunately, there are growing numbers of intelligent black-hats with university degrees spread around the globe, many of them operating in countries where legal employment does not pay as well and the chances of being caught are slim.

But more troublesome is that it has become easier than ever before to be a hacker capable of inflicting great harm on networks and committing cyber crime. The Internet has created a repository of knowledge where anyone is able to learn the fundamentals of subverting computer systems, with numerous tutorials available that spell out in nearly layman's terms how to perform a buffer overflow or a man in the middle attack. Interestingly, the greatest problem is not those who will take the time to learn and find new exploits. In fact this group will probably remain a small, highly intelligent network of researchers and security groups focused solely on finding holes in software. In this, it is preordained, that even if someone is motivated to learn how exploits work, finding a new exploit takes a degree of investigation, skill and diligence that most are not willing to invest.

The real threat comes from the profound ease at which anyone can run a programme like "MetaSploit," a framework for running exploits against targets that allows new modules to be imported and run automatically. The attacker literally needs to know nothing about how computers work, besides how to operate one. In fact, for almost all attacks, the hard work is done by a small group of people, and then released into the public domain, allowing almost anyone to just run the attack. Botnets are no longer handcrafted software made by one group who truly understood the fundamentals, but instead are opensource collaborative efforts that aim to make it as easy as possible to control remote computers, such as BotNET, eggheads and CSharpBot, all available from SourceForge. Thus, the barrier to entry to the field is so low that it allows almost anyone to experiment and join the swelling ranks of cyber criminals.

With the learning curve so low, it should prompt discussion on the need for a new paradigm of thought in how to pre-empt and deal with criminals, in a way that is no longer tied to traditional methods. For example, for someone to break into a house, not only do they need to plan the opportune moment, but they may also have to be aware of lock picking, security system evasion and possess a degree of gumption to overcome moral thresholds. In opposition, the ease of cyber crime seems inversely proportional to the lucrativeness that it bestows and moreover, these trends show signs of accelerating. Beyond the "who" and the "why" of future cyberattacks, the "how" will also change as operating systems become more secure and harder to exploit. With the damage that comes with each new security hole released, Microsoft, Apple and open source vendors have finally begun to seriously focus on security. Of course that hasn't stemmed the flow of vulnerabilities discovered, but techniques such as address space randomisation to stop buffer overflows, advanced and automatic code reviews and more training will reduce the ability to compromise a machine through operating system protocols over time. The real danger in the future lies with user applications, which are created by individuals or small groups without the knowledge or training required to implement security correctly.

Especially dangerous are web applications that can be installed on web servers. The traditional problem with these types of security vulnerabilities was finding susceptible hosts. But with Google, a programme can automatically search for sites with a specific version of a programme installed and then launch an attack. If remote code can be executed, the programme may not be able to take over the whole system, but it can run programmes as the user which may be enough to install bots and automatically replicate. The first instance of such an attack occurred in December of 2004 with the Santy worm that attacked a popular bulletin board system by searching through Google to find hosts with a specific file that was vulnerable. Such attacks aim their weapons at the least secure and vetted of software created. Although the installed base of such systems may be small, with "Google Hacking," they can still be quickly located and exploited.

Another avenue of attack that will open up will be through embedded systems, such as cell phones, mobile devices and other electronics that may connect to the Internet for the most mundane of purposes. Software is usually recreated for each iteration of a device as it is specifically designed for the hardware. This allows for security problems to creep back in over time that may have been eliminated before.

As these devices start to allow consumers to make purchases, while storing valuable information, they will become more attractive for criminals. The incentives now to do so are low, so security researchers have only seen "proof-of-concept" viruses, like the one that infected cellphones running a version of the Symbian OS that could spread automatically. It appears organised crime has not moved into this area due to the lack of research and understanding of how such attacks can be made profitable. Much as with the Internet, it will take time to exploit successfully. In the same vein, eventually automobiles, home electronics devices, refrigerators and almost all devices can and will use the Internet in order to perform maintenance, download upgrades or monitor performance.

These will present opportunities for maliciousness and blackmail that doesn't equate in the same way as the purely virtual environment of the Internet. If someone enters their car, controlled by a foreign agent that demands a wire transfer or else the car will be crashed at high speeds, a situation arises that people will no longer accept. Whether such a scenario will occur is debatable, but the possibility will certainly exist.

MITIGATING CYBER CRIME ACTIVITY

Although it is inevitable that cyber crime will increase and continue to explore new vectors for undermining privacy, authentication and law enforcement, there will also be valid and useful attempts for mitigating the abilities of criminals, as well as the effects of cyber crime. These solutions will take form in better software, anti-spyware and anti-virus software integrated into operating systems and more user education regarding phishing and identify theft. These solutions will come primarily from software vendors themselves. On the other side, legislators will work with banks to reduce and prevent fraud, putting some of the liability with those most able to prevent it. Finally, advanced solutions coming out of research and academia will try to inhibit the inherently anonymous and insecure nature of the Internet.

With Microsoft's upcoming release of Vista, the latest version of their operating system, they'll have a new chance to focus on not only improving the general security of the system through fundamental changes, but also in providing methods for eliminating common problems, such as botnets, spyware and phishing attacks. In October of 2005, Microsoft began working together with the FTC to educate customers about botnets and the danger of allowing a computer to turn into a zombie. To deal with the problem of phishing, Microsoft released a programme in July of 2005 called the "Microsoft Phishing Filter," which aims to invalidate the ability of phishers to reach Microsoft customers by dynamically notifying them when there is a high chance that what is being viewed is a phishing attack. Finally, Microsoft released their "AntiSpyware" programme in January of 2005, to be included with Vista as well, that automatically scans your computer for programmes that match spyware signatures or that try to perform suspicious actions, like modifying system functionality or trying to run upon computer start up. If cyber crime continues to grow to epidemic proportions, as all indications seem to point to, legislation will invariably step in, but more importantly, those with the most to lose will become more involved.

This includes credit card companies, banks, lending operations and other organisations dealing with monetary transactions. While also serving as a bank in many capacities. With only an e-mail address and a password required to send money, this low hanging fruit has been one of the most heavily exploited realms for phishing attacks. In response, Paypal has offered at least a thousand dollars of purchase protection and a supposed one hundred per cent protection against unauthorised payments sent from an account. A fraud investigation team responds to queries and according to their web site, they have software that automatically monitors every transaction for inconsistencies.

This last measure used by Paypal has also become fertile ground for credit cards companies, as their systems have become powerful at identifying fraudulent purchases though the use of neural networks, a type of software emerging out of the field of artificial intelligence. In some cases, this software has been able to reduce fraud by thirty per cent or more. It's important to remember that the systems are not perfect solutions, but do address a large portion of illegal activity. Combined with other efforts, the goal is to reduce the effect of fraud, while making it more difficult to achieve. Legislation will attempt to do its part as well, even though it has moved notoriously slowly when dealing with cyberthreats. The past few years have seen laws specifically crafted for spam and dealing with attacks that threaten the integrity of the infrastructure of the Internet. If the botnet problem continues to grow, coupled with identify theft, surely more action will be taken. Although, it is still unclear how effective it will be without a significant contribution to cyberforensic development and funding for the various governmental enforcement agencies responsible for handling cyber crime matters.

Another issue discussed in the Legal Policies section is the need for more international cooperation in locating, extraditing and prosecuting foreign criminals when possible, as the current system leaves much to be desired. Finally, as with any dangerous and difficult problem, there will be new and inventive ways to handle security issues coming out of research. One contribution that has limited, but not eliminated many common security flaws that are exploited, is the use of randomisation in dealing with code, data and other programmatic necessities. By introducing a factor of unpredictability, it can make the work of a hacker much more difficult and prone to error, limiting the ability of those who do not posses the skill to effect a novel attack. Other interesting proposals have included trace back systems that can remove the anonymous identity of data traveling through the Internet, devising a system for fast and accurate discovery of the source of even one packet of data. Stopping distributed denial of service attacks and worm discovery has also been proposed as a method that can be automated and integrated into the backbone of the Internet, high speed routers.

By analysing similar patterns coming from separate locations, such detectors can realise an attack while it is in its infancy and isolate infected hosts. There is also still room for ISPs to actively monitor and discourage botnets, spam and DDoS attacks from occurring. As the first link in the chain for many zombie hosts, as well as attackers, they are in a prime position for stopping spam, either by blocking outgoing mail, which most users have no need for, or by identifying when one host is sending out a large amount of data that does not match expected behaviour. Additionally, if they noticed that a number of hosts were acting in concert, with regards to the data being disseminated from those machines, they may assume with likelihood that they are being controlled remotely. Consequently, the ISPs can examine logs to find who is sending the commands and initiate a complaint with the F.B.I. The problem holding back this kind of proactive approach has not been technical in nature, but rather legalistic, as it can be considered an invasion of privacy. Furthermore, such methods are being used to track down minor copyright violations, instead of focusing on more substantial problems, such as cyber crime and identify theft.

LOOKING AHEAD

The future of the Internet is still up for grabs between criminals and normal users. Fears of a cyber-apocalypse still abound, while the potential extent of damage that can be caused by wide scale fraud is nearly unbounded. These anxieties should be rationally tempered with the knowledge that the problems are being addressed, although perhaps not fast enough. The usefulness of the Internet has proved itself in numerous and myriad ways that will hopefully be enough to ensure it does not become a wasteland of criminal activity and a bastion for the malicious.

The government still has an important role to play, but most of the prevention needs to be done by commercial entities producing software and those with the ability to stop fraud. Relying on consumer education programmes will only affect a percentage of possible victims. The others need to be automatically protected through measures that do not stress and require considerable participation. Security needs to be easy and effective if it is do work. Whether cyber crime is still a pertinent issue ten years from now is unknowable in a sense, but if the Internet will continue to grow, it must be solved so that the realities of cyber crime will be proportional to real-world crimes, if not better.

GLOBAL STATE OF WAR TO CONVERGENCE SECURITY

Michael Hardt and Antonio Negri have noted that war in the modern state system "was a limited state of exception" conducted between states with sovereign political authority, not by individuals or non-sovereign groups, However, the current state of affairs is one in which "the exception has become the rule" with the lines between war and peace, warrior and non-combatant, becoming increasingly blurry. The result is what they describe as a perpetual, indeterminate, interminable, and global state of war.

While the emergence of this global state of war was in evidence prior to the attacks of September 11, 2001, the "global war on terrorism" that resulted from those attacks has become the quintessential example of the phenomenon that they describe. The GWOT is a war against "abstract concepts," "sets of practices," and "indefinite, immaterial enemies" that "serve[s] to mobilise all social forces" in response to threats for which "there is little difference between outside and inside, between foreign conflicts and homeland security". One result has been a shift in focus from defence to security in Western nations. This involves a shift from emphasising the defence of the political and territorial sovereignty of the state from external threats to emphasising the need to secure all aspects of social, political, economic, and cultural life in the face of proliferating risks, vulnerabilities, and threats that transcend traditional boundaries.

"This notion of security is a form of biopower, then, in the sense that it is charged with the task of producing and transforming social life at its most general and global level". Security-as-biopower works at all levels of society and results in a state of conflict that suffuses all of society, that is "indeterminate, both spatially and temporally," and which allows for the possibility that "all of humanity can in principle be united against an abstract concept or practice such as terrorism". As war invades the normal functioning of everyday life, even mundane activities like washing one's hands or having up-to-date antivirus on one's computer become acts of "national security." In short, when war permeates all of society, which must be secured in its entirely on every possible front, then everyone is a potential "warrior."

Biopower, which Hardt and Negri see as "above society, transcendent, as a sovereign authority imposes its order," is contrasted with "biopolitical production". Biopolitical production is a networked, collaborative form of production based in openness, free flows of information, and sharing of common resources that is at the heart of the new economy. They point to the Internet-enabled labour of the open-source software movement as a prime example of biopolitical production.

Biopolitical production, they argue, "tends itself to become political decision-making" and "makes democracy possible for the first time today" by "banish[ing] sovereignty from politics". They also point to "post-Fordist," networked guerrilla movements like the Zapatistas as examples of biopolitical production, which implies that practices of biopolitical production can be found in practices of conflict. But they only identify biopolitical practices of conflict among those groups that are resisting Western, neo-liberal globalisation and existing forms of politics based in sovereignty and war. They limit the work of security-asbiopower to the state.

But the cases of convergence security examined are examples of biopolitical production in service to state interests, or even the outsourcing of biopower to private actors. To explore our cases, as suggested, draw on convergence theory as developed in media studies. Henry Jenkins' theory of "convergence" is central to contemporary efforts to understand the production of media and entertainment content often identified as the "immaterial goods" most exemplary of the new economy and its collaborative, information and communication technology (ICT) enabled practices of biopolitical production. Convergence is about technological, organisational, and cultural changes.

It involves producers and consumers both adapting to technological changes, which results in changes in and among traditional producer organisations, as well as changes in the relationship between traditional producers and consumers. Jenkins has predicted that while "we are mostly using this collective power through our recreational life...soon as suggested, be deploying those skills for more 'serious' purposes" like political and military affairs. Convergence can already be seen in military affairs and the production of security. The effects of convergence within and among traditional producers of security can be seen in efforts to "transform" both the U.S., military via the adoption of "network-centric warfare" and the U.S., intelligence community via increased reliance upon open source information and collaborative work processes. Self-organising, online volunteer groups like the ones examined are examples of the changing relationships between producers and consumers of security. As with Jenkins' "convergence culture" or Toffler's "prosumer," we do not see the elimination or complete domination of one group by the other, but neither do we see the emergence of a space of completely open and equal participation. Instead, we see both topdown and bottom-up change that often leads to ambivalent, ambiguous, and sometimes contentious relationships among producers and consumers, with producers at once recognising that they must rely upon the labour of consumers while simultaneously seeking to maintain control and consumers labouring out of a combination of passion, fear, patriotism, and frustration with producers, but nonetheless dependent upon the producers for the security that they ultimately seek.

COUNTERING THREATS THROUGH CYBER SPACE

In the United States, surveillance has been at the heart of changes in traditional defence, as well as attempts to counter so-called "asymmetric" security threats. Guided by the principle that "what can be seen can be hit," battlefield surveillance was at the heart of the U.S., "revolution in military affairs" during the 1970s, 1980s, and 1990s. Two asymmetric threats in particular have caught the imaginations of those within the United States who have worked consistently to increase government surveillance capabilities: the threats of terrorism and cyber attack.

The idea that information-age conflict in general, and the fight against terrorism in particular, constitute a global "battle for hearts and minds" has been popular among U.S., defence and security professionals for at least a decade. Various observers have worried about terrorist use of the Internet as a tool for fundraising, organising, recruiting, and propaganda. It is in this spirit that Arquilla has urged the U.S., government to remove terrorist web sites from the Internet. Likewise, it is in this spirit that groups of self-organised, online volunteers engage in various types of online activities in support of the U.S., "war on terrorism," including intelligence gathering and counter-propaganda activities.

The work of Shannen Rossmiller and her group Phoenix Global Information Systems is the most notable example of intelligence-focused, volunteer cyber-counterterrorism. In response to the terrorist attacks of September 11, 2001, Rossmiller, a municipal judge from a small town in Montana, began trolling jihadist web sites to learn more about those who had attacked the United States and what they might be planning next. In January 2003, Rossmiller joined forces with at least six other individuals whom she met in the online discussion forum. They created a web site and began calling themselves 7-Seas Global Intelligence.

Members of 7-Seas live in the United States, Canada, Australia, and Singapore and include an economist, a physicist, a computer systems engineer, a corporate security consultant, and a private investigator. Rossmiller and members of 7-Seas have used a number of techniques to gather intelligence about terrorists online. These have included creating multiple false personas complete with pictures and detailed life histories. To appear as convincing as possible to her targets, Rossmiller has learned Arabic, studied the Quran, and read Arabic literature. They also employ translation software, tools to map the IP addresses of the online jihadists with whom they interact, software to mask their own IP addresses and make it appear that they are located in the Middle East or South Asia, and even spyware that is remotely installed on the computers of some of those that they investigate.

While their initial goal was to predict future terrorist attacks, they soon shifted to gathering and analysing information from terrorist web sites, forums, and chat rooms, and then turning that information over to authorities.

Rossmiller's efforts in particular have contributed to two high-profile arrests of would-be terrorists, including the 2004 case of Specialist Ryan Anderson, a Washington state National Guardsman who attempted to sell classified information about vulnerabilities of U.S., weapons systems to an al-Qa'ida member that he met online.

That al-Qa'ida member was actually Rossmiller. Anderson is now in prison serving five consecutive life sentences, the harshest penalty yet dealt to an American in the war on terrorism. In another case, and again posing online as a member of al- Qa'ida, Rossmiller uncovered a plot by Pennsylvania resident and al-Qa'ida sympathiser, Michael Reynolds, to blow up several gas pipelines and oil refineries in the United States. Reynolds was convicted and is now serving fifty seven years in prison. Rossmiller is reported to have provided information to U.S., law enforcement or intelligence in as many as 240 other cases, leading to the detention of dozens of suspects worldwide and even some arrests and deportations of terrorism suspects from the United States.

For all the success that Rossmiller and 7-Seas has had, there remains a great deal of ambivalence, ambiguity, and tension in their relationship with authorities. On the one hand, the volunteers are motivated in part by calls by authorities to be vigilant. They believe authorities' claims about the seriousness of the threat of terrorism and want to help. One the other hand, they are also motivated by feelings that the government is either unable or unwilling to counter extremists' use of the Internet. Similarly, while Rossmiller has received a great deal of praise and assistance from authorities—the FBI has compensated her for her expenses, provided her with Arabic translation services, and provided her with security, a former Secretary of Commerce has said that she deserves a medal, she has been consulted by the Defence Intelligence Agency, and she has been an invited speaker at an FBI cyber security conference—these agencies have also sometimes expressed concern or doubt about her work and the work of others like her.

For her part, Rossmiller has at times complained that her work is being undervalued by authorities and has been clear to assert her independence from the state. But for all the tensions between authorities and volunteers, and for all that Rossmiller and 7-Seas have tried to distance themselves from the authorities, they nonetheless seek both approval and profit from the authorities. Both 7-Seas and later Phoenix Global Intelligence Systems have sought government contracts and intelligence and security consulting work for government clients.

In 2009, Rossmiller announced at an FBI-sponsored cyber security conference that she had formed a company and was seeking a partnership with a defence contractor to offer cyber-intelligence training and services to the government. She has been encouraged to do so by former CIA Director, James Woolsey. In the end, there are real reasons for tension and for concern. Both sides are right. The authorities likely cannot monitor and analyse that much Web content, making the work of the volunteers indispensable.

However, the volunteers do not have the ability to physically arrest suspects or materially disrupt terrorist planning or operations in any significant way, making the capabilities of the state indispensable in achieving their goals. Additionally, there are clear difficulties in making the relationship work. Sometimes authorities and volunteers can work at cross purposes. If authorities rely too much on volunteers, or if the role of volunteers becomes formally institutionalised, then their main value can be compromised. Finally, Michael Reynolds' defence strategy—i.e., claiming that he too was just trying to catch terrorists online like Rossmiller—also points to some of the potential difficulties in this new relationship between producers and consumers of security online.

COUNTERING THREATS TO CYBER SPACE

Other groups have worked to counter threats to cyber space. This includes efforts to investigate and analyse cyber attack incidents such as denial of service attacks and targeted use of malware. Founded in August 2008 by former intelligence analyst Jeffrey Carr, Project Grey Goose was an experiment in online, volunteer, open source intelligence (OSINT) aimed at investigating possible Russian government involvement in the large-scale cyber attacks that hit the country of Georgia during the Russian military invasion earlier that month. On August 22, 2008, Carr used his blog to announce the project and to put out a call for volunteers.

The final cadre of twelve that was listed in the group's October 2008 report was comprised primarily of current and former members of the intelligence community, academic researchers, and defence and security professionals. Contributors to a second Grey Goose report released in early 2009 largely fit the same demographic profile. The group has described their OSINT methodology as relying on "data mining" and "machine translation" of "foreign language forums and social media sites," technical analysis of "serverlevel data," "an examination of geopolitical events occurring around the time of the cyber attacks," and "a review of the Nation State's military doctrine related to Information Warfare." They believe that the open source nature of their work is a distinct advantage, allowing them to work more quickly and with greater participation from international volunteers.

The two Grey Goose reports have had a substantial impact on shaping perceptions of Russia's involvement in the 2008 Georgia cyber attacks, as well as shaping public debate about the threat of cyber war. Members and supporters of Project Grey Goose even believe that data that they turned over to authorities may have prevented some cyber attacks, as well caused the Kremlin "to reduce its support of various [hacker] groups". Jeffrey Carr has become a sought-after expert on issues of cyber war, resulting in his publication of the book *Inside*

Cyber Warfare for O'Reilly Media in 2009. Carr's book is now on the Commander's recommended reading list for members of U.S., Strategic Command, the parent organisation of the newly-formed U.S., Cyber Command.

Once again, the case of Project Grey Goose indicates the ambivalence and ambiguities that often exist between producers and consumers of security. Like Rossmiller and others, Carr has argued that bureaucratic inefficiencies often prevent government from effectively countering "terrorism in cyber space". One of those limitations, he argues, is that state actors do not yet understand the power of either the Internet, open sources of information, or collaborative processes of knowledge production.

Thus, governments have proven ill-equipped for countering terrorists online or meeting the challenge of cyber attacks. He sees Project Grey Goose as exemplary of the value of applying the open source software development model to intelligence work and hopes that "it will prove that we do not have to wait for official channels to adopt innovative solutions". Carr and his supporters identify Project Grey Goose as an example of what they call a "security trust network" (STN). Michael Sinkowitch, an executive at Fujitsu Australia who specialises in national security and intelligence, has defined STNs as "expert affiliations of interested organisations and individuals that can investigate and mitigate cyber crime threats".

Alexander Klimburg, a fellow at the Austrian Institute for International Affairs and a contributor to Carr's 2009 book, defines them as the liberal, democratic, Western antithesis to Russian and Chinese "patriotic hackers." Where "patriotic hackers" are seen as beholden to or controlled by the state and composed of malicious actors with a dubious moral code, STNs are defined as free to "choose when and if" to support a government, as trustworthy and credible partners for government, and as "shar[ing] a common moral code" based in "doing the right thing" and "operating within the remits of the law". Carr, Sinkowitsch, and Klimburg all see STNs like Project Grey Goose as examples of the security-producing "informal groups and volunteer networks" that Klimburg speaks about in the epigraph to this chapter.

In the realm of cyber security in particular, Klimburg has claimed that most work is already being done by STNs and business with "government bringing up the rear". He has claimed that STNs are particularly good at addressing the "attribution problem" in cyber security—i.e., figuring out the origin of a cyber attack, which is "a notoriously difficult task". Sinkowitsch has gone so far as to claim that cyber security STNs are able to "defeat, or at the very least limit the damage of, these adversaries [i.e., cyber attackers of various sorts]". But like the other cases of convergence security examined here, STNs too are ultimately dependent upon their relationship to the state.

Even Sinkowitsch admits that "There is not much they [STNs] can do about stopping the threats". Though STNs are theoretically free to choose when and if they work with the state, in practice having an impact requires working with the state. Since, the original call for volunteers for Project Grey Goose, Carr has solicited volunteers for a project he calls "Grey Balloons," which is an open-ended project to create a standing pool of volunteers that are ready and able to help the U.S., intelligence community with whatever challenges it might face. Grey Balloons is a reflection of Carr's "hope that a bridge could be established connecting intelligence community professionals with independent volunteers with the necessary expertise". Finally, as in the case of Rossmiller and cyber-counterterrorism, there is profit to be made in assisting the state.

In 2009, Project Grey Goose became Grey Logic, "a consultancy and information services provider to governments". It is perhaps unsurprising then that Sinkowitsch and Klimburg have encouraged Western governments to promote and support the formation of STNs as a necessary component of their national cyber security strategies. Finally, there are real reasons for concern when it comes to STNs. When questioned about the legal status of STNs and whether their work borders on vigilantism, Sinkowitsch claimed that there is no legal problem with what STNs do because they rely on information that is freely available on the Web; they are merely collecting and analysing it in a different, more effective way.

But recent scandals over advertiser use of social media content, as well as the case of a defence contractor mining and analysing social media content to smear supporters of WikiLeaks and political opponents of the U.S., Chamber of Commerce, indicate that there are legitimate privacy and legal concerns when volunteers begin doing their own online intelligence work on behalf of the state or powerful corporate interests.

THE INTERNET AND NATIONAL SECURITY AGENCIES

By now, nearly every federal agency within the U.S. government has some department or division responsible for computer security. But the pre-eminent agencies of the field are still the agencies charged with national security, such as the National Security Agency, the Central Intelligence Agency, the Federal Bureau of Investigation, and, to a lesser extent, the Justice Department and the Secret Service within the Treasury Department. It is important to acknowledge that it is the character of these agencies, their histories and their other responsibilities that give the subject of computer security in the United States a particular kind of atmosphere, largely that of the military and national security community itself.

Thus, the "command and control" model of computer security has tended to dominate the U.S. government's approach. In 1987, the Computer Security Act of the U.S. Congress apportioned responsibilities for computer security to the National Institute of Standards and Technology (NIST), of the U.S. Department of Commerce, for non-classified computer systems; and to the

National Security Agency (NSA) for classified systems. This law was the result of a certain level of alarm, on the part of Congress and civil libertarians, during the Reagan administration because of a pair of White House national security directives that pointed towards NSA control over all computers in the U.S. The Computer Security Act was an attempt to mark a boundary for civilian control of unclassified information systems. However, since the Computer Security Act the U.S. National Security Agency has worked diligently to regain and secure its supremacy over computer security policy.

A 1989 "Memorandum of Understanding" between NSA and NIST shifted power back to NSA, and in 1994 President Clinton issued Presidential Decision Directive 29, which set up the Security Policy Board, which has recommended that all computer security functions for the government be merged under NSA control. At the same time that NSA has attempted to impose its own standards on computer security in the U.S., the Justice Department's Federal Bureau of Investigation has tended to extend its responsibilities beyond domestic law enforcement to international crime, counter-terrorism, and counter-intelligence. While officials of the NSA are largely unknown to the public, FBI Director Louis Freeh is a common face in the news, often called upon to testify and make the government's case for control over encryption and computer security in the name of national security.

The 1993 bombing of the World Trade Center in New York City, which was apparently connected to a foreign conspiracy in the Middle East, strengthened the FBI's role in monitoring international terrorism immeasurably. Freeh also points to international drug cartels, new foreign sources of organised crime, the international terrorist activities of so-called "rogue states," the frightening potential for the uncontrolled proliferation of small nuclear weapons, and other threats to make the case that the FBI now has a host of new targets. These two phenomena of recent years have tended to blur the line between domestic security and national security, a blurring that has produced crises of constitutional protections in the past. But Congress has been persuaded by the federal law enforcement and national agencies.

The Intelligence Authorisation Act of 1997 states:

- ... elements of the Intelligence Community may, upon the request of a United States law enforcement agency collect information outside the United States about individuals who are not United States persons. Such elements may collect such information notwithstanding that the law enforcement agency intends to use the information collected for purposes of a law enforcement investigation or counterintelligence investigation.

Whitfield Diffie, the co-inventor of public key encryption, and his co-author Susan Landau, in their 1998 book Privacy on the Line, comment: "This wording carefully steers clear of permitting the intelligence community to spy on

Americans directly, but opens the way for unprecedented collaboration between the intelligence and law enforcement communities". The boundary-free character of the Internet will likely intensify the merging of conventional law enforcement activities inside the U.S. and the activities of national security agencies. The front line in the debate about this trend is encryption policy. In September of 1997, the U.S. Congress' House National Security Committee voted to strengthen controls on the export of digital encryption, reversing a trend towards relaxing such controls, one of the chief goals of the high tech industry. Committee members cited the warnings they received in "classified briefings" as the main reason for their vote.

Congressman Mike Oxley, a Republican of Ohio, told The New York Times, "I would find it difficult to believe that a member who heard the briefing could walk away not committed to addressing security issues. Frankly, I wish everyone interested in this issue could have heard for themselves the alarming briefing that members of our committee heard". Constraints of space prevent a comprehensive or even adequate review of the encryption debate here. In summary, the U.S. government's position is that law enforcement and national security authorities need to retain the ability to intercept and interpret communications, including digital data, in order to fulfill their responsibilities to protect the United States from crime and foreign threats. As such, the federal government has proposed a series of arrangements that have all included the concept of "escrowed keys," meaning the ability of authorised officials to acquire an encryption key to unlock scrambled data. Opponents of this scheme, which is the traditional approach in military cryptography, argue that public key encryption, without escrowed keys, is the only safeguard for privacy and authenticated electronic commerce.

These opponents also argue that criminals and foreign adversaries will have no incentive to use encryption with escrowed keys — *i.e.*, the "key escrow" approach will provide keys to the communications of people who obey the law, while others will have easy access to unbreakable encryption algorithms. The ready availability of public key encryption, argue government critics, means that "the horse is out of the barn" already. Moreover, they point out, the task of security in the computer age is for each person, or each computer administrator, to be responsible for computer security, because the task is too immense and complex for bureaucratic oversight. The argument has been framed as one in which the protective schemes are characterised as a choice between armies or locks, and each of these has its attendant interest group. While the Congress has been largely sympathetic to and supportive of the federal law enforcement and national security agencies, another front has opened up in the U.S. courts.

In early 1997, in a case heard before the United States District Court for the Northern District of California, Bernstein v. United States Department of

State, U.S. District Court Judge Marilyn Hall Patel ruled that national security considerations cannot be used to censor cryptographic schemes on the Internet. Daniel Bernstein, a graduate student, created an encryption algorithm called "Snuffle." After four years of correspondence with the U.S. State Department, Bernstein learned that his source code and all other material about "Snuffle" except a research paper were in violation of export control laws and could not be posted to the Internet. Bernstein sued the State Department, claiming that this ban violated his First Amendment rights. Judge Patel agreed with Bernstein, and wrote a stinging rebuke of the government's position. Patel ruled that computer source code is protected as free speech by the First Amendment, and that the government's attempt to ban such speech amounted to "prior restraint," which is unconstitutional. Judge Patel specifically prevented the U.S. government from using claims of a breach of national security to impose prior restraint on the distribution of encryption source code.

The U.S. government has appealed the Bernstein decision to the U.S. Supreme Court, and it is there that a final ruling is expected. If the Supreme Court upholds Judge Patel's ruling, this may close the encryption debate for the foreseeable future; after such a ruling, all encryption source code could be posted to the Internet without intervention by national security or law enforcement agencies. This would effectively kill the means by which such agencies now control the distribution of non-escrow encryption algorithms. On the other hand, if the Supreme Court overturns the Bernstein decision, this will reinforce the role of national security agencies in shaping the future of the Internet. Because of this, the Bernstein case is being watched very closely by both sides of the encryption debate.

The dispute over encryption has put into stark relief the dual nature of the national security mission: the responsibility of such agencies to protect national technological assets and also retain the ability to intercept and interpret digital communications. In the era of the Internet, these two responsibilities are in conflict with each other, thus posing significant dilemmas to national security officials. On the one hand, these agencies are urging businesses, other government agencies, and individuals to protect their computer data from attack.

On the other hand, these agencies seek to control the way these people protect such data in order to protect law enforcement and national security agency access to this data. Not surprisingly, both businesses and individuals are hesitant to implement encryption schemes that require turning over keys to people they don't know or whose motives they don't fully comprehend. Because of this hesitancy, the first mission of the security agencies, that of increasing protection for U.S. computer systems, is stymied. General Marsh, the chairman of the President's Commission on Critical Infrastructure Protection, has told the press he hopes the dispute about encryption policy is resolved soon, because he believes, with justification, that this ongoing dispute is obstructing the implementation of greater security for computer systems. Members of the commission have hinted at their support for a loosening of encryption controls, but have also leaked the information, to The New York Times, that "they are under fairly strict orders' to fall in line with the FBI's push for key recovery". Business executives are understandably reluctant to invest in security systems that may be superseded by other technologies or blocked by court rulings.

The U.S. federal government's rapid transition from one policy recommendation to another — such as from DES to the "Clipper chip" to key escrow to "key recovery — has not helped foster confidence in the business community. And of course, some influential business organisations, such as the Business Software Alliance are allied with civil libertarians and other opponents of U.S. government policy in the case of encryption standards. Despite the hopes of General Marsh and others, at present the encryption debate in the United States is so polarised that compromise solutions are not visible nor likely to emerge soon. This polarisation has been exacerbated by some ideological and political trends in the U.S. Republican conservatives who now control the U.S. Congress are more sympathetic to law enforcement and national security arguments than was true of the Congress just a few years ago.

For example, for many years the U.S. House Subcommittee on Civil and Constitutional Rights was chaired by Rep. Don Edwards, a Democrat and a former FBI agent who was highly critical of any law enforcement encroachment on civil liberties. But Congressman Edwards has retired, and conservative Republicans have taken his place as committee chairmen. Another new phenomenon is the emergence of a new breed of "cyberlibertarians — typically young, talented technologists who reject most of the assumptions of the national security establishment. Some of the more radical of these ideologues have argued that the Internet is the beginning of the end of the nation-state, let alone the end of the national security state. This perspective is not just an isolated intellectual discourse, either: the "cypherpunk" movement, for example, has complex and extensive ties to outlaw hackers, most of them young men, some of whom have adopted the intellectual framework of "cyberlibertarianism" as an ideological justification for criminal penetrations of government computers — casting themselves as "Thomas Paines" of the digital revolution. Such "counterculture" attitudes are widely shared by educated young people all over the world, perhaps a natural attitude of young people rebelling against authority.

But when this attitude is combined with the fact that these same people are the most technically adept in the world, and a number of them are affluent or even wealthy because of this skill — once again, national security officials are confronting a new and alien environment, one dramatically different from eras of the past, when business leaders and skilled technologists were typically undisturbed by the alleged imperatives of national security. Now, when confronting young leaders of the digital revolution, national security authorities are in hostile territory. The end of the Cold War has given new impetus to calls for a dismantling of national security institutions, and the Internet, with its idealistic potential for global communications between planetary citizens, has come along at just the right time to fuel such ideas. Widespread use of phrases like "the digital revolution" and "Third Wave civilization" reinforce the popular notion that the "information age" entails an overturning of old regimes, including, perhaps, the centuries-old competition between nation states.

For these reasons, in addition to the prosaic clash of interests between the government and pragmatic corporations that are part of a global marketplace, the encryption debate is the leading edge of a much larger philosophical debate about the role of the state in the information age. It is unfair, of course, to characterise national security authorities as "dinosaurs" due for extinction, the way they are characterised by some of the "cyberlibertarians" — even a small dose of the daily news is enough to convince most people that there are in fact real threats that continue to justify the need for some national security protections. On the other hand, there is no compelling reason to assume that the missions and structures and traditions and size of national security institutions created during the decades of the Cold War need persist into eternity. Many critics of national security agencies argue reasonably and persuasively that the Cold War should be regarded as an anomaly in U.S. history, a struggle that imposed sacrifices in democratic values that need not be sustained or repeated in the absence of a threat equivalent to the Soviet Union.

These critics have quite rightly put on the table for debate the question of whether the "national security state" is an essential or necessary political form for nations in the 21st century, particularly in an era in which the Internet is challenging many assumptions and norms inherited from a pre-Internet period, that of World War II and the decades of the Cold War. It may seem grandiose to suggest that complex technical debates such as those surrounding digital encryption or the prospect of "cyberwar" are the most important political debates of our time. But this is in fact the case. This is not actually all that surprising, when one considers the catalyst of such debates: the Internet itself, one of the most remarkable, promising, and at the same time vexing creations of human enterprise in the history of the world.

THE INTERNET AND THE MILITARY IN HISTORICAL CONTEXT

As is common, popular knowledge by now, the Internet was first launched as a research project funded and managed by the U.S., Department of Defence Advanced Research Projects Agency (ARPA) in the late 1960s. In 1983, the Defence Communications Agency split the network into two parts, ARPANET and MILNET, the former for the research community and the latter for non-classified military communications. ARPANET's name was changed to the Internet, and management was turned over to the National Science Foundation.

It was also in 1983 that the network adopted TCP/IP, which was perhaps the most important technical decision in the history of the Internet to date, allowing a vast expansion of the Internet that continues at an amasing rate of growth today. There is a persistent myth surrounding the history of the Internet that it was designed to "sustain a nuclear attack," and that this was the chief research interest of the Internet's Pentagon sponsors. As described in the definitive history of the Internet, When Wizards Stay Up Late, by Katie Hafner and Matt Lyon, the story that lies behind this myth is somewhat complicated.

Paul Baran, a RAND Corporation researcher who joined that Air Force-sponsored thinktank in Santa Monica, California, in 1959, "developed an interest in the survivability of communications systems under nuclear attack," write Hafner and Lyon. "He was motivated primarily by the hovering tensions of the cold war, not the engineering challenges involved.... Baran knew, as did all who understood nuclear weapons and communications technology, that the early command and control systems for missile launch were dangerously fragile". At this time, during the late 1950s and early 1960s, the RAND Corporation was the primary source of strategic thinking for U.S., nuclear policy, and the institution was already heavily dependent on computer technology, producing many of the earliest computer models of nuclear war. RAND researchers were working on sustainable communications systems before Baran joined their ranks, without much success.

It was Baran's theoretical work on distributed networked systems that pointed towards a solution. Baran came up with three theoretical innovations that became fundamental to the development of the Internet: a distributed network, network redundancy, and message disaggregation. This was a radical departure from the then universal model of communications based on centralised switching and open, direct circuits. Baran's work was understood by only a handful of communications experts in the United States, and it was poorly received by the people in charge of improving defence communications, most of whom came from careers rooted in the more conventional model. He halted his work in 1964, convinced that the agencies responsible for military communications would botch the job even if they adopted his ideas.

"So I told my friends in the Pentagon to abort this entire programme — because they wouldn't get it right," he told Hafner and Lyon. Instead, he decided to wait for the right moment, with some different kind of organisation. His opportunity emerged a few years later, when Larry Roberts, one of the ARPA officials in charge of investigating computer networks in the late 1960s, discovered Baran's RAND papers. However, note Hafner and Lyon, "Nuclear war scenarios, and command and control issues, weren't high on Roberts' agenda".

Roberts was intrigued by Baran's theoretical ideas of a distributed network from a purely research point of view. Roberts was also interested in a network that would tie together several of ARPA's chief research sites, universities and other institutions conducting experiments funded by the agency. It was Roberts who laid the first foundations of the Internet, relying on contributions from many different sources, including Baran, who became a consultant to the project. Thus, while Baran's work was motivated by the goal of building a communications network that could survive a nuclear war, this motivation was only a small part of the flow of ideas that built the technical foundations of the Internet.

Even more important is the fact that the Internet was never linked to any critical military application or system. The Internet never played a role in controlling nuclear weapons, for example. The communications network that connected U.S., nuclear facilities, such as between the North American Air Defence Command in Cheyenne Mountain, Colorado — the hub of the country's "early warning" system — and the launch control headquarters of the Strategic Air Command in Omaha, Nebraska, was deliberately isolated from the Internet. The scenario portrayed in the popular movie "War Games," in which a teenage computer whiz taps into the nation's nuclear arsenal from his home computer, was never possible in real life.

The Defence Department built its own global communications network, the World-Wide Military Communications System (WWMCs, pronounced "Wimmix"), which shared little with the Internet and was not connected to it; indeed, WWMCs was notoriously unreliable and was eventually abandoned. For a variety of reasons, the development of the Internet, even when it was funded by the Pentagon, scarcely attracted the attention of military planners or national security officials.

In the 1960s and 1970s, ARPA was an agency nearly unto itself, run primarily by and for academic researchers who were distant from military culture. ARPA's character began to change in the 1980s, but in the early days of the Internet, the system was viewed almost universally as a research programme, not as a precursor to a communications network tied to national security. In fact, it was this research character that contributed to the ease with which the Internet was absorbed by the civilian sector and now by commercial enterprises. The Internet was not burdened with security classifications, black budgets, or secret technical specifications. And, ironically enough, it was this very openness of the Internet's development that reduced its importance in the eyes of career military officers and high national security officials, who were conditioned to believe that anything significant in their fields must be classified and secret. In short, while the Internet and the concept of "national security" share common roots in history, they developed along separate and divergent paths. This makes it all the more interesting that these paths are now converging again, but in a way that makes the Internet problematic and even threatening to national security.

THE NEW INTERSECTION OF NATIONAL SECURITY AND THE INTERNET

In September of 1997, the President's Commission on Critical Infrastructure Protection released a preliminary report calling for a vast increase in funding to protect eight key elements of U.S., infrastructure: electric power distribution, telecommunication, banking and finance, water, transportation, oil and gas storage and transportation, emergency services and government services. "These are the life support systems of the nation," said the Commission's chairman, retired Air Force General Robert T. Marsh. "They're vital, not only for day-to-day discourse, they're vital to national security. They're vital to our economic competitiveness world wide, they're vital to our very way of life."

"The Internet provides an access point into all these infrastructures," said Marsh. Commission member John T. Davis, representing the National Security Agency, said the government should develop a secure "Next Generation Internet" for official use. The commission recommended doubling the current federal R&D budget of $250 million for protecting these systems, with increases of $100 million each year after 1999 to $1 billion per year by 2004. In February, 1998, U.S., Attorney General Janet Reno unveiled a $64 million plan to build a new "command center" to fight "cyber attacks" against U.S., computer systems. This new "command center" is called the National Infrastructure Protection Center, a Justice Department response to the report from the President's Commission on Critical Infrastructure Protection. These are just some of the more recent and visible results of concern over "cyber war," "infowar," "cyberterrorism," and other, related threats now perceived by law enforcement personnel and national security officials as new and important terrain. And these authorities commonly view the Internet as the "highway" upon which these threats will be borne.

The character of the Internet has been dramatically transformed over the past five years, as everyone knows. What began as a communications network for scientists, academics, engineers, and specialists is now a vast, global, communications medium that rivals the public telephone network, television broadcasting, and even radio. The Internet-using population, worldwide, is now over 60 million people, and Matrix Internet Data Services, an Internet demographic consulting company in Austin, Texas, has predicted that, by the year 2002, there could be more than 700 million people using the network. Senior executives in large telecommunications companies, an industry which is now the largest in the world, routinely report that data traffic will soon surpass voice traffic, and that packet-switched networks, like the Internet, may eventually supersede the circuit-switched telephone network worldwide. The Internet "model," of packet-switching, distributed communication, and unmanned digital nodes, appears to be the bedrock for nearly all future communications. Of particular importance to those charged with national security is the fact that increasing levels of international commerce are conducted over the Internet, and also increasing levels of government service. International funds transfers, now surpassing over a trillion dollars a day, are carried by computer networks.

Power grids, banks, government databases, large corporate enterprises, news networks, transportation facilities, and many other essential components of civilised life are increasingly "on the net," delivering services or conducting critical communications over the Internet. Disruption of such services or communications could, someday it is feared, resemble or approach in severity an actual physical attack such as a military strike or a major terrorist incident. At present, the potential for a computer attack that would produce a major national calamity is controversial. Most computer attacks documented so far have been merely intrusions or annoyances. In many cases, vulnerability to computer attack is shrouded in secrecy or proprietary prudence.

In other cases, vulnerability may be exaggerated to enhance the status and commercial value of computer security firms or to improve the negotiating position of government agencies that are seeking more funding or clout. What is important now, however, is that officials of the U.S., government and experts in the private sector are arguing, persistently, that the growth of the Internet, and its expanding capabilities, combined with the fact that it is increasingly embedded in "critical national infrastructures," makes protection of computers on the Internet a matter of national security. In other words, regardless of the current threat, the future indicates growing vulnerability and thus a growing urgency for protection and vigilance. Jamie Gorelick, U.S., Deputy Attorney General, told the host of TV's "Nightline" news talk show, Forrest Sawyer, in December of 1997, "My own assessment, Forrest, is that we have a couple of years before there is a really serious threat. We have seen indications in criminal activity, in the plans of foreign nations, in the plans of terrorist groups that lead us to believe that we should be about the process of hardening our computers against attack". In yet another irony, what may contribute to the threat of computer attack in the U.S., is the country's unrivaled military superiority. General Marsh said on the same "Nightline" programme, "Nobody around the world today would attempt to defeat us on the battlefield. Instead, they will be seeking means to find vulnerabilities in our systems that they can exploit and do serious harm without having to confront us in the conventional armed way of the past." If the Internet does prove to be a viable means for nations to attack one another, nations capable of such threats will be able to afford a credible threatening status far more cheaply than if they needed vast arsenals of missiles and tanks. A relatively modest investment in the skills of a handful of network trespassers and hackers would become a substitute for immense investments in weaponry. As such, the sources of credible threats could proliferate.

This "new terrain" of computer warfare or cyberterrorism poses some serious and unfamiliar challenges to national security authorities. First, all forms of warfare in the past have involved a threat to geographically specific assets by equally geographically specific threats — such as massed armies or ballistic missiles. One of the chief characteristics about computer attacks is their ambiguity in nearly every dimension: it's difficult to ascertain where the attack is coming from, who is behind it, what the motive is, whether it is the work of a determined enemy or merely a curious trespasser, etc. Penetrations that come from trespassers inside the U.S., may not be benign or "domestic." Before the war in the Persian Gulf, for example, there was a report of a U.S., hacker breaking into Pentagon computers and then offering to sell the information to Saddam Hussein (who didn't buy it because he didn't believe it was genuine). It's not even clear what the term "cyberwar" describes. If it means an organised and coordinated attack on computer systems by another state government, that may be too high a threshold; it's unlikely we'll see an unequivocal example of this soon, except perhaps by the U.S., attacking an enemy's computers. "Cyberterrorism" may be more likely, but, as in the distinction between war and terrorism by other means, this prospect might call for solutions different than protection from "cyberwar." If a computer attack were to occur in the midst of some other crisis of national security, says Roger Molander, an expert now at the RAND Corporation, the very ambiguity of the attack may complicate decision-making tremendously. This is a murky world for national security officials.

Second, the United States has historically avoided major military attacks because of its relative isolation from belligerents, a kind of "continental defence." Most of the country's history in military strategy has been to keep conflict as far from the U.S., mainland as possible. But the Internet poses a new dilemma: its global character, and the way it works, allows easy access to almost any networked computer inside the United States, including those running critical systems, from nearly anywhere else in the world. For a determined adversary, there are now millions of entry points to the U.S., heartland, and requiring no logistical effort, in contrast to the obstacles facing adversaries in the past.

Third, because of the fact that computer attacks can come from both inside and outside the U.S., and the fact that the origins of such attacks are difficult to identify promptly, jurisdictional controversies and overlap among law enforcement and national security agencies are already rampant. The U.S., has had a long tradition, for fifty years at least, of separating the jurisdictions of agencies responsible for domestic threats from those responsible for foreign threats. If the Internet is factored into their responsibilities, these jurisdictional boundaries are rendered exceedingly vague and arbitrary, leading to confusion and conflicting interests.

Finally, the biggest issue of all, for the most part, in the past, the U.S., military and its national security allies, such as intelligence agencies, have been charged with protecting military assets first, and using these as offensive weapons or deterrents against enemies. In a "cyberwar" scenario, however, conventional military assets will be useless, and there may be no appropriate offensive weapons available. The military and law enforcement and national security agencies are increasingly faced with protecting private assets, such as corporate computer systems, or other information systems far outside the jurisdiction of the federal government.

Given the nature of U.S., democracy, the federal government's powers for forcing protection schemes on private companies or other governmental entities are limited. And, as demonstrated by the ongoing debate over encryption restrictions, the government may have interests quite different from those of private companies, especially those that compete in the global marketplace. Indeed, given the evolving nature of global enterprise, it's commonly unclear where a U.S., company stops and a foreign counterpart or partner begins. The Internet does tend to erase national borders, as does global commerce.

The U.S., defence establishment has traditionally been able to circumscribe what constitutes a "national asset," but this is getting more and more difficult to do. For all these reasons, many of which have emerged only in the past half decade, the Internet is a new factor in national security assessment. And, given the significant influence of national security agencies in setting national political agendas, and in shaping technological trends, this new friction between the Internet and national security is likely to affect the way the Internet develops for the foreseeable future. At stake is whether the Internet can retain its democratic, global, and egalitarian features, or whether it will be absorbed into older patterns of national competition for power and status.

THE LEGAL LANDSCAPE FOR THE PROTECTION OF PRIVACY

Although not specifically referenced in the Constitution, the Right to Privacy is considered a 'penumbral right' under the Constitution *i.e.* a right that has been declared by the Supreme Court as integral to the Fundamental Right to Life and Liberty. In addition, although no single statute confers a cross-cutting 'horizontal' right to privacy various statutes contain provisions which either implicitly or explicitly preserve this right. The following sections provide an overview of both constitutional and statutory safeguards to privacy in India.

CONSTITUTIONAL PROTECTIONS FOR PRIVACY

Although the Indian Constitution does not contain an explicit reference to a Right to Privacy, this right has been read in to the constitution by the Supreme Court as a component of two Fundamental Rights: the right to freedom under Article 19 and the right to life and personal liberty under Article 21. It would be instructive to provide a brief background to each of these Articles before delving deeper into the privacy jurisprudence expounded by the courts under them. Part III of the Constitution of India is titled 'Fundamental Rights' and lists out several rights which are regarded as fundamental to all citizens of India.

Article 13 forbids the State from making "any law which takes away or abridges" the fundamental rights. Article 19(1)(a) stipulates that "All citizens shall have the right to freedom of speech and expression". However this is qualified by Article 19(2) which states that this will not "affect the operation of any existing law, or prevent the State from making any law, in so far as such law imposes *reasonable restrictions* on the exercise of the right ... in the interests of the sovereignty and integrity of India, the security of the State, friendly relations with foreign States, public order, decency or morality, or in relation to contempt of court, defamation or incitement to an offence". Thus the Freedom of Expression guaranteed by Article 19(1)(a) is not absolute, but a qualified right that is susceptible, under the Constitutional scheme, to being curtailed under specified conditions. The other important Fundamental Right from the perspective of privacy jurisprudence is Article 21 which reads "21. No person shall be deprived of his life or personal liberty except according to procedure established by law." Where Article 19 contains a detailed list of conditions under which Freedom of Expression may be curtailed, by contrast Article 21 is thinly-worded and only requires a "procedure established by law" as a pre-condition for the deprivation of life and liberty.

However, the Supreme Court has held in a celebrated case *Maneka Gandhi vs. Union of India* that any procedure "which deals with the modalities of regulating, restricting or even rejection of a fundamental right falling within Article 21 has to be fair, not foolish, carefully designed to effectuate, not to subvert, the substantive right itself. Thus, understood, "procedure" must rule out anything arbitrary, freakish or bizarre." Shortly after independence, in a case challenging the constitutionality of search and seizure provisions, the Supreme Court dealt a blow to the right to privacy in India, holding that "When - the Constitution makers have thought fit not to subject to Constitutional limitations by recognition of a fundamental right to privacy, analogous to the American Fourth Amendment, we have no justification to import it, into a totally different fundamental right."

Notwithstanding this early setback, five decisions by the Supreme Court in the succeeding 5 decades have established the Right to Privacy in India as flowing from Article 19 and 21. The first was a seven-Judge bench decision in

Kharak Singh V. The State of U.P decided in 1964. The question for consideration in this case was whether "surveillance" under Chapter XX of the U.P.Police Regulations constituted an infringement of any of the fundamental rights guaranteed by Part III of the Constitution. Regulation 236(b) which permitted surveillance by "domiciliary visits at night" was held to be violative of Article 21.The meanings of the word "life" and the expression "personal liberty" in Article 21 were elaborately considered by this court in Kharak Singh`s case. Although the majority found that the Constitution contained no explicit guarantee of a "right to privacy", it read the right to personal liberty expansively to include a right to dignity.

It held that "an unauthorised intrusion into a person's home and the disturbance caused to him thereby, is as it were the violation of a common law right of a man - an ultimate essential of ordered liberty, if not of the very concept of civilization". In a minority judgement in this case, Justice Subba Rao held that "the right to personal liberty takes in not only a right to be free from restrictions placed on his movements, but also free from encroachments on his private life. It is true our Constitution does not expressly declare a right to privacy as a fundamental right but the said right is an essential ingredient of personal liberty Every democratic country sanctifies domestic life; it is expected to give him rest, physical happiness, peace of mind and security. In the last resort, a person's house, where he lives with his family, is his "castle" " it is his rampart against encroachment on his personal liberty."

This case, especially Justice Subba Rao's observations, paved the way for later elaborations on the right to privacy using Article 21. In 1972, the Supreme Court decided one of its first cases on the constitutionality of wiretapping. In *R. M. Malkani vs State Of Maharashtra* the petitioner's voice had been recorded in the course of a telephonic conversation where he was attempting blackmail. He asserted in his defence that his right to privacy under Article 21 had been violated. The Supreme Court declined his plea holding that "The telephonic conversation of an innocent citizen will be protected by Courts against wrongful or high handed' interference by tapping the conversation. *The protection is not for the guilty citizen against the efforts of the police to vindicate the law and prevent corruption of public servants.*"

The third case in the series, *Govind vs. State of Madhya Pradesh*, decided by a three- Judge Bench of the Supreme Court, is regarded as being a setback to the right to privacy jurisprudence. Here, the court was evaluating the constitutional validity of Regulations 855 and 856 of the Madhya Pradesh Police Regulations which provided for police surveillance of habitual offenders which including domiciliary visits and picketing of the suspects. The Supreme Court desisted from striking down these invasive provisions holding that "It cannot be said that surveillance by domiciliary visit-, would always be an unreasonable restriction upon the right of privacy. It is only persons who are suspected to be habitual criminals and those who are determined to lead a criminal life that are subjected to surveillance."

The court went on to make some observations on the right to privacy under the constitution:

- "Too broad a definition of privacy will raise serious questions about the propriety of judicial reliance on a right that is not explicit in the Constitution. The right to privacy will, therefore, necessarily, have to go through a process of case by case development. Hence, assuming that the right to personal liberty. the right to move freely throughout India and the freedom of speech create an independent fundamental right of privacy as an emanation from them it could not he absolute. It must be subject to restriction on the basis of compelling public interest. But the law infringing it must satisfy the compelling state interest test. *It could not be that under these freedoms the Constitution-makers intended to protect or protected mere personal sensitiveness"*

This case is important since it marks the beginning of a trend in the higher judiciary to regard the right to privacy as "not being absolute". From *Govind* onwards, 'non-absoluteness' becomes the defining feature and the destiny of this right. This line of reasoning was continued in *Malak Singh v State Of Punjab and Haryana* where the Supreme Court held that surveillance was lawful and did not violate the right to personal liberty of a citizen as long as there was no 'illegal interference' and it was "unobstrusive and within bounds". Nearly fifteen years separate this case from the Supreme Court's next major elaboration of the right to privacy in *R. Rajagopal vs. State of Tamil Nadu*. Here the court was involved a balancing of the right of privacy of citizens against the right of the press to criticize and comment on acts and conduct of public officials. The case related to the publication by a newspaper of the autobiography of Auto Shankar who had been convicted and sentenced to death for committing six murders. In the autobiography, he had commented on his contact and relations with various high-ranking police officials – disclosures which would have been extremely sensational. Sometime before the publication, he appears to have been induced to write a letter disclaiming his authorship of the autobiography.

On this basis, the Inspector General of Prisons issued a letter forbidding the newspaper from publishing the autobiography claiming, inter alia, that the publication of the autobiography would violate the prisoner's privacy. Curiously, neither Shankar himself, nor his family were made parties to this petition. The Court decided to presume, somewhat oddly, that he had "neither written his autobiography" nor had he authorised its publication.

The court then proceeded on this assumption to enquire whether he had any privacy interests that would be breached by unauthorised publication of his life story.

The right of privacy of citizens was dealt with by the Supreme Court in the following terms:

- The right to privacy is implicit in the right to life and liberty guaranteed to the citizens of this country by Article 21. It is a "right to be let alone". A citizen has a right to safeguard the privacy of his own, his family, marriage, procreation, motherhood, childbearing and education among other matters. None can publish anything concerning the above matters without his consent - whether truthful or otherwise and whether laudatory or critical. If he does so, he would be violating the right to privacy of the person concerned and would be liable in an action for damages. Position may, however, be different, if a person voluntarily thrusts himself into controversy or voluntarily invites or raises a controversy.
- The rule aforesaid is subject to the exception, that any publication concerning the aforesaid aspects becomes unobjectionable if such publication is based upon public records including court records. This is for the reason that once a matter becomes a matter of public record, the right to privacy no longer subsists and it becomes a legitimate subject for comment by press and media among others. We are, however, of the opinion that in the interests of decency an exception must be carved out to this rule, *viz.*, a female who is the victim of a sexual assault, kidnap, abduction or a like offence should not further be subjected to the indignity of her name and the incident being publicised in press/media.

On this reasoning, the court upheld that the newspaper's right to publish Shankar's autobiography, even without his consent or authorisation, to the extent that this story was able to be pieced together from public records. However, if they went beyond that, the court held, "they may be invading his right to privacy and will be liable for the consequences in accordance with law." Importantly, the court held that "the remedy of the affected public officials/public figures, if any, is *after the publication*" The final case that makes up the 'privacy quintet' in India was the case of *PUCL v. Union of India*, a public interest litigation, in which the court was called upon to consider whether wiretapping was an unconstitutional infringement of a citizen's right to privacy. The case was filed in light of a report brought out by the Central Bureau of Investigation on the 'Tapping of politicians' phones' which disclosed several irregularities in the tapping of telephones.

On the concept of the 'right to privacy' in India, the Court made the following observations:

- The right privacy - by itself - has not been identified under the Constitution. As a concept it may be too broad and moralistic to define it judicially. Whether right to privacy can be claimed or has been infringed in a given case would depend on the facts of the said case."

However, the Court went on to hold that "the right to hold a telephone conversation in the privacy of ones home or office without interference can certainly be claimed as right to privacy". This was because "conversations on the telephone are often of an intimate and confidential character...Telephone conversation is an important facet of a man's private life. Right to privacy would certainly include telephone-conversation in the privacy of one's home or office. Telephone-tapping would, thus, infract Article 21 of the Constitution of India unless it is permitted under the procedure established by law."

The court also read this right to privacy as deriving from Article 19. "When a person is talking on telephone, he is exercising his right to freedom of speech and expression.", the court observed, and therefore "telephone-tapping unless it comes within the grounds of restrictions under Article 19(2) would infract Article 19(1)(a) of the Constitution." This case made two important contributions to communications privacy jurisprudence in India – the first was its rejection of the contention that 'prior judicial scrutiny' should be mandated before any wiretapping could take place. Instead, the court accepted the contention that administrative safeguards would be sufficient. Secondly, the Court prescribed a list of procedural guidelines, the observance of which would save the wiretapping power from unconstitutionality.

In 2007, these safeguards were formally incorporated into the Rules framed under the Telegraph Act. Thus, to conclude this section, it may be observed that the right to privacy in India is, at its foundations a *limited* right rather than an absolute one. This limited nature of the right provides a somewhat unstable assurance of privacy since it is frequently made to yield to a range of conflicting interests – rights of paternity, national security etc which happen to have a more pronounced standing in law. In March 2002, the National Commission to Review the Working of the Constitution submitted its report and recommended amending the Constitution to include a slew of new rights including the Right to Privacy.

The new Right to Privacy would be numbered Article 21-B and would read: "Every person has a right to respect for his private and family life, his home and his correspondence. Nothing in clause (1) shall prevent the State from making any law imposing reasonable restrictions on the exercise of the right conferred by clause (1), in the interests of security of the State, public safety or for the prevention of disorder or crime, or for the protection of health or morals, or for the protection of the rights and freedoms of others." There has, so far been no move to amend the constitution to give effect to this recommendation.

STATUTORY PROTECTIONS FOR PRIVACY

Although such a move is under consideration, India does not currently have a sui-generis statute that safeguards privacy horizontally across different contexts. However various statutes dealing with issues as diverse as banking and finance, professional ethics of lawyers, doctors and chartered accountants, information technology and telephony etc contain provisions which either explicitly or impliedly protect privacy and offer victims remedies for their breach. Details of some of these sector-specific privacy provisions are provided in later sections of this report. In this section we propose to deal mainly with privacy protections under the Information Technology Act, with special focus on Data Protection provisions and certain other miscellaneous laws which protect privacy.

The Information Technology Act

The Information Technology Act 2000 contains a number of provisions which can be used to safeguard against online/computer related privacy. The Act provides for civil and criminal liability with respect to hacking and imprisonment of up to three years with fine for electronic voyeurism, Phishing and identity theft, Offensive e-mail. Disclosure by the government of information obtained in the course of exercising its interception powers under the IT Act is punishable with imprisonment of up to two years and fine Section 72A of the IT Act penalises the unauthorised disclosure of "personal information" by any person who has obtained such information while providing services under a lawful contract. Such disclosure must be made with the intent of causing wrongful loss or obtaining a wrongful gain and is punishable with imprisonment which may extend to 3 years or a fine of ₹ 500,000 or both.

SUPERVISORY AUTHORITY FOR PRIVACY LAWS AND COMPLAINTS

India does not have a national regulatory body to specially oversee the enforcement of privacy protections. However several sector-specific tribunals and adjudicatory authorities are empowered to determine issues of privacy that arise within their jurisdiction. Thus, for instance, the State Information Commission and the Central Information Commission established under the Right to Information Act, 2005 adjudicate issues relating to privacy that arise in the course of requests for information under that Act. More than 700 decisions of the Central Information Commission between 2005 and 2011 directly reference the word 'privacy' – indicating that this is a frequent venue for the determination of a range of privacy issues in India. The District, State and National Consumer Dispute Redressal Commissions can act as fora for the redressal of consumer privacy complaints.

The Human Rights Act 1993 grants victims or their representatives the right to approach the Human Rights Commission for relief for the violation, or the negligence in the prevention of violation of a human right by a public servant.

Human rights have been defined in the Act to mean "the rights relating to life, liberty, equality and dignity of the individual guaranteed by the Constitution or embodied in" the International Covenant on Civil and Political Rights and the International Covenant on Economic, Social and Cultural Rights. Since, the right to privacy is considered a fundamental right attached to the right to life, and is also explicitly affirmed in Article 17 of the ICCPR, this is definitely a subject on which the Human Rights Commission could provide a forum for redress. Since the Information Technology Act contains the clearest provisions relating to Data Protection and Privacy in India, it would be instructive to examine briefly the enforcement mechanism under that Act. Violation of privacy and data protection under the Information Technology Act entails both civil and criminal remedies. We provide a brief overview of the adjudicatory apparatus for both.

CIVIL COMPLAINTS UNDER THE IT ACT

Section 46 of the Information Technology Act empowers the Central Government to appoint "Adjudication Officers" to adjudicate whether any person has committed any of the contraventions described in Chapter IX of the Act and to determine the quantum of compensation payable. Accordingly, the Central Government has designated the Secretaries of the Department of Information Technology of each of the States or Union Territories as the "Adjudicating Officer" with respect to each of their territories. However, a pecuniary limit has been placed on the powers of Adjudicating Officers, and they may only adjudicate cases where the quantum of compensation claimed does not exceed ₹ 5 crores.

In cases where the compensation claimed exceeds this amount, jurisdiction would vest in the "competent court", under the Code of Civil Procedure. The AO is empowered with all the powers of a civil court – including the powers of summoning and enforcing attendance of witnesses, requiring the discovery and production of records, compounding complaints etc. Although the powers of the AO under the Act are very extensive, they have been used very sparingly in the 11 years since the passage of the IT Act. No compilation of the orders of AOs of various states exists either online or offline and they are only sparingly reported in newspapers. Among the cases that do get reported, however, there are encouraging signs of the Act being used to provide compensation to those who suffer due to data breaches by companies. In April 2010, the Adjudicating Officer of the State of Tamil Nadu passed an order for compensation against a leading bank for its failure to install a foolproof internet banking system. An amount of ₹ 4,60,000 had been illegally transferred out of the complainant's account and subsequently withdrawn by unknown persons. The AO observed that as a there was "unauthorised access to the petitioner's account.., loss of data and account information of the petitioner, damage to electronic information of the petitioner which resulted in financial loss, denial of access to his account".

Further, the AO held that "The Respondent bank has failed to put in place a foolproof Internet Banking System with adequate levels of authentication and validation which would have prevented unauthorised access.. that has led to serious financial loss to the petitioner".

Pursuant to this determination the respondent bank was ordered to pay an amount of ₹ 1,285,000 – which included the amount lost, interest, litigation expenses and travel expenses of the complainant. In May 2011, the same bank was ordered by the same Adjudicating Officer to pay an amount of ₹ 237,850 for a similar incident where the complainant's money was illegally transferred out of his account. The IT Act provides for the constitution of a Cyber Appellate Tribunal to hear appeals from cases decided by the adjudicating officer. Within twenty five days of the copy of the decision being made available by the Adjudicating Officer, the aggrieved party may file an appeal before the Cyber Appellate Tribunal. Section 57 provides that the appeal filed before the Cyber Appellate Tribunal shall be dealt with by it as expeditiously as possible and endeavour shall be made by it to dispose of the appeal finally within six months from the date of receipt of the appeal.

According to the Tribunal's web site, the CAT currently has 12 cases listed as 'pending' before it. It has disposed 8 cases, 7 of which were disposed on the same day – May 26 2010 – and in every case, the case was remanded back to an Adjudicating Officer for determination of facts. Some of these cases complain of privacy violations or seek reliefs which have implications on privacy. For instance, in *Mascon Global Limited V. CCA, Google etc*, disposed by the CAT on May 28, 2010, the appellant had sought details about an e-mail account from Google which was purportedly being used to send defamatory e-mails.

The CAT remanded the case to the Adjudicating Officer, which according to it was the appropriate forum to decide the case. In another case, widely reported in the press, a man filed a complaint of hacking against his estranged wife alleging that she had, with the aid of her professional colleagues, hacked into his and his father's e-mail account in order to obtain evidence in support of a dowry harassment case that she had filed against them. The Adjudicating Officer in the first instance had dismissed the complaint believing her assertion that the man and his father had themselves given her the password– a contention which was not denied by the complainant. On appeal, however, the man contended that he had not, in fact, given his wife the password.

The CAT ordered the case to be re-heard by the AO. Although the complaint alleged 'hacking' by the woman, the case in fact refers to a privacy grievance of the complainant. Section 62 gives the right of appeal to a High Court to any person aggrieved by any decision or order of the Cyber Appellate Tribunal on any question of fact or law arising out of such order.

8

Naxalite Violence and the Economic Development

Since its independence in 1947, India has faced numerous insurgencies within its borders at various points in time. One of the longest running insurgencies in India is the Naxalite insurgency. Using the synthetic control method of analysis developed by Abadie and Gardeazabal, we present the first estimates of the economic cost in terms of lost income per capita due to the Naxalite insurgency in the affected states, as well as the gains in terms of recaptured income per capita of a unique, robust security response to the Naxalite insurgency in one of the affected states *i.e.* Andhra Pradesh. With the ultimate objective of "seizing political power *i.e.* state power", the Naxalite movement started in Naxalbari, a small village in West Bengal in 1967, and then spread steadily across the country during the rest of the 20th century.

The rate of spread of the movement has become alarming in the recent past. By the Indian Government's own estimate, Naxalite activity has increased from 76 districts in 9 states in 2005 to 182 districts in 16 states in 2007, prompting Prime Minister Manmohan Singh to observe that the Naxalite insurgency is the single biggest internal security threat facing the country. Although there is a large literature measuring the economic costs of terrorism in different regions across the world, little research has been done to assess the economic costs of Naxalite violence. This paper attempts to fill this gap. Further, several states in India are affected by Naxalite violence, yet only one state raised a unique, specially trained police force dedicated to combating the Naxalite insurgency.

This natural experiment gives us a unique opportunity to measure the direct economic benefits of a robust localized security response to the Naxalite insurgency. We find that as a group, states affected by Naxalite violence lost on average 12.48 per cent of their per capita NSDP per year over the period 1980 to 2000. The average pcNSDP of these states was ₹10,200/- per year during this period, and the average loss of pc NSDP due to Naxalite violence was of the order of ₹1,273/- per year.

Despite the magnitude of the Naxalite problem, none of the affected states save Andhra Pradesh instituted a specialized police force, dedicated to combating the Naxalite menace. The introduction of such a force known as the Greyhounds in 1989 by Andhra Pradesh yielded a "security dividend" equal on average to 17.23 per cent of its pcNSDP over the period 1990 to 2000. The average pcNSDP of Andhra Pradesh was ₹12,884/- per year during this period, and the average gain of pcNSDP due to the Greyhounds force was of the order of ₹2,221/- per year. Placebo tests indicate that our results are significant. To the best of our knowledge, this is the first study that directly estimates the economic benefits of a unique security response undertaken by a state to an extremist threat.

LITERATURE REVIEW

Sandler and Enders report several avenues through which terrorism can impose economic costs on a state. Specifically, terrorism may "... divert foreign direct investment, destroy infrastructure, redirect public investment funds to security, or limit trade". Naxalite violence appears to have imposed economic costs on Indian states through all of these avenues.

For example, the blog Naxal Terror Watch documents incidents of Naxalites destroying pipelines transporting iron ore slurry in Chattisgarh, destroying road construction machinery in Bihar, forcing the closure of bank branches in Jharkhand, disrupting power supply by damaging hydroelectric power stations in Orissa, impeding interstate commerce by routinely preventing the repair of national highways and damaging railway infrastructure in Jharkhand and Orissa, degrading telecom service by destroying mobile phone towers, and discouraging the free flow of labour across regions by administering a "kidnap and extortion empire" in their area of operation, among other things. Joshi reports that investments of the order of ₹130bn were tied up in just the power and steel industries in projects that could not be completed in the state of Chattisgarh on account of Naxalite violence. In their excellent surveys, Blattman and Miguel, Frey, Luechinger and Stutzer, Llusa and Tavares and Sandler and Enders cite several papers that capture the wide range of macroeconomic and microeconomic effects that armed conflict in general and terrorism in particular may have.

We summarize some of these effects below. Macroeconomic effects may include reduced per capita GDP growth *e.g.* Blomberg, Hess and Orphanides, higher inflation, lower tax revenues, lower domestic investment, and higher expenditure on defence at the cost of lower expenditure on education and health *e.g.* Gupta *et al*, depressed exports and non-durable consumption *e.g.* Eckstein and Tsiddon, reduced bilateral trade flows *e.g.* Nitsch and Schumacher, reduced foreign direct investment inflows *e.g.* Enders and Sandler, depressed aggregate savings *e.g.* Fielding, significant negative abnormal stock returns both domestically and internationally *e.g.* Chen and Siems, etc. Microeconomic effects may include lower tourist inflows *e.g.* Enders and Sandler, lower tourism receipts *e.g.* Enders, Sandler and Parise and Sloboda, lower regional tourism market share *e.g.* Drakos and Kutan, depressed demand for domestic airline travel services *e.g.* Ito and Lee, depressed demand for hotel room stays *e.g.* Fleischer and Buccola, reduced visits to coffee shops, restaurants and pubs, and reduced usage of public transport *e.g.* Becker and Rubinstein, reduced long term investments in agriculture *e.g.* Singh, reduced enrolment in school *e.g.* Shemyakina, reduced height for age z-scores *e.g.* Bundervoet *et al* etc.

Although there is a large and growing literature on the economic consequences of terrorism, to the best of our knowledge, there is none in the Indian context save Singh. This India sized hole in the literature needs to be addressed on a war footing since "... no nation has suffered more from terrorism than India". In the Indian context, since not all districts of the Naxalite affected states are affected by Naxalite activity, it is possible that Naxalite violence redistributes economic activity and income from affected districts to non-affected districts, but without depressing the overall level of economic activity in the state. In that case, we would expect to find effects on GDP at the district level, but not at the state level. For example, Abadie and Gardeazabal find that the per capita GDP of a sub national region *i.e.* the Basque country in Spain declined by over 10 percentage points after the outbreak of terrorism. However, this paper does not use district level GDP data to investigate district level effects of Naxalite violence. We are concerned with the macroeconomic consequences of Naxalite violence at the state level, as measured by the loss in pcNSDP. In any study of the economic costs of terrorism, there are always endogeneity concerns in that while terrorist violence may depress GDP growth, reduced GDP growth may in turn spur terrorism. In the Indian context, Borooah finds that high incidence of poverty, low levels of literacy, and large amounts of forest cover are the main correlates of Naxalite activity at the district level in India.

Borooah however does not control for possible endogeneity, and notes that while poverty may lead to Naxalite activity, Naxalite activity by discouraging investment may contribute to poverty. However, Subramanian argues that "the real aim of Naxalites is nether the domain of economics nor state welfare. It is a political movement having its goal as the seizure of political power *i.e.* state power". If this is indeed the case, then the causation would tend to flow from Naxalite violence to low levels of GDP, and not vice versa. In Section 6, we argue that endogeneity issues are unlikely to be a serious concern for this study.

NAXALITE IN INDIA: AN INTRODUCTION

The word *Naxal*, Naxalite or Naksalvadi is a generic term used to refer to various militant Communist groups operating in different parts of India under different organizational envelopes. In the eastern states of the mainland India

(Jharkhand, West Bengal and Orissa), they are usually known as, or refer to themselves as Maoists while in southern states like Andhra Pradesh they are known under other titles. They have been declared as a terrorist organization under the Unlawful Activities (Prevention) Act of India (1967). Leaders of the movement have been found to have hideout located in China.

The term 'Naxal' derives from the name of the village Naxalbari in the state of West Bengal, India, where the movement had its origin. The Naxals are considered far-left radical communists, supportive of Maoist political sentiment and ideology. Their origin can be traced to the split in 1967 of the Communist Party of India (Marxist), leading to the formation of the Communist Party of India (Marxist–Leninist). Initially the movement had its centre in West Bengal. In later years, it spread into less developed areas of rural central and eastern India, such as Chhattisgarh, Orissa and Andhra Pradesh through the activities of underground groups like the Communist Party of India (Maoist). For the past 10 years, it has grown mostly from displaced tribals and natives who are fighting against exploitation from major Indian corporations and local corrupt officials.

In 2006 India's intelligence agency, the Research and Analysis Wing estimated that 20,000 armed cadre Naxalites were operating in addition to 50,000 regular cadres and their growing influence prompted Indian Prime Minister Manmohan Singh to declare them to be the most serious internal threat to India's national security. In February 2009, the Indian Central government announced a new nationwide initiative, to be called the "Integrated Action Plan" (IAP) for broad, co-ordinated operations aimed at dealing with the Naxalite problem in all affected states, namely (Karnataka, Chhattisgarh, Orissa, Andhra Pradesh, Maharashtra, Jharkhand, Bihar, Uttar Pradesh, and West Bengal). Importantly, this plan included funding for grass-roots economic development projects in Naxalite affected areas, as well as increased special police funding for better containment and reduction of Naxalite influence in these areas.

In 2009, Naxalites were active across approximately 180 districts in ten states of India. In August 2010, after the first full year of implementation of the national IAP programme, Karnataka was removed from the list of naxal affected states. In July 2011, the number of Naxal affected areas was reduced to 83 districts across nine states. In December of 2011, the national government reported that the number of Naxalite related deaths and injuries nationwide had gone down by nearly 50 per cent from 2010 levels.

HISTORY

The term Naxalites comes from Naxalbari, a small village in West Bengal, where a section of the Communist Party of India (Marxist) (CPM) led by Charu Majumdar, Kanu Sanyal and Jangal Santhal initiated a violent uprising in 1967. On May 18, 1967, the Siliguri Kishan Sabha, of which Jangal was the president, declared their readiness to adopt armed struggle to redistribute land to the landless. The following week, a sharecropper near Naxalbari village was attacked by the landlord's men over a land dispute. On May 24, when a police team arrived to arrest the peasant leaders, it was ambushed by a group of tribals led by Jangal Santhal, and a police inspector was killed in a hail of arrows. This event encouraged many Santhal tribals and other poor people to join the movement and to start attacking local landlords.

Charu Majumdar, inspired by the doctrines of Mao Zedong, provided ideological leadership for the Naxalbari movement, advocating that Indian peasants and lower class tribals overthrow the government and upper classes by force. A large number of urban elites were also attracted to the ideology, which spread through Majumdar's writings, particularly the 'Historic Eight Documents' which formed the basis of Naxalite ideology. In 1967, Naxalites organized the All India Coordination Committee of Communist Revolutionaries (AICCCR), and later broke away from CPM. Violent uprisings were organized in several parts of the country. In 1969, the AICCCR gave birth to the Communist Party of India (Marxist-Leninist) (CPI(ML)).

Practically all Naxalite groups trace their origin to the CPI(ML). A separate offshoot from the beginning was the Maoist Communist Centre, which evolved out of the *Dakshin Desh* group. The MCC later fused with the People's War Group to form the Communist Party of India (Maoist). A third offshoot was that of the Andhra revolutionary communists, mainly represented by the UCCRI(ML), following the mass line legacy of T. Nagi Reddy, which broke with the AICCCR at an early stage. During the 1970s, the movement was fragmented into disputing factions. By 1980, it was estimated that around 30 Naxalite groups were active, with a combined membership of 30,000.

Violence in West Bengal

Ca.1970 the Naxalites gained a strong presence among the radical sections of the student movement in Calcutta. Students left school to join the Naxalites. Majumdar, to entice more students into his organisation, declared that revolutionary warfare was to take place not only in the rural areas as before, but everywhere and spontaneously. Thus Majumdar declared an "annihilation line", a dictum that Naxalites should assassinate individual "class enemies" (such as landlords, businessmen, university teachers, police officers, politicians of the right and left) and others.

Throughout Calcutta, schools were shut down. Naxalites took over Jadavpur University and used the machine shop facilities to make pipe guns to attack the police. Their headquarters became Presidency College, Kolkata. The Naxalites found supporters among some of the educated elite, and Delhi's prestigious St. Stephen's College, alma mater of many contemporary Indian leaders and thinkers, became a hotbed of Naxalite activities. The chief minister,

"'Siddhartha Shankar Ray'" of the Congress Party, instituted strong counter-measures against the Naxalites. The West Bengal police fought back to stop the Naxalites. The house of Somen Mitra, the Congress MLA of Sealdah, was allegedly turned into a torture chamber where Naxal students from Presidency College and CU were incarcerated illegally by police and the Congress cadres. CPI-M cadres were also involved in the "state terror". After suffering losses and facing the public rejection of Majumdar's "annihilation line", the Naxalites alleged human rights violations by the West Bengal police, who responded that the state was effectively fighting a civil war and that democratic pleasantries had no place in a war, especially when the opponent did not fight within the norms of democracy and civility.

Large sections of the Naxal movement began to question Majumdar's leadership. In 1971 the CPI(ML) was split, as the Satyanarayan Singh revolted against Majumdar's leadership. In 1972 Majumdar was arrested by the police and died in Alipore Jail. His death accelerated the fragmentation of the movement.

Reasons for Failure, 1967–1975

In a methodical study, Dr. Sailen Debnath has surmised the consequences and reasons of failures of the Naxalite movement organised by Charu Majumdar and Kanu Sanyal. He writes "The Naxalite movement, though continued intensively from 1967 to the middle of the 1970s and resurfaced after some years, could not go a long way achieving anything commendable because of the following reasons:"

- The Naxalites wanted to surround the towns and cities by the villages, *i.e.*, they wanted to encircle the urban centres with organized peasant forces of the villages. If the peasant militia could have occupied the cities, the so-called bourgeois government would fall making the passage to the coming of a socialist government; but the Naxalites could not and did not come up to a stage capable of organizing the peasants and thereby encircling the towns.
- Majumdar gave sole importance to secret organization and armed training of its members for the purpose of eliminating class enemies. As the Naxalites did not have mass level organization, they lacked mass support. With only a few armed elements, and those not properly educated in the party line, little could be accomplished.
- "Khatam" (the action of eliminating the so-called class enemies in villages) was a wrongheaded attempt at political mobilization based on the individual murders of a select few people whose political class and character was never adjudged by their socio-economic conditions or the properties they possessed but very often only by their political affiliation or by the name and colour of the party or parties they

directly or indirectly belonged to. For example, in Jalpaiguri and Alipurduar they killed some petty jotdars who otherwise could have been comrades in action against the capitalists or could be friends in a revolution for radical change.

- Recruitment in the Naxalite party took place in the absence of proper judgement and scrutiny of the political characters and behaviours of the recruits. It was not uncommon for recruits into the Naxalite party to vent their personal animosities by identifying their personal enemies as class enemies, to be killed with the help of the Naxalite organization.
- The ruling Congress party inserted spies inside the unguarded Naxalite organization to gather information about its secret bases and arrest its supporters. Government intelligence personnel and police disguised as Naxalite sympathizers infiltrated the party's inner organization and arrested many of its leaders, including Charu Majumdar. Thus police had information about the movements of Majumdar after he had gone underground in 1970, and he was arrested in Calcutta in July 1972. He died in jail days after his arrest, probably in the night of 27 or 28 July. It is not known how he died, although the government reported that he died of a heart attack.

2000 Onwards

In a 2004 Indian Home Ministry estimate numbers were placed at that time at "9,300 hardcore underground cadre... [holding] around 6,500 regular weapons beside a large number of unlicensed country-made arms". In 2006, "Figures (in that year) put the strength of the movement at 15,000, and claim the guerrillas control an estimated one fifth of India's forests, as well as being active in 160 of the country's 604 administrative districts." India's Research and Analysis Wing, believed in 2006 that 20,000 Naxals were involved in the growing insurgency.

Today, some Naxalite groups have become legal organisations participating in parliamentary elections, such as the Communist Party of India (Marxist-Leninist) Liberation. Others, such as the Communist Party of India (Maoist) and the Communist Party of India (Marxist-Leninist) Janashakti.

On 6 April 2010 Naxalites launched the most deadly assault in the history of the Naxalite movement by killing 76 security personnel. The attack was launched by up to 1,000 Naxalites in a well-planned attack, killing an estimated 76 CRPF policemen in two separate ambushes and wounding 50 others, in the remote jungles of Chattisgarh's Dantewada district in Eastern/ Central India. On 17 May, Naxals blew up a bus on Dantewda-sukhma road in Chhattisgarh, killing 15 policemen and 20 civilians. In third Major attack by Naxals on 29 June, at least 26 personnel of Indian Centre Reserve Forces (CRPF) were killed in Narayanpur district of Chhattisgarh. Despite the 2010 Chhattisgarh ambushes, the most recent central government campaign to contain and reduce the militant Naxalite presence appears to be having some success. States such as Madhya Pradesh have reported significant reduction in Naxalite activities as a result of their use of IAP funds for rural development within their states.

In late 2011, the death of Kishenji, the military leader of Communist Party of India (Maoist) was killed in an encounter with the joint operation forces, which was a huge blow to the Naxalite movement in Eastern India. In March 2012 maoist rebels kidnapped two Italians in the eastern Indian state of Orissa, the first time Westerners were abducted there. 12 CRPF personnel were killed on 27th March 2012 in a landmine blast triggered by suspected Naxalites in Gadchiroli district of Maharashtra.

NAXALISM AND ITS EFFECTS ON ECONOMY

The Naxalites may pose a graver threat to India's economic power, potentially more damaging to Indian companies, foreign investors and the state than pollution, crumbling infrastructure or political gridlock. The growing Maoist insurgency over large swathes of the mineral-rich countryside could soon hurt some industrial investment plans. Just when India needs to ramp up its industrial machine to lock in growth and when foreign companies are joining the party — Naxalites are clashing with mining and steel companies essential to India's long-term success. The other reason for sounding the alarm stems from the increasingly close proximity between the corporate world and the forest domain of the Naxalites.

There is a growing concern over the widening reach of Naxalites as they operated in 30 per cent of India, up from 9 per cent in 2002. The terror groups have already begun operating and attacking industries on the edge of Maharashtra, Andhra Pradesh, Chattisgarh, Orissa Tamil Nadu, Jharkhand and Madhya Pradesh. Naxalites are now planning to penetrate India's major cities, and are looking to encircle urban centres, find sympathy among students and the unemployed and create armed, secret, self-defence squads that will execute orders. While Corporate were apathetic to security before 26/11, it has become a real issue now. Corporate and investors have a larger stake in securing a country, thus it is suggested that a vulnerability assessment be done and investments made in foolproof security.

CORPORATE/INDUSTRIAL INVESTIGATION & REPORT WRITING

In the wake of rising cases of corporate frauds and scams, corporate investigation services have become the need of the hour to ensure that you take a prudent decision, prior to finalize your business partners or big clients. Over the years, corporate investigation in India has emerged into a big and reliable industry that provides excellent investigation service without raising any suspicion. Corporate investigation agencies in India conduct external and internal investigations for small scale corporations to the big-wigs of the industry.

As far as internal investigation services are concerned, these corporate investigations in India do investigations regarding the use of drugs in work place. Besides this, these corporate investigation agencies also ensure that employees have been following the devised code of conduct. In external investigations, these corporate investigation agencies in India work well to expose any criminal scheming outside the corporation. On the other hand, they ensure that the company is not incurring any losses due to fraud billing of the products by the suppliers. Besides keeping an eye over the associates, these corporate investigation agencies in India also keep track of the activities revolving in and around the distributors, agents and contractors.

In special investigation cases, these corporate investigation agencies in India also scrutinize the actions of the company's competitors. Over the years, these corporate investigation agencies in India have exposed many frauds and scams. Consequently, they have helped corporate houses to grow well without incurring any losses due to any fraud committed by their associates or employees. This is the reason why there is a demand for these corporate investigation agencies which has been increasing day by day. Generally, most of these corporate investigation agencies have a dedicated team of highly-trained professionals, who are capable to get into the facts without raising any sort of suspicion.

ACQUISITION OF LAND & ESTABLISHMENT OF INDUSTRIES IN REMOTE AREAS - A SECURITY PERSPECTIVE

India today is facing a critical situation in relation to land - use planning. Even though the food grain production recorded almost a fourfold increase in the postindependence decades, shortage of rice, pulses and oilseeds is growing. Shortages of pasturelands, firewood and fast depletion of the forest wealth are assuming serious proportions. As a consequence of various development endeavors ecological imbalances *e.g.* soil erosion, rapid situation of dams, shortage of ground water, land and water pollution, water logging etc. are growing adversely effecting the agricultural productivity.

Unless special efforts are made towards preservation of the land, water and vegetative resources of the country and its long term sustainable use is planned, the food grains and other basic needs of the country's population cannot be met, food security and self-reliance cannot be assured and enhanced livelihood security to the oiling millions in India cannot be ensured. Plagued with the problem of stagnant agriculture and shortage of food grains production in drought years, India accepted the green revolution technology under the advice of various foreign aid agencies. In the short-run, gains in productivity were achieved. However, this petrochemical-based technology is not sustainable because it is resulting in depletion and deterioration of land and water resources.

The non-sustainable nature of the green revolution, white revolution technology and the fast depletion of natural resource base led the Ministry of Agriculture and the Planning Commission to take serious cognizance of the problems of planning and management of country's natural resources. The Ministry of Agriculture initiated in 1987 an extensive research project "Perspective plan for Conservation, Management and Development of Land resources in the country" on a zonal basis. The Planning Commission set up in 1988 Agro-climatic Regional Planning Units. Before the recommendations of the various zonal studies were taken up for serious deliberations the NEP era set in. NEP is in obvious contradiction with the policy of Land use regulation.

Need for a Firm Land-Use Policy

The experience in Maharashtra, Gujarat, Andhra Pradesh, Karnataka, Tamil Naidu and most other states of India. The states are removing special restrictions under 'no development zone' declared to protect agricultural lands, hill ranges and coasts, 'reverse forest areas' 'biodiversity conservation areas', tribal areas and regulatory measures in relation to land-use, contradicting the stipulations of the state TRP Acts, Forest Acts, CRZ and other regulations promulgated by the Ministry of Environment and Forests and even the provisions under the Indian Constitution. The states are competing to attract MNC's giving those special concessions and gifting away lands and forests.

Unless the Central Ministry of Agriculture, Ministry of Environment and Forests and the Planning Commission intervene and halt this indiscriminate spread of industry, mining tourism and other urban encroachments into coastal lands, hilly tracts, forests, and tribal homes and the Indian Ocean, the natural resources of the country would be squandered and plundered by the MNC's and the toiling masses ruined. Two pronged strategy has to be planned to avert this disaster. On the one hand, the protective legislation in relation to land, forests and environment has to be strictly adhered to. Today the Ministry of environment is giving a provisional clearance to MNC's and State Governments for several ecologically harmful projects even without insisting on submission of scientific environmental impact studies and its evaluation.

On the other hand, policy measures have to be formulated and implemented for preservation, augmentation and proper utilization of the land, forest, water and other natural resources of the country. The judicious approach under tropical conditions would be to put stress on conservation and enrichment of the natural renewable resource base. For this it is necessary to deepen our understanding of how the biochemical systems exchange matters with the surroundings all the time, the process of recycling between land surfaces, water surface and the atmosphere, the process of recycling between soil, plant and animal life, the hydrological cycle and energy flows. Holistic understanding will give us clues to simple, inexpensive but efficient techniques beneficial in the long run.

Holistic approach will show the way of nitrogen fixation through biological agents, soil enrichment by composting waste products, higher productivity through inter-cropping and crop rotation, pest control through diversity, maximization of food basket through multivariate crops and multipronged culture - *viz.* forestry, agriculture, horticulture, animal husbandry, poultry, fishery, all interwoven and supporting one another. The variegated needs of the Indian society can be maximized through judicious use of processes of recycling and symbiosis.

ACCESS MANAGEMENT

Access management is a simple concept. Every business has information that needs to be protected from unauthorized disclosure. To protect information, companies define policies that govern who can access specific classes of business and/or personal information.

For example, if a manager seeks to access the salary of a subordinate, they should have authorization to do so, however, they should not be authorized to access the same information about a chief executive. That is, there is a policy that specifically governs the release of an employee's salary. Or is there? The answer is: "Probably not." What exists is a written policy related to disclosure of proprietary business information. Because human beings are skilled at generalizations, we expect someone in authority to be able to classify the request for salary information and make a decision.

As part of your quest for an access management strategy, consider the following questions:

- Who should be responsible for access policy?
- What kind of access policy do you require?
- What resources do you need to protect?
- How do I plug in the access management solution?

Who Should be Responsible for Access Policy

To implement an application access management solution, you must ensure that access policies exist and are unambiguous. Although access controls will be enforced by technology, defining access policy is the responsibility of the business. For this reason, access policy related to release of sensitive information and/or application features should be documented using business terminology. During the analysis of these business requirements, concise rules will be defined governing who has access to specific classes of business or personal information and under what circumstances.

This analysis often requires a significant classification effort in three areas:

- Information,
- Application features
- People.

Many companies already have an information protection group tasked with ensuring that business policies are in place to ensure the protection of business and personal information. Such an organization can play an important role in ensuring that access policy is consistent across business applications. If each application group does this classification independently, inconsistencies in policy may occur. But can an internal organization define access policy? Increasingly the answer is no. Legislation regarding confidentiality and privacy requires that individuals be allowed to define who personal information is released.

BOMB THREAT MANAGEMENT

Bombs and the threat of their use have become the primary weapons of the terrorist. They are also used as a means of retaliation by employees with real or fancied grievances, as well as by criminal extortionists. This report provides information on the general guidelines that can be used in developing a plan to reduce the risk of bombing incidents. Information on handling bomb threats and procedures for evacuating a facility and conducting bomb searches are also included. A bomb threat is an effective means of disrupting business. The problems are intensified when the incident involves an actual explosive or incendiary device.

Although there is no foolproof means of securing a premises against a bomb threat, a good security plan, correctly executed, will enable a business to deal with an incident properly. Bombs and the threat of their use has become the primary weapon of the terrorist. They are also used as a means of retaliation by employees with real or fancied grievances, as well as by criminal extortionists. Trends in bombing incidents can usually be linked to political and/or social unrest. For example, in the 30month period between May 1976 and December 1978, the Red Brigade, an Italian terrorist organization, carried out bombing attacks against 10 computer centers because of their belief that "computers represent instruments of the capitalist system." Recently, as a result of political unrest in the Middle East, terrorists have threatened to bomb U.S. targets throughout the world.

Purpose of a Bomb Threat

The only reasonable explanations for a call reporting that a bomb is to go off at a particular location are:

- The caller has definite knowledge or believes that an explosive or incendiary device has been or will be placed and may want to minimize personal injury or property damage.

- The caller may be either the person who placed the device or someone else who has become aware of such information.
- The caller wants to create an atmosphere of anxiety and panic which will, in turn, possibly result in a disruption of the normal activities at the facility where the device is purportedly located.

When a bomb threat call has been received, there will be a reaction to it. If the call is directed at a business where there has been no organized, advance planning to handle such a threat, the call may result in panic. Panic is defined as a "sudden, excessive, unreasoning, infectious terror." Panic is caused by fear - fear of the known or the unknown. It is one of the most contagious of all human emotions. Panic can also be defined, in the context of a bomb threat call, as the ultimate achievement of the caller. Once a state of panic has been reached, the potential for personal injury and property damage is dramatically increased.

Emergency and essential facilities may be shut down or abandoned and the community denied their use at a critical time. Leaving facilities unattended can lead to destruction of the facility and the surrounding area. Large chemical manufacturing plants, power plants, unattended boilers, and other such facilities often require the constant attention of operating personnel. Other effects of not being prepared, or not having an organized plan to handle bomb threat calls, can result in a lack of confidence in the leadership. This will be reflected in lower morale and productivity, or reluctance on the part of employees to continue employment at a location that is being subjected to bomb threat calls.

A BRIEF HISTORY OF THE NAXALITE MOVEMENT

This section draws heavily from Kujur and Hindustan Times. The Naxalite movement traces its roots to Naxalbari, a small village in West Bengal. In March 1967, a tribal farmer was attacked by local landlords over a land dispute. A peasant uprising followed, led by revolutionaries of the Communist Party of India *i.e.* CPI(M) in several states of India, namely Andhra Pradesh, Bihar, Jammu and Kashmir, Karnataka, Kerala, Orissa, Tamil Nadu, Uttar Pradesh, and West Bengal. The West Bengal government, despite being led by CPI(M), crushed the rebellion within West Bengal.

However, the revolutionaries within the CPI(M) split to form the *All India Coordination Committee of Communist Revolutionaries* (AICCCR) in 1968. The AICCCR rejected parliamentary elections and called for an armed uprising against the state. Due to internal conflicts, the AICCCR split, and a new organization called the Communist Party of India *i.e.* CPI(ML) was formed in 1969. At the same time, another organization, later known as the *Maoist Communist Center* (MCC) was formed in Bihar under the name Dakshin Desh. Although, the CPI(ML) continued armed struggle against the Indian state throughout the 1970s, the movement was riven by internal conflicts, suffered from further splits, and soon disintegrated. Of the various factions to emerge from the CPI(ML), the two most prominent ones were the Communist Party of India Liberation *i.e.* CPI(ML) Liberation in 1974 and the Communist Party of India – Marxist Leninist, also known as the *People's War Group* (PWG) in 1980. While the CPI(ML) Liberation did not rule out the possibility of armed revolution against the state, it did participate in the electoral process, even winning an election in Bihar in 1989. The PWG and the MCC on the other hand, completely rejected the democratic system and continuously waged a "people's war for the "people's government". Consequently, all the major violent organizations of the Naxalite movement were in place by 1980.

Kujur notes that in the following years, "intra-organizational conflict and rivalry among different groups touched several high points, resulting in the loss of a considerable number of cadres of rival groups". With regard to the states' response to the Naxalite problem, Kujur observes that "... while the Naxal movement has mostly been characterized by fragmented groups and innumerable splits, successive governments at the national and state levels were never able to follow a uniform approach to deal with the problem of Naxalism ...". In addition to a lack of uniform or even unified response, no Naxalite affected state except Andhra Pradesh created a dedicated security force tasked mainly with countering the Naxalite menace. All other Naxalite affected states relied on some combination of their regular state police forces as well as reinforcements from central police organizations, which were not specially trained in either counter insurgency or jungle warfare operations, resulting in an inability to check the spread of the Naxalite movement.

Only the Andhra Pradesh Government raised a specially trained state police force known as the Greyhounds in 1989, whose main purpose was to combat the Naxalite insurgency. Recruited from the state police force, the Greyhounds are wellequipped and specially trained in counter-insurgency methods and in the recent years have been widely accredited with bringing the Naxalite violence in Andhra Pradesh under control. Given the evolution of the Naxalite movement in India and the states' responses to the same, this paper asks two main questions. First: what is the economic cost of Naxalite violence in the Naxalite affected states, as measured by lost pcNSDP? This question assumes importance because there is no study in the Indian context measuring the economic costs of extremist violence.

Second: to what extent did the creation of the dedicated anti-Naxalite police force known as the Greyhounds mitigate the loss of pcNSDP due to Naxalite violence in Andhra Pradesh? This question assumes importance for two reasons. First: the creation of the Greyhounds is a natural experiment that gives us an opportunity to directly measure the economic benefits of a unique targeted security response to a violent insurgency. Other papers have measured the economic costs of violence, usually in a regression framework, but no paper has exploited an explicit change in the Government's approach to handling extremist violence as a natural experiment to measure the economic benefits of a unique security response.

Second: in the recent past, motivated by the Andhra Pradesh example, several Naxalite affected states namely Chhattisgarh, Jharkhand, Orissa, Madhya Pradesh, Bihar and Maharashtra are in the process of creating dedicated security forces along the lines of the Greyhounds to tackle the Naxalite menace. This is being done even though there is no study that establishes whether the Greyhounds have either reduced Naxalite violence levels, or mitigated the economic costs of Naxalite violence. We investigate the latter aspect.

DATA

The first objective of this study is to estimate the economic costs of Naxalite violence in Naxalite affected states, as measured by lost pcNSDP; while the second objective is to measure the extent to which the creation of the dedicated anti-Naxalite police force known as the Greyhounds mitigated the loss of pcNSDP due to Naxalite violence in Andhra Pradesh. The outcome variable of interest for both objectives is real pcNSDP at 1999 prices. The variables used to predict growth of pcNSDP are the same for both objectives, and include proxies for human capital and infrastructure indicators. For the first objective, we take 1980 as the first year of the treatment period. This is because 1980 is the first year by which all the major violent Naxalite organizations had come into existence. The pre-treatment period is therefore 1970-1979 and the treatment period is 1980-2000. The treated unit is constructed by taking a simple average of the variables for Andhra Pradesh, Bihar, Madhya Pradesh, Maharashtra, Karnataka, Orissa, Uttar Pradesh and West Bengal, these being the states most severely affected by Naxalite violence during the treatment period. An alternate way of determining the treatment period could have been to use data on the state-wise levels of Naxalite violence to determine the period after which the Naxalite violence escalated in the Naxalite affected states as a group.

Unfortunately, except for Andhra Pradesh, this data is not available for the other Naxalite affected states. Note that some of the variables from were used for the analysis were measured in 1981, even though the treatment period for the first objective begins in 1980. At the cost of some bias in the estimates, we treat such variables as being measured in 1979 *i.e.* as being measured prior to the treatment for the first objective. Since these variables are unlikely to change much over the course of two years, we feel confident that the bias in our estimates on account of treating the post treatment values of these variables as pre-treatment values will not be too severe.

While choosing the potential controls we drop:

- States that had missing data for the period 1970-2000 (Chhattisgarh, Chandigarh, Uttaranchal and Jharkhand),

- States that faced some other significant form of violence during this period (the North-Eastern States, Sikkim, Punjab and Jammu and Kashmir), and
- States that are too small (Lakshadweep Islands, Andaman and Nicobar Islands, Daman and Diu, Dadra and Nagar Haveli).

After dropping these states, the sample of potential controls consists of nine states: Tamil Nadu, Rajasthan, Kerala, Gujarat, Himachal Pradesh, Haryana, Goa, Delhi and Pondicherry. For the second objective, we take 1989 as the first year of the treatment period. This is the year in which the Greyhounds police force was raised by the Andhra Pradesh government. This gives us 1970-1988 as the pre-treatment period and 1989-2000 as the treatment period. The treated unit is Andhra Pradesh, and the potential control units are the other Naxalite affected states *i.e.* Bihar, Madhya Pradesh, Maharashtra, Karnataka, Orissa, Uttar Pradesh and West Bengal. Since our objective is to measure the extent to which the operations of the Greyhounds force mitigated the extent of loss of pcNSDP in Andhra Pradesh due to Naxalite violence, it is necessary to retain as potential controls only those states that suffered from Naxalite violence but which did not constitute a Greyhounds type dedicated anti-Naxalite force.

RESULTS

First Objective

Consider the results for the first objective *i.e.* measuring the loss of pcNSDP in Naxalite affected states due to Naxalite violence. The trajectory of pcNSDP of the Naxal States and that of a simple average of all control states. The average pcNSDP for the Rest of India lies well that of the Naxal States in both pre and post treatment periods, indicating that simply using the Rest of India as a comparison group for the Naxal States would not be appropriate. Even before the formation of the major violent Naxalite groups, the Naxal States were consistent under performers relative to the Rest of India.

Even though the Naxal States were consistent underperformers relative to the Rest of India, we argue that endogeneity between low income levels and Naxalite violence is unlikely to be a serious problem for the study. Between 1970 and 1979 *i.e.* during the pre-treatment period, Maharashtra had on average higher income levels than Gujarat, Himachal Pradesh, Kerala, Rajasthan and Tamil Nadu. Similarly, during the pretreatment period, West Bengal had on average higher income levels than Rajasthan and Tamil Nadu. Despite having higher income levels than some of the control states, both Maharashtra and West Bengal went on to become Naxalite affected, while none of those control states with lower income levels went on to become Naxalite affected. Although this is by no means definitive evidence, it tends to support the argument that causation flows from Naxalite violence to low levels of GDP, and not vice versa.

The synthetic Naxal States *i.e.* the synthetic control unit, is constructed as a weighted average of the states in the potential control group that most closely resembles the Naxal States in terms of:

- Pre-treatment values of pcNSDP and
- Pre- treatment values of pcNSDP growth predictors.

The synthetic control does a fairly good job of mimicking the real Naxal States both in terms of:

- Pre-treatment values of pcNSDP, and
- Pre-treatment values of pcNSDP growth predictors.

On the other hand, the Rest of India is quite different from the Naxal States. The optimal weights are positive for only two states – Tamil Nadu, Rajasthan; and zero for all the other states. The trajectory of pcNSDP of the Naxal States and the synthetic control for the period 1970-2000. In the pre-treatment period 1970-1979, the pcNSDP of the synthetic control behaves very similarly to that of the actual Naxal States. In the treatment period, the pcNSDP of the synthetic control continues to the track the movement of pcNSDP of the Naxal States till 1984, after which it begins to diverge from the Naxal States, with the gap increasing rapidly over time and peaking towards the end of the 1990s.

What does this divergence mean for the actual and potential evolution of pcNSDP for the Naxal states? Recall that the evolution of pcNSDP for the synthetic control is what the evolution of pcNSDP would have been for the Naxal States if they had not been subjected to Naxalite violence. The main implication of figure is that Naxalite violence resulted in a loss of pcNSDP for the Naxal States from 1984 onwards, with the loss becoming more severe over time, and peaking towards the end of the 1990s.

We can quantify the loss of pcNSDP for the Naxal States in two ways:

- Percentage average loss, and
- Average percentage loss.

The former is the average yearly gap between pcNSDP of the Naxal States and that of the synthetic control expressed as a percentage of the average yearly pcNSDP of the Naxal States over the treatment period *i.e.* 1980-2000. The latter is the average of the yearly percentage gap between pcNSDP of the Naxal States and that of the synthetic control over the treatment period. The average yearly gap between pcNSDP of the Naxal States and that of the synthetic control was ₹1,273/-, and the average yearly pc NSDP of the Naxal States was ₹10,200/- over the treatment period. Naxal States consequently experienced a percentage average loss of 12.48 per cent of their pcNSDP over this period.

The loss at the end of the period was ₹3,114/-, and the maximum loss observed was ₹3,340/- in 1998. Naxalite violence has therefore had a large negative impact on the pcNSDP of the affected states. Implicit in the calculation of the economic costs of Naxalite violence is the assumption of no spillover between units *i.e.* outcomes of control units are not affected by the treatment administered to the treated unit. This assumption may be violated in the following ways in the present context. For example, it is possible that Naxalite violence may have driven away investment from non Naxalite affected states by tarnishing the image of India as a whole as an investment destination. This would artificially lower our estimates of the treatment effect by lowering the pcNSDP of the synthetic control.

There is no evidence however that such an effect exists for India. Another possibility could be that investment is driven away from the Naxalite affected states to the non Naxalite affected states within India. To the extent that the investment went to the non Naxalite affected states that comprise the synthetic control, this would artificially raise our estimates of the treatment effect by increasing the pcNSDP of the synthetic control. Our estimate of the treatment effect would then constitute an upper bound on the true treatment effect. As AG argue, the bias in the estimate due to this effect would be smaller the larger is the size of the control units with respect to the treated unit. Since the control states had on average 1.47 times greater pcNSDP than the treated states during the pre-treatment period, it is unlikely that the extent of such bias is high in the present context.

Following ADH, we assess the robustness of our results by using different combinations of predictors of pcNSDP when constructing the synthetic control. We find that our results remained robust to the use of measures of state level credit utilization from scheduled commercial banks, percentage share of NSDP from agriculture, the percentage of population below the poverty line, and area under cultivation of foodgrains. Following AG and ADH, we assess the significance of our results by conducting a series of placebo tests that involve iteratively applying the synthetic control method to each of the nine control states. In each iteration of the placebo test, we treat a different control state as the treated state, and assign the actually treated state to control state status.

Each placebo test yields a measure of the treatment effect for a control state, and the tests as whole yield a distribution of treatment effects for the control states. If the placebo tests yield pcNSDP gaps for the control states similar in magnitude to the pcNSDP gap estimated for the Naxal States, then we conclude that there is no significant effect of Naxalite violence on the pcNSDP of the Naxal States. If however the placebo tests yield pcNSDP gaps smaller in magnitude to the pcNSDP gap estimated for the Naxal States, then we conclude that there is a significant effect of Naxalite violence on the pcNSDP of the affected States.

pcNSDP Gap in Naxal States and the placebo gaps for all the control states. The estimated pcNSDP gap between each control state and its synthetic counterpart is represented by the grey lines. The black line represents the estimated pcNSDP gap between the Naxal States and its synthetic counterpart.

It is clear from figure that the estimated pcNSDP gap for the Naxal States is large in comparison to the distribution of pcNSDP gaps for the control states, with the exception of one control state *i.e.* Pondicherry. Also, the synthetic control method provides a good fit for pcNSDP both in the Naxal States and in the control states in the pre-treatment period, with the exception of Pondicherry.

The pre-treatment MSPE for the Naxal States is just 323.74, while the median pre-treatment MSPE for control states in the placebo runs is just 583.26, indicating relatively good pre-treatment fits. The pretreatment MSPE for the Pondicherry placebo run is however relatively large at 1591.65, while that for Delhi is the largest at 4727.46. The poor pre-treatment fits in the placebo runs for Pondicherry and Delhi cast doubt on the reliability of the post treatment fits for Pondicherry and Delhi. As ADH observe, "... placebo runs with poor pre-treatment fit do not provide information to measure the relative rarity of estimating a large post treatment gap for a state that was well fitted prior to treatment."

Therefore, where we drop placebo runs for states that give pre-treatment MSPEs that are at least three times higher than the pre-treatment MSPE for the Naxal States *i.e.* we drop the placebo runs for Delhi, Haryana, and Pondicherry. The pc NSDP gap for the Naxal States is now the largest of all the pcNSDP gaps.

Second Objective

Next we measure to what extent – If any – the creation of the Greyhounds, a dedicated anti-Naxalite police force, mitigated the loss of pcNSDP due to Naxalite violence in Andhra Pradesh. The trajectory of pcNSDP of Andhra Pradesh and that of a simple average of the control states. Recall that the control states are the other states that are affected by Naxalite violence but which did not set up a dedicated anti-Naxalite police force.

The treatment year is 1989, being the year in which the Greyhounds police force was raised. The pre-treatment period is then 1970-1988, and the treatment period is 1989-2000. The average pcNSDP for the Control States lies well that of Andhra Pradesh in both the pre-treatment and treatment periods, indicating that simply using the rest of the Naxalite affected states as a comparison group for Andhra Pradesh would not be appropriate. Even before the formation of the Greyhounds force, Andhra Pradesh was a consistent underperformer relative to the rest of the Naxalite violence affected states. The synthetic Andhra Pradesh *i.e.* the synthetic control unit is constructed as a weighted average of the states in the potential control group that most closely resemble Andhra Pradesh in terms of:

- Pre-treatment values of pcNSDP and
- Pre-treatment values of pcNSDP growth predictors.

The pre-treatment characteristics of Andhra Pradesh to those of the synthetic control and also to the simple average of controls. The synthetic control does a fairly good job of tracking the real Naxal States both in terms of:

- Pre-treatment values of pcNSDP, and
- Pre-treatment values of pcNSDP growth predictors.

On the other hand, the simple average of control states is quite different from Andhra Pradesh. The weights given to each state in the control group when constructing the synthetic Andhra Pradesh. The optimal weights are positive for Bihar, Karnataka, Madhya Pradesh and Orissa; and zero for the other states.

The trajectory of pcNSDP of Andhra Pradesh and the synthetic control for the period 1970-2000. In the pre-treatment period 1970-1988, the pcNSDP of the synthetic control behaves very similarly to that of Andhra Pradesh till 1987. In the treatment period, the pcNSDP of the synthetic control diverges sharply from that of Andhra Pradesh, with the gap increasing rapidly over time all the way till the end of the study period.

What does this divergence mean for the actual and potential evolution of pcNSDP for Andhra Pradesh? Recall that the evolution of pcNSDP for the synthetic control is what the evolution of pcNSDP would have been for Andhra Pradesh if it had not raised the Greyhounds force. The main implication of figure is that the establishment of the Greyhounds force paid immediate and rich dividends to Andhra Pradesh in terms of raising its pcNSDP to levels higher than could have been achieved in the absence of a dedicated anti-Naxalite force. The pcNSDP "dividend" seems to be increasing steadily from year to year all the way till the end of the study period.

The average yearly gap between pcNSDP of Andhra Pradesh and that of the synthetic control was ₹2,221/-, and the average yearly pc NSDP of Andhra Pradesh was ₹12,884/- during the treatment period. Andhra Pradesh consequently experienced a percentage average gain of 17.23 per cent of its pcNSDP during this period. The maximum gain observed was ₹4,409/- at the end of the period. The Greyhounds force has therefore had a large positive impact on the pcNSDP of Andhra Pradesh. The assumption of no spillover between units may be violated in the present context in the following ways. Anti-Naxalite operations by the Greyhounds in Andhra Pradesh may have resulted in the movement of Naxalites from Andhra Pradesh to the surrounding Naxalite affected states, where the absence of specially trained and equipped security forces would have meant a less threatening security environment for Naxalites.

An example of such an instance occurred in 2007 when Naxalites from North Telangana and Nallamala regions in Andhra Pradesh state retreated to Dantewada in response to the increased tempo of Greyhounds operations in Andhra Pradesh.

Although this incident occurred after the study period ended, such instances may have occurred during the study period as well. To the extent that such displaced Naxalites indulged in insurgency activity in their temporary refuge across state borders, the pcNSDP of the other Naxalite affected states would have decreased. This would result in an over estimate of the Greyhounds treatment effect. Unfortunately, there is no publicly available data on the extent of Naxalite activity in any state except Andhra Pradesh during the treatment period. As a result, there is no way to know the extent of such bias in the calculated treatment effect.

The calculated treatment effect must therefore be interpreted as an upper bound on the true treatment effect. Another source of violation of the assumption of no spillover between units could have been if the Greyhounds offered support to the police forces of other states to tackle the Naxalite insurgency. Such support could be in the form of training, joint operations, material supply, deputing officers to other state police forces etc. To the extent that the Greyhounds offered such support, the effect of the Greyhounds on pcNSDP would not have been confined to Andhra Pradesh, but would have extended to all other states whose police forces were supported by the Greyhounds.

This would have artificially raised the pcNSDP of the other Naxalite affected states and thus biased the estimate of the treatment effect downwards. Priyadershi notes that the Greyhounds started offering training to the police forces of other Naxalite affected states from 2000. To avoid this source of bias, we terminate the analysis at the year 2000. As before, we assess the robustness of our results by using different combinations of predictors of pcNSDP when constructing the synthetic control. We find that our results remained robust to the use of measures of state level credit utilization from scheduled commercial banks, the percentage share of NSDP from agriculture, the percentage of population below the poverty line, and area under cultivation of foodgrains.

As before, we assess the significance of our results by conducting a series of placebo tests that involve iteratively applying the synthetic control method to each of the nine control states. The estimated pc NSDP gap between each control state and its synthetic counterpart is represented by the grey lines. The black line represents the estimated pc NSDP gap between the Andhra Pradesh and its synthetic counterpart. It is clear from that the estimated pc NSDP gap for Andhra Pradesh States is large in comparison to the distribution of pc NSDP gaps for the control states, with the exception of one control state *i.e.* Maharashtra.

It is clear that the synthetic control method provides a good fit for pc NSDP both in Andhra Pradesh and in control states prior to the treatment period, with the exception of Maharashtra. The pre-treatment MSPE for Andhra

Pradesh is just 279.10, while the median pre-treatment MSPE for control states in the placebo runs is just 514.54, indicating relatively good pre-treatment fits. The pre-treatment MSPE for the Maharashtra placebo run is largest at 2112.54, while that for Bihar is also relatively large at 1633.12. The poor pre-treatment fits in the placebo runs for Maharashtra and Bihar cast doubt on the reliability of the post treatment fits for Maharashtra and Bihar. Therefore, where we drop placebo runs for states that give pre-treatment MSPEs that are at least five times higher than the pre-treatment MSPE for Andhra Pradesh *i.e.*, we drop the placebo runs for Bihar and Maharashtra. The pc NSDP gap for Andhra Pradesh is now the largest of all the pc NSDP gaps.

Bibliography

A.K. Gaur: *Biotechnology Research in Age of Terrorism*, Cyber Tech Publication, Delhi, 2010.

A.L. Bhatia and S.K. Kulshrestha: *Bioterrorism and Biological Warfare*, Pointer Publication, Delhi, 2009.

Abha Avasthi: *Dimensions of Violence and Terrorism*, Bharat Publication, Delhi, 1998.

Anil Bhat: *Assam : Terrorism and the Demographic Challenge*, Knowledge World, Delhi, 2009.

Caesar Roy: *Definition of Terrorism*, Kalpaz Publications, Delhi, 2014.

Farooq Sobhan: *Countering Terrorism in Bangladesh*, The University Press Limited, Delhi, 2008.

G.C. Satpathy: *Biological Weapons and Terrorism (2 Vols-Set)*, Kalpaz Publication, Delhi, 2004.

James W. Jones: *Blood That Cries Out from the Earth : The Psychology of Religious Terrorism*, Oxford University Press, Delhi, 2008.

Jayant Malik: *Cyber Crime and Terrorism*, Swastik Publication, Delhi, 2011.

Karan Raj: *Dictionary of Terrorism and Bioterrorism*, Ivy Publication, Delhi, 2002.

L.R. Reddy: *Bio Terrorism*, APH Publication, Delhi, 2002.

M G Chitkara: *Combating Terrorism*, APH Publication, Delhi, 2003.

M. K. Dhar: *Black Thunder: Dark Nights of Terrorism In Punjab : A Novel*, Har-anand Publications, Delhi, 2010.

Manas K Mandal and Updesh Kumar: *Countering Terrorism: Psychosocial Strategies*, Sage Publication, Delhi, 2012.

Maroof Raza: *Confronting Terrorism*, Penguin Books, New York, 2009.

P K Das: *Cross-Border Terrorism In South Asia*, Sumit Enterprises, Delhi, 2007.

Paul Grishman: *Cyber Terrorism: The Use Of The Internet For Terrorist Purposes*, Axis Publications, Delhi, 2010.

Prateep K. Lahiri: *Decoding Intolerance : Riots And The Emergence Of Terrorism In India*, Roli Books, Delhi, 2009.

R. C Mishra: *Bioterrorism: Threat of Massive Global Destruction*, Authors Press, Delhi, 2002.

R.K. Pradhan: *Cyber Crime and Cyber Terrorism*, Manglam Publication, Delhi, 2010.

Rahul K Bhonsle: *Beyond Bin Laden : Global Terrorism Scenarios*, Vij Books, Delhi, 2011.

Rajiva Wijesinha: *Declining Sri Lanka: Terrorism and Ethnic Conflict: the Legacy of J R Jayewardene (1906-1996)*, Cambridge University Press, New York, 2005.

Randhir Pal: *Cyber Terrorism and Military Preparedness: An International Prospective*, Swastik Publication, Delhi, 2012.

Roberto Toscano: *Between Terrorism And Global Governance*, Har-anand Publications, Delhi, 2009.

S K Shiva: *Counter Terrorism*, Authorspress, Delhi, 2003.

S.K. Sinha: *Contemporary Psychological Research on Terrorism*, Pearl Books, Delhi, 2011.

S.P. Singh: *Combating Bio-Terrorism : With Special Reference to Anthrax Bacteria*, Reliance Books, Delhi, 2002.

Satish Kumar Rai: *Biological and Chemical Terrorism*, Signature Books International, Delhi, 2011.

Sudhir Manav: *Democratic Response to Terrorism*, Swastik Publications, Delhi, 2012.

Ved Bhatnagar: *Challenges to India's Integrity : Terrorism, Casteism, Communalism*, Rawat Publication, Delhi, 1998.

Vinod Saighal: *Dealing with Global Terrorism : The Way Forward*, Sterling Publication, Delhi, 2003.

William M. Carpenter and David G. Wiencek: *Asian Security Handbook : Terrorism and the New Security Environment*, Pentagon Press, New York, 2007.

Index